State, Space, World

SELECTED ESSAYS

Henri Lefebvre

Edited by Neil Brenner *and* Stuart Elden
Translated by Gerald Moore, Neil Brenner, *and* Stuart Elden

University of Minnesota Press
Minncapolis • London

For publication information on previously published material in this book, see pages 309–11.

Every effort was made to obtain permission to reproduce material in this book. If any proper acknowledgment has not been included here, we encourage copyright holders to notify the publisher.

Published by the University of Minnesota Press
111 Third Avenue South, Suite 290
Minneapolis, MN 55401–2520
http://www.upress.umn.edu

Library of Congress Cataloging-in-Publication Data

Lefebvre, Henri, 1901–1991.
    State, space, world : selected essays / Henri Lefebvre ; edited by
Neil Brenner and Stuart Elden ; translated by Gerald Moore,
Neil Brenner, and Stuart Elden.
        p. cm.
    Includes bibliographical references and index.
    ISBN 978-0-8166-5316-4 (hc : alk. paper) — ISBN 978-0-8166-5317-1
(pb : alk. paper)
    1. Social sciences—Philosophy. I. Brenner, Neil. II. Elden,
Stuart, 1971– III. Title.
    H61.15.L43 2009
    300.1—dc22

                                    2008044595

Printed in the United States of America on acid-free paper

The University of Minnesota is an equal-opportunity educator and employer.

16 15 14 13 12 11 10 09   10 9 8 7 6 5 4 3 2 1

Contents

State, Space, World

Acknowledgments

We are grateful to Gerald Moore for his collaboration on the translations and to Jason Weidemann for his support and patience as our editor. We also thank Carrie Mullen, formerly of the University of Minnesota Press, for supporting an earlier version of this project many years ago. This book has its distant origins in a special section of the *Antipode* journal, which we organized in 2001. We are grateful to the journal's editors at that time, Jamie Peck and Jane Wills, for encouraging our initial collaboration and for their editorial suggestions and support. Kanishka Goonewardena, Stefan Kipfer, Joe Painter, and Nathan Sayre participated in the panel discussion "Lefebvre, Politics, and the State" at the Association of American Geographers meeting in April 2005, which helped to situate and shape this project. The process of tracking down and negotiating rights with French publishers has sometimes been difficult, and we are grateful to a number of friends and colleagues for generously helping us in our efforts to navigate this task. These include Vincent Berdoulay, Maurice Blanc, Sebastian Budgen, Nick Entrikin, Terry Freiberg, Rémi Hess, Stephen Kalberg, Stefan Kipfer, Stathis Kouvelakis, Elizabeth Lebas, Dave McBride, Tristan Palmer, Christian Schmid, Ellen Snooks, and Łukasz Stanek. Reports from Stefan Kipfer and Nick Entrikin for the publisher provided a number of useful suggestions. Finally, thanks are due to David Madden for his careful work on the index.

N.B. and S.E.

State, Space, World

Introduction
State, Space, World
Lefebvre and the Survival of Capitalism

NEIL BRENNER AND STUART ELDEN

HENRI LEFEBVRE'S STATE THEORY IN CONTEXTS

Commenting on the long history of interpretations of Marx, Henri Lefebvre wrote that "the correct line of thought is to situate the works and the theoretical or political propositions within the global movement of the transformation of the modern world."[1] It seems appropriate to view Lefebvre's own formidable intellectual and political legacy—whether in France, in the English-speaking world, or beyond—in directly analogous terms. Since the early 1970s, when Anglo-American urbanists and geographers first began to discuss and appropriate Lefebvre's approach to urban spatiality, his many post-1968 writings have inspired considerable debate and any number of critical appropriations in the English language. From those early discussions of Lefebvre's urban theory through the critical engagements with his approach to sociospatial theory during the 1980s, to the more recent appropriations of his work in the context of debates on the condition of postmodernity, the body and sexuality, everyday life, the production of scale, urban and antiglobalization struggles, the transformation of citizenship, and the right to the city, Lefebvre's writings have served as central reference points within a broad range of theoretical and political projects.[2] Clearly, this diversity of readings and appropriations reflects not only the extraordinary richness of Lefebvre's ideas, but also the changing intellectual, political, and social contexts in which his work has been read and debated during the last three and a half decades.

Yet, while most of Lefebvre's writings on cities and on sociospatial theory have now been translated into English and extensively discussed, his equally innovative works on state theory, the spatiality of modern statehood, and the process of globalization have received much less attention. This neglect is surprising on the one hand, for these are writings that explicitly develop, complement, and critique his work on cities, the urban, and space; yet it is entirely understandable on the other, for most of his central texts on these matters have yet to be translated or were originally published in rather dispersed, difficult-to-obtain English-language sources.[3] Indeed, although Lefebvre's contributions to the study of the state, state spatiality, and globalization have occasionally been acknowledged—as illustrated, for instance, in Nicos Poulantzas's respectful tribute in his 1978 work, *State, Power, Socialism*[4]—they have been almost systematically neglected in scholarly discussions of Lefebvre's work, both in English *and* in French.[5] These writings encompass, most centrally, Lefebvre's sprawling but sporadically brilliant four-volume text, *De l'État* (1976–78; On the State); yet they extend to include chapters of other major theoretical books, including, for example, *Une pensée devenue monde* (1980; A Thought Become World) and *Le retour de la dialectique* (1986; The Return of the Dialectic), as well as a series of academic articles, political essays, interviews, and book reviews generated between the mid-1960s and the mid-1980s.[6] They represent an essential theoretical and political reference point within the corpus of Lefebvre's mature writings on sociospatial theory.

The period under consideration here was thus a remarkable phase of Henri Lefebvre's long intellectual and political career. Emerging from what he calls the "eruption" of 1968,[7] and freed from the membership of the Parti Communiste Français (PCF) that had constrained him a decade before, Lefebvre systematically began to rethink the political aspects of his work. This extended through works on the urban, philosophy, and everyday life. Then, having published his momentous and now widely disseminated book *La production de l'espace* (The Production of Space) in 1974, Lefebvre immediately embarked on an equally ambitious project on the theory and historical geography of the modern state on a world scale. The result of this inquiry, which appeared in France between 1976 and 1978, was *De l'État*. Why the state? For Lefebvre the answer is straightforward—"because the State, and everything that it concerns and implies, is to be found at the heart of modernity and the so-called modern world."[8]

De l'État is a comprehensive study of the state in history, theory, and contemporary politics. It has never been translated into English and is both out of print and neglected in France. Complexities associated with legal rights to the work have hindered both a French reprint and either a full or abridged English translation. Over the more than 1,600 pages of this book, Lefebvre discusses theories of the state and analyzes the state in the modern world, adding significantly to the literature on this topic both within Marxism, as a continuation of a tradition that runs from Lenin and Luxemburg through Gramsci to Miliband and Poulantzas, but also more generally within contemporary political and philosophical inquiry. Among its many highpoints are analyses of state theory, the development of the modern state, the relation between the state and space, the state mode of production, and the process of *mondialisation.* This last term, as will be discussed more fully below, cannot be translated adequately as "globalization," as it stresses a notion of the "world," *le monde,* that the English term obscures. This concept became increasingly central to Lefebvre's vision of the possibilities for, and constraints on, political, social, and cultural transformation from the mid-1970s until the end of his life. In the course of his epic intellectual odyssey in the four volumes of *De l'État,* Lefebvre elaborates explicitly state-theoretical readings of themes to which he had long devoted his attention in previous decades, including architecture and monumentality, the city and the urban, spatial inequality and the world market, capitalist growth and crisis, class struggle and political representation, citizenship, and the everyday. Here Lefebvre also offers a detailed study of the question of *autogestion* (another untranslatable term that is discussed more fully below) as a model of grassroots democracy or workers' control in the context of a wide-ranging analysis of oppositional sociopolitical mobilization in neighborhoods, cities, regions, rural peripheries, national states, and ultimately on a world scale.

In addition to their relevance for understanding Lefebvre's evolving philosophical and theoretical concerns, the volumes of *De l'État* and related publications from the same period provide a remarkable window into his evolving political orientations, particularly in relation to the dominant political organizations of the Left, in France, Western Europe, and beyond, during the high point of Eurocommunism and Fordist national developmentalism in the West and state socialism (including its Soviet and Maoist forms) in Eastern Europe, the USSR, China, and parts of the postcolonial periphery. Along with dissident Marxist contemporaries such as Herbert Marcuse and André Gorz, Lefebvre was one of the great antiproductivist theoreticians of the twentieth century, and especially after his break with the PCF in the late 1950s, this political stance profoundly informed his relation to all political organizations and social movements. His foundational rejection of the logic of commodification and capital accumulation—with their destructive consequences for social space, everyday life, and the natural environment—permeates many of the texts included here, where he insists repeatedly on the limits of productivist ideologies of the Right *and* the Left. More specifically, it is Lefebvre's theoretical understanding of the state's role in stimulating and managing economic growth—analyzed in the following chapters and in volume 3 of *De l'État* through the concept of the "state mode of production" (*mode de production étatique*, hereafter SMP)—which underpins his powerful critique of European social democracy *and* Soviet-style state socialism. This state-theoretical conception also grounds his vision of what an alternative to the productivist world of commodification and capital accumulation might entail—development instead of growth; a politics of difference instead of state-imposed abstraction, homogeneity, and consumerism; and radical grassroots democracy, or *autogestion,* instead of technocracy and ruling class hegemony.

The present volume thus makes available for the first time a collection of Lefebvre's most essential writings that are associated broadly with the intellectual project of *De l'État.* While we hope that an English-language version of the latter book may someday be published, the selections included in the present volume are intended to provide an overview of some of Lefebvre's major state-theoretical preoccupations from the mid-1960s until the mid-1980s, including those he explored at length in the four volumes of *De l'État.*[9] Accordingly, in preparing this book, we have carefully excavated the entirety of Lefebvre's writings from the period dating from his first explicit theorizations of the state until the last years of his life. On this basis, we have selected a series of crucial texts, primarily but not exclusively from the 1970s and early 1980s, that most clearly elaborate his major arguments on these themes.

Of the fifteen essays in this volume, ten are translated here for the first time (chapters 1, 2, 3, 5, 6, 9, 10, 12, 13, and 15). Of the five previously translated essays, one is a foundational text that is presented here in a new, corrected translation (chapter 7); and three are products of the current editors' previous work: two of the latter are crucial chapters of *De l'État* that are presented here in longer forms than their earlier abridged English renderings (chapters 11 and 14); and the other is reprinted from an earlier collaborative project between the editors (chapter 4). The editors were not involved in the translation of chapter 8, a classic text from the 1970s that is reintroduced here after a long period of neglect, and for which no French text is extant. Taken as a whole, the chapters in this book represent a broad variety of textual styles and modes of engagement—they range from initial sketches of an overall problematic, preliminary reviews of other theorists' writings, and a spirited interview, to well-crafted scholarly essays, polemical political interventions, and detailed studies of the economic, geographical, and political aspects of the reconfiguration of the state on a worldwide scale.

The heterogeneous character of the volume—its composition from diverse types of materials dating from an almost two-decade period of extraordinary intellectual productivity and political engagement in Lefebvre's life—is intended to enable readers to glimpse the development, deployment, and elaboration of some of Lefebvre's key ideas in an unusually broad range of contexts. Equally, their arguments resonate closely with one another, often in unexpectedly illuminating ways, through their specific positioning within this book. Indeed, we would suggest that they acquire a qualitatively new, possibly more enduring significance when read in the synthetic context of this volume, for they set into relief Lefebvre's theoretical agendas, conceptual deployments, political orientations, and intellectual experiments—not to mention some of his stylistic quirks—in ways that may not be readily apparent in an isolated reading of any one among these texts.

Our purpose in assembling these writings is derived not only from a desire to enhance scholarly understanding of Lefebvre's ideas among English-language readers. For even though Lefebvre's analyses of state, space, and world were elaborated in the period just prior to, and in the midst of, the crisis of North Atlantic Fordism, we believe that they contain insights and political orientations that can be mobilized productively to illuminate the present global formation of neoliberalizing capitalism and neoconservative geopolitical reaction in the early twenty-first century. This is a matter that deserves more exhaustive treatment elsewhere, but at the end of this chapter, we provide some initial reflections on the contemporary relevance of Lefebvre's work.

In this introduction, we sketch several important theoretical and political contexts in relation to which the texts included in this book must be situated. On this basis, we survey some of the major concepts and intellectual orientations elaborated by Lefebvre in this volume. This contextually sensitive reading is supplemented within each of the following chapters through short editorial prefaces and, where appropriate, extensive editorial footnotes intended to clarify some of Lefebvre's intellectual and political references, many of which may be obscure to Anglo-American readers. After surveying the organizational structure of the volume, we offer some brief reflections on the relevance of Lefebvre's arguments in the present volume to critical analyses of the contemporary geohistorical moment. For the purposes of this introduction, we do not attempt to provide a comprehensive critical evaluation of Lefebvre's work on state, space, and world; this is a task that deserves to be confronted more systematically elsewhere. This volume is intended to facilitate such a critical assessment, both within Anglo-American scholarship and beyond. In a brief appendix, we present some suggestions for further reading of texts by Lefebvre that complement and develop those included here.

OPENINGS: 1968 AND THE EXPLOSION OF MARXISM

As Stefan Kipfer has argued, Lefebvre's politics were forged under the influence of four key experiences during the postwar period: "(1) the critique of Stalinism in France and Eastern Europe before and after his expulsion from the PCF at the end of the 1950s; (2) a critical engagement with Situationist avant-gardism in the 1950s and 1960s; (3) a brief flirtation with the alternative Communism of Yugoslavia and China; and (4) his contribution to New Left politics in France both before and after 1968."[10] Most of the essays included in this volume are enmeshed within this fourth layering of Lefebvre's political identity, which he articulated most powerfully and systematically during the post-1968 period. In this period his political perspective encompassed diverse modes of political–intellectual engagement, or, in the words of his colleague and biographer Rémi Hess, from "grassroots militantism to a critique of the state."[11] Interestingly, although Lefebvre had written on the state previously in several works from the 1950s and 1960s, he claimed that those analyses needed to be rethought in the light of the events of May 1968 in Paris.[12]

During the 1970s, Lefebvre developed many of his most seminal theoretical ideas in close conjunction with his involvement in political struggles and debates within the French, European, and emergent global Left. The dialectical interaction of Lefebvre's theoretical and political projects is particularly apparent in the texts included in this book, in which issues of conceptualization, interpretation, strategy, and praxis are explored in an exceptionally immediate relation to one another. Indeed, Lefebvre's writings on the state during the post-1968 period develop important theoretical foundations for a number of political projects—for instance, radical political decentralization, grassroots democratic governance, and the transformation of everyday life—which he had already begun to advocate and theorize in some of his earlier works. Additionally, Lefebvre's post-1968 writings on the state represent an important extension and concretization of his earlier studies of the production of space and, perhaps most importantly, they articulate an impassioned call to arms in the name of an anti-Stalinist *and* anti-social-democratic form of radical-democratic political praxis. Lefebvre's analyses of the state during this period can thus be read as an expression of his sustained efforts to clarify both theoretically and practically the possibility for transformative political praxis under the highly fluid global, European, national, and local conditions of that tumultuous decade.

The post-1968 period witnessed a number of dramatic transformations within the French and European Left that significantly conditioned Lefebvre's political outlook and theoretical orientation. Lefebvre would subsequently describe these transformations as an "explosion" (*éclatement*) of Marxism in which the rigidly enforced, dogmatic unity of Marxian theory associated with Stalinism was definitively splintered into a multitude of autonomous strands and currents.[13] Although, as Lefebvre noted, this explosion of Marxism had begun to erupt as early as the late nineteenth century in the bitter debates between Marx, Lassalle, and Bakunin,[14] it continued in wavelike succession well into the late twentieth century, rippling through a broad constellation of urban and national contexts, creating a worldwide culture of Marxisms competing for ideological influence within intellectual and political life. The legacy of Khrushchev's 1956 "secret speech," which condemned the crimes of Stalin, provided an additional impetus to this pluralization and differentiation of the Left, as did the Sino-Soviet split beginning in 1959 and the unrealized possibilities of the Non-Aligned Movement that had emerged following the 1955 Bandung conference. In the post-'68 period, the worldwide explosion of Marxism occurred in sites scattered throughout the globe, from Prague, Belgrade, London, Chicago, and Berkeley to Mexico City, Calcutta, and Beijing, but Paris was arguably one of its most vibrant global flashpoints. Here, as Sunil Khilnani remarks, "[t]he "long decade" between the revolutionary efflorescence of May 1968 and the Socialist Party's election to government in 1981 produced the most dramatic and decisive realignment in the political affiliations of French intellectuals that has occurred in recent times."[15]

Always a bit of a heretic when it came to the prospect of grounding himself in any singular intellectual or ideological tradition, Lefebvre had enthusiastically embraced the explosion of Marxism well before the global eruptions of 1968, developing his own, eclectic critique of capitalism that synthesized ideas from Marx, Lenin, and the Surrealists as well as from a host of non-Marxist thinkers such as Hegel, Nietzsche, Heidegger, and Kostas Axelos, among many others.[16] At the same time, Lefebvre's writings of the post-1968 period are single-mindedly persistent in their emphasis on the radically new, worldwide horizon, both for thought and for action, that had been opened up as of the late 1960s. Indeed, by the late 1970s Lefebvre would invoke the worldwide extension and heterogenization of Marxism as one of the important expressions of the more general, late twentieth-century process of "becoming worldwide" that he attempted to grasp using the concept of *mondialisation*.[17]

For Lefebvre, then, the 1970s was a period of immense uncertainty, geopolitical danger, and potential planetary destruction, a "space of catastrophe," as he ominously described it, drawing on the terminology of the French mathematician René Thom at the end of *De l'État* (see chapters 3 and 11). Many geopolitical tendencies, crises, and conflagrations at the time further accentuated the world-historical disillusionment of the European and global Left— these included U.S. support for Israel in the Yom Kippur war and the resultant global oil crisis; civil wars across the Middle East and Africa; the consolidation of military-industrial complexes in both West and East under a reintensifying Cold War; the entrenchment of military dictatorships in postcolonial states in Africa, South America, and parts of East and Southeast Asia; the ongoing neocolonial war in former French Indochina; the 1973 CIA-backed Pinochet coup in Chile; and the ever-present threat of worldwide nuclear annihilation. But despite these disturbing trends, threats, and conflicts, it was also, Lefebvre hastened to insist, a conjuncture of extraordinary political promise, in which established political institutions, conventions, and assumptions were being widely called into question, and thus, one in which genuine alternatives, including radical ones, could be envisioned, debated, and even put into practice. It was therefore a time of intense intellectual, ideological, and cultural experimentation, one that Lefebvre would embrace with—as he put it in a postcard scribbled off to his old friend and comrade Norbert Guterman in New York—a "youthfulness of heart."[18] Now entering his seventh decade— Lefebvre was born in 1901—he embarked with youthful excitement upon one of the most brilliantly creative periods of his long, productive life.

In 1976, responding to an ostensibly biographical question posed by one of his young interviewers, Lefebvre forcefully insisted that his own ideas were evolving during the post-1968 period not due to changes in his own subjective intellectual orientation, but rather because of an unavoidable need to decipher ongoing transformations of the modern world "as a bundle of contradictions" (see chapter 6). And, indeed, in the selections included in this book, we find Lefebvre engaged in a variety of theoretical dialogues, conceptual innovations, analytical maneuvers, and thematic realignments that at once build on some of his earlier political–intellectual commitments and adapt them creatively to the radically changing worldwide conjuncture he was living through. The intricate choreographies of Lefebvre's intellectual and political evolution during this period have yet to be thoroughly explored by his commentators, and surely deserve much more systematic investigation elsewhere.[19] For present purposes, in the interest of contextualizing Lefebvre's arguments in the texts below in both theoretical and political terms, our concern is to set into relief just a few of the most essential positions and concepts he stakes out. These should be viewed not as the product of a fixed, dogmatic stance, but rather as dynamically evolving engagements within perpetually shifting material and ideological contexts grounded in theory, oriented toward practice, and guided by his ever-youthful political imagination. Before turning to the substantive themes explored in this book, we first consider some of the major theorists in relation to whom Lefebvre positioned his analyses of the modern state.

DIALOGUES: MARXISM AND BEYOND

Lefebvre forged his theoretical approach to the modern state in explicit dialogue with Marx and other Marxists, as well as with several prominent late nineteenth- and early twentieth-century critics of the Marxian tradition and philosophers positioned, or who positioned themselves, entirely outside it. Lefebvre's writings on the state, including most of those collected here, contain ample examples of each type of engagement. Lefebvre's excursions into other writers' works are not merely exegetical: his goal throughout is to derive insights that enable him to pursue some of his own overarching theoretical questions regarding the nature, history, geography, contradictions and evolutionary trajectory of the modern state. The latter are wide ranging and encompass an extraordinarily broad range of philosophical, theoretical, methodological, historical, and political themes.[20]

Unlike many of his contemporaries, Lefebvre was always concerned with reading Marx's early and later writings in dialogue, rather than privileging the earlier "humanist" writings or the later "scientific ones." In particular, in developing his approach to state theory, Lefebvre made extensive use of the *1844 Manuscripts, On the Jewish Question*, Marx's historical and political writings, the three volumes of *Capital*, the *Grundrisse*, and perhaps most essentially, the *Critique of the Gotha Program*, which he once described as Marx's

"political last will and testament."[21] Using these other writings enabled Lefebvre to excavate creatively and forcefully Marx's views on state theory, the
analysis of modern state formation, the critique of contemporary political
forms, and the dynamics of sociopolitical mobilization (see chapters 1 and 2).
Indeed, in 1975 Lefebvre suggested that his work had attempted to engage
with Marx's writings as a whole around two key themes: alienation—a key
focus in his multivolume series *Critique of Everyday Life*—and the state.[22]

In so doing, however, Lefebvre does not hesitate to point out some of the
major ambiguities in Marx's analysis of the state. According to Lefebvre's
analysis in volume 2 of *De l'État*, Marx produced different accounts of the
modern state in part because it was being constituted and transformed before
his very eyes—he was a witness to its transition during the consolidation of
industrial capitalism and the expansion of the world market, and also to the
reconstitutions of state power wrought by Bismarck and Napoleon.[23] Of these
different accounts, Lefebvre draws attention to three in particular. First, he
mentions Marx's well-known theorization of the state as an economic and
political instrument of the dominant class, that is, as a "collective capitalist."
Second, he suggests, Marx analyzes the state as being apparently autonomous
from the social relations of production, yet also parasitically dependent on
them. Third, Lefebvre notes Marx's emphasis on the state's direct involvement
in the creation and regulation of productive forces, tasks that include the
promotion of economic growth and the management and even production
of civil society.[24] Yet, in underscoring some of these quite different ways of
theorizing the state, Lefebvre does not follow the route of Marxist scholars
who have tended to defend one version of these theorizations against the others—as illustrated, for instance, by the positions adopted in the Miliband-
Poulantzas debates of the late 1960s and early 1970s, or by those elaborated
in the German state derivation debates of the late 1970s.[25] Lefebvre suggests,
rather, that textual support for a range of perspectives on the state may be
gleaned from Marx's writings, and that these perspectives may in turn be
productively mobilized to explore different issues within state theory and the
critique of political economy.[26] Lefebvre's analytical strategy is thus to draw
on Marx's work in order to open up perspectives through which to elaborate
his own ideas.

Lefebvre also devotes considerable attention in *De l'État* and elsewhere to
Hegel's distinction between state and civil society, as elaborated in the *Philosophy of Right*, and its subsequent appropriation and reinterpretation by Marx.[27]

Lefebvre suggests that the topic of the state was Marx's "point of rupture" with Hegel, for it was precisely around this issue that their intellectual projects collided and then dramatically diverged.[28] Like both Hegel and Marx, Lefebvre considers the differentiation of state and civil society to be a fundamental feature of the modern world. Crucially, however, Lefebvre sides with the young Marx in viewing this differentiation as an expression of an historically specific form of political alienation within capitalist society, the result of what he terms "the fissure between man and citizen."[29] Concomitantly, like the mature Marx, he understood this differentiation not as a static structural divide, but rather as an evolving terrain of intensive class conflict and sociopolitical struggle regarding the nature of economic growth, political representation, and citizenship (see chapter 1). Thus, while Lefebvre acknowledges that Marx and Hegel must be linked together theoretically, he insists that their views of the state must be clearly distinguished in both sociological and political terms. Indeed, one of Lefebvre's major objections to institutionalized forms of Marxism—Stalinism and the PCF being the central targets— is their systematic obscuring or misreading of the state–civil society distinction based on a neo-Hegelian totalization of state power.[30] Accordingly, rather than embracing the state as the historical embodiment of Reason, as it is for Hegel, or, in Stalinist terms, as a "dictatorship of the proletariat," Lefebvre affirms Marx's view that the conflicts associated with modern political life cannot, and indeed should not, be overcome.

But this poses a further question, which Lefebvre poses most concisely and bluntly in chapter 4 of this volume, namely: "which State do we want?" In confronting this issue, Lefebvre draws not only on Marx but also on Engels and, still more centrally, on Lenin. Indeed, Lefebvre devotes a significant portion of chapter 2 of this volume and a lengthy chapter of volume 2 of *De l'État* to excavating Lenin's political and state-theoretical writings, particularly *State and Revolution,* for insights into the question of what a postcapitalist state might look like. This issue was, Lefebvre suggests, one of Lenin's lifelong preoccupations.[31] Invoking Lenin's work, Lefebvre argues that socialists must seek out a state form that "withers away," not in the sense of disappearing, but of being transformed into a mechanism for grassroots, radically democratic collective decision-making. This approach to the question of the state, Lefebvre argues, has been either forgotten or radically distorted during the course of the twentieth century, particularly in the Stalinist and social-democratic period. Lefebvre thus forcefully counterposes his reading of Marx,

Engels, and especially Lenin on the "withering away" of the state to official
social-democratic, "state socialist," and Stalinist orthodoxies that, paradoxically, promoted a strengthening of the power of the state, whether in liberal-
pluralist or violently authoritarian forms.[32] As we shall see below, Lefebvre's
reappropriation of the notion of the withering away of the state from the
Marxist tradition also constitutes a key precondition for his subsequent theorization of *autogestion* during the course of the 1970s.

In addition to forging his ideas on the state within this broad Hegelian–
Marxist context, through his intense and probing dialogue with Lenin, and
his ongoing effort to criticize the orthodoxies of the official Marxisms associated with Stalin and the PCF, Lefebvre attempted to situate his analyses in
relation to those of writers working in other intellectual traditions. Sometimes,
this entailed fiercely polemical forms of engagement, in which Lefebvre did
not hesitate to accuse some of his most eminent contemporaries of engaging
in various forms of mystification or at least misrecognition. For instance,
Lefebvre is singularly dismissive of Louis Althusser, the founding figure of
structuralist Marxism, whose influence was peaking around the time *De
l'État* was published. In volume 2 of that work, Lefebvre scornfully charac-
terizes Althusser's structuralist Marxist theory as an extreme form of "neo-
Stalinism";[33] in volume 4 he argues that Althusser's theory of "ideological
state apparatuses" serves to mask not only the "ideologization of Marxism"
by the Soviet state, but also the role of structuralism as a "dominant ideology
of State capitalism" in the West.[34]

Lefebvre is likewise rather cursory, if generally less polemical, in his treatment of Michel Foucault's work. Lefebvre's main criticism was that Foucault
neglected to consider the state's role in producing and maintaining power
relations and in generating the types of changes documented in his historical studies of, for instance, madness and incarceration. Thus, while Lefebvre
concedes that "the philosopher" Foucault had produced a "strong book" in
History of Madness, he faults the study for neglecting to examine the role of
the state and capitalism in engendering the shifts examined therein.[35] Nearly
a decade after *De l'État,* without directly naming him, Lefebvre clearly had
Foucault in mind as one of the "speculative philosophers who have diluted
the concept [of power] by finding it all over the place, in every form of 'subordination,' and by forgetting about where power has its 'real' seat: in the
state, in constitutions and institutions."[36]

In contrast to his treatment of Althusser and Foucault, Lefebvre engaged more carefully, if selectively and always critically, with certain key ideas from such philosophers as Nietzsche, Heidegger, and Axelos. For instance, Lefebvre frequently cites Nietzsche's claim in *Thus Spoke Zarathustra* that the state is the "coldest of all cold monsters."[37] For Lefebvre, Nietzsche's critique of the state's mystifying claim to represent the popular will proved useful in advancing his own arguments against liberal-pluralist, social-democratic, and Stalinist ideologies. Thus, in a Nietzschean formulation, Lefebvre subsequently characterized Khrushchev's vision of the "state of the entire people" as a "monster."[38] In the 1975 book *Hegel, Marx, Nietzsche ou le royaume des ombres* (Hegel, Marx, Nietzsche, or the Kingdom of Shadows) Lefebvre explains that these three thinkers provide three different ways to understand the world. For Lefebvre, Hegel is an affirmative theorist of the state, whereas Marx and Nietzsche offer powerfully complementary albeit somewhat contradictory critiques of this politico-institutional formation—Marx from the perspective of society and social relations, and Nietzsche from that of culture or civilization.[39] Elsewhere, and just as importantly, Lefebvre appropriates and critiques Nietzsche's notion of the "will to power," suggesting that it can be productively redeployed to decipher the power struggles associated with class relations under modern capitalism and, more generally, the mortal violence that is endemic to the modern state form.[40]

Finally, it is worth mentioning the important influence of some of Heidegger's key ideas to Lefebvre's thought. In various writings, Lefebvre discusses and criticizes Heidegger's analyses of everyday life, space, politics, and being. Indeed, much like his long engagement with Marx's thought, Lefebvre's dialogue with Heidegger lasted from the 1920s until the end of Lefebvre's life. While many aspects of this dialogue are of interest, most central in the present context is the question of the world, an essential aspect of Lefebvre's state theory (see part II of this volume). But this was a multilayered dialogue, mediated profoundly through the work of Axelos, a Greek émigré to France and translator and interpreter of Heidegger, who became one of Lefebvre's major philosophical interlocutors during the 1960s. It was above all through his engagement with Axelos's provocative and often poetic meditations on the concept of the world in pre-Socratic Greek thought and in Heidegger's work that Lefebvre elaborated the philosophical foundations for his own conceptualization, both in *De l'État* and elsewhere. As chapters 12, 13, and 14 show, Axelos and Lefebvre engaged in a vigorous, if contentious, conversation concerning how best to theorize the emergent space of the world that they were both increasingly concerned to understand during the last quarter of the twentieth century. Heidegger's philosophy remained a major reference point throughout this conversation, albeit often only implicitly. Thus, even though Heidegger is rarely cited by Lefebvre in *De l'État,* his ideas are crucial to one of the most fascinating and provocative chapters of the entire work, namely the final chapter of the final volume (translated in chapter 14).[41]

All of the themes highlighted above are tightly interwoven throughout Lefebvre's writings on state, space, and world; references and citations to these major intellectual interlocutors therefore recur in many of the chapters included in this volume. We now consider three politico-theoretical and philosophical issues that, in our reading, lie at the heart of Lefebvre's approach to the state during the post-1968 period: state power and *autogestion,* the state mode of production and antiproductivist state theory, and state space and *mondialisation.*

STATE POWER AND *AUTOGESTION*

The classical Marxist concept of the withering away of the state, especially with its fundamental reworking by Lenin in *State and Revolution,* was a significant theme of Lefebvre's writings in the 1960s (see chapters 1 and 2). However, during the 1970s, he returned to the same constellation of issues through the closely related but analytically distinct concept of *autogestion,* which had by then become a central topic of political debate and ideological struggle throughout the French and European Left (see, in particular, chapters 4, 5, and 6).

The term *autogestion* literally means "self-management," but its French connotation may be captured more accurately as "workers' control." The project of *autogestion* can be traced to the antistatist socialist movements of the nineteenth century; it was subsequently debated among contributors to Cornelius Castoriadis's journal *Socialisme ou Barbarie* in the 1950s and again in the 1960s in discussions within the French Left concerning the Yugoslav system of industrial democracy and the Algerian independence movement.[42] During the events of May 1968, *autogestion* became a popular rallying cry for the noncommunist and anarchist Left, including Lefebvre himself, who discussed it enthusiastically in a number of the texts and interviews included in this volume.[43] In order to underscore its contextually specific meaning, which might be rendered most effectively as "grassroots control," we have preserved the original French term throughout these translations.

In approaching Lefebvre's writings on *autogestion*, it is important to recognize that, as of the 1970s, this notion had been adopted by any number of dissident factions of the French and European Left that explicitly rejected the hierarchical, statist authoritarianism of the PCF. Thus, the main noncommunist trade union federation CFDT (Confédération Française Démocratique du Travail), guided by the editor and philosopher Pierre Rosanvallon, promoted *autogestion* as a means to enhance workers' control at the site of production.[44] Likewise, the dissident socialist Michel Rocard and the CFDT trade unionist Edmond Maire, both of whom were strongly influenced by the events of May 1968, advocated *autogestion* as a form of radical democratic political mobilization to counteract the hierarchical, state-centered orientations of both the PCF and the newly formed Parti socialiste (PS). Perhaps most importantly for Lefebvre's own thinking, the regionalist thinker Robert Lafont promoted an urbanistic and regionalist strand of the *autogestion* discussion, advocating a radical decentralization of political power, enhanced local control over basic economic and administrative tasks, and an abolition of the divide between governors and governed.[45] Yet, despite its deeply entrenched statist tendencies, even the PCF tentatively adopted a politics of *autogestion* in conjunction with its experiments with Eurocommunist ideology, particularly between 1975 and 1978. Even before then, as Lefebvre quipped in *The Survival of Capitalism*, the notion of *autogestion* had become the ideological focal point for "a great outburst of confusion."[46] As Khilnani explains, it had become an "infinitely plastic idea" that encompassed, at one and the same time, antistatist and statist political projects, antiproductivist and productivist visions of modernization, and grassroots and liberal-parliamentary forms of political participation.[47]

However, even though Lefebvre recognized the degree to which *autogestion* had become a "hollow slogan" within the French Left as it was appropriated by pseudo-radical political organizations that were committed substantively neither to democratization nor to a radically democratic socialism,[48] he argued that *autogestion* represented the essential basis for radical-democratic transformation under contemporary conditions. In these texts, Lefebvre undertakes a rigorous theorization and historical–geographical contextualization of this concept, which he viewed until the end of his life as one of the foundational impulses for a genuinely socialist political practice. The roots of this contention arguably lie in Lefebvre's lifelong concern to elaborate a critically revised Marxian approach to the philosophy of praxis in the context of twentieth-century capitalism.[49] Lefebvre had articulated the foundations for this project in his writings on the critique of everyday life, in his detailed historical analysis of the Paris Commune of 1871, in his interpretation of the French student revolts of 1968, as well as in his various critical commentaries on Marxian theory.[50] Indeed, Lefebvre's concept of *autogestion* may be interpreted as his own reworking of the concept of the "withering away of the state," as elaborated in his reading of Marx, Engels, and Lenin in chapters 1 and 2 of this volume. He views *autogestion* as a form of direct democracy, a grassroots political practice that "is born spontaneously out of the void in social life that is created by the state."[51] To the extent that the apparatuses of the modern state are redefined into mechanisms of grassroots democracy, Lefebvre argues, the state is "withering away in the Marxist sense" (see chapter 4, "The State and the World Market"). It bears repeating here that the key issue, for Lefebvre, is less the erosion of state power as such than the possibility of its qualitative transformation into a radically decentralized, participatory institutional framework that not only permits social struggles and contradictions, but actively encourages and provokes them (see chapter 4, "The State and the World Market"; see also chapter 5, passim). The political utopia envisioned by Lefebvre is thus one in which the state would serve not as an instrument for capital accumulation, bureaucratic domination, and everyday violence, but rather as an arena for—as he put it at the end of *De l'État*—"spatial (territorial) *autogestion*, direct democracy, and democratic control, affirmation of the differences produced in and through that struggle" (see chapter 11).

For Lefebvre, then, *autogestion* is not only a project of radically democratic governance but a conflictual, contradictory process through which participants continually engage in self-criticism, debate, deliberation, conflict, and struggle; it is not a fixed condition but a level of intense political engagement and "revolutionary spontaneity" (see chapter 5) that must "continually be enacted" (see chapter 4). Lefebvre therefore firmly distances himself from the various meanings and associations that were linked to projects of *autogestion* within France, Yugoslavia, and elsewhere: *autogestion*, Lefebvre insists, is not a magic formula, a system, a model, or a panacea; it is not a purely technical or rational operation; it will not solve all the workers' problems; it encounters countless obstacles and threats; and it is in constant danger of degenerating or being assimilated into considerably less radical projects of "co-management" (*co-gestion*; see chapters 4 and 5). In this manner, Lefebvre promotes *autogestion* less as a fully formed postcapitalist institutional framework than as a political orientation through which various sectors of social life—from factories, universities, and political associations to territorial units such as municipalities and regions—might be subjected to new forms of decentralized, grassroots democratic political control through the very social actors who are most immediately attached to them.

THE STATE MODE OF PRODUCTION AND ANTIPRODUCTIVIST STATE THEORY

Lefebvre believed that states throughout the world had been undergoing profound transformations during the twentieth century, and that these transformations were, as of the 1970s, producing distinctive institutional realignments, strategic dilemmas, and political conflicts. To grasp such transformations and their implications for political strategy, Lefebvre introduces the notion of the "state mode of production," which he elaborated at greatest length in volume 3 of *De l'État* and which he summarizes concisely in chapters 4 and 11 in the current volume. For Lefebvre, the notion of the SMP provided a more appropriate way of grasping the relation between capitalism and the state in the modern world than other state-theoretical orientations that were popular in the 1970s, including Althusserian structuralism, the thesis of State Monopoly Capitalism (nicknamed "Stamokap" theory in West Germany), and the "power elite" theory associated with C. Wright Mills.[52]

The essence of the SMP concept is an insight that Lefebvre was already beginning to develop a decade earlier (it is evident, for instance, in chapters 1 and 5, texts that were written in the mid-1960s): states have come to play a key role in the management and maintenance of capitalist growth at all spatial scales, from the local to the worldwide; therefore, the critique of capitalism necessarily entails the critique of modern state power. Lefebvre describes the consolidation of the SMP as *the* significant event of the twentieth century, since it is a way of understanding fascism, Stalinism, and Western liberal-democratic models such as the U.S. New Deal and European social democracy.[53] For Lefebvre, then, the concept of the SMP is intended as a means to describe what might be termed *state productivism*, which in his view had come to prevail on a world scale during the course of the twentieth century, independently of fluctuations of political regime or ruling coalition: "A qualitative transformation occurs from the moment in which the State takes charge of growth. . . . From this moment forward, economic failures are attributed to the State" (see chapter 4). Accordingly, in volumes 3 and 4 of *De l'État*,

Lefebvre examines the dynamics, geohistory, and consequences of twentieth-century state productivism at some length, with reference both to the Stalinist state apparatuses of the East and to the neo-capitalist, social-democratic state apparatuses of the West.

In the essays included below, Lefebvre devotes particular attention to the social-democratic form of the SMP, which he interprets as the long-term historical outcome of the Lassallian political project that had been promoted by reformist social-democratic parties during the early twentieth century. Lassalle, Lefebvre contends, was a "Hegelian who thought he was a Marxist," yet it is his vision of state socialism that has become dominant in twentieth-century political practice.[54] Ever since social-democratic parties first gained access to the national parliamentary systems of Western European bourgeois democracies, social-democratic control over the machinery of state power has been deployed consistently, if unevenly, as a means to redistribute the social surplus to the working class on a national scale. This social-democratic politics of national redistribution, Lefebvre suggests, has in turn masked a profound transformation of state-economy relations, in which the state has become ever more deeply imbricated in producing, maintaining, and reproducing the basic socio-institutional and territorial preconditions for capital accumulation.

The conception of social democracy as a deradicalizing form of collaboration with the capitalist class enemy dates to Marx's 1875 *Critique of the Gotha Program* and to the subsequent bitter debates between Kautsky, Bernstein, Lenin, and Luxemburg within the Second International over the question of participation within liberal-democratic systems.[55] However, Lefebvre's central concern over a half-century later was to assess the politico-institutional *consequences* of this strategy of social-democratic redistribution coupled with aggressive, often violent, state productivism. From his vantage point in the late 1970s the key issue was less the role of social democracy as a reformist or deradicalizing political strategy than its long-term structural impacts on the nature of state power, the spatial infrastructures for economic growth, and everyday life within neo-capitalism. Lefebvre's claim, in this context, is that social-democratic political strategies, which were initially deployed experimentally during the first half of the twentieth century, have now been directly inscribed into the capitalist state form. Throughout Western Europe, Lefebvre argues, the social-democratic class compromise has thus served as a key political anchor for the consolidation of state productivism as a deep structure of the global capitalist system.

One of Lefebvre's recurrent concerns in part I of this volume is to critique the French and European Left for its failure to recognize and critically interrogate its own role in the creation of a social-democratic crystallization of the SMP. Drawing on Marx's critique of Lassalle in the *Critique of the Gotha Program*, Lefebvre suggests that social-democratic strategies of redistribution are deeply inadequate, because they do not attempt to undermine capitalist relations of production and their associated political basis in the SMP. Around the same time in which Lefebvre was elaborating this point, David Harvey developed a closely analogous critique of American political theorist John Rawls's theory of justice, because it failed to address problems of inequality created at the stage of production and attempted to deal with redistribution entirely separately and subsequently.[56] In effect, as Lefebvre and Harvey both point out, social-democratic practice and liberal theories of distributive justice fail to address the underlying issue—which, for Lefebvre, was that of "the survival of capitalism."[57] Clearly, Lefebvre considered the ideological nuances within the French Left to be of paramount strategic and political importance, but he developed his analysis at a higher level of abstraction in order to interrogate theoretically the very institutional field within which the sociopolitical forces of the Left were situating themselves, and which was essential to securing capitalism's continued survival. While Lefebvre accepts that the Left has generally been able to manage economic growth more equitably than the Right, he insists that it has done so within parameters dictated by its supposed opponents: "What the 'left,' apart from a few exceptional people, has been proposing for years is the same thing that the government has been proposing . . . : a higher rate of growth, fairer distribution of the national income, etc."[58] Thus, rather than challenging the destructive logic of commodification and capital accumulation, and thereby undermining capitalist relations of production, the Left has usually embraced the priorities of promoting stable economic growth and securing a more equitable distribution of the social surplus.[59] One of the core political implications of Lefebvre's state theory is the contention that a basis-democratic appropriation and socialist transformation of state power cannot effectively occur unless the productivist logic of the SMP is challenged directly—this "interruption of economic growth," for Lefebvre, is a key institutional precondition for the transformation of everyday life.[60] In this sense, then, Lefebvre's critique of the social-democratic formation of SMP must be viewed as an important extension and historical contextualization of his advocacy for, and theorization of, *autogestion*.

STATE SPACE AND *MONDIALISATION*

Lefebvre's conception of the SMP was not only a tool of political critique: it also figured crucially in his substantive analysis of twentieth-century state forms and state strategies in *De l'État* and elsewhere. In particular, the notion of the SMP underpinned Lefebvre's analysis of the state's role in the production and transformation of capitalist spatiality, in the changing spatialities of state institutions and practices, and still more generally in the consolidation of a new, worldwide horizon for social and political action, which, as discussed above, he described using a philosophically laden version of the concept of *mondialisation.*

In Lefebvre's framework, state institutions are understood to play an essential role in the production, regulation, and reproduction of a vast range of capitalist spaces—from factories, industrial farms, housing estates, commercial zones, suburban enclaves, and large-scale urban ensembles to roads, canals, tunnels, port facilities, bridges, railway networks, highway grids, airports and air transport corridors, public utilities systems, and diverse techno-institutional infrastructures for communication and surveillance (see chapters 7, 10, and 11). According to Lefebvre, the state's unparalleled capacities to channel large-scale, long-term investments into the built environment for industrial production, collective consumption, commodity circulation, transportation, and communication—coupled with its sovereign legal power to plan and regulate the social uses of such investments—give it a privileged institutional position in the production of capitalist spatiality. "Only the state," Lefebvre notes, "can take on the task of managing space 'on a grand scale'" (see chapter 11). The notion of the SMP, which remains merely implicit in the major state-theoretical passages of his 1974 classic, *The Production of Space,* thus provides an important extension and deepening of Lefebvre's approach to sociospatial theory.

Lefebvre's theorization of the SMP is also closely tied to an insightfully suggestive analysis of the spatiality of state institutions and interventions themselves (see, particularly, chapters, 9, 10, and 11). Lefebvre's theorization of state space—"*l'espace étatique*" (see chapter 11)—is richly multifaceted: it encompasses several intertwined dimensions to which Lefebvre alludes intermittently, but not systematically, in *The Production of Space, De l'État,* and many of the chapters included in part II, especially chapter 11. A careful excavation of these texts reveals that state space, for Lefebvre, encompasses each of the following elements:

- the production of the territory of the nation–state in which capitalist social relations may unfold, appropriately mapped, managed, and manipulated;
- the production of political spaces, politically meaningful architectural forms, and symbolic representations of state power within such territories;
- the production of "mental spaces" composed of popular representations of state power and its associated geographies;
- state strategies to shape, reproduce, and control patterns of industrial development, land use, energy production, transportation, and communication within and beyond their territories;
- the mobilization of new forms of scientific knowledge (*savoir*) and technocratic expertise to facilitate and steer the aforementioned interventions;
- the mobilization of state strategies of colonization through which states attempt to extend capitalist social relations "internally" onto previously marginalized zones within the national territory as well as "externally" onto peripheralized regions of the consolidating world economy;
- and finally, the *mondialisation* of the state form itself through the establishment of a worldwide interstate system in which the tensions of capitalism and inter-state relations may be mediated and managed through diverse international institutions.

Lefebvre's analysis of the SMP thus flows into a rich exploration of how states engage in, and are in turn shaped and reshaped by, the production of space. However, while his analysis opens up many specific realms of inquiry into the historical, institutional, and representational geographies of state space, Lefebvre insists that the link between the SMP and space must ultimately be understood with reference to the still broader process of *mondialisation*. He argues that it is on the terrain of the world, and its associated "space of catastrophe," that the spatial dimensions of state power in neo-capitalism are most directly articulated. As Lefebvre indicates in chapter 11, "the political conception of space makes possible an understanding of how history and its by-products enter into the worldwide process [*le mondial en marche*] and are thus transformed" (see chapter 11). In chapter 14, the final chapter of *De l'État*, Lefebvre takes this proposition a step further by suggesting that, even as the state itself becomes worldwide, it is also increasingly forced to manage, arbitrate, and even oppose the tumultuous social forces that are being articulated on the newly established worldwide scale —leading in turn to new conflicts, crises, wars, and even catastrophes (see chapter 11).

Lefebvre's conceptualization of *mondialisation* encompasses but also transcends his focus on the state, opening up onto a broader series of questions about contemporary historical and spatial formations. Before proceeding to consider these questions, several terminological issues must first be clarified. Lefebvre's conceptual vocabulary of this period is replete with a number of words that link to the core French term of *le monde*—the world. These include *mondial, mondialité,* and *mondialisation,* which present significant translation difficulties. It is tempting to suggest that they can be straightforwardly rendered as "global," "globality," and "globalization." But the latter two terms are more recent in English, and they carry resonances Lefebvre does not intend, while he is in fact careful to distinguish between the *global*—which for Lefebvre effectively means the general—and the *mondial.* As a consequence, words that depend on "*monde*" in French have been translated with variants on the English term "world"—"worldwide" for *mondial* and "worldness" for *mondialité.* For *mondialisation,* we have retained the French, since "worldization" strikes us as an ugly barbarism, and "becoming-worldly" risks inflecting the term with an excessively philosophical determination. While stylistically awkward, the phrase "process of becoming worldwide" initially appears to capture the sense of *mondialisation.* But this too falls short because it misleadingly implies that the "worldwide" is an endpoint that can be achieved definitively, at which point the process in question would terminate. By contrast, Lefebvre's notion of *mondialisation* implies a continual, ongoing making and remaking of worldwide social space—a meaning that is likewise implied in his use of the verb *se mondialiser.*[61] While Lefebvre contends that the question of "worldness" may initially appear to be concerned with spatiality more than temporality, he insists that these three terms—worldness, spatiality, temporality—need to be understood as a trinity.[62] Readers should keep in mind, therefore, the simultaneously philosophical and political–economic resonances of these terms, which Lefebvre uses in order to grasp what might be termed—in analogy to his concept of the production of space—the *production* of world. In both cases, production is to be understood as an ongoing, contradictory, and contested process rather than as a linear sequence with a clear beginning and end.

Given the above considerations, we have preserved Lefebvre's key distinction between the *global* and the *mondial* throughout this translation. In making this distinction, drawing on his earlier arguments in *The Urban Revolution,* Lefebvre is suggesting that the global is a *level,* while the worldwide is a *scale.*

The global (level) refers to a mode of analysis that is focused on the general or the whole; it is linked to understandings of totality and stands in contrast to more specific levels of analysis.[63] By contrast, Lefebvre conceives the worldwide (scale) as a basis for recognizing the simultaneous extension, differentiation, and fragmentation of social relations across the entire earth under contemporary capitalism, a process he also attempts to describe with reference to mathematician René Thom's notion of a "hierarchical stratified morphology" (see chapter 11). Lefebvre's argument here is that *mondialisation* must be understood not as a linear homogenization of social life across the planet, or as a simple enlargement of the scope for socioeconomic activity, but rather with reference to the tangled, constantly changing articulation among different scales, from the local, regional, and the national to the worldwide and the planetary, and their associated social, political, and economic relations.[64]

Lefebvre also links his account of state space to a multiscalar interpretation of newly emergent patterns of neocolonialism and uneven spatial development: his claim is that inter-class relations within established nation–states are now being superseded by new types of center–periphery relations, hierarchization, fragmentation, and differentiation on a worldwide scale. On the national level, Lefebvre suggests that "colonisation, which like industrial production and consumption was formerly localised, is made general. Around the centres there are nothing but subjected, exploited and dependent spaces: neo-colonial spaces."[65] Outside established states, the political decolonization of European empires is replaced with a still more insidious form of colonization: one in which dominant states and multinationals impose relations of dependence and hierarchy within and beyond these new so-called independent states.[66] On a worldwide scale, new sectors of production and exploitation, including tourism, the arms trade, information technology, and energy, are constituted as mechanisms to accelerate, expand, and intensify the extraction of surplus value.[67] It is through the latter, he argues, that "the mode of production actualizes its inherent nature, as a totality on a worldwide scale (that of the worldwide market)."[68]

As noted, Lefebvre's work on the world contains philosophical as well as political–economic dimensions. Lefebvre considered Heidegger's suggestions concerning the world to be extremely powerful, but he was not satisfied with their remoteness from concrete political engagements. Lefebvre contends that Axelos built on Heidegger's somewhat cryptic philosophy, elaborating its insights in powerful and suggestive ways. One of the analyses Lefebvre considered most productive was Axelos's 1961 book, *Marx penseur de la technique: De l'aliénation de l'homme à la conquête du monde* (Marx, Thinker of Technology: From the Alienation of Man to the Conquest of the World). Lefebvre reviewed this Heideggerian reading of Marx for the journal *Esprit* in 1962.[69] In that review, Lefebvre suggested that through technology humans are conjoined to the process of "becoming worldwide and planetary [*devenu mondial et planétaire*]" and that, as a consequence, they may "finally to be able to enjoy or command [*jouir*] the Earth."[70]

Building on Axelos's ideas, Lefebvre distinguishes between the earth—*le terre*—and the world—*le monde*. The earth is the foundation, "a unity of cycles, self-regulating stable systems: waters, winds, air, light, soils, and sediments." The world is "the whole of the devices [*l'ensemble des dispositifs*] assembled by humans [that] begins to cover the earth" (see chapter 12). Thus the earth, planet earth, becomes the "world" through our intervention. This commanding of the earth opens possibilities but comes at a profound cost. Axelos therefore declares that "modernity leads to the planetary era. This era is global and worldwide, errant, leveling and flattening, planning, calculating, and combinative."[71] Modern technology is the means through which many of these feats are realized, but the prior determination of the essence of modern technology—in Heidegger's terms—makes this development possible. Positing the world as something controllable, calculable, and amenable to human designs comes prior to any actual implementation of these goals.

But, in contrast to Axelos's treatment of these issues, Lefebvre's approach to the concept of world is much more explicitly political, building on theoretical foundations only to subject them to radical critique. And in contrast to Heidegger, Lefebvre's arguments do not have a reactionary conservative intention. Rather than simple critique he recognizes the possibilities inherent to the process of taking struggle to a worldwide level. Thus for Lefebvre, Axelos's work ran the same risk as Heidegger's: he had a tendency to lapse into speculative metaphysics (see chapter 6), and to avoid concrete problems such as those of the reproduction of social relations and the survival of capitalism.[72] Nonetheless, Axelos's writings on the question of the world were enormously productive for Lefebvre's more concrete analyses. Specifically, Lefebvre finds Axelos's work concerning the world valuable in at least three registers. First, Lefebvre appreciated Axelos's argument that the world was not simply a totality, an agglomeration of all of the things within it and acting on it. Rather, the world is an object to be thought on its own terms, as world itself, rather than through any external determination. Second, Lefebvre appropriates Axelos's conception of the continual making and remaking of worldwide relations, a process captured by the notion of *mondialisation*. Crucially this notion of *mondialisation* cannot be understood simply as a process of globalization. Rather *mondialisation* is the precondition of globalization, its condition of possibility: it is the prior grasping of the world as a whole, both in thought and in practice, which makes possible the spatial extension of economic, political, and cultural phenomena across the surface of the globe. Third, Lefebvre discusses at some length the notion of play or the game—*le jeu*—in relation to his concept of the world (see chapter 13). Play or game is a term Axelos developed in part via Heidegger, but much more explicitly in dialogue with another German philosopher, Eugen Fink.[73] For all these thinkers the recurrent reference is Heraclitus, who suggested that the world, or time, is "like a child playing a game."[74] These three themes are developed in three chapters in part II—in two explicitly focused on Axelos (chapters 12 and 13); and in the final chapter of *De l'État*, entitled "The Worldwide Experience" (chapter 14).[75]

Yet, for Lefebvre, in contrast to the philosophers with whom he was in dialogue, *mondialisation* cannot be appropriately understood without a sense of its relation to the state and capitalism. The world needs to be understood on its own terms, through its continual making and remaking and through a sense of play or game—but Lefebvre insists that each of these in turn need to be interpreted politically and economically. What all of this means is that, for Lefebvre, the emergence of worldness and the process of *mondialisation* do not entail an erasure of difference but rather an intensified hierarchization, differentiation, and fragmentation of social life at all spatial scales. The notions of hierarchization, differentiation, and fragmentation recur in many places in this book, as Lefebvre seeks to grasp how the production of space, patterns of state spatial organization, and geographies of sociopolitical struggle are being reshaped under late twentieth-century capitalism.

Finally, it is useful to underscore how Lefebvre's writings on the SMP, state space, and *mondialisation* enrich and clarify his widely cited notion of the "survival of capitalism"—a phrase connoting afterlife (*survie*) as much as endurance—which has here already been invoked. In an oft-quoted but cryptic comment made in *The Survival of Capitalism*, first published in 1973, Lefebvre rather generically refers to "the production of space" as the key to this question: "What has happened is that capitalism has found itself able to

attenuate (if not resolve) its internal contradictions for a century, and consequently, in the hundred years since the writing of *Capital*, it has succeeded in
achieving 'growth.' We cannot calculate at what price, but we do know the
means: *by occupying space, by producing a space.*"[76] This comment is rather
brief, and not clearly elaborated, and David Harvey thus speaks for many
when he notes that while the production of space is evidently the key to understanding capitalism's survival, Lefebvre "unfortunately failed to explain exactly
how or why this might be the case."[77] Our response—which comes through
as Lefebvre's in this collection—is that the role of the state is central. Given
Lefebvre's analyses of issues such as the state mode of production, state space,
and the state's role in the process of *mondialisation*, it is clear that the state
represents *the* link between the survival of capitalism and the production of
space. It is therefore in *De l'État* and, for English-language readers, in this
volume, that Lefebvre offers an analysis of "how or why" capitalism has sur-
vived during the twentieth century.

STRUCTURE AND ORGANIZATION OF THE BOOK

As the preceding discussion indicates, Lefebvre's essays on state theory engage with diverse interlocutors, intellectual traditions, and philosophical and
political debates; they cover a broad range of substantive themes in a variety
of historical and geographical contexts; and they articulate several distinctive
yet interconnected perspectives for political practice, imagination, and mobilization. For this reason, the editorial classification of the texts assembled
here presents a challenge. While we considered organizing this book chrono-
logically, to set into relief the temporal evolution of Lefebvre's ideas, we ultimately decided on a division of the volume that, while attuned to each essay's
historical situatedness, emphasizes two distinct yet interconnected conceptual problematics—first, "State, Society, *Autogestion*"; and second, "Space, State.
Spatiality, World." Whereas the former problematic encompasses Lefebvre's
treatment of state institutions and the broad ensemble of social forces and
political struggles that shape them, the latter problematic encompasses his
account of the spatiality of political life in its widest sense, at all spatial scales,
including state institutions, forms of state intervention, forms of political representation, and political struggles. To be sure, spatial categories figure crucially in nearly all of Lefebvre's writings included in this book; at minimum
they serve as diagnostic tools for the understanding of the contextual situatedness of state institutions, state strategies, and political struggles. However,

the spatiality of states and political strategies becomes a more explicit object of analysis in the essays included in part II, where Lefebvre develops a reflexively spatialized analytical lens to investigate the geohistory of state formation under capitalism and, more specifically, the new geographies of state power, political contestation, and popular mobilization that were crystallizing during the post-1968 period in France, in Europe, and on a worldwide scale. Thus, although the dating of each essay in the table of contents enables readers to pursue a chronological path through the book, we have positioned the chapters among and within each of the book's two parts according to a substantive logic rather than a sequential one.[78] The two parts of the book are, however, closely linked through their common engagement with the task of theorizing the state itself, its historical development, and its contemporary restructuring, and still more generally, its changing relation, in diverse historical–geographical contexts, to the problematic of social, political, and cultural transformation.

The contributions to part I of the book allow a thorough examination of Lefebvre's work as a social theorist of the modern state, with specific reference to Marxian debates on state power and capitalism within Western Europe and globally during the 1960s and 1970s. In these essays, Lefebvre situates himself in relation to the key aspects of the state-theoretical writings of Marx and Lenin, as well as in relation to debates among other key nineteenth- and early twentieth-century reformist and revolutionary theorists. In so doing, Lefebvre also repeatedly lambastes state socialist and Stalinist misappropriations of Marxist (and, it should be added, Leninist) ideas on the state and democracy, arguing that the radical core of such ideas remains as relevant as ever to revolutionary theory and practice under late twentieth-century capitalism. Just as importantly, Lefebvre here elaborates some of the intellectual foundations for the analyses of state restructuring under late twentieth-century capitalism that he would subsequently undertake over the next decade and a half in the four volumes of *De l'État*.

Part I opens with a translation of two remarkable but largely unknown 1964 lectures—"The State and Society" (chapter 1) and "Sources of Marxist–Leninist State Theory" (chapter 2)—in which, through a reinterpretation of some classic texts in the history of Marxian political thought, Lefebvre consolidates the foundations for his approach to state theory and democratic transformation. These tightly argued, didactic essays are followed by a schematic piece entitled "The State in the Modern World" (chapter 3), which would

later reappear as the introduction to volume 1 of *De l'État,* in which Lefebvre
outlines the general architecture of the epic four-volume excursion he had
just begun to undertake. While chapter 3 is, in effect, an annotated table of
contents to that long, sprawling work, it reveals the audacious scope and
ambition of Lefebvre's thought on the state generally. It may also serve, therefore, as a broad conceptual mapping of the intellectual and strategic terrain
Lefebvre was attempting to explore in all of the essays included in this book.
The next three chapters of part I are devoted to more specific topics—first, a
substantial analysis of transformations of the French and European state
through social-democratic political strategies during the 1970s (chapter 4);
and second, an essay and an interview on the question of *autogestion* (chapters
5 and 6). These chapters illustrate Lefebvre's consistent efforts to apply his
theoretical apparatus to the practical-political and strategic issues that faced
the European Left during the period of economic restructuring and Eurocommunist political experimentation in the 1970s. Taken together, then, the six
chapters in part I survey some of Lefebvre's major state-theoretical concerns,
demonstrating the breadth of his analysis; his relation to other traditions of
state theory, particularly within Marxism; his interest in the historicity of
modern statehood and state forms; and his engagement with a still broader
set of questions regarding the nature of modern state power, its transformation during the course of the twentieth century, and the possibility for its
radical-democratic "withering away" through a process of *autogestion.*

   In the chapters included in part II of the volume, Lefebvre builds on the
state-theoretical foundations elaborated on in part I in order to explore state
spatial strategies in worldwide context, with specific reference to the new geographies of state power, political struggle, and uneven spatial development
that were emerging around the world, and on a worldwide scale, during the
second half of the twentieth century. In the most general sense, these chapters demonstrate how Lefebvre's engagements with state theory, state formation, state restructuring, and radical politics were in continual relation with
the problem of space. As indicated previously, a key contribution of the essays
included in part II is to clarify and elaborate in detail Lefebvre's thesis that
state institutions have come to play an increasingly essential role in the production of space and thus, in facilitating the survival of capitalism. Just as important, several chapters in part II emphasize the distinctively geographical
dimensions of *autogestion,* which Lefebvre now views as a process operating
not only at the level of the individual firm or enterprise but also, increasingly,

as a territorial mode of self-governance for communities, towns, and even entire subnational regions (see chapters 8, 14, and 15). In this sense, then, the contributions to part II explore the politics of spatiality in several of its core dimensions—the spatiality of capitalist growth, crisis, and contradiction; the spatiality of state strategies oriented toward the regulation of those tendencies; and finally, the spatiality of social forces oriented toward their radical-democratic transcendence.

Part II opens with three broad-ranging essays on sociospatial theory, and then moves to more focused inquiries into the distinctive spatialities of states, politics, *mondialisation,* and social mobilization in worldwide context. The first two essays have been available in English for some time but have generally been neglected in the appropriation of Lefebvre's writings on space. The first is translated anew to update the error-laden version that was originally published in the mid-1970s and to render its terminology consistent with this book as a whole and with more recent developments in Lefebvre studies (chapter 7). The second resonates closely with arguments from *The Production of Space,* but presents them in a more explicitly political and state-theoretical perspective (chapter 8). Indeed, what is most significant about the opening pair of chapters of part II is their demonstration that Lefebvre's work on the problematic of spatiality was always explicitly and reflexively political, and animated by a series of arguments regarding the role of state strategies in the production and transformation of sociospatial forms and practices. In subsequent chapters of part II, this political analysis of spatiality is further broadened to consider the worldwide, if unevenly articulated and internally contradictory, dimensions of capitalist spatiality; the state's role in the management of worldwide processes and their contradictions; and finally, the increasingly worldwide parameters of capitalism, state action, and oppositional political struggles. Thus, chapters 9 through 15 introduce and elaborate a series of key concepts Lefebvre used to confront these issues—the world, the worldwide, the planetary, the state mode of production, state spatiality, and *mondialisation.* Chapters 12 and 13 demonstrate how Lefebvre's concern with the concept of the world—and with closely derivative terms such as *mondialisation*— emerged from an intensive philosophical engagement with the works of Axelos. Finally, the last two contributions to this part of the book link the preceding concerns back to the problematic of the SMP, state restructuring, state space, state strategies, politico-spatial transformation and *autogestion* in long-term geohistorical perspective.

In assembling and introducing this group of texts, our role as editors has been both to frame the context and to highlight some of the key insights of Lefebvre's work. Accordingly, through brief introductory prefaces and editorial endnotes to each translation, we have provided contextual information to illuminate the intellectual, social, and political milieus in which Lefebvre's arguments were situated. Much of this, we believe, has generally been opaque to English-language readers and deserves greater attention in engagements with his ideas. In addition, Lefebvre's references to texts are often seriously incomplete, and, at times, incorrect. As far as practicable, we have sought to identify and complete these references.

Translating Lefebvre's writing has posed significant challenges, not least due to its dense theoretical argumentation, its many implicit or covert references, its often-elusive organizational structure, and its frequent digressions. Indeed, even French-language readers often express frustration with the difficulties of deciphering some of Lefebvre's more meandering or vague formulations. We now know that many of Lefebvre's writings were produced through dictation—as Andy Merrifield notes, he "blasted out his books 'jerkily, hastily, nervously'"—and this practice may at least partially explain some of the stylistic quirks, infelicities, and apparent carelessness of certain passages.[79] Yet, the apparent awkwardness of some of Lefebvre's more elusive formulations may also hide deeper, dialectical secrets. In chapter 12, Lefebvre makes the following comment about Kostas Axelos:

> The writings of Kostas Axelos happen to irritate many readers, exasperating some of them. And furthermore one never knows, in reading his books, exactly where and when we encounter an essential thought or mere wordplay. Axelos knows this. Behind this ambiguity, we glimpse his laughter, the laughter of the Sphinx before the young Oedipus (the reader). A demon of dialectics, he uses and abuses this game. Although not exactly Latin, is not a certain rhetoric an integral part of his thought? What right do we have to reproach him for it, in an age where everything is thrown into question, including language? No one can guarantee that word games are always facile, inoffensive and merely amusing.

In penning these lines, we suspect that Lefebvre may well have been thinking of himself as much as of Axelos. Accordingly, so as to preserve some of the complexities and challenges of his own way of writing, we have sought, as much as has been feasible, to maintain Lefebvre's own occasionally ambiguous or vague formulations, turns of phrase, and wordplays in the translations included here, even if this occasionally means permitting a certain degree of imprecision in some sentences or passages.

Beyond Fordist Marxism? The Futures of Lefebvre

The Eurocommunist movements and *autogestion* debates of the mid-1970s in France, Italy, and Spain may be viewed as the high point of a distinctively Fordist form of western Marxism that prevailed, albeit in variegated forms, throughout much of the postwar period. In Western Europe and North America, the main reference point for this Fordist crystallization of Marxist theory and practice was the specific framework of social, political, and economic organization that had been consolidated between the early 1950s and the early 1970s: the critique of capitalism was articulated, under these conditions, as a critique of the Fordist regime of accumulation, the closely associated bureaucratic apparatuses of the Keynesian welfare national state and the entrenched patterns of everyday power, class domination, and popular alienation with which those socio-institutional forms were intertwined.[80] Yet Lefebvre's analyses of the postwar capitalist formation were not confined to Western Europe and North America. Throughout his work he references, and occasionally analyzes, the changing nature of state power in Eastern Europe and the Soviet Union. Additionally, in volume 3 of *De l'État,* he suggests several ways in which the concept of the SMP might illuminate politico-institutional transformations in the national states of Latin America, Africa, and Asia.

Nonetheless, like many of the major critical theorists of the postwar period, Lefebvre's most important works, including almost all of those included in this volume, were tightly embedded within the theoretical grammar of Fordist Marxism. Whereas Lefebvre's initial analyses of the "bureaucratic society of controlled consumption" were explicitly focused on the political–economic order of the 1950s and 1960s,[81] even his later studies of neo-capitalism, the SMP, and state space implied that the restructuring processes of the 1970s represented a consolidation and intensification of the postwar capitalist order rather than its destabilization or transcendence. In several of his state-theoretical writings, Lefebvre mentions the politics of neoliberalism, but in so doing he is more frequently referring to a specific ideological strand within the French Right than to the worldwide capitalist class offensive that has underpinned the successive waves of state retrenchment and economic restructuring of the post-1970s period. Although the four volumes of *De l'État* and

most of the contributions to this volume were published while the basic institutional foundations of postwar Fordism were being dismantled in France
and elsewhere, Lefebvre does not attempt in these works to examine systematically the global economic crises of the 1970s or their ramifications for the
forms, functions, and spatialities of the modern state.[82]

These contextual limitations of Lefebvre's theoretical framework arguably
deserve to be examined much more closely in scholarship devoted to or influenced by his work. Certainly, we would urge readers to keep them in mind
in absorbing Lefebvre's arguments in the present volume. Nonetheless, we
would also suggest that recognizing the contextual boundedness of Lefebvre's
theoretical framework can open up potentially fruitful possibilities for its
application and redeployment under the *after*-Fordist, neoliberalizing conditions of the present day. What, we might ask, would a Lefebvre-inspired interpretation of the current round of worldwide sociospatial restructuring entail?
More specifically, in what ways might Lefebvre's writings on state, space, and
world help illuminate the current conjuncture of global neoliberal domination, neoconservative geopolitical reaction, and their strategic dilemmas for
progressive or radical social forces? And how successfully is Lefebvre's work
able to "travel," to offer insight into very different geographical regions?

In the present context, we cannot attempt to pursue these demanding questions in detail. Instead we conclude this introductory essay by noting, in highly
stylized terms, six possible ways in which Lefebvre's contributions to this volume might remain relevant to the concerns of contemporary Left-radical
scholars, social theorists, and activists.

The New Politics of Space

In the early 1970s Lefebvre reflected on the elaborate, nationwide system of
spatial planning that had been constructed in France and throughout much
of Europe during the preceding decade and a half (see chapters 7 and 11). For
Lefebvre, the proliferation of state strategies to manage urbanization—at once
on European, national, regional, and local scales—revealed the inherently
political character of capitalist spatiality. Such strategies, he argued, involved
the mobilization of diverse forms of technocratic knowledge and politico-
institutional power in order to produce, manipulate, manage, and regulate
the geographies of production, exchange, transportation, and biological reproduction within each national, regional, and local territory. Just as important,

Lefebvre insisted, despite the technocratic, bureaucratic, and apolitical veneer associated with such strategies, they unleash intensely dysfunctional side-effects and bitter disputes at all scales, and across the ideological spectrum. Spatial relations thus constantly escape any attempt to subsume them under a fixed framework, whether through planning, regulation, or design.

Although Lefebvre's analysis of state spatial strategies was clearly focused on the various institutional mechanisms of spatial Keynesianism, the nationally redistributive system of urban and regional planning that prevailed during the postwar period throughout France and much of Western Europe, we would argue that his analytical approach remains remarkably salient even in a post-Keynesian period. To be sure, the nature of state spatial strategies has undergone a sea change: the nationalizing, homogenizing politics of spatial redistribution of the 1960s and 1970s that Lefebvre portrayed in such a negative light have been widely marginalized or abandoned, and in the meantime, during the post-1980s period new, aggressively developmentalist forms of locational policy have emerged that target major urban and regional spaces for transnational capital investment.[83] Consequently, nationalized systems of spatial planning and infrastructural investment are being fragmented and redifferentiated as states attempt to reposition local growth poles strategically within supranational circuits of capital investment rather than within nationally self-enclosed territorial economies. Yet, even as the forms, mechanisms, and goals of state spatial strategies have been fundamentally reoriented and rejigged, Lefebvre's underlying intuitions regarding the endemically political character of space continue to resonate as powerfully as ever. His famous aphorism "There is a politics of space because space is political [*il y a politique de l'espace, parce que l'espace et politique*]" (see chapter 7) remains as useful a commentary on the spaces of neoliberalism and interlocality competition as it was on the geographies of Fordist-Keynesian capitalism. Indeed, it is precisely because patterns of spatial organization continue to have such strategic significance to capital, states, and social forces at all scales that such concerted political strategies are being mobilized to reshape them. The politics of space thus remain as contradictory and contentious as ever, and their consequences for everyday life remain to be fought out in diverse territorial arenas and at a variety of spatial scales. Lefebvre's reflections on the politics of space from over three decades ago arguably remain an indispensable methodological and political guide for exploring such issues.

Neoliberalism as a Reconstitution of the State Mode of Production

Lefebvre's analysis of the SMP can be fruitfully redeployed to decipher the forms of state institutional restructuring that have been unfolding on a world scale throughout the last two decades. As discussed above, Lefebvre interprets the SMP as the outgrowth of a historical class compromise that was consolidated through social-democratic political strategies during the mid-twentieth century and grounded in a combination of aggressive state productivism and a class-based politics of redistribution. The post-1970s round of state restructuring can be plausibly understood as a systematic assault on the state's redistributive functions coupled with a marked intensification of the productivist, commodifying aspects of the SMP—that is, its role in promoting, financing, subsidizing, and regulating capitalist growth. Indeed, as contemporary analyses of "competition states" imply, we may currently be witnessing the emergence of an historically new form of the SMP in which the state's role as an agent for the commodification of its territory—at once on national, regional, and urban scales—has acquired an unprecedented supremacy over other regulatory operations within the state's institutional architecture.[84] Although this productivistic orientation of state power was clearly evident during the post-war period, the currently emergent hyperproductivist form of the SMP appears to entail a significant enhancement of the state's role in mobilizing space as a productive force, coupled with a major recalibration of the social power relations that are mediated through the state apparatus. In an era in which public discourse on the state is dominated by the neoliberal utopia of free, deregulated markets, powerless states, hypermobile capital, and unconstrained exploitation, Lefebvre's theory of the SMP provides a powerful analytical lens through which the evolving political, institutional, and geographical dimensions of actually existing state productivism can be critically decoded.

Development versus Growth: Beyond Left Productivism

Postwar forms of social democracy in Western Europe and beyond were grounded in the assumption that egalitarian redistributive goals could be attained within the parameters of a political system that was structurally dependent on capital accumulation for its own survival. However, as the current period of worldwide capitalist restructuring has rather brutally illustrated, the social-democratic project was premised on historically and geographically contingent socio-institutional conditions and power relations that appear now to have been largely superseded through the creatively destructive forward movement of global capital. Whereas many traditional Left political parties struggled throughout the 1970s and into the 1980s to defend the redistributive arrangements associated with the Fordist-Keynesian settlement, much of the centrist or mainstream Left today appears to have embraced some version of the neoliberal consensus, often in the guise of so-called Third Way programs that, despite their attention to the social disruptions triggered by capitalist restructuring, nonetheless promulgate an economic policy repertoire that is almost indistinguishable from that of the neoliberal Right.

Under these conditions, Lefebvre's critique of state productivism from the 1970s provides a timely warning against the tendency—which is quite rampant even within contemporary left-wing political discourse—to narrow the field of political discussion to the issue of how to promote capitalist growth and thus to vacate the problematic of criticizing and ultimately transforming the logic of capitalism itself as an objectified form of abstract domination and socio-ecological destruction. Clearly, the politico-institutional frameworks within which capitalist growth occurs have massive ramifications for everyday life and must remain a key focus of any progressive, egalitarian, and democratic politics. Nonetheless, from a radical-democratic socialist perspective, it would be politically fatal to accept the capitalist form of development as an unquestioned or self-evident end in itself. As is evident in several chapters, Lefebvre insisted on a distinction between (qualitative) development and (quantitative) growth, and he forcefully and consistently rejected the capitalist equation of the latter with the former (see chapters 1, 4, 8, 9, 11, and 14). In an era in which putatively progressive parties across Europe and North America have become powerful agents, enforcers, and apologists for various kinds of soft neoliberalism, Lefebvre's dissident critique of state productivism over three decades ago provides a welcome reminder of one essential ingredient within any radically democratic socialist politics: the critique of the capitalist growth dynamic—"production for production's sake, accumulation for accumulation's sake"—in the name of alternative frameworks for the production of everyday life.[85]

States, Territory, and Violence under "Globalization"

Contrary to mainstream arguments for globalization to be understood as a process of deterritorialization, in which inherited geographical frameworks are said to be dismantled and overcome, Lefebvre's writings provide a conceptual basis for interpreting contemporary geopolitical developments as the latest expression of a continual making and remaking of territory during the long-term history of the modern world. From this perspective, territory must be understood not as a fixed container of political action and international relations, but rather as a dynamic and constitutive dimension and stake of struggle, one that is currently being reconfigured rather than eroded.[86] Lefebvre's understanding of state violence—embodied in his assertion that "violence is inherent to political space, not only as an expression of (political) will to power, but due to a permanent reign of terror . . ."[87]—is valuable in this respect: it helps to explain why territorial disputes continue to permeate global politics even when, according to dominant neoliberal ideologies, such disputes represent threats to economic stability, and thus to prosperity. It is telling that just as global capital has sought to divert decisions in the economic sphere to putatively independent institutions such as the World Bank and the International Monetary Fund (IMF), so too did it do so much earlier in the political realm, establishing the United Nations as "a clearinghouse for territorial disputes,"[88] or more recently as "a post-war management tool for territories ravaged by military interventions decided in Washington."[89] Particularly in the post–Cold War period, there is a clear attempt to create international institutions that appear to be independent of particular states, even though U.S. political and economic elites have an obvious interest and role in the divestment of these decisions.[90]

Against this background, due to his sustained attention to the produced, contested, and violently contradictory character of state space and state sovereignty, Lefebvre's writings offer some valuable insights into some of the new patterns of territorial conflict, at various spatial scales, that have emerged under post–Cold War capitalism. These trends are illustrated, for instance, by the way in which the United Nations, the United States, and other geopolitical powers generally oppose the breakup of existing territorial settlements, while at the same time offering justifications for international intervention within them. The process of using geopolitical force, particularly but not exclusively by the United States, in the interests of global capitalism—as opposed to narrow understandings of the national interest—is something Lefebvre merely anticipated, but it can be seen in a range of contemporary events, notably the Iraq war that began in 2003. While traditional theories of imperialism tended to focus on state accumulation through colonial dispossession, studies of the "new imperialism" require several crucial issues to be taken

into account: the global scale and ambition of these strategies, the tension between the logics of global capital and nation–state territory, and the fact that
the intended outcome of contemporary geopolitical strategies is no longer
crude territorial expansion, but rather the free passage of goods, energy, and
military power across the globe.[91] Lefebvre's state theory, and in particular its
understanding of the violence inherent to the state of territory, provides a solid
theoretical foundation for a systematic consideration of precisely these issues.

Radical Democracy and the Critique of the State

In a paper originally published shortly after Lefebvre completed the final volume of *De l'État,* West German state theorist Claus Offe noted the apparent
convergence between leftist and neoconservative accounts of the crisis of the
Keynesian welfare state.[92] At that time, the critique of the state was one of the
major ideological battlegrounds on which the politics of capitalist restructuring were being fought out in Western Europe. Today, however, the project
of a critique of the state appears to have been monopolized almost entirely
by the neoliberal and neoconservative Right, with its persistent demand for
greater governmental efficiency, lean management, fiscal discipline, market
rationality, and political recognition of the putative "rights" of capital. Mean-
while, the left-wing critique of the state seems to have all but disappeared
as progressives struggle desperately to salvage the remaining vestiges of the
Keynesian settlement and to manage the polarizing effects of neoliberal policies. Such struggles no doubt remain significant, even essential; however, as
Lefebvre's analysis indicates, they need not be premised on a wholesale re-
treat from the project of a critique of the state. Indeed, as we observe state
institutions becoming leaner, meaner, and increasingly undemocratic as they
indulge in the "dangerous obsession"[93] of promoting global territorial competitiveness, a critique of the state must surely remain central to any radically
democratic politics.

    Although Lefebvre's conceptualization of *autogestion* is quite multifaceted,
one of its core components is the affirmation of grassroots democracy as an
ongoing, limitless project at all geographical scales and within all sectors of
social and political life—including, crucially, within state institutions themselves. During the last two decades, neoliberal regimes have systematically
undermined mechanisms of democratic accountability and political legitimation that were won during many centuries of popular struggle. Currently,
this U.S.-dominated "new constitutionalism" supporting the extension of

corporate capitalist power, fiscal austerity, heightened social polarization, intensified exploitation, and untrammeled financial speculation is being extended onto a global scale through the initiatives of autocratic, unaccountable institutions such as the IMF, the World Bank, the World Trade Organization, the Organisation for Economic Co-operation and Development, the World Economic Forum, and so forth.[94] Under these circumstances, the project of a democratization of the state remains particularly urgent at all spatial scales. Lefebvre's sustained critique of the state in the name of a politics of social and territorial *autogestion*—and, more generally, his impassioned call for the "withering away" of a state form dominated by ruling class interests—could potentially provide an important normative reference point for the rejuvenation of political struggles oriented toward a comprehensive *redemocratization* and even *hyperdemocratization* of state institutions and all other governance arrangements.

Toward a Politics of the Possible

One of the hallmarks of neoliberal politics is the appeal to the supposed "external constraints" of the global economy, which are generally represented as being objective, abstract, and quasi-natural forces that are autonomous from political decisions and independent of human control. This neoliberal political program is perhaps most concisely expressed in the infamous Thatcherite dictum, "there is no alternative." Lefebvre's writings on the state contain a systematic critique of this necessitarian logic, which was embodied in his own time by Stalinist ideologues in the PCF such as Guy Mollet and Maurice Thorez, the "men of the State" associated with the Jean-Moulin Club (chapter 1) and social-democratic technocrats such as Jacques Attali (chapter 4), all of whom took for granted extant institutional frameworks and thus provided "an apology for the existing reality" (see chapter 1, "The Myth of Consumer Society").

By contrast, Lefebvre advocated the path of the "Statesman," who repeatedly calls "into question the existing institutions . . . in order to pose the problem of the State, which entails a critique of the existing type of State" (see chapter 1). Invoking disparate examples, from the political strategizing of Lenin to the cultural experiments of the Surrealists and the grassroots militancy of *autogestion* movements, Lefebvre insisted on the need to excavate everyday life for political possibilities that point toward alternative, more progressive, democratic, and egalitarian futures. Indeed, in the final pages of *De l'État,* Lefebvre reinforces this imperative by advocating an *"urgent utopia . . . ,* a style of thinking turned toward the possible in all areas" (see chapter 14; italics in original). For Lefebvre, the formation of the Paris Commune in 1871 and the French student revolts of 1968 represented defining political conjunctures within the modern world that revealed such latent possibilities for radical democracy, *autogestion,* and utopian practices, even if they were realized only fleetingly and incompletely in current institutional arrangements.[95] Concomitantly, Lefebvre's interest in the diverse experiments in *autogestion* that were percolating throughout French society during the post-1968 period—in factories, schools, universities, trade unions, cities, regions, and so forth—stemmed from his conviction that they represented the elements of a "social pedagogy"[96] within everyday life that pointed beyond the extant and toward alternative futures grounded in more progressive, democratic, and egalitarian ways of organizing social space and time.

In an epoch in which, in Habermas's apt formulation, the "exhaustion of utopian energies" continues to haunt the global Left,[97] Lefebvre's dialectical utopianism provides a salient reminder that everyday life under capitalism is permeated with utopian possibilities and strivings—of both reactionary and progressive variants, and with foreboding, benign, or emancipatory ramifications.[98] This is the Lefebvre who, consistent with his description of Marx, is a thinker of the possible.[99] This characterization should be understood in two senses—first, as a thinking through of what makes something possible, its historical conditions; and second, as an opening up of what might be (or become) possible within that context. This is another iteration of Lefebvre's notion of the regressive-progressive mode of analysis, in which he argues that historical examination is key to strategies of transformation. A thorough understanding of how we got where we are can give us considerable insight into how we might go beyond it, changing paths toward a different future. Lefebvre sums up this point with admirable precision in the injunction that "utopia today is the possible of tomorrow."[100] Similarly, as Lefebvre declared in 1959: "If we define communism not as a being or a 'state' (the pun is intentional) but as movement, and in movement, towards a possible future, established as such, then I lay claim to being an excellent communist."[101]

The revolution Lefebvre once sought has not happened; as he said to Catherine Régulier in a volume of dialogues, "the revolution is not what it used to be."[102] Nonetheless, oppositional social movements continue to emerge around the world that challenge some of the basic institutional arrangements of

modern capitalism and insist relentlessly that "another world is possible." The
global justice movement represents one of the most prominent examples of
this multiscalar, multicentered trend, the nature of which remains a matter
of intense academic and political disagreement.[103] We would argue that, even
in a radically different geopolitical conjuncture than that to which his critique of the state was a response, Lefebvre's politics of the possible provide a
potentially fruitful point of orientation for the understanding of such movements, which have oriented their struggles less toward abstract utopian visions
than toward unrealized possibilities embedded within extant social and political institutions. Lefebvre's intellectual framework thus appears to contain
rich resources for deciphering the failures of radical and revolutionary movements and the worldwide "space of catastrophe" that has subsequently been
established—a situation he once described with reference to the notion of
"the schema of the worst," the dialectical inversion of his theory of the possible (see chapter 10, "The State and the Worldwide System of States"). Just
as important, Lefebvre's framework suggests a theoretically grounded yet
historically specific orientation for understanding the restless anticapitalist
mobilizations, struggles, and experiments that continue to percolate throughout diverse institutional and territorial arenas around the world in the early
twenty-first century.

With these six possible applications of Lefebvre's ideas in mind, and antici-
pating others that will hopefully be sparked in the minds of individual readers, this book is offered as a contribution to present and future discussions
and debates regarding Lefebvre's multifaceted intellectual and political lega-
cies for contemporary times. This introduction and the critical apparatus with
which we have supplemented the translations seek to provide a framework
for understanding the contexts in which Lefebvre was thinking and writing.
We additionally hope that the juxtaposition of these essays may provide a
spur to future thinking about how Lefebvre's ideas, nearly two decades since
his death, might speak to the contemporary moment, even if much remains
to be thought in his wake. Lefebvre obviously cannot be expected to have
anticipated contemporary theoretical debates or political–economic trends,
and we reiterate that his conceptual, interpretive, and political orientations
were very much situated within the times and places in which he lived and
worked. The limitations of his work—theoretically, politically, historically,
and geographically—need to be carefully interrogated. Indeed, it is precisely

when they are effectively contextualized in time and space, we would argue, that the writings presented here offer analytical tools for thinking through our own volatile geohistorical moment. This contextually embedded yet forward-looking mode of engagement is perhaps the most fitting way of appropriating Lefebvre's remarkable intellectual and political legacy. The futures of Lefebvre remain to be forged through his readers, including, we hope, those of this book.

NOTES

1. Henri Lefebvre, "Marxism Exploded," *Review* 4, no. 1 (1980): 23.

2. The Anglo-American reception of Henri Lefebvre's work is vast and constantly expanding. References to even a small fraction of the literature that makes use of his ideas would be overwhelming. Two important initial statements in English were Mark Gottdiener, *The Social Production of Urban Space*, 2nd ed. (Austin: University of Texas Press, 1994 [1985]); and Edward W. Soja, *Postmodern Geographies: The Reassertion of Space in Critical Social Theory* (London: Verso, 1989). For general overviews of Lefebvre's work, which also provide detailed references to more specific lines of interpretation and appropriation, see the following works: Rob Shields, *Lefebvre, Love, and Struggle: Spatial Dialectics* (New York: Routledge, 1999); Stuart Elden, *Understanding Henri Lefebvre: Theory and the Possible* (London: Continuum, 2004); Andy Merrifield, *Henri Lefebvre: A Critical Introduction* (New York: Routledge, 2006); and, most recently, Kanishka Goonewardena, Stefan Kipfer, Richard Milgrom, and Christian Schmid, eds., *Space, Difference, Everyday Life: Reading Henri Lefebvre* (New York: Routledge, 2008). A useful overview of the French-language discussion is *Espaces et Sociétés* 76 (1994), a special issue devoted to Lefebvre's work. Rémi Hess's biography is invaluable: *Henri Lefebvre et l'aventure du siècle* (Paris: A. M. Métaillié, 1988).

3. There are currently two collections of Lefebvre's essays available in English—*Writings on Cities*, ed. Eleonore Kofman and Elizabeth Lebas (Oxford: Blackwell, 1996); and *Key Writings*, ed. Stuart Elden, Eleonore Kofman, and Elizabeth Lebas (New York: Continuum, 2003)—but they deal with his writings on the state and the world only indirectly in the first instance and as one aspect among many in the second.

4. Nicos Poulantzas, *State, Power, Socialism*, trans. Patrick Camiller (New York: New Left Books, 1978), 50, 190.

5. In *Social Production of Urban Space*, Gottdiener offers a useful initial exploration of some of Lefebvre's ideas on the state, but he does not discuss Lefebvre's major work on this topic, *De l'État*, 4 vols. (Paris: Union Générale d'Éditions, 1976–78). To our knowledge, the only systematic studies of Lefebvre's state theory are two German texts: Hajo Schmidt's *Sozialphilosophie des Krieges: Staats- und subjekttheoretische Untersuchungen zu Henri Lefebvre und Georges Bataille* (Essen: Klartext, 1990); and Corel Wex's doctoral thesis, "Logistik der Macht: Henri Lefebvres Sozialtheorie und die Räumlichkeit des Staates" (Phillips-Universität Marburg, 1999). Elden, *Understanding Henri Lefebvre*, 211–56, and Merrifield, *Henri Lefebvre*, 121–42, each contain a chapter devoted to

Lefebvre's state-theoretical writings. Neil Brenner has written several articles that explicate and apply Lefebvre's state theory to debates on contemporary globalization, sociospatial theory, and state spatial restructuring. See, in particular, "State Territorial Restructuring and the Production of Spatial Scale," *Political Geography* 16, no. 4 (1997): 273–306; "Global, Fragmented, Hierarchical: Henri Lefebvre's Geographies of Globalization," *Public Culture* 10, no. 1 (1997): 137–69; "Between Fixity and Motion: Accumulation, Territorial Organization and the Historical Geography of Spatial Scales," *Environment and Planning D: Society and Space* 16 (1998), 459–81; "The Urban Question as a Scale Question: Reflections on Henri Lefebvre, Urban Theory and the Politics of Scale," *International Journal of Urban and Regional Research* 24, no. 2 (2000): 361–78; and "Henri Lefebvre's Critique of State Productivism," in Goonewardena et al., *Space, Difference, Everyday Life*, 231–49.

6. Lefebvre's works cited here are *De l'État*; *Une pensée devenue monde: Faut-il abandonner Marx?* (Paris: Fayard, 1980); and *Le retour de la dialectique: Douze mots-clefs pour le monde moderne* (Paris: Messidor, 1986).

7. Henri Lefebvre, *L'irruption de Nanterre au sommet*, 2nd ed. (Paris: Éditions Syllepse, 1998 [1968]), translated by Alfred Ehrenfeld as *The Explosion: Marxism and the French Upheaval* (New York: Modern Reader, 1969).

8. Henri Lefebvre, "State," in *Key Writings*, 61 (originally from *Le retour de la dialectique*).

9. According to Rémi Hess's bibliography, *De l'État* has been translated into Spanish, Italian, Portuguese, and Serbo-Croatian. See Hess, *Henri Lefebvre et l'aventure*, 333.

10. Stefan Kipfer, "Marxism, Everyday Life and Urbanization" (unpublished manuscript, Department of Political Science, York University, 1996), 34.

11. Hess, *Henri Lefebvre et l'aventure*, 284. Unless otherwise indicated, translations are our own.

12. See particularly Henri Lefebvre, *La somme et reste*, 3rd ed. (Paris: Méridiens Klincksieck, 1989 [1959]); and his *The Sociology of Marx*, trans. Norbert Guterman (New York: Columbia, 1968). The latter work contains an extensive treatment of Marx's state theory or, as Lefebvre then termed it, his "political sociology." For the suggestion that these analyses need supplanting, see Lefebvre, *De l'État*, 2:255 n.1.

13. Lefebvre, "Marxism Exploded." A decade before, the journal *Arguments* (later edited by Axelos and to which Lefebvre was a contributor) had said that they were launched at the time of the *éclatement*—the explosion or destruction—of Stalinism. See "Manifeste," *Arguments* 1 (December 1956–January 1957): 1.

14. Lefebvre, "Marxism Exploded," 21.

15. Sunil Khilnani, *Arguing Revolution: The Intellectual Left in Postwar France* (New Haven: Yale University Press, 1993), 121.

16. For a more detailed analysis of these and other influences, see our discussion below and Elden, *Understanding Henri Lefebvre*; see also Elden, "Between Marx and Heidegger: Politics, Philosophy and Lefebvre's *The Production of Space*," *Antipode* 36, no. 1 (2004): 86–105.

17. See chapter 14 of this volume; and our own discussion later in the present chapter.

18. See Merrifield, *Henri Lefebvre*, xxxi.

19. For some important recent elaborations, see Goonewardena et al., *Space, Difference, Everyday Life.*

20. See the outline of *De l'État* included in chapter 3.

21. See Lefebvre, *Sociology of Marx*, 183. Lefebvre's most detailed treatment of the history and development of Marxist state theory in the nineteenth and twentieth centuries can be found in volume 2 of *De l'État*, whose subtitle is "the Marxist theory of the State from Hegel to Marx via Stalin."

22. Henri Lefebvre, *Les temps des méprises* (Paris: Stock, 1975), 192. See *Critique of Everyday Life*, trans. John Moore and Gregory Elliott, 3 vols. (London: Verso, 1991–2006).

23. Lefebvre, *De l'État*, 2:177.

24. Lefebvre, *De l'État*, 2:216–37.

25. For an excellent overview of the Poulantzas-Miliband debates, see Clyde Barrow, "The Miliband-Poulantzas Debate: An Intellectual History," in *Paradigm Lost: State Theory Reconsidered*, ed. Stanley Aronowitz and Peter Bratsis, 3–52 (Minneapolis: University of Minnesota Press, 2002). On the German state derivation debates, see John Holloway and Sol Picciotto, *State and Capital: A Marxist Debate* (Austin: University of Texas Press, 1979); and Bob Jessop, *The Capitalist State* (Oxford: Blackwell, 1982), 78–141. In 1976 Lefebvre is explicitly critical of his own earlier attempt, a decade earlier in *The Sociology of Marx*, to derive a single unitary theory of the state from Marx. See Lefebvre, *De l'État*, 2:255 n.1.

26. For a contemporaneous English-language interpretation of these and other aspects of Marx's state theory, see Bob Jessop, "Recent Theories of the Capitalist State," *Cambridge Journal of Economics* 1 (1977): 353–73; and Jessop, *Capitalist State*, 1–31.

27. Lefebvre, *De l'État*, 2:118–64; see also chapters 1 and 2.

28. Lefebvre, *Sociology of Marx*, 26.

29. See chapter 2; and Lefebvre, *De l'État*, 2:120. See also Lefebvre, *Sociology of Marx*, 127–34.

30. In 1959, shortly after his departure from the PCF, Lefebvre wrote that "Marxism has been turned into a metaphysics of the party and the State, elevated into absolutes that demand unconditional allegiance. . . . Marxism, imprisoned within categories it had critiqued and dismantled, has itself become a system, an entity" ("Being a Communist," in *Key Writings*, 231–32; originally from *La somme et le reste*, 3rd ed. (Paris: Méridiens Klincksieck, 1989 [1959]), 684).

31. See V. I. Lenin, *The State and Revolution: The Marxist Theory of the State and the Tasks of the Proletariat in the Revolution* (Moscow: Progress Publishers, 1965), 18–24, 79–80. Lefebvre's analysis of Lenin's work in *De l'État* can be found in volume 2, 329–64; see also his *Pour connaître le pensée de Lénine* (Paris: Bordas, 1957).

32. See especially chapter 1, where Lefebvre also develops his critique of "state socialists." The notion of the withering away of the state is regularly attributed to Marx, but a closer formulation is actually found in Engels, who states explicitly that "the state is not 'abolished,' it withers away" (see *Socialism: Utopian and Scientific* [Peking: Foreign Languages Press, 1975], 94). Analogously, in one of his early texts on Hegel, Marx suggests

that "the political state disappears [*untergehe*] in a true democracy" (see Karl Marx, "Critique of Hegel's Doctrine of the State," in *Early Writings*, trans. Rodney Livingstone and Gregor Benton [Harmondsworth: Penguin, 1975], 88). Although his discussion of Stalin occupies relatively few pages of this lengthy text, the importance of the Stalinist experience for Lefebvre's approach to state theory should not be underestimated. As he noted in a passing comment in *De l'État:* "Stalin? One may devote but a few pages to him, since the objective and purpose of this entire work is an examination of 'Stalinism,' its conditions and its consequences" (2:393). On this theme, see also Lefebvre, *De l'État*, 1:281–96; 2:389–97.

33. See Lefebvre, *De l'État*, 1:153, 160. Lefebvre's criticisms of Althusser's reading of Marx also run through a number of essays in his book *Au-delà du structuralisme* (Paris: Anthropos, 1971).

34. See Lefebvre, *De l'État*, 4:339–40.

35. See Michel Foucault, *History of Madness*, trans. Jonathan Murphy and Jean Khalfa (London: Routledge, 2006); the original French text is *Folie et déraison: Histoire de la folie à l'âge classique*. Lefebvre's comments are in *De l'État* 1:160–64; 2:42–43; 4:408.

36. Lefebvre, *Key Writings*, 61–62; the reference is to an excerpt from Lefebvre's 1986 book, *Le retour de la dialectique*. See also Lefebvre's *Critique of Everyday Life*, 3:126, where he says that the state is no longer content to "surveiller et punir" (literally, "to survey and to punish"); the latter phrase is the original French title of Foucault's *Discipline and Punish*. A closely analogous yet rather more detailed and sympathetic critique of Foucault from the same period is developed by Poulantzas, *State, Power, Socialism*, esp. 146–53. A more recent engagement with Foucault's work, which takes into account his recently published lecture courses, is Bob Jessop, "Foucault on State, State Formation, Statecraft," in *State Power*, 140–56 (Cambridge: Polity, 2008).

37. Friedrich Nietzsche, "Thus Spoke Zarathustra," in *The Portable Nietzsche*, ed. and trans. Walter Kaufmann (Harmondsworth: Penguin, 1954), 160. This formulation is cited by Lefebvre in many places, including *De l'État*, 3:52; and *La fin de l'histoire*, 2nd ed. (Paris: Anthropos, 2001 [1970]), 89.

38. See Lefebvre, *De l'État*, 3:240.

39. Henri Lefebvre, *Hegel, Marx, Nietzsche ou le royaume des ombres* (Paris: Casterman, 1975; excerpts in Lefebvre, *Key Writings*, 42–49); and see his early study *Nietzsche* (Paris: Éditions Sociales Internationales, 1939).

40. See also Lefebvre, *De l'État*, 3:165–69. Lefebvre's relation to Nietzsche's thought is explored by Andy Merrifield in "Lefebvre, Anti-Logos and Nietzsche: An Alternative Reading of *The Production of Space*," *Antipode* 27, no. 3 (1995): 294–303.

41. The references to Heidegger in *De l'État* all concern the world, and while seen as important he is continually outweighed by Axelos. See Lefebvre, *De l'État* 3:133; 4:416–17, 433. The last two references are in chapter 14 of this volume. On Lefebvre's relation to Axelos, see the discussion and references that follow.

42. For a detailed overview by two of Lefebvre's contemporaries (one of whose interviews with him appears in chapter 6 of this volume), see Yvon Bourdet and Alain Guillerm, *L'Autogestion* (Paris: Editions Seghers, 1977).

43. See, in particular, chapters 2, 4, 5, 6, 8, 11, 15; and Lefebvre's chapter "On Self-Management," in *The Explosion*, 84–90.

44. Pierre Rosanvallon, *L'âge de l'autogestion* (Paris: Seuil, 1976).

45. Lefebvre refers to Lafont's thinking on secessionist movements in the Occitan region of France several times in volume 4 of *De l'État*. Some of Lafont's key works included *Décoloniser en France, les régions face à l'Europe* (Paris: Gallimard, 1971); *La révolution régionaliste* (Paris: Gallimard, 1973); and *Autonomie: De la région à l'autogestion* (Paris: Gallimard, 1976).

46. Henri Lefebvre, *The Survival of Capitalism*, trans. Frank Bryant (New York: St. Martin's, 1976), 40.

47. Khilnani, *Arguing Revolution*, 182. See also Bernard Brown, *Socialism of a Different Kind: Reshaping the Left in Postwar France* (Westport, Conn.: Greenwood Press, 1982).

48. Lefebvre, *Survival of Capitalism*, 120.

49. Horst Müller, *Praxis und Hoffnung* (Bochum: Germinal, 1986).

50. Henri Lefebvre, *Critique of Everyday Life; Everyday Life in the Modern World*, trans. Sacha Rabinovitch (Harmondsworth: Allen Lane, 1971); *La proclamation de la commune* (Paris: Gallimard, 1965); and *The Explosion*.

51. Lefebvre, *Survival of Capitalism*, 120.

52. Lefebvre cites various exemplars of these positions in *De l'État*. The structuralist position is represented by Louis Althusser, Etienne Balibar, Roger Establet, Pierre Macherey, and Jacques Rancière, *Lire Le Capital*, 2 vols. (Paris: Maspero, 1965), abridged as *Reading Capital*, trans. Ben Brewster (London: NLB, 1970). Stamokap theory is represented by Paul Boccara, *Études sur le capitalisme monopoliste d'État, sa crise et son issue* (Paris: Édition Sociales, 1973). Lefebvre develops a fascinating and highly suggestive critique of C. Wright Mills's *The Power Elite* (New York: Oxford University Press, 1956) in *De l'État*, 1:215–22. Lefebvre claims that, despite its substantive critique of liberal pluralist ideology, Mills's theory "self-destructs" due to its inadequate conceptualization of state power in the United States and beyond.

53. Lefebvre, *De l'État*, 3:300; 4:22.

54. Lefebvre, *Sociology of Marx*, 181; see, among others, Lefebvre, *De l'État*, 2:277; and chapters 4 and 11 in this volume.

55. Adam Przeworski, *Capitalism and Social Democracy* (Cambridge: Cambridge University Press, 1985).

56. David Harvey, *Social Justice and the City* (Oxford: Basil Blackwell, 1973), 15, 108–9.

57. See Lefebvre, *Survival of Capitalism*.

58. Lefebvre, *Survival of Capitalism*, 126.

59. Lefebvre, *The Explosion*, 128.

60. Lefebvre, *Survival of Capitalism*, 124–25.

61. Lefebvre also occasionally uses the term *devenir-monde*, which literally means "becoming-world." Where there might be confusion on which term is used in the original text, we have included the French in brackets.

62. See Lefebvre, *De l'État*, 4:326; chapter 14 in this volume.

63. See Henri Lefebvre, *The Urban Revolution*, trans. Robert Bonnano (Minneapolis: University of Minnesota Press, 2003), chap. 4.

64. See chapters 9, 11, and 14; as well as Lefebvre, *De l'État*, 2:67–70; 3:164; 4:165–66; and Lefebvre, *The Production of Space*, trans. Donald Nicolson-Smith (Oxford: Blackwell, 1991), 86–87.

65. Lefebvre, *Survival of Capitalism*, 84–85.

66. Lefebvre, *De l'État*, 4:178–79.

67. See particularly Lefebvre, *De l'État*, 2:322–23.

68. Lefebvre, *De l'État*, 2:322. For a discussion and application of Lefebvre's notion of colonization, see Stefan Kipfer and Kanishka Goonewardena, "Colonization and the New Imperialism: On the Meaning of Urbicide Today," *Theory and Event* 10, no. 2 (2007). For an appropriation of Lefebvre's sociospatial theory to analyze the dialectical interplay between colonial geopolitical economies and anticolonial nationalisms, see Manu Goswami, *Producing India: From Colonial Space to National Economy* (Chicago: University of Chicago Press, 2003).

69. Kostas Axelos, *Marx penseur de la technique: De l'aliénation de l'homme à la conquête du monde* (Paris: Éditions de Minuit, 1961), translated by Ronald Bruzina as *Alienation, Praxis and Technē in the Thought of Karl Marx* (Austin: University of Texas Press, 1976); Lefebvre, "Marxisme et technique," *Esprit* no. 307 (1962): 1023–28.

70. Lefebvre, "Marxisme et technique," 1026.

71. Kostas Axelos, *Arguments d'une recherche* (Paris: Éditions de Minuit, 1969), 174.

72. Lefebvre, *Survival of Capitalism*, 70–71.

73. Kostas Axelos, *Le jeu du monde* (Paris: Minuit, 1969); Eugen Fink, *Spiel als Weltsymbol* (Stuttgart: Kohlhammer, 1960). See also Axelos, "*Mondialisation* without the World: Interviewed by Stuart Elden," *Radical Philosophy* no. 130 (2005): 25–28; and Axelos (trans. Gerald Moore), "The World: Being Becoming Totality," *Environment and Planning D: Society and Space* 24, no. 5 (2006): 643–51.

74. Hermann Diels, *Die Fragmente der Vorsokratiker: Griechisch und deutsch,* ed. Walther Kranz, 6th ed. (Berlin: Weidmann, 1952), 162, fragment 52.

75. For accounts of Axelos and his relation to Lefebvre, see Stuart Elden, "Kostas Axelos and the World of the Arguments Circle," in *After the Deluge: New Perspectives on Postwar French Intellectual and Cultural History,* ed. Julian Bourg, 125–48 (Lanham, Md.: Lexington Books, 2004); and "Lefebvre and Axelos: *Mondialisation* before Globalisation," in Goonewardena et al., *Space, Difference, Everyday Life,* 80–93.

76. Lefebvre, *Survival of Capitalism*, 21.

77. David Harvey, *The New Imperialism* (Oxford: Oxford University Press, 2003), 87. Harvey's own confrontation with this issue is found most extensively in *The Limits to Capital* (Oxford: Basil Blackwell, 1982), as well as in many of his subsequent writings. For an overview, see Harvey, *Spaces of Capital: Towards a Critical Geography* (New York: Routledge, 2001).

78. A chronological reading would follow this sequence: chapters 1, 2, 12, 5, 7, 9, 3, 6, 11, 14, 8, 4, 10, 13, 15.

79. Merrifield, *Henri Lefebvre*, xxii. Merrifield is quoting a phrase from *La somme et le reste*, 46, in which Lefebvre describes his own writing style.

80. The term "Fordist Marxism" is derived from Bernd Röttger, *Neoliberale Globalisierung und eurokapitalistische Regulation: Die politische Konstitution des Marktes* (Münster: Westfälisches Dampfboot, 1997). For analogous conceptualizations, see also Noel Castree, "Envisioning Capitalism: Geography and the Renewal of Marxian Political Economy," *Transactions, Institute of British Geographers* 24, no. 2 (1999): 137–58; and Moishe Postone, *Time, Labor, and Social Domination: A Reinterpretation of Marx's Critical Theory* (New York: Cambridge University Press, 1996). It can be argued that Fordist Marxism also assumed distinctive politico-ideological forms in Eastern Europe, where it culminated in the Prague Spring and in the work of dissident writers such as Rudolf Bahro; and in the imperialist/postcolonial periphery, where it was expressed in the form of Left critiques of the national-developmentalist projects associated with the Bandung alliance.

81. See Lefebvre, *Everyday Life in the Modern World*.

82. Lefebvre does, however, briefly allude to this new context in chapter 15 of this volume.

83. See Neil Brenner, *New State Spaces: Urban Governance and the Rescaling of Statehood* (Oxford: Oxford University Press, 2004).

84. See Joachim Hirsch, *Der nationale Wettbewerbsstaat* (Berlin: Edition ID–Archiv, 1995); Bob Jessop, *The Future of the Capitalist State* (London: Polity, 2003); and Phil Cerny, "Paradoxes of the Competition State," *Government and Opposition* 32, no. 3 (2005): 251–74.

85. Other important contributions to this antiproductivist line of critique include André Gorz, *Critique of Economic Reason* (London: Verso, 1989); Postone, *Time, Labor, and Social Domination*; John Friedmann, *Empowerment: The Politics of Alternative Development* (Cambridge, Mass.: Blackwell, 1992); and John Holloway, *Change the World without Taking Power: The Meaning of Revolution Today* (London: Pluto, 2002).

86. This issue has been explored in increasingly sophisticated ways by several contemporary political economists and political geographers. For an excellent overview of this emergent literature, see David Newman and Anssi Paasi, "Fences and Neighbors in the Postmodern World: Boundary Narratives in Political Geography," *Progress in Human Geography* 22, no. 2 (1998): 186–207. An important recent statement is Saskia Sassen, *Territory, Authority, Rights: From Medieval to Global Assemblages* (Princeton: Princeton University Press, 2006).

87. See chapter 9, and Lefebvre, *Production of Space*, 280. For a discussion dependent in part on Lefebvre, see Mark Neocleous, "Off the Map: On Violence and Cartography," *European Journal of Social Theory* 6, no. 4 (2003): 409–25.

88. Neil Smith, *American Empire: Roosevelt's Geographer and the Prelude to Globalization* (Berkeley: University of California Press, 2003), 379.

89. Gilbert Achcar, *The Clash of Barbarisms: The Making of the New World Order*, trans. Peter Drucker, expanded ed. (Boulder, Colo.: Paradigm, 2006), 103.

90. In addition to the references in the previous notes, see Neil Smith, *The Endgame of Globalization* (London: Routledge, 2005); Matthew Sparke, *In the Space of Theory: Postfoundational Geographies of the Nation–State* (Minneapolis: University of Minnesota Press,

2005); and John Agnew, *Hegemony: The New Shape of Global Power* (Philadelphia: Temple University Press, 2005).

91. See Giovanni Arrighi, *The Long Twentieth Century: Money, Power and the Origins of Our Times* (London: Verso, 1994); David Harvey, *The New Imperialism* (Oxford: Oxford University Press, 2003); and Stuart Elden, *Terror and Territory: The Spatial Extent of Sovereignty* (Minneapolis: University of Minnesota Press, 2009).

92. See Claus Offe, "'Ungovernability': The Renaissance of Conservative Theories of Crisis," in *Contradictions of the Welfare State*, 65–87 (Cambridge, Mass.: MIT Press, 1984).

93. Paul Krugman, "Competitiveness: A Dangerous Obsession," *Foreign Affairs* 73 (1994): 28–44.

94. Stephen Gill, "Globalization, Market Civilisation and Disciplinary Neoliberalism," *Millennium* 24, no. 3 (1995): 399–423.

95. See above all, Lefebvre, *La proclamation de la commune*; and *The Explosion*.

96. Lefebvre, *Survival of Capitalism*, 121.

97. Jürgen Habermas, "The New Obscurity: The Crisis of the Welfare State and the Exhaustion of Utopian Energies," in *The New Conservatism: Cultural Criticism and the Historians' Debate*, trans. Shierry W. Nicholsen, 48–70 (Cambridge, Mass.: MIT Press, 1992).

98. On which see also David Harvey, *Spaces of Hope* (Berkeley: University of California Press, 2000).

99. Lefebvre, *Une pensée devenue monde*, 215.

100. Henri Lefebvre and Catherine Régulier, *La révolution n'est plus ce qu'elle était* (Hallier: Éditions Libres, 1988), 21. This argument is developed in Elden, *Understanding Henri Lefebvre*, esp. 241–44.

101. Lefebvre, "Being a Communist," *Key Writings*, 234 (originally in *La somme et le reste*, 687).

102. Lefebvre and Régulier, *La révolution*.

103. For an excellent overview of the latter, see William Fisher and Thomas Ponniah, eds, *Another World Is Possible: Popular Alternatives to Globalization at the World Social Forum* (London: Zed, 2003); and Louise Amoore, ed., *The Global Resistance Reader* (New York: Routledge, 2005). A prominent, if highly controversial, interpretation of such movements can be found in Michael Hardt and Antonio Negri's *Empire* (Cambridge, Mass.: Harvard University Press, 2000), and its sequel, *Multitude: War and Democracy in the Age of Empire* (Cambridge, Mass.: Harvard University Press, 2004).

Part I

State, Society, Autogestion

1   The State and Society

This essay, the earliest included here, represents one of Lefebvre's first sustained engagements with state theory. It was delivered as a lecture and published in a socialist academic and political magazine in the mid-1960s. The essay is framed around the critique of Stalinism in the Soviet Union, and, more specifically, a critique of the Stalinist model of the state, both in theory and in practice. Lefebvre's key goal is to understand, in theoretical terms, the qualitative growth in state power and activity during the nineteenth and twentieth centuries. This mode of analysis would later prove crucial to Lefebvre in his contextualization and critique of Stalinism in some of the key chapters of De l'État. Lefebvre's essay provides a sweeping overview of several key themes in state theory that would occupy his attention for much of the next two decades, and which recur throughout the present volume. These include:

- The relationship between social-scientific studies of the state and the consolidation or expansion of the modern state;
- The relationship between political elites ("men of the State"), critics of state power ("Statesmen"), and the status quo;
- The expanding role of the state in the promotion of economic growth during the history of modern capitalism;
- The interplay between economic growth, political development, and social forces;
- The diverse configurations of state power and social class relationships that underpinned the process of state formation in major capitalist countries (especially England, France, and the United States);
- The critique of right-wing and left-wing technocratic understandings of the modern state;

• The insistence on a critical standpoint that does not take contemporary
political–economic institutions for granted but instead continually seeks
out alternative visions of social life.

Lefebvre concludes the essay by critiquing the corruption and perversion of
socialist "democracy" in the Soviet Union. He thus begins to allude to the theme
of *autogestion* that is addressed more directly in subsequent chapters of this
volume.—*Eds.*

AN ESSENTIAL PROBLEM

This presentation is only the first in a series devoted to the problem of the
State, so it does not claim to be exhaustive or to resolve all problems. It could
well be that at the end of this series of presentations, the problems of the
State will appear in a slightly new light. In fact, I think that, for several supporting reasons, we are entering into a period where many controversial questions, many questions whose horizons remain sealed off, will be posed anew.
A heavy mortgage, a very heavy mortgage, which weighed both on action and
on socialist thought, is in the process of being paid off, and of being paid off
definitively. The Twenty-first Congress of the Soviet Communist Party marked
a setback compared to the Twentieth, but the Twenty-second Congress of this
party has resumed—and with what force and what intensity—the unblock-
ing of the situation and the politics of de-Stalinization.[1]

We have not yet seen the consequences, either in theory or in practice, of
this Twenty-second Congress, and I will perhaps presently have occasion to
return to them.

I think that new horizons, very broad horizons, are beginning to open up,
both for thought and for the unity of democratic forces. The liquidation of
Stalinism is nothing other than the liquidation of a certain conception of the
State, identified with Marxism by the Stalinist era and by Stalin. This conception of the State, attributed to Marxism, is in the process of disappearing
in theory and in practice, despite the repositioning of one and fluctuations in
the other. The State, knowledge of the State, its description and detailed analysis, are incontestably the indispensable elements of every politics; but not only
of politics, since they are also indispensable to philosophy, history, sociology,
and all the sciences of social reality. But if this knowledge is indispensable for
the social sciences, it is even more so for political action, properly speaking.
It is from this understanding that political goals, interests, and objectives, and
the means of political action are determined.

Every political program must choose between two directions: either it proposes an action within a certain framework that it accepts, a framework determined by the State; it therefore fits within the existing State. Or alternatively it proposes to bring changes to the existing State framework and can even propose to change it completely. This, of course, presupposes an understanding of what one wants to change, which is to say an understanding of both institutions and apparatuses, an understanding of laws and also an understanding of techniques for their application within the framework determined by the State. What are properly called political techniques, the techniques of application in an institutional framework, concern the functioning of these institutions and these laws in their application to a reality that is always more mobile, more indecisive than the political framework of the State. These techniques propose to adapt reality, to confront it with social practice, in this framework, and to oblige this social practice to enter into the mold, as it were, into the forms offered to it by the State.

The State and Social Sciences

Broadly, then, knowledge of the State is the essential given of political action. It is equally the essential given of a totality that various social sciences describe and analyze. Together, the social sciences—sociology, history, political economy—are in a relation of perpetual interaction with the State and understanding of the State. In part, they result from these relations because they operate on the givens of social life and of social practice in frameworks determined by the State. Sometimes, by contrast, they contribute to the possibilities of acting on these givens.

Between the social sciences and the frameworks of the State there is therefore a perpetual movement of interaction. And here, I am going to introduce a distinction that I consider important: the State, as we understand it, as we live it in our everyday life, in our experiences, in our relations with these institutions, this State has nowadays become a reality so complex, so dominant, that it has itself become the object of certain sciences, or certain disciplines that aspire to become scientific.

This complexity is proved, for example, by a simple fact: knowing who makes the decisions, where they are made, and so forth, necessitates very probing and very difficult studies.

Let's take a concrete example from among the essential decisions: seven or eight years ago, why was the EDC, the European [Defense] Community, more

military than economic in nature, rebuffed by a vote in the Chamber?[2] Who
was behind it? Who came to rebuff the EDC? And how did this political operation take place? And yet it is very difficult to answer such a question, which
could require entire books. Let's take a simpler case: how and why was the
new faculty of sciences set up on the site of Halle aux Vins (the wine market),
why didn't it come to occupy the ground set aside for it, and how did the
wine merchants defend themselves?[3] And yet, here too, one could write an
entire book to arrive at such knowledge.

The State apparatus has become so complex that it is itself an object of science, and the theory of decision is part of the science of the State.

STATESMEN AND MEN OF THE STATE

There are therefore specialists who know the State admirably well, both in
practice, through the cogs that constitute it, and in theory. These theoreticians
busy themselves with defining the statist and institutional framework in which
sovereignty, authority, and power are exercised. They bring them together in
a theory of constitutions, for example, and they can write many volumes, some
of which are quite brilliant, on any subject. I will call them collectively men
of the State [*les hommes de l'État*].

Every politician [*homme politique*], past and present, is a Statesman [*homme
d'État*], which is to say a man who acts politically, either within a framework
determined by the State, or to bring about change in this institutional framework. But a Statesman [*homme d'État*] is not necessarily a man of the State
[*homme de l'État*]. I hope presently to show you the meaning of this distinction. In my view there are two types of politician: men of the State and Statesmen, just as there are two types of intellectual, two types of economist, two
types of sociologist, and historian. There are those who accept the existing
State as a central given of reality, as a central given of the moral sciences, who
think as a function of this given and who pose all the problems related to the
knowledge of society, to science and reality itself as a function of this given.
And there is another type of intellectual: he who, directly or indirectly, calls
into question the existing institutions, and who departs from a scientific study
of reality, of life and social practice, in order to pose the problem of the State,
which entails a critique of the existing type of State.

Obviously there is no socialist thought that does not call into question
the existing State and existing reality, in relation to one another and through
one another. There is no socialist political thought that does *not* pose the

problematic—to use, if you'll excuse me, a word slightly tainted by philosophy—there is no socialist thought that does not pose the State as a problematic, and which does *not* demand through a detailed and maximally sustained analysis which of the institutions of the existing State are atrophied and dead, which are contestable, which are transformable and utilizable, which have a future, and which must be created for the State to be transformed and correspond to new requirements.

This analysis of institutions, some of which are atrophied and dead, others of which are contestable and open to criticism but transformable, some of which have a future and others of which have to be created from scratch, this analysis forms a part of socialist political thought. Someone who does not begin with this critique of the existing State apparatus is simply someone who operates within the framework of existing reality, who does not propose to change it and who absolutely does not deserve the title of socialist, whatever their knowledge and skills.

There is, moreover, a critical element missing from such an understanding, and I think that one can pose it as an axiom in the social sciences that there is no true science without the critique of existing reality. There are, in any case, many people who move through existing reality with ease and who adapt themselves to it, who find that the social framework of the existing State suits them. These are men of action, politicians, at times extremely realistic, but no less opportunistic and generally more than moderate, they are accepting of the bourgeoisie, the bourgeois State, with all the consequences of this acceptance. There is therefore, in my opinion, at least—and we will be able to discuss this presently—an incompatibility between being a man of the State and a socialist.

A socialist, a socialist politician can and must be a Statesman. There is an incompatibility between what I call the quality, the property of being a man of the State and the quality of being a socialist. And the socialist politician knows how to handle social forces, understands the dynamic of social forces within the framework of the existing State. He proposes to utilize them, to employ them to change this State. And it is thus that he can be a Statesman without being a man of the State. Typical of those men who would be Statesmen without being men of the State is Lenin, in my opinion. Lenin was a great Statesman, with an admirable understanding of all forms of the State and a no less admirable understanding of the social forces one finds behind and beneath the political realities of institutions, but he was not a man of the State.

There is not a single line of Lenin that does not contain a probing critique of existing institutions and existing political reality. The distinction between men of the State and Statesmen can initially appear a bit subtle. It seems to me that if we reflect on the case of Lenin, the distinction appears almost crudely obvious. Now that I have introduced this distinction, to which I shall return later, I would like very quickly to examine for you the place of the State in history and to give a schema that could then allow much more developed studies.

THE STATE AND THE PROCESS OF ECONOMIC GROWTH

Here is the theoretical position that will allow me to give you the general schema:

First point: There is a process of economic accumulation that begins in Western Europe in the Middle Ages, toward the end of the Middle Ages, emerging, so to speak, in the era wrongly called the Renaissance, which has developed and accelerated up until the present, where this accumulation of capital and the means of labor, technology, and knowledge, where this cumulative process becomes irresistible and moreover begins to extend itself over the whole world. The first point, then: there is a process of accumulation that begins in the Middle Ages and has intensified, bit by bit, in accordance with a well-known curve.

Second point: This process of intensification has incontestably assumed a capitalist form. This took place from the moment of the Renaissance in Western Europe, in the sixteenth and seventeenth centuries, under conditions that have not yet been perfectly elucidated. The history of the sixteenth and seventeenth centuries is not exactly clear. But ultimately we still broadly know why and how this process assumed a capitalist form.

Third point: This capitalist form was, historically, inevitable and probably necessary in Western Europe, in historical and social conditions where the process of accumulation unfurled, which is to say in a territory already occupied by an economic, social, and political organization: that of feudalism.

Fourth point: The political form assumed by this process of economic accumulation was equally necessary and inevitable—even in the absence of these anterior conditions, these feudal antecedents. For example, in the United States, where feudalism did not exist as it did in Europe, the cumulative process nonetheless assumed a capitalist form.

Fifth point: This form is not absolutely necessary. There is no absolute necessity in history. There are only relative necessities, and today we can perfectly well conceive the passage from a relatively primitive economy to a socialist economy under certain favorable conditions. I am alluding to new States, let's say Guinea, with a question mark, because it is not at all certain that the passage from a tribal economy, a primitive economy, to a socialist economy is being realized. Although this could be a theoretical possibility.

Sixth point: This process of accumulation constitutes the central axis around which one can lay down the elements of modern history, political history, and the history of the State in different contemporary States.

In relation to this cumulative role, what might the place and the role of the State have been? What happened, for example, in England? Economic growth and the process of economic accumulation have been spontaneous or quasi-spontaneous since the Middle Ages, and economic growth was forged in this spontaneity; the properly capitalistic State, the bourgeois State, came only after economic growth. Economic growth preceded the State. This meant that, throughout extremely acute class struggles and even revolutions such as those of Cromwell, given that economic growth preceded the State and was prior to the formation and crystallization of a State, a political compromise could initially be made between the bourgeoisie and feudalism, a compromise that tends to extend to these two dominant classes and to the proletariat, to the working class itself. English democracy is constituted on a kind of political compromise between active social forces, and this compromise was only possible because economic growth preceded the constitution of the State and the State apparatus. England has the dual characteristic of representing both a political compromise and the most evolved, most sophisticated form of bourgeois democracy, with these two characteristics going together. But where does this dual character come from? From the fact that the State apparatus is posterior to economic growth.

The case of the United States is a bit different but presents several analogies, all the same. In the United States, too, economic growth does not occur through the support of the State. It is not the State that stimulates, that creates, that encourages economic growth; as in England, economic growth precedes the constitution of a general State apparatus, a federal State apparatus, an apparatus of the State as a whole, and that, furthermore, is why the United States and England are the countries where the State was the least present, the least active, at least up until quite recently.

The case of France is curious and interesting. In France, the State apparatus finds itself riding the horse, as it were, of the growth process. For in France, the bourgeoisie is born of economic growth but helps itself to the State apparatus both for the accumulation of capital and to affirm its domination over the course of this very growth.

Here is what I mean: the English bourgeoisie is a commercial bourgeoisie, the French bourgeoisie is a bourgeoisie that consolidates itself by introducing itself, in the sixteenth century, into the apparatus of the State—it buys offices and responsibilities, for example; it helps itself to the State apparatus in order to facilitate economic growth; the accumulation of capital notably takes place by way of taxes. The mutual imbrication of the State apparatus and the bourgeoisie is therefore much more profound in France than in England. The State apparatus is immediately much more heavy. Since the monarchy, France has been the country of state centralization and a bourgeoisie that penetrates the State apparatus, seizes it, and helps itself both to economic growth and to its own domination; the bourgeoisie can thus deliver a much more fierce class struggle in France than in England. Compromise between classes does not exist, and France becomes what one might dare to call the "classic" (this is a formula of Engels) country of class struggle.[4]

On account of the arrangement of social forces and their relation to the political institution, to the State apparatus itself, in countries like Germany, Italy, and Russia, the process of economic growth succeeds the constitution and crystallization of the State apparatus. In all of these countries, in fact, the economic role of the state has been considerable. Economic growth takes place increasingly by means of the State, and the State becomes the stimulant of economic growth. This is absolutely not the case in England. And we arrive at last at the limit case, the case of underdeveloped countries, where the constitution of the State precedes economic growth, where these countries still have but a primitive economy; already having a State, they are heading toward industrialization. It is, you see, exactly the opposite situation from that of a country like England, where economic growth precedes the crystallization of the modern State.

It is evident that the problem of the State does not arise in at all the same way in a country where the State follows growth, where the crystallization of the State follows economic development, and in countries where it precedes economic growth. In countries where the State precedes growth, let's say in the countries that are on the whole underdeveloped, it is theoretically possible to pass from a primitive economy to a socialized economy; everything depends on those who are governing the State, but it is thus the State itself and the State apparatus that becomes both the site and the stake of social strug-gles, and a danger arises: that of the formation of a bourgeoisie that would not be a trading or commercial bourgeoisie, but a bourgeoisie linked directly to the State apparatus, a bureaucratic bourgeoisie, that is to say, an entirely new social formation.

So, the closer we get to the end of the initial point of departure of my argu-ment, the more the arrangement of social forces changes. In England the bour-geoisie is strictly commercial and financial. In the countries that are situated between the two extremes, the bourgeoisie is penetrated by statist elements [d'éléments étatiques], precisely because it penetrates the State itself. Ultimately, on the other hand, we have the great danger, not yet realized, of a bourgeoisie that has become part of the State [une bourgeoise étatisée], a bureaucratic bourgeoisie. I don't know if I am explaining this schema clearly. It is not a schema destined to resolve all the problems of the modern State, but to deter-mine the general framework within which they can be posed. In the highly particular case of France, the State apparatus is, relatively speaking, very heavy, but it is also a country, however, where social and political forces act on the inside of this framework in such a way that political problems are posed—dare I say it—in an exemplary manner. And that is why Marx and Engels could say it was the classic country of class struggles. Class struggles play out inside of the State in an almost transparent, almost visible, manner; it is a privileged site. Whereas in other countries, class struggles are less apparent, less visible on the inside of the State apparatus. It is this that gives French political life, seen from the outside, the impression of confusion and agita-tion, which is nothing other than the aspect of its transparency, the external face of its transparency and even of its fecundity.

ECONOMIC, SOCIAL, AND POLITICAL

I thus come to a number of ideas that are very simple and which are destined to illuminate the problem.

First idea: There is a dialectical interaction between the economy, which is to say economic growth, and the development of the political element. It is this dialectical interaction that determines the nature, the internal structure, the role, and above all the weight of the State; the structure of the State therefore depends, in the long run of course, and considered over vast historical peri-ods, on the movement of the conjuncture, which is to say on this interaction.

Second idea: This dialectical interaction between the economic and the

political is not exercised directly. It exerts itself through the intermediary of
mobilized social forces. Social forces are the mediation, the intermediary element between the economic and the political. The particular characteristics
of the State in France, in England, in Germany, in Italy, and in Russia are
determined by mobilized social forces and not directly and immediately by
economic growth and economic questions. In other words, class struggle plays
a major role. Class struggles, in the broadest sense of the term, which is to say
not only referring to revolutionary periods, periods of intensity, but to periods of reciprocal weight, of reciprocal pressure, of the multiple actions of the
classes present, through their leaders, through their politicians, and through
their ideas and their ideologies; it is a perpetual relation that must not be
reduced to those periods of intensity.

This means, and I believe that this is very important, that it is always the
social that holds the secret of the political, that holds the reasons of the political and of the state [*l'étatique*] rather than the political in itself or, conversely,
the economic taken separately. Between the economic and the political there
is always a level of social forces that must be analyzed.

Finally, another very simple idea: the possibility of a political movement,
which is to say the eventual choice between political possibilities, narrowly
depends on the social forces that are mobilized or mobilizing, and the intensity of their action.

And this is what I mean to say a bit more precisely: if social forces stag-
nate, if they do not mobilize in some form or other, if they balance each other
out, if they neutralize each other, the State still remains a bloc. An apparently
monolithic bloc. There are no fissures, there is no crack in the State apparatus. There is no movement and there are no political possibilities in these
stagnant periods, except action on the inside of the State, through the acceptance of its structures. It is, as such, the moment for men of the State. They
win, they dominate. These men of the State furthermore contribute to im-
mobilizing the social basis of the political apparatus. The structures of the
State are not only structured within the State. They also serve to structure
social forces and economic life, practical life, and society as a whole. But once
social forces begin moving, everything happens, as if under this house, under
this edifice that seemed solid and balanced, the earth begins to move. And
there promptly appear fissures where once we saw a vertical rock face. And
what appeared to be a simple crack in the walls promptly becomes a crevasse
and deepens. Everything immediately shifts in this gigantic edifice, in this State

apparatus, and the bloc begins to move. And so there appears the possibility of changing something in this bloc, though not without difficulty, not without danger. It is in this moment that Statesmen, who are not exactly men of the State, can intervene. They understand, they can see the possibilities, and they can choose between these possibilities. They know moreover that these possibilities are strictly determined by the movement of the masses, without which the edifice of the State would remain a bloc.

This means primarily that there are degrees of democracy and of revolution. The degree of democracy, or more exactly the degree of the democratization of public life, of political and social life is quite precisely proportional to the intensity of the struggle for democracy. Democracy is nothing other than the struggle for democracy. The struggle for democracy is the movement itself. Many democrats imagine that democracy is a type of stable condition toward which we can tend, toward which we must tend. No. Democracy is the movement. And the movement is the forces in action. And democracy is the struggle for democracy, which is to say the very movement of social forces; it is a permanent struggle and it is even a struggle against the State that emerges from democracy. There is no democracy without a struggle against the democratic State itself, which tends to consolidate itself as a bloc, to affirm itself as a whole, to become monolithic and to smother the society out of which it develops.

The State always has a tendency to atrophy, even when it emerges from democracy, to inject democracy and introduce democracy into its structures, which must be avoided. Thus the term "democratic state" must be taken with some reservations, as must other customary labels such as "worker State," "peasant State," and "proletarian State."

Finally, the depth of a revolution, like the depth of democracy, varies with the social forms that have mobilized and with the intensity of this mobilization. There are degrees of revolution, as there are degrees of democracy, and they are moreover the same. One could put this in the form of an axiom, a political axiom: social forces determine the possibilities that the talent or the genius of leaders lead to realization.

Men of the State and Technocrats

That said, it is certain that we have to deal nowadays with many men of the State. Why? Because of the realist tendency to accept existence, to work, to operate within the framework of existing reality, within the frameworks of institutions, within given institutions. This positive tendency, this realist tendency, is extremely strong; there is nowadays an almost spontaneous positivism that pushes individuals to act within and consequently to accept existing frameworks. Furthermore, the critical aspect of thought in general, and of Marxist thought in particular, has been cast into the shadows and hidden away. It is often Marxists themselves who have become men of the State, uniting a verbal critique and violent phraseology with vast opportunism in practice. The deterioration of Marxist thought and action has therefore greatly contributed to orienting many people and thought in general toward this type of positivism, toward this realism. And the tendency is thus sufficiently widespread to blur the problematic—still the philosophical term, but at least it points quite well to what is meant here—to blur the precise problematic of the modern State, and to construe it reductively, either as a political tactic or as a somewhat moralizing critique.

I find a first example of this tendency in a book published by the Club Jean-Moulin, *The State and the Citizen*.[5] I'll speak about this book with courtesy, though the authors do not always merit this courtesy because they come to speak, at times, in disparaging terms of men whom they suspect of being adversaries or harboring potential critiques. This book is very interesting and it is important. It is often brilliant, always intelligent, at times profound, and also, at times, extremely naïve. But, it collapses, if one can say such a thing, through incoherence. A specific example:

This incoherence is due to the fact that it involves the juxtaposition of extremely different ideological formulas. Some of its authors, whom we all know from elsewhere—and this is an open or jester's secret—are men of the State. They don't hide it, furthermore. In this instance, the distinction between men of the State and Statesmen assumes a particular meaning and a particular pattern. And if these are men of the State, I will read you a small paragraph that demonstrates it admirably, and with exquisite naivety, with the delightful naivety of technocrats who pursue not the myth but the fairytale of the twentieth century, the folklore of technocracy. This charming little paragraph is entitled "The State As It Is." We are therefore fully within our subject: "Neither the analysis of the role of the State and political institutions, nor the study of the part that numerous intermediary groups play in it, could suffice for a serious awareness of the problems of modern democracy. The only acceptable measure of our judgments on institutions is, in fact, the individual, the citizen." This is very well intentioned, but we must look closer at whether there is a more precise meaning. "We tried not to forget this, when demonstrating the functioning of the cogs in the contemporary State"—this refers back to previous articles—"but we referred to a relatively abstract image of its needs, of its desires, and it is now important to make it more precise, to confront the reality, or at least what we can know of it, through an investigation of the social sciences and through reflection."[6] I find that this is truly a modern fairy tale, to imagine the State facing off against the citizen, both with needs and desires that clash with and confront each other. And this in place of ruthlessly seeking to overcome the fissure between the State and the citizen! The State is treated as a proper personality, facing the individual, with the same characteristics as the individual but on a greater scale. This is the surrendering of political reflection to the State. It is a way of placing oneself on the inside of the State. This is exactly what I call the thought of men of the State. They place themselves on the inside of the State in order to accept its existing frameworks, and in order to judge reality against the standard of the State, rather than making reality the criteria by which we judge the State.

The Myth of Consumer Society

I believe that in this thought there is an internal principle, which is the internal coherence of the State. And this book notably accepts another myth of modern times, which is that of consumer society. We are supposedly in a consumer society, and modern industry, industrial society would tend toward this consumer society, whatever the structure of production. More precisely, the structure of production loses considerable importance in the face of a generalized consumer society. I think nowadays that this consumer society, which brackets and ignores the relations of production, this consumer society is the current myth corresponding to what individualism was in the time of free, competitive capitalism.

During the latter period of free, competitive capitalism, the ideological appearance of society was individualism, the individual acting for and by himself. And this appearance was not entirely an appearance and a mystification. There was something real in it. In fact, this society of free, competitive capitalism perhaps demanded of individuals a bit more initiative and individual energy than the preceding and succeeding societies. And yet individualism was only an appearance and an illusion, the hanging curtain behind which the reality of capitalism concealed itself. Today, monopoly capitalism gives the appearance of a consumer society where everything is made for the consumer, where the needs of the consumer are the very rule of capitalist production. This conceals the reality of this production and the fact that capitalist producers manufacture the consumers themselves, if only through advertising or through studies of the market, in such a way that the consumer in question is the most alienated man there could ever be. Yet he believes himself to be a free individual, an individual close to self-completion and self-realization.

The idea that the State has no more to do than plan and manage consumer society, which is taken as the governing idea that animates this book, will serve us, I think, as a criterion for separating out socialist thought from that which is not. It is impossible for socialist thought to accept, to this extent, the apology for the existing reality, and not only the existence of this current society with its tendencies and its capitalistic orientation, but the sparkling appearance that it gives itself, which must first be destroyed to arrive at the underlying truth of the relations of production. It is easy to say that in appealing to the consciousness of the working class, to class struggle, to union action and to the analysis of the relations of production, is to go backward, toward the nineteenth century. However, the critical analysis of current reality remains within these frameworks of thought. To come to understand current reality, we must depart from Marxist thought, from the Marxist method, push it toward an analysis of the current reality and tear off a veil of appearances that is no longer the same as thirty, forty, or fifty years or a century ago, at the time of free competitive capitalism, a veil of appearances that is no less colorful, nor less coarse than a century ago.

What I reject in the political and economic analysis of the book by the Club Jean-Moulin is their total acceptance of the existence of the State with its current tendencies, with its contemporary orientation within the framework of capitalism, and their claim to be the theorists of consumer society, again within the framework of capitalism. Our critical analysis is precisely part of the denunciation of these appearances and the discovery of the reality that they hide, namely the reality of capitalism, monopoly control (it is no longer competitive capitalism with its appearance of individualism, it is monopoly capitalism, with its appearance of consumer society). Clearly, the State plays the role of the manager of consumer society. This society is held, machinated, more profoundly than ever by big capitalism, and it is of this above all that we must take into consideration in order to be able to change this society. We thus have in this book a veritable criterion, the line of demarcation between a thought that one could call neo-technocratic or neo-capitalist, or whatever else one might like to call it, but which is not socialist thought. This is because the critical element that—without having completely disappeared since it is represented even among the members of the Unified Socialist Party (PSU)—is blurred and diminished by the apologists for what exists and finally by those whom I call men of the State.[7]

STATE SOCIALISTS

Outside this circle of intelligent men who are not free from the framework of the State and from society such as it is, there is here, even in France, a long tradition of State socialism. State socialism, which is to say socialism that accepts the frameworks of the existing State in order to insert itself within it, this socialism has a long tradition. And this tradition is double sided. On the one hand, it is the opportunism of the socialist party and of traditional social democracy. On the other hand, it is also the opportunism of the Stalinist party, the party in the grip of, dominated and oriented by Stalinists. In fact, if one looks into the ideology of these two parties, into what they have in common—which is to say the acceptance of the existing State in State socialist thinking—one sees that this tradition is grounded not in Marx but in Ferdinand Lassalle. Guy Mollet is a Lassallian who is not unaware of that fact, and Maurice Thorez is a Lassallian who doesn't know it. Both accept the profound thought of Ferdinand Lassalle on the State apparatus and the necessity of inserting oneself into this apparatus in order to act within its framework.[8] Perhaps you will tell me that it is precisely true of Guy Mollet, but that it isn't true of Maurice Thorez. And yet, if one looks over the last twenty or the last five years of History, one nonetheless finds proof of my assertion.

The Lassallism of the Left coincides with Stalinism. Stalin was a State socialist who considered the State and the Russian State as the supreme goal of History, as the actualization, the end point of History. It was a State socialism that endeavored to consolidate the State by all means. This, as I will show you in the next presentation, is radically different from the thought of Marx.[9] With regard to Maurice Thorez, if we consult the thought of Lassalle, we perceive that it consisted in a certain number of affirmations. Lassalle spoke of the antiquated law of salaries. Maurice Thorez speaks of absolute pauperization with an obstinacy as great as Lassalle talking about antiquated laws. And when, a few years ago, ten or fifteen years ago, Maurice Thorez was vice president of the council and charged with outlining the status of public administration, he could simultaneously uphold Marxist thought on a theoretical level (according to which we must break up the State apparatus) while working in practice to consolidate the State apparatus by outlining the status of public administration. Certainly, the large numbers of civil servants in France and the extraordinary expansion of the State cause a great many problems, very serious problems; however, working to consolidate the state while outlining the status of public administration is nothing but a means to elude these problems: this entails nothing other than promoting the consolidation of State power while nonetheless professing the phraseology, if I might say so, of the destruction of the existing State.

KHRUSHCHEV AND THE RESTORATION OF DEMOCRACY

Stalinism in general, and the Stalinism of Thorez in particular, ambiguously blends together a language (or, if you will, an ideology) that is revolutionary and a practice that is highly opportunistic. Leftist phraseology conceals a right-wing practice. Sectarian ideology conceals an opportunistic practice. And it is the same for Stalinism, the essence of Stalinism for thirty or forty years, and it is this that the Twenty-second Congress of the Communist Party of the Soviet Union is in the process of dissociating and flushing down into the forgotten dungeons [oubliettes] of History.[10] This liquidation of a leftist phraseology molded onto a politics of the Right, the one concealing the other, is drawing to an end, which is to say that one can finally see an open, transparent, democratic politics, in which theory and practice will be linked in a coherent manner. I think that Khrushchev, in his speech, went incomparably further than has been reported in the French and communist press. Khrushchev made a veritable appeal to the Russian people, over the head, I would say, of the State apparatus, over the party. He made a direct appeal to the people and invited the people to control the State apparatus and the functioning of the party. This is the essence of democracy in the modern State, this essence of democracy in the modern State, which has equally been passed over by the men of the Club Jean-Moulin, who furthermore do not even pose, in their otherwise sometimes very detailed book, a question as important as that of the representative nature of governmental agencies. Who must be represented in the State? Who and how? Which are the agencies, the organs that constitute life, the very tissue of democratic life in a country? We must clearly say that the problem was difficult to resolve, since in the most socially and politically advanced countries—the USSR—the problem has been blurred and ultimately replaced by its contrary, by the contrary solution to the solution sought by the proponents of Marx and Lenin, replaced by a pure and simple bureaucratization of the State apparatus.

Now, all these problems will be revisited in a renewed light, and democracy will appear in its true face, which is to say with the social providing and containing the secret of the political, with the social containing the meaning of the political, first point; and second point, the people's control—with the people understood not as an amorphous mass, but as men reunited in their actual social groups, living on the basis of real life. This sense of people's control over the State apparatus, over the political parties, which is to say over the whole of the political superstructure—that is what defines modern democracy.

Translation by Gerald Moore, Neil Brenner, and Stuart Elden

NOTES

1. [The Twentieth Congress of the Communist Party of the USSR was held in February 1956. It was famous for the "secret speech" of Khrushchev denouncing the crimes of Stalin. The Twenty-first Congress was held less than a year later, in early 1957, and was more of a consolidating move on Khrushchev's part, given an attempted coup against him. The Twenty-second Congress was held in October 1961. In it, Khrushchev took particular aim at Albania's continued Stalinist orthodoxy, which in turn provoked a critical reaction from the Chinese. It was one of the contributing factors to the Sino-Soviet split.—Eds.]

2. [This was a proposal for a common European security policy, proposed by the French prime minister René Pleuven as an alternative to West Germany's accession to NATO. A treaty was signed in 1952, although a vote in the French parliament defeated it. The countries that signed it were the same six that, five years later, signed the Treaty of Rome founding the European Economic Community.—Eds.]

3. [The Halle aux Vins was part of the Halles market area of Paris. The Jussieu Campus of the Université de Paris VI and VII was eventually constructed on this site and opened in 1970–71, despite the dispute Lefebvre discusses here. Lefebvre returns to a discussion of the development of this area in "The Other Parises" in *Key Writings*, 154–55.—Eds.]

4. [Friedrich Engels, "Preface to the Third German Edition of The Eighteenth Brumaire of Louis Bonaparte," in Karl Marx and Friedrich Engels, *Selected Works in One Volume* (London: Lawrence and Wishart, 1968), 95.—Eds.]

5. [The Club Jean-Moulin, a group of politicians and political advisors, was named after a French resistance fighter who killed himself when captured by the Germans. The text Lefebvre refers to is Club Jean-Moulin, *L'État et le citoyen* (Paris: Seuil, 1961).—Eds.]

6. See Club Jean-Moulin, "Thesis," in *L'État et le citoyen*, 185. [This is the opening section of part 2 of the book. The section entitled "The State As It Is" actually appears on 95.—Eds.]

7. [The Unified Socialist Party (Parti Socialiste Unifié—PSU) was founded in 1960 by several dissident socialist groups, some of which had left the PCF following the Soviet invasion of Hungary in 1956. At the time of the present essay, the PSU was a relatively new presence on the landscape of the French Left, but it later supported the French student movement in May 1968 and, under Michel Rocard's leadership, developed a political program based on *autogestion.—Eds.*]

8. [Guy Mollet (1905–75), was a socialist politician and French prime minister from 1956 to 1957. Maurice Thorez (1900–1964) was general secretary of the French PCF from 1930 to 1964. When Lefebvre refers to the "Stalinist party" he means the PCF. Ferdinand Lassalle (1825–64) was a German revolutionary who met Marx in 1848. Lassalle later established the Universal German Working Men's Association, which subsequently became the German Social Democratic Party. His ideas and legacy were criticized by Marx in the *Critique of the Gotha Program*, a text frequently cited by Lefebvre.—*Eds.*]

9. [See chapter 2.—*Eds.*]

10. [An *oubliette*, derived from *oublier*, to forget, was a dungeon whose only entrance was a trapdoor in the roof.—*Eds.*]

2 The Withering Away of the State

The Sources of Marxist–Leninist State Theory

This essay was published alongside the preceding one and stems from the same intellectual and political context. Initially a seminar paper, it retains elements of the spoken form (including several somewhat rambling sentences), even while elaborating a series of key theoretical and political points that lay at the heart of Lefebvre's vision of politics and the state. Central to Lefebvre's agenda here is the reassessment of Marxian theory following his break with the French Communist Party (PCF) and his ongoing critique of Stalinist theory and practice. The essay is framed around a detailed analysis of the Marxist–Leninist notions of the dictatorship of the proletariat and the withering away of the state. Lefebvre suggests that these concepts, appropriately reinterpreted, can help illuminate the dilemmas and contradictions of the current conjuncture. In order to dismantle the Stalinist misappropriation of these ideas, the essay surveys at length their development and elaboration in key texts by Marx, Engels, and later by Lenin. Lefebvre's detailed exegeses of these concepts is obviously linked to his subsequent, more sustained engagements with their ideas in other book-length works. Yet, while this essay shows Lefebvre engaging with the details of specific texts in a way he only rarely did, this piece is not merely exegetical. Lefebvre's interpretations of the concepts of the dictatorship of the proletariat and the withering away of the state lay the foundations for his subsequent critique of the modern (capitalist) state (described in later chapters of this book as the "state mode of production") and his broader vision of popular grassroots democracy or *autogestion*.

Throughout this text, Lefebvre cites Marx from the Jules Molitor edition and translation of *Oeuvres Philosophiques,* 6 vols. (Paris: Alfred Costes, 1927–37). He regularly modifies the translation and is often explicitly critical of it. He is less critical of the edition he uses for Lenin. In the footnotes below, we cite

the standard English editions of Marx, Engels, and Lenin. We have occasionally
modified the translations, in order to better follow the idiosyncrasies of
Lefebvre's renderings. The current subtitle of the piece was the title in its
original 1964 publication. We have provided a new title to highlight what is
arguably the essay's main substantive theme.—*Eds.*

The Leninist theory of the State is both the theory of the dictatorship of the
proletariat and the theory of the withering away [*dépérissement*] of the State.
It is therefore the theory of the dictatorship of the proletariat and simultaneously and correlatively the theory of the withering away of the State that
we are going to analyze this evening.

The fact that this theory is both the theory of the dictatorship of the proletariat and that of the withering away of the State seems to me of the greatest
contemporary relevance. Of course, when one speaks of the dictatorship of
the proletariat, one must know what one is talking about. It is not a question
of just any old dictatorship. It is not a question of the form that the dictatorship of the proletariat took in the Soviet Union under Stalin. The Stalinist
theory, or rather practice, of the dictatorship of the proletariat has been a
deviation, a distortion, and, to use a word that has become banal, the Stalinist practice of the dictatorship of the proletariat was a *revisionism* of the genuine Leninist theory of the dictatorship of the proletariat and the withering
away of the State. Stalin retained only one of the two terms in Marxist–
Leninist theory, and in so doing distorted it. In Stalin the dictatorship of the
proletariat was combined with a theoretical superfetation that was absolutely
not in Marx and Lenin, namely that during the construction of socialism,
there was a worsening of class struggle, and hence the necessity of consolidating the State.[1] This Stalinist distortion of the Marxist–Leninist theory
must today be critiqued in light of the authentic theory of Marx and Lenin.

THE DICTATORSHIP OF THE PROLETARIAT

When speaking of the dictatorship of the proletariat, we must know exactly
which theory is under consideration, whether it is Stalinist theory and practice or Marxist–Leninist theory. The essential text with which I'm going to
begin is found in the Moscow edition of Lenin, *The Selected Works*. Lenin cites
The Communist Manifesto and says: "According to Marx and Engels, as we
have seen, the first stage in the workers' revolution is the 'constitution of the
proletariat as the ruling class,' and 'the conquest of democracy.'"[2] Note the

two terms: the constitution of the proletariat as the ruling class and the conquest of democracy. Which is to say that the constitution of the proletariat as the ruling class is also the conquest of democracy: "The proletariat will use its political supremacy to wrest, by degrees, all capital from the bourgeoisie, to centralize all instruments of production in the hands of the State, that is, of the proletariat organized as the ruling class; and to increase the total of productive forces as rapidly as possible."[3]

Having cited this text, Lenin comments on it by way of a probing analysis. We see formulated here one of the most remarkable and one of the most important ideas of Marxism on the subject of the State, that of the dictatorship of the proletariat, as formulated by Marx and Engels after the Paris Commune.

We subsequently find here a definition of the State that is of the highest interest, and which is also among the numerous forgotten ideas of Marxism: "The State"—which is to say the proletariat organized as ruling class—"this definition of the State has never been explained in the prevailing propaganda and agitation literature of the official Social-Democratic parties" (this refers to the socialist parties of the Second International, since the Third did not yet exist).[4] "More than that," Lenin adds, "it has been forgotten, for it is absolutely irreconcilable with reformism, and it is a slap in the face of the common opportunistic prejudices and the petit bourgeois illusions regarding the 'peaceful development of democracy.' The proletariat needs the State. All the opportunists, the social-chauvinists, and the Kautskyists" (thus concerning Lenin's polemics against the social democrats) "repeat this, reassuring themselves that it is what Marx taught. But they 'forget' to add that in the first place, according to Marx, the proletariat needs only a State which is withering away, i.e. one which is constituted in such a way that it begins immediately to wither away and cannot but wither away; and second that the workers have need of the State, which is to say of the 'proletariat organized as the ruling class.'"[5]

Here is thus a doctrine in two very neat parts that complement one another. The proletariat must have a State. This State is not that of the bourgeoisie, it is that of the proletariat organized as the ruling class. But this State is such that it begins immediately to wither away and cannot but wither. The passage is categorical.

THE WITHERING AWAY OF THE STATE: A FUNDAMENTAL IDEA OF MARX

Now, in order fully to comprehend the origins of this fundamental theory, one must go further back in the history of Marxist thought, because the theory of the dictatorship of the proletariat and the withering away of the State in Lenin has its deepest roots in the thought of Marx himself and in the Marxist critique of the Hegelian doctrine of the State.

There is, however, no shortage of theorists who believe that the dictatorship of the proletariat is outdated, that it is consequently without importance, that it must be relegated to the background, that after all it is more important to show in the critique of Marx and Engels the progressive realization of reason in the State, the fact that this Reason is not realized statically and definitively in the Hegelian State, that one can therefore advance the theory of Reason in the State, bring it closer to modern reality by throwing away the theory of the withering away of the State. We will soon demand answers from ourselves, as it were, on this evidently very serious point. I think that if the theory of the withering away of the State is false, it must be abandoned, thrown overboard. If ever it were proven that the State could not be made to wither away, that the State is destined to prosper and to flourish until the end of time, then Marxism as a whole would have to jump ship. The dialectic would have no more meaning, for the revolutionary dialectic of Marx and Lenin is just that. If it were true, the socialist revolution would capitulate in the face of democracy. The whole of Marxism would eventually collapse. One could not even give a precise meaning to the theory of supersession [dépassement], that is, of the concrete realization of philosophy. Philosophy would continue to be speculative, the State would continue to be constructed over society in one way or another, history would continue to follow its course, perhaps attenuating its contradictions, but in so doing giving birth to others. The revolution, in the sense of Marx and Lenin, would no longer make sense.

THE CRITIQUE OF THE STATE IN MARX

It is therefore essential to return quickly to the Marxist analysis of the State in general and to the analysis of the withering away of the State in particular. We find this in Marx and Engels's critiques of the Hegelian doctrine (in a series of texts that we are going to survey) and above all in the works of the young Marx. I'm going to show you that, beginning with the earlier works, the thesis of the withering away of the State is found from the outset. In fact, I am looking not at the unpublished work of Marx, entitled *Critique of the Hegelian Philosophy of the State*, but at a little article published in Paris in 1844 and which, written in 1843, is called "Critique of Hegel's Philosophy of Right":[6] "The criticism of the German philosophy of State and Right, which attained its most consistent, richest, and final formulation through Hegel, is both a critical analysis of the modern State and of the reality connected with it."[7] Let us weigh up each term thoroughly: it is the critical analysis of the modern State, not the philosophy of Hegel, but the State to which this philosophy is effectively linked, whose ideology it embodies. It is therefore not the critical analysis of a theory, but rather of the modern State itself, and of the reality with which it stands together.

"The resolute negation of the whole manner of the *German consciousness in politics and right* as *practiced* hitherto, the most distinguished, most universal expression of which, raised to the level of *science*, is the *speculative philosophy* of right itself. If the speculative philosophy of right, that abstract transcendent *thinking* on the modern state, the reality of which remains a thing of the beyond, if only beyond the Rhine, was possible only in Germany [though published in Paris], inversely the *German* thought-image of the modern state which makes abstraction of *real man* was possible only because and insofar as the modern state itself makes abstraction of *real man*, or satisfies the whole of man only in imagination."[8] This last phrase in fact signifies that political man, the citizen, the political citizen, is only a political fiction in which the real man, the total man, is completed only in the imagination. Man realizes himself not at the level of the State, nor in the State, nor in that which depends on the State, but in freeing himself from the State. The formula is as neat as possible.

In *On the Jewish Question,* from around the same time, when he was twenty-five, Marx wrote:

> Only where the political State exists in its completely developed form can the relation of the Jew, and of the religious man in general, to the political State . . . stand out in all its specific character and purity. The criticism of this relationship ceases to be a theological criticism as soon as the State ceases to adopt a *theological* attitude to religion, as soon as it adopts the attitude of a state towards religion, i.e., politically. Criticism then becomes *criticism of the political state.*[9]

So, we keep coming back to the idea of a general critique of every political State. Still in the same text: "In the religion of State, the State limits itself in making a place for religion at its core. The political emancipation of religion is not the emancipation of religion taken to its end without contradiction, because political emancipation is not the complete, contradiction-free mode of human emancipation."[10] I repeat: "The political emancipation of religion is not the emancipation of religion taken to its end," which is to say that when there is separation between Church and State, for example, it is not an emancipation, a liberation, an enfranchisement that goes all the way—because "political emancipation is not the complete, contradiction-free mode of human emancipation." The limit of political emancipation immediately appears in the way the State can enfranchise itself up to a point without man being enfranchised by this, in the way the State can be a free State without man being free. This applies to all States that acquire their independence, for example the new States: the people believe that, once they have national independence, they will immediately become free.[11] Yet one can be enslaved in a free State. The State can therefore be emancipated from religion even if the great majority of citizens continue to be subjected to religion, on account of their being privately subjected. The relation between the State, especially the free State, and religion, is only the relation between the men who constitute it and religion. It follows that man is enfranchised up to a point through the mediation of the State; that is politically, so that he raises himself above this limit only partly in contradiction with himself; even when he proclaims himself atheist by the mediation of the State, which is to say when he proclaims the State atheist, he remains religiously limited. The State is the mediator between man and the freedom of man, which is to say that, at best, the State, when it is freed from whatever fetters, like State religion, is only ever a mediation between man and himself, which is to say an intermediary stage in the realization and enfranchisement of the human being.

The Fissure between Man and Citizen

These works of the young Marx are written in a very antiphrastic[12] and somewhat too visibly dialectical style. Ultimately, it is almost a procession of dialectical thought. Thus the contradictions are exposed, but in a way that shocks, is intended to shock, which is to say in a style that is written rather than spoken, and these citations can seem difficult.

There is a fundamental text, again from the same period, in which Marx criticizes the internal fissure that produces itself between man and citizen, private man and public man, a fissure that is also a separation of the individual from society, and of the individual from himself, once there is a political State.

When the political State has achieved its true development, man leads a double life, a heavenly one and an earthly one, not only in thought and consciousness, but in reality, in life. He has a life both in the political community, where he is valued as a communal being, and in civil society, where he acts as a private individual, regards other men as means, degrades himself to a means, and becomes the plaything of alien powers. The relation of the political State to civil society is just as spiritual as the relation of heaven to earth.[13]

What we see, here, is the political State realizing its full development, the most modern State, therefore the most democratic State. The State is, in its essence, of the same nature as religion, even when it is separated from religion and struggles against it. Which is to say that every State ideology is a religiosity, and this is why the cult of personality of Stalin was a religiosity, because it was a cult of the State and not a cult of the personality of Stalin. It was a cult of the State through the personality of Stalin. An element of religiosity therefore necessarily attaches itself to that. This analysis is found in Marx. There is a religiosity of State linked to the existence of the State itself because the State is, in relation to real life, in the same relation as the sky to the earth, which is to say above real life, looming over it. It triumphs over it in the same way that religion vanquished the world of the profane. There is an admirable description of what happened here in Stalinist ideology, where anti-Stalinism was vanquished like religion vanquishes the world of the profane, by recognizing it, by sating the need for it: "In his most immediate reality, in civil society, man is a secular being. Here where he regards himself, and is so regarded by others, as a real individual he is an illusory phenomenon. In the State, on the other hand, where man counts as a species being, he is an imaginary member in an imaginary sovereignty, he is deprived of his real life and endowed with an unreal universality."[14] This is a critique of the Rights of Man and the Citizen.[15] Marx initially criticizes the division of rights into the rights of man and the rights of the citizen. The rights of the citizen are abstract, fictitious. They only give the individual an imaginary sovereignty that lies outside of real individuality, and in an unreal universality, whereas the rights of man are essentially the rights of the egoistic individual, and ultimately, in bourgeois society, the rights of the owner and of private property.

Here are two other passages taken from *On the Jewish Question:*

In moments of particular self-consciousness political life tries to suppress its presuppositions, civil society and its elements, and to constitute itself as the real, species life of man. However, this is only possible by coming into violent contradiction to its own conditions, only by declaring the revolution to be permanent.[16]

An astonishing passage!

Political Life versus Real Life

Political life suppresses its own conditions, which is to say everyday life, economic life, the life of real individuals. It suppresses its own conditions when it wants to intensify itself, when it asserts itself over the banal existence of the life of the family, of couples, and everyday life in general. It suppresses it, it denies its own internal contradiction by—in a stupefying phrase—"declaring the revolution to be permanent," a phrase that should provoke much discussion.

The drama of politics thus inevitably ends in the restoration of religion, of private property, and of elements of civil society, just as war ends in peace. There is obviously a question of Jacobinism, but there is also a much deeper drama: there is a critique of the French Revolution, a far-reaching critique. It is a critique of every State and every politics. We are familiar with these periods where political life is so intense that it suppresses its own conditions and announces a permanent revolution that ends up in the restoration of religion, for example. "The members of the political state are religious" (I emphasize religious) "because of the dualism between their individual life and their species life, between life in civil society and political life. They are religious because men treat the political life of the state, an area beyond their real individuality, as if it constituted their real life."[17]

Marx's critique goes an astonishingly long way. It is a critique of political life itself. I will say that it is the critique of the life of the militant, of a certain militantism that poses as total life, which engages itself so completely that it separates itself from all that is not political, that it claims to transcend all that is extrapolitical. Men are religious "insofar as religion here is the sprit of civil society, the expression of separation and alienation of man from man. Political democracy is Christian insofar as man, not merely one man but every man, counts as a sovereign and supreme being; but it is man as he appears uncivilized and unsocial, man in his partial existence, in short, man as he is, lost, alienated, delivered over to inhuman elements and relations, man who is no longer a real species being. The fantasy, dream, and postulate of Christianity, the sovereignty of man, but of man as born of an alien essence and distinct from actual man, becomes in democracy a tangible reality, a real presence, a profane reality."[18] Marx reiterated several times, notably in the *Critique of the Hegelian Philosophy of the State,* that democracy is, in relation to all forms of the State, what Christianity is in relation to all other religions. Christianity brings man to the fore, but it is alienated man. Just as democracy brings man to the fore, but it is alienated man, not real man. It is not flourishing man. Why? Because it is a political State.

CRITIQUE OF THE RIGHTS OF MAN

And it is here that Marx reappropriates the critique of human rights.[19] The rights of man are distinguished, as such, from the rights of the citizen: "But what is a man, as distinct from a citizen? Nothing other than a member of civil society. Why is the man of civil society called man, simply, and his rights, the rights of man? How is this fact to be explained? From the relation of the political State to civil society, from the very essence of political emancipation."[20] "The so-called rights of man, the rights of man as different from the rights of the citizen, are nothing but the rights of the member of civil society, i.e., egoistic man, man separated from other men and the communal essence."[21] . . . "The freedom in question is that of man treated as an isolated and self-sufficient monad"[22]—remember that Marx had read a lot of Leibniz— "The right of man to freedom is not based on the relations between man with man, but rather upon the separation of man from man. It is the right of such separation, the right of the circumscribed individual, withdrawn into himself. The practical application of the rights of man to freedom is the right of man to private property . . . '[Article 16 (Constitution of 1793)] Thus the right of man to property is the right to enjoy his possessions and dispose of the same arbitrarily, without regard for other men, independently from society.' . . . It is the right to selfishness. This individual freedom and its latter application form the basis of civil society. It leads each man to see in other men not the realization but the limitation of his own freedom."[23] . . . Thus none of the so-called rights of man goes beyond egoistic man, man as he is in civil society."[24]

This persists throughout *The Jewish Question* in relation to the problem of the emancipation of Jews and their participation in the political State: "Political man"—this is not a question of the professional politician, but of man insofar as he participates in politics—"is only the abstract, fictional man, man as an allegorical or moral person . . . All emancipation is bringing back man's world and his relationships to man himself. Political emancipation is the reduction of man, on the one hand to a member of civil society, an egoistic and independent individual, on the other, to a citizen, a moral person."[25] And here comes an equally important citation:

> Only when the real individual man reabsorbs the abstract citizen into himself and, as an individual in his empirical life, in his individual work and individual relationships become a species being; only when he recognizes and organizes his *forces propres* [own forces] as social forces, and consequently no longer separating social forces from himself in the form of political forces; it is only then that he accomplishes human emancipation.[26]

I note that the respective pages in the Molitor translation, volume 3 of the so-called "philosophical works" (one always says the philosophical works, though in reality they contain a critique of philosophy), are very poor. The sentence is incomprehensible and even truncated, so I have rectified the translation. It is thus only when the real man has taken back into himself, which is to say when he has reconquered himself, when he has put an end to this political alienation, when he has taken back into himself and recovered the forces separated from him, when he has taken the abstract citizen back into himself, and when he has become as an individual man, in his empirical life, in his individual work, in his individual relationships, when he has become species being, which is to say humanity, the human species, it is only because he has recognized and organized his own forces as social forces—and we shall presently see the precise meaning of this term—and no longer separates social force from himself in the form of political force, which is to say only when there is nothing more outside him, beyond him, raised above him, in the form and the force of the political: the State, when he has recovered the alienated forces in his politics, in political life, "it is only then that he accomplishes human emancipation." To my mind, this text is decisive.

Democracy and the People

I would like to cite for you a few extracts from the *Critique of the Hegelian Philosophy of the State*. Above all, this one: "The real relation of the family and of civil society with the State is conceived by Hegel as their intimate, imaginary activity" (same observation as previously).[27] The family and civil society are presuppositions of the State; they are its properly active elements. Yet, in Hegelian speculation, the relationship is reversed. When the subject is made an idea, which is to say a conscious and ultimately supraconscious reality, an absolute Idea, real subjects like civil society and families, whatever the circumstances, become unreal moments of the Idea, with a very different significance. And it is here that the critique of Hegel's panlogical mysticism, of the Hegelian manner of hypostatizing the absolute Idea construed as a subject, neatly appears.[28] Hegel does not develop his thought around the object; he deduces the object from a thought that is realized in itself, in the sphere of logic, and thus, Marx says, political categories are born as logico-metaphysical categories of the most abstract variety.

But here is another text that closely reiterates what I've just told you: "Democracy is the resolved riddle of all constitutions. . . . Hegel starts from the state and makes man the subjectified state; democracy starts with man and makes the state objectified man. Just as it is not religion that creates man but man who creates religion, so it is not the constitution that creates the people but the people that create the constitution. . . . In a certain respect the relation of democracy to all other forms of the state is like the relation of Christianity to all other religions. . . . Similarly, democracy is the essence of all state constitutions[29] socialized man as a *particular* state constitution. Democracy stands to the other constitutions as the genus stands to its species; except that here the genus itself appears as an existent, and therefore as one *particular* species over against the others whose existence does not correspond to their essence. . . . In monarchy, for example, and in the republic as merely a particular form of the state, political man has his particular and separate existence beside the unpolitical man, man as a private individual. Property, contract, marriage, civil society appear here (as Hegel shows quite rightly with regard to these *abstract* state forms, but he thinks that he is expounding the idea of the state) as *particular* modes of existence alongside the *political* state, as the *content* to which the *political state* is related as organizing form."[30] The State, in this theory, thus appears as a form organizing a formless content. This is a theory we encounter very often, and it comes from Hegel. "In democracy," Marx continues, "the political state as particular is itself merely a particular content, like a particular form of existence of the people . . . The French have recently interpreted this by saying that in true democracy the *political state disappears.*"[31]

Marx and Lenin are in agreement with this theory, since they think that true democracy is the disappearance of democratic politics itself. Marx retains here an idea of Saint-Simon, according to which the accomplishment of democracy is the end of the State.[32] You are familiar with the famous parable of Saint-Simon: if one took from a country ten state officials, ten generals, and ten princes, the State would continue to function in exactly the same way. But if one took the ten principal intellectuals, the ten principal technicians and the ten principal directors of industry, it could no longer work. This is the famous Saint-Simonian parable according to which the State is useless beyond a certain level of social development. Marx does not cite him, but it is incontestably Saint-Simon to whom he refers. Remember, the critique of the State, of the Hegelian philosophy of the State, was not published; it is a draft. Marx does not give the citation, the reference, but it is extremely clear: "the modern French have interpreted this by saying that in true democracy, the political State disappears." The phrase alludes to Saint-Simon, perhaps also to Fourier and J.-B. Say.[33]

This idea was "in the air" in France during this era, notably following the writings of Saint-Simon. From this time onward, there is therefore a question of the end of the State. The critique of Hegel is not only a critique of the Hegelian conception of the State in order to substitute for it a Marxist theory of the State; the critique of the Hegelian philosophy of the State is already the theory of the withering away and the disappearance of the State. This is a much more fundamental critique, which goes much further than a simple analysis of some reticent remarks.

THE CONTRADICTIONS OF THE STATE

Apropos of Hegel, Marx analyzes at length the relation Hegel makes between the estates [*états*], small "e," which is to say the trades, the corporations ("to take up a trade [*prendre un état*]," as they used to say and which is still said a bit in the provinces, perhaps even in Paris) and the State. The estates were not the idea of classes, in the strict sense of the term, nor of the State [*l'État*] in general—with a capital "E"—but of the trades, the corporations, even of the groups, like the third estate.[34] In German this is *Stände*, whereas the State is *Staat*. In French there is a certain confusion in the vocabulary, which is why I must explain that Marx examines in Hegel the relation between the estates (with a small "e") and the State (with a capital "E").

And here is the important point. The principal characteristic of this relationship between the estates and the State in Hegel—and Marx indicates this with irony—is that the lack of goods and the state of work form less a state of civil society than the terrain on which rest and move every circle·of this society, which is to say that it already substitutes for a Hegelian analysis a Marxist analysis of the base (or superstructure?) of the State. Marx cites a text of Hegel that he turns back against itself with his usual ingenuity.

Hegel writes:

> It is important to underline that a frequent and dangerous prejudice consists in representing the estates from the point of view of their opposition to government, as if that were their essential position. Organically, which is to say, taken in its totality, the elementary role of the estates is only affirmed through the function of mediation. Through the latter, opposition is reduced to an appearance. If, in appearing, an opposition concerned not only the surface but really became a substantial opposition, the State would be in the throes of disappearing.[35]

This text is extremely curious, and you will immediately see what Marx can draw from it. What Hegel means is that, if we consider the trades, the corporations, what we would nowadays call the unions, ultimately civil society, in their opposition to the government, we make an error, a dangerous error. What must be considered are the elements taken as a whole, which is to say integrated into the State. So, what appears is the mediation, the conciliation; opposition becomes of secondary importance. We glimpse something of the link between these particular estates and the State in general, which is to say the fact that they are taken in their totality, that they are only the elements of a totality. If by chance the opposition became real, which is to say that if there were real contradictions between the estates and the State at the heart of society, the State would verge on disappearing, it would be undermined by contradictions. Which is to say that Hegel, with his extraordinary but always bounded genius, perfectly perceived the point where his theory would turn back against him. He who said that there are contradictions everywhere understood that if there are contradictions internal to the State, it is the State that will explode into pieces and then finally disappear: there will be no more State. The whole work of Marx consists in pushing the Hegelian dialectic further than Hegel; this is why he comments on the text with the greatest care, precisely because it shows that oppositions are very real and inevitably become or even already are contradictions, and that the State will consequently explode into pieces. The State is destined to disappear. This critique of the State therefore goes a very long way. I note in passing that it includes a critique of philosophy, which is to say both of materialism and of spiritualism insofar as

they are philosophical representations that correspond to political representations and to ideas that reign in the representative State itself. I refer, for those
who would like to follow it up, to the pages on the critique of philosophical
representations and those on the critique of political representations.[36] There
is a link between the representations, the abstractions of philosophy, and the
abstractions of politics. This is to say that the theory of the supersession of
philosophy is linked to the theory of the supersession of political abstraction,
which is to say the withering away of the State.

I shall not dwell on the critique of political formalism. So here is an important passage in a letter from Marx to Ruge, in September 1843, responding to
all kinds of concerns that show Marx is not completely rejecting the Hegelian
thesis according to which the State is reason incarnate.

The State is proof that human reason is objective . . . Much as the reason
of the State is revolting, the State has reason to exist, several reasons for existing, but only up to a point, beyond which reason itself, human reason, requires the disappearance of the State.

And this is what Marx says in the letter to Ruge: "Reason has always existed,
but not always in a rational form. The critique . . ." (I indicate to you in passing that when Marx writes, he employs the word "critique" in an extremely
strong sense, as a matter of fundamental critique, of radical critique, a critique that reaches to the roots, as he himself said, to the very roots of man)
"critique can therefore begin from any form of theoretical and practical consciousness and, out of the proper forms of existing reality, develop the true
reality as its ultimate goal and objective. Now, as regards real life, even where
it is not consciously pregnant with the demands of socialism, in all its modern forms the political State contains the demands of reason."[37] There is thus
something rational in the State, in its functioning and organizational capacities, even where it is not yet socialist, impregnated with the demands of socialists, Marx says. Everywhere it presupposes the realization of reason, up to a
point. Everywhere there is a State, the State gives itself as the incarnation of
reason, and up to a certain point it is, in its men, in its organizations, in its
specialists, in its administrators and even in its police. But everywhere "it also
falls foul of the contradiction between its theoretical definition and its real
presuppositions. Thus the social truth emerges everywhere out of this conflict of the political State with itself."[38] Keep hold of the term "social truth."
There is no State without internal conflict, which is to say that the State carries within it the seeds of its self-destruction. Thus, the social truth emerges

everywhere. "Just as religion is the summary of all the theoretical struggles of humanity, so is the political State the summary of its practical struggles. So *sub speciae rei publicae* (from a republican, that is, political, form)—the political State thus gives expression to all social struggles, needs, and truths."[39]

In developing Marx's thought, we must introduce here the idea of several layers of truth, or several series of interconnected truths, each one through a critique of the preceding reality and level. There is a philosophical truth that emerges from the philosophical critique of religion, and there is a political truth of philosophical representations. And there is finally a social truth of politics and philosophy.

The State must be examined from up close. It cannot be transformed or broken down in just any old way. We must examine it as a summary, as a compendium of social needs, of accomplished or current social struggles, of the truths of society. The critique of the State must begin from the fact that there is a social truth of the State, which contains within it that which the State encompasses, but masks, dissimulates, which is to say transposes: social needs, social struggles, social truths. There is a social truth of philosophy, just as there is of politics. "The working class, in the course of its development, will substitute for an old civil society an association that will exclude classes and their antagonism. There will no longer be political power, properly speaking, since political power is precisely the official expression of antagonism in civil society." This comes from *The Poverty of Philosophy* (1845).[40]

Engels later returns to this critique of the Hegelian theses in *The Origin of the Family, Private Property, and the State.* "The state is therefore by no means a power imposed on society from without; just as little is it 'the reality of the moral idea,' 'the image and the reality of reason,' as Hegel maintains."[41] The State is the product of society at a certain stage of its development. It constitutes the admission that this society is caught up in an insoluble contradiction with itself, that it is broken down into irreconcilable antagonisms from which it is unable to rid itself; for these antagonisms (the classes that have contradictory economic interests) not to devour one another and not to devour society in a sterile struggle, a force has become necessary, which, giving the appearance of sitting above society, moderates conflict, keeps it within its limits of order. This force that emerges from society, yet gives the appearance of sitting above it and increasingly distances itself from it, is the State.

The Marxist theory of the State thus differs radically from the Hegelian theory: it begins with a critique of the Hegelian notion of the State. The texts cited above lead us clearly to understand the impact of this critique. The State is not that which crowns society, realizes it or brings it to completion, that which elevates it to the level of reason or the moral idea, it is simply the product of antagonisms, contradictions internal to society, and it is a force that erects itself over society in order to resolve these contradictions in appearance, and in fact in order to put itself in the service of the ruling class. The State does not arbitrate conflicts, it moderates them by keeping them within the limits of the established order. A few pages later, Lenin cites the following from Engels's text:

> The state, therefore, has not existed from all eternity. There have been societies which have managed without it, which had no notion of the state or state power. At a definite stage of economic development, which was necessarily bound up with the cleavage of society into classes, the state became a necessity because of this cleavage. We are now rapidly approaching a stage in the development of production at which the existence of these classes not only will have ceased to be a necessity, but will become a positive hindrance to production. They will fall as inevitably as they once arose. The state inevitably falls with them. The society which organizes production anew on the basis of free and equal association of the producers will put the whole machinery of state where it will then belong: into the Museum of Antiquities[42]

The End of the State

The State is thus not the result of timeless reason; it is thus not the result of an action of the society that rears it, that elevates its essence or its deepest nature, so to speak, to the highest degree. It is the product of history. And like all products of history, like philosophy, like every kind of form and culture, it is born, develops, and subsequently withers away and dies. The analysis of the history of the State is the analysis of its birth, its growth, its peak, and its decline. At its peak, its completion carries within it the necessity of its loss, its disappearance. In the society that emerges from socialist revolution, the State becomes useless.

"The first act by virtue of which the State really constitutes itself the representative of the whole of society—the taking possession of the means of production in the name of society—this is, at the same time, its last independent act as a State," writes Engels in *Anti-Dühring*, a text that is also cited by Lenin: "State interference in social relations becomes, in one sphere after another, superfluous and then dies out of itself. In the place of the government of persons, steps the administration of things and the management of the processes of production. The state is not 'abolished.' *It withers away.*"[43] This text of Lenin is partly directed against the social democrats, the reformists, and evolutionists.

Like that of Engels, it is also directed against the anarchists, against Bakunin and the leaders of anarcho-syndicalism. The State is not abolished through the act of revolution; the previous State, the State of the bourgeoisie must be fragmented and replaced with a new type of State, but this State must wither away. The State is not abolished by the act of revolution, but the State created through the act of revolution, through the historical act of revolution, is a State that withers away. This is the doctrine in all its clarity and simplicity. The passages furthermore multiply in Lenin. Lenin adds: "But it never enters the head of any of the opportunists who shamelessly distort Marxism that Engels is consequently speaking here of *democracy* 'ceasing of itself,' or 'withering away.'"[44] The idea here that perhaps becomes more subtle to grasp is that it is the democratic State itself that withers away and must wither away. The State of democracy is not a State that is abolished because it is a State. It is not the definitive State that would progressively improve toward socialist-democracy, it is just this socialist–democratic State that would disappear, that is withering away. "This seems very strange at first sight," notes Lenin himself. "But it is 'incomprehensible' only to those who have not thought that democracy is *also* a state and that, consequently, democracy will also disappear when the state disappears. Revolution alone can 'abolish' the bourgeois state. The state in general, i.e., the most complete democracy, can only 'wither away.' . . . Having formulated his famous proposition that 'the state withers away,' Engels at once explains specifically that this proposition is directed against both the opportunists and the anarchists."[45] "The opportunists," Lenin argues, "have applied makeup to bourgeois democracy, and the opportunist tendency lacks an understanding of the socialist critique of every State."[46]

THE STALINIST DISTORTION

Thus Lenin, like Marx—as we have just seen in the texts of Marx—is quite categorical: socialist thought criticizes every State. There is no question of a workers' State, a stable and strengthened proletarian State, before which socialist thought would accordingly bow down. This is the Stalinist distortion, the Stalinist revision of the Marxist–Leninist theory. Socialist thought, socialist critique, Marxist critique, which is to say radical critique, bears down against every State, because every State whatsoever, including the most democratic, is still a machine elevated above society, erecting itself above it and incorporating elements of constraint. The elements of constraint in question are inevitable in the moment of revolution, when it is a case of wresting from the bourgeoisie the possession, the ownership of the means of production and the management of social affairs, the power of decision, as we say nowadays, in contemporary language. But the State that emerges from this revolution must be submitted to radical critique. Socialist thought is fundamentally a critique of any and every State. Marx, Engels, and Lenin are categorical on this point.

Personally, I find Stalinist-era thought guilty of having abandoned this fundamental theory, and consequently of having entirely sidetracked Marxist theory, even of having transformed it into State ideology, of having transformed into a philosophy of State, whereas Marxist thought was a critique of every philosophy, likewise a critique of every State, a theory of the supersession of philosophy, likewise a theory of the withering away of the State. This is to say that the theory, the fundamental critique that must begin again from the relevant texts of Lenin, goes much further than a political critique. It is also a critique of a whole period of the past, of these works, of supposedly philosophical works, for example.

The Dictatorship of the Proletariat

The texts subsequently offered by Lenin are increasingly precise. He asserts two aspects of the problem: (1) The dictatorship of the proletariat, which is to say the proletariat's taking possession of the management of social affairs, deepened democracy, which is to say democracy really functioning for and through the majority. Constrained throughout the period of the dispossession of the bourgeoisie, the final act that it can accomplish, and (2) the State subsequently withers away. This is to say that these different aspects form an organic unity: the dictatorship of the proletariat; the deepening, extension, and concretization of democracy; and the withering away of the State. These are three aspects of the same revolutionary process in the thought of Marx and Lenin. Lenin states: "only one who *extends* the acceptance of class struggle to acceptance of the *dictatorship of the proletariat* is a Marxist,"[47] and on this point he cites a highly celebrated and very famous text of Marx, a letter to Weydemeyer in 1852: "What I did that was new was to prove: (1) that the existence of classes is only bound up with particular historical phases in the development of production, (2) that the class struggle necessarily leads to the dictatorship of the proletariat, (3) that this dictatorship itself only constitutes the transition to the abolition of all classes and to a classless society,"[48] which is to say, in this context, a society without a State.

This means that today, as a Marxist, this criterion remains essential for me and, as far as I am concerned, I FULLY RECOGNIZE the necessity of the dictatorship of the proletariat. And when one of my former friends and communist comrades tries to embarrass me by saying: do you recognize the necessity of the dictatorship of the proletariat? I reply: perfectly, and more than ever. But which dictatorship of the proletariat? The one of which Marx and Lenin speak, or the one that has been put into practice by Stalin? Because the equivocation persists even after the Twenty-second Congress of the Communist Party of the USSR.[49] And I know very well where I want to go with this in this presentation; for it is a question of getting to the roots of the debates and their difficulties, or, if you prefer, the compromises.

THE STATE IN THE PROCESS OF WITHERING AWAY

Subsequently, in *The State and Revolution,* Lenin takes things further: The idea of Marx is that the working class must break up, demolish, break up the machinery of State right away, and not limit itself to a mere taking of possession, for Lenin, following Engels, indicates that there exists a kind of tradition of State socialism, which we moreover know goes back to Lassalle, Ferdinand Lassalle, and not to Marx, and which consists in integrating the socialist movement into the existing State, which is obviously the criterion of political opportunism. I have explained myself briefly on this point elsewhere, three weeks or a month ago.[50] Lenin returns endlessly to the theory of the withering away of the State, which is here a matter of transforming quantity into realized quality as methodically and as fully as is possible to conceive. Through revolution, bourgeois democracy becomes proletarian. The State, which is to say the special force destined to repress a determinate class, is transformed into something that is no longer properly a State, but repressing the bourgeoisie and breaking down its resistance remains no less a necessity. This necessity is especially imposed on the Commune. And one of the causes of its undoing is that this was not done with sufficient determination. I suggest here that the Commune, from which we continually draw inspiration and to which so many references are made, the Commune is cited by Marx and by Engels as an example of the withering away of the State, or an act envisaging the withering away of the State. "The organ of suppression is now the majority of the population, and not a minority, as was always the case under slavery, serfdom, and wage slavery. And since the majority of people *itself* suppresses its oppressors, a 'special force' for suppression is no longer necessary! In this sense, the state begins to wither away. Instead of the special institutions of a privileged minority (privileged officialdom, the command of the standing army), the majority itself can directly fulfill all these functions, and the more the functions of state power are devolved upon the people generally, the less need there is for the existence of this power."[51] A remarkable formulation: the more the functions of State power are exercised by the whole of the people, the less necessary this power becomes. This is what Lenin himself calls the revolutionary dialectic of Marx. The theory of the State aims at the end of the State and, more generally still, the political theory of Marx aims at the end of all politics.

Freedom and the State

There is no possible freedom so long as there is a State apparatus, Lenin shows, following Engels and Marx. Even in a democracy, the State is incompatible with freedom in that every State is a force of constraint. So long as there is a State there is no freedom—this is one of the fundamental tenets of Marxism. Monsieur Roger Garaudy was able to write a whole book on freedom not only by presenting freedom, human freedom as accomplished in Stalinist Russia, but by completely passing over in silence the theory of the withering away of the State and the principal ideas of Marxism, namely that there is no freedom, no true freedom, so long as there is a State, even the most democratic of States.[52] This is the revolutionary dialectic, for which, Lenin adds, there has never been a fashionable vocabulary. The theory of the State, the class State, the rupture of this class State, the break in history that this new State, which is a withering State, represents, fills the whole of Lenin's book right up until the final pages, entitled "The Abolition of the Parasitic State," and it is always a question of the experience of the Commune to which the greatest importance must be attached, not only as an attempt to seize power by the armed proletariat, but as a remarkable example of an attempt at withering away the State.[53] Cited by Lenin, Marx writes with regard to the Commune that, in spite of its disadvantages, the communal constitution of which the people dreamed, which is to say the autonomy, the semiautonomy of the

principal and even the smallest communes of towns, "the Communal Constitution would have restored to the social body all the forces hitherto absorbed
by that parasitic excrescence, the 'State,' feeding on and clogging the free
movement of society."[54]

You see how far the theory, the critique of the State, goes. Marx reproaches
the anarchists for wanting to go too fast, for leaping ahead of the historical
era that is the era of transition, the era of the dictatorship of the proletariat,
but he would declare himself in agreement with the anarchist tendency on
the point that there is no freedom so long as there is a State and that the State
itself is a parasitic excrescence looming over society, the State as State apparatus. It is obvious that this whole side of the Marxist–Leninist theory was
kept under wraps during the Stalinist period. It does not yet give us a complete analysis of the historical phenomenon named Stalinism. Every historical
phenomenon has causes. Every historical phenomenon must be explained,
and the personality of Stalin is only one aspect of the historical period marked
by Stalinism, which has a whole set of causes and effects, which we are still
far from seeing clearly. It has always been inevitable that, under these historical conditions, this whole aspect of the Marxist–Leninist theory would remain obscure. I think that the moment has come, today, at the end of 1961,
after the end of the Twenty-second Congress of the Communist Party of the
USSR, to bring it to into the light and restore to it its true meaning. And this
whole part of the analysis is based on the experience of the Commune.

Lenin later cites several texts of Engels in which, he argues, Engels touches
on this critical point in history where democracy, deepened and thereby taken
to its limits, is on the one hand, transformed into socialism and on the other,
clamors for socialism, always, for Lenin, in accordance with this dialectic that
grasps all the aspects of the question. At a certain point in its development,
democracy traverses a critical period, a limit, where, on the one hand, it tends
to be transformed into socialism, but by no means spontaneously because it
must be deepened to be transformed into socialism, because if it does not go
further, it will collapse back into itself; it is obliged to turn into socialism
under the pain of disappearance. I think that for some time we have been
around and about this critical point where the resultant democracy must turn
into socialism, and where, on the other hand, it clamors for socialism, and I
believe that our political analyses must begin precisely from this idea that we
are at this point, at this elementary position, at this frontier, moreover on this
frontier that, like every slightly dangerous frontier, is somewhat difficult to

cross. In a text subsequently cited by Lenin, Engels states that "To develop democracy *to its logical conclusion*, to find the *forms* for this development, to test them *by practice*, and so forth—all this is one of the component tasks of the struggle for the social revolution. Taken separately, no kind of democracy will bring socialism."[55] This is important for situating the relations between forces and ideas at present, and there is no need to look far to find analogies; for example, a man of politics [*tel homme politique*] sympathetic to socialism and wanting to develop democracy in a corresponding way will never arrive at socialism, and his democratic values will never give rise to socialism. But, Lenin adds, in life, democratic values will never be viewed separately, it will be viewed as part of a whole, it will also exert an influence over the economy, it will stimulate its transformation, it will endure the influence of economic development, etc. Such is the dialectic of living history, which is to say that unequal and unequally distant forces enter into play in the dialectic of living history, each of which finds itself up against its own frontiers and limits, but the situation is changing, and it is a question of grasping how it develops in the sense of socialism.

These ideas of Engels, rehearsed by Lenin on the explosion, the collapse of State power, such as it has hitherto been, and its replacement by a new and truly democratic power, are outlined in detail in the third chapter of Marx's work on the Commune, *The Civil War in France*. But it was necessary to dwell more than briefly on these themes, because in Germany in particular, super-stitious faith in the State has passed from philosophy into the consciousness of the bourgeoisie and even that of many workers. According to the philoso-phers' teachings, the State is the realization of an idea. In philosophical terms, it is the reign of God over the earth, the domain where eternal justice and truth are realized and must be realized, hence the superstitious respect for the State and everything that touches the State, a sovereign respect rooted all the more easily when one is accustomed from birth to imagine that the common interests and affairs of the whole of society could not be ruled over or safe-guarded otherwise than has hitherto been done, which is to say by the State. I think that this superstitious faith in the State, which in the time of Engels spread throughout Germany, following the State socialism of Ferdinand Las-salle, since when it spread prodigiously and contaminated a good proportion of Marxist thought itself, it extended to the Soviet Union with Stalinism and it even put down strong roots in France, through both Guy Mollet and Maurice

Thorez. I think that one, Maurice Thorez, is a left-leaning Lassallian, and the other, Mollet, a right-leaning Lassallian.[56]

I have arrived here at the end of what I wanted to show during this lecture: the foundations of the Leninist theory, its roots in Marx and Engels. We see the theory take shape, constitute itself, reinforce itself, analyze events, become deepened through the experience of 1848, the experience of the Commune, but retain the dialectical elements that deepen each in their own way. The creation by the working class and its political allies of an improved and more consequential democracy, a critical point attained by this democracy during the process of its deepening, its expansion and realization; a dictatorship of the proletariat coinciding with a deepened and extended democracy; and finally the withering away of the State coinciding with the dictatorship of the proletariat, the dictatorship of the proletariat creating only a withering State, destined to wither away and unable not to wither away. Such is the summary of the Marxist–Leninist theory of the withering away of the State.

Translation by Gerald Moore, Neil Brenner, and Stuart Elden

NOTES

1. [Superfetation—in Lefebvre's French *superfétation*—is a medical term referring to the formation of a new fetus when one is already present. Lefebvre is using it to refer to Stalin's unjustified theoretical insemination of Marxist terms.—*Eds.*]

2. V. I. Lenin, *The State and Revolution,* in *Selected Works* (London: Lawrence and Wishart, 1947), 2:167, translation modified. [The reference is to Karl Marx and Friedrich Engels, *The Communist Manifesto* (London: Penguin, 2002), 243, translation modified.—*Eds.*]

3. Marx and Engels, *Communist Manifesto,* 243, translation modified.

4. Lenin, *State and Revolution,* 156, translation modified.

5. Lenin, *State and Revolution,* 156, translation modified.

6. [The latter is generally understood to be the introduction to the former. In other words, Marx wrote a long manuscript of which he published only the first part. The longer manuscript is generally given the title "Critique of Hegel's Philosophy of Law" or "of Right," not "of State" as Lefebvre has it.—*Eds.*]

7. Karl Marx, "Critique of Hegel's Philosophy of Law: Introduction," in Karl Marx and Friedrich Engels, *Marx and Engels: 1843–44—Collected Works* (New York: International Publishers, 1975), 3:181, translation modified.

8. Marx, "Critique of Hegel's Philosophy of Law: Introduction," 3:181, translation modified. [The phrase in brackets is Lefebvre's.—*Eds.*]

9. Karl Marx, "On the Jewish Question," in Marx and Engels, *Marx and Engels: 1843–44—Collected Works,* 3:150, translation modified.

10. Marx, "On the Jewish Question," 3:151–52, translation heavily modified in line with Lefebvre's rendering.

11. [Written in 1964, this clearly applies particularly to the contemporary context of decolonization in Africa and elsewhere.—*Eds.*]

12. [Antiphrasis is the use of a word in the exact opposite of its usual meaning.—*Eds.*]

13. Marx, "On the Jewish Question," 3:154, translation modified.

14. Marx, "On the Jewish Question," 3:154, translation modified.

15. [*La déclaration des droits de l'homme et du citoyen,* from 1789, was one of the fundamental texts of the French Revolution, and, along with the U.S. Declaration of Independence, one of the founding documents of more general human rights discussion.—*Eds.*]

16. Marx, "On the Jewish Question," 3:156, translation modified.

17. Marx, "On the Jewish Question," 3:159, translation modified.

18. Marx, "On the Jewish Question," 3:159, translation modified.

19. [Marx does indeed cite and critique *La déclaration des droits de l'homme et du citoyen* at this point. See Marx, "On the Jewish Question," 3:161.—*Eds.*]

20. Marx, "On the Jewish Question," 3:162, translation modified.

21. Marx, "On the Jewish Question," 3:162, translation modified.

22. Marx, "On the Jewish Question," 3:163, translation modified.

23. [This passage does not appear in the *Collected Works*. It can be found in Karl Marx, "On the Jewish Question," in Karl Marx, *Early Writings,* trans. and ed. T. B. Bottomore (London: C. B. Watts, 1963), 25, translation modified. Lefebvre does not note that there is a quotation within Marx's text from the 1793 constitution.—*Eds.*]

24. Marx, "On the Jewish Question," *Collected Works,* 3:164, translation modified.

25. Marx, "On the Jewish Question," 3:167–68, translation modified.

26. Marx, "On the Jewish Question," 3:168, translation modified. [Marx's text includes *forces propres* in French.—*Eds.*]

27. Marx, "Critique of Hegel's Philosophy of Law," in Marx and Engels, *Marx and Engels: 1843–44—Collected Works,* 3:8, translation modified.

28. [Panlogical is the doctrine that the universe is the realization of the *logos,* reason, or language. In Marx, "Critique of Hegel's Philosophy of Law," 3:7, this phrase is rendered "logical, pantheistic mysticism."—*Eds.*]

29. [Lefebvre writes "every political constitution" in place of "state constitutions."—*Eds.*]

30. Marx, "Critique of Hegel's Philosophy of Law," 3:29–30, translation modified.

31. Marx, "Critique of Hegel's Philosophy of Law," 3:30, translation modified. [Lefebvre's rendering diverges some way from Marx's own text; we have followed Lefebvre's version. The passage in Marx actually reads "the political state as particular is merely particular; as general, it is the truly general, i.e., not something determinate in distinction from the other content. The French have recently . . ."—*Eds.*]

32. [The Comte de Saint Simon (1760–1825) was a French socialist, influential to and criticized by Marx for his utopian ideas.—*Eds.*]

33. [Charles Fourier (1772–1837) was another utopian socialist criticized by Marx.

Lefebvre edited a book on his work (*Actualité de Fourier: Colloque d'Arcs-et-Senans sous la direction de Henri Lefebvre* [Paris: Anthropos, 1975]). Jean Baptiste Say (1767–1832) was a French economist.—*Eds.*]

34. [Through the medieval and early modern period the term "third estate" was used to describe the common people, after the first two estates of the nobility and the clergy. The notion of the third estate was particularly widely discussed during the French Revolution, following the polemical text by Abbé Sieyès, *Qu'est-ce que le tiers état?* (What Is the Third Estate?) published in 1789.—*Eds.*]

35. *Philosophy of Right,* sect. 302, remark, cited by Marx, "Critique of Hegel's Philosophy of Law," 70, translation modified. [Lefebvre references both the Molitor edition (4:146–47), though he modifies the translation, and refers to the French edition of the *Philosophy of Right, Principes de la philosophie du droit,* trans. André Kaan (Paris: Gallimard, 1963), 334–35. He notes parenthetically in the text that "the translator of this last volume renders 'états' as 'assemblies' and 'orders,' which does not illuminate this question!"—*Eds.*]

36. [The most sustained account of representation in this essay can be found in Marx, "Critique of Hegel's Philosophy of Law," 3:120–24. Marx's most extensive discussion of political representation is found in "The Eighteenth Brumaire of Louis Bonaparte."—*Eds.*]

37. Karl Marx, "For a Ruthless Critique of Everything Existing (Letter to Arnold Ruge)," in *The Marx-Engels Reader,* ed. Robert C. Tucker (New York: W. W. Norton, 1972), 9, translation modified.

38. Marx, "For a Ruthless Critique," 9, translation modified.

39. Marx, "For a Ruthless Critique," 9, translation modified.

40. Marx, "The Poverty of Philosophy," in Karl Marx and Friedrich Engels, *Marx and Engels: 1845–48—Collected Works* (New York: International Publishers, 1976), 6:212, translation modified.

41. Friedrich Engels, *The Origin of the Family, Private Property, and the State* (New York: Pathfinder Press, 1972), 158–59, translation modified.

42. Engels, *Origin of the Family,* 162, translation modified, cited by Lenin, *State and Revolution,* 150.

43. Friedrich Engels, *Herr Eugen Dühring's Revolution in Science (Anti Dühring)* (Chicago: Charles H. Kerr and Co, 1935), 292, translation modified.

44. Lenin, *State and Revolution,* 152, translation modified.

45. Lenin, *State and Revolution,* 152, translation modified.

46. Lenin, *State and Revolution,* 153, translation modified.

47. Lenin, *State and Revolution,* 163, translation modified.

48. Karl Marx, "Marx to J. Weydemeyer in New York," March 5, 1852, in Karl Marx and Friedrich Engels, *Selected Works in One Volume* (London: Lawrence and Wishart, 1968), 679, translation modified.

49. [See chap. 1 n.1—*Eds.*]

50. [This is a reference to the talk published as chapter 1 of this volume.—*Eds.*]

51. Lenin, *State and Revolution,* 169, translation modified.

52. [Roger Garaudy (1913–) was a member of the PCF who converted to Islam in 1982 and was prosecuted for Holocaust denial in 1998. The book Lefebvre is referring to is *La liberté* (Paris: Éditions Sociales, 1955), but in the year Lefebvre gave this lecture, Garaudy also published *Karl Marx* (Seghers, Paris, 1964).—*Eds.*]

53. [Lefebvre's study of the Commune appeared one year after the present chapter was published: *La proclamation de la commune* (Paris: Gallimard, 1965).—*Eds.*]

54. Lenin, *State and Revolution*, 177; Karl Marx, "The Civil War in France," in Marx and Engels, *Selected Works in One Volume*, 293, translation modified.

55. Lenin, *State and Revolution*, 194. [Lefebvre seems to think this is a citation from Engels, but this is not how Lenin presents it. The text Lenin is discussing is Engels's 1891 introduction to Marx's *Civil War in France*, which can be found in Marx and Engels, *Selected Works in One Volume*, 252–62.—*Eds.*]

56. [See chap. 1 n.8.—*Eds.*]

3   The State in the Modern World

This essay was published as Lefebvre embarked upon on his massive, four-volume work *De l'État;* it is nearly identical to its first chapter (published in volume 1 of that work in 1976) and provides a broad survey of the book as a whole. While the essay reads somewhat like an annotated outline—indeed, that is basically what it is—it is a remarkable piece since it illuminates the sheer breadth and audacious intellectual ambition of Lefebvre's book. Given that *De l'État* is unlikely ever to be translated into English in its entirety, this essay will provide English-language readers with a unique glimpse into some of the core agendas and arguments contained in that work. Interestingly, even though Lefebvre drafted this essay before completing the book in question, he did not significantly modify his original outline. It thus provides a fairly accurate mapping of the book's complex, if often meandering, intellectual terrain.—*Eds.*

This work, entitled *On the State,* comprises four parts. This article is a plan of it that is sufficiently detailed to show its direction: it presents a resume of the whole rather than a simple "table of contents." The following paragraphs indicate the themes treated, not chapters. This is to say that individual volumes do not exactly follow the indicated order.

PART 1: THE STATE IN THE MODERN WORLD

1. *The problematic of the State and the mystery of the State:* How can it be defined? How can we respond to the question: "what is the State and State power [*l'étatique*]?"

Enumeration of hypotheses. The State? A conscience, the consciousness of the nation? A "moral" or "legal" person? A "substance" or a set of relations? A reality? A firm? A "subject"? An "object"? Or the name for an absence, a simulation? For "being" or collective presence?

Would it be the "reflection" or the result of a social structure (classes)? A sum of functions? The exercise of Power? Or "something" else, to be discovered and defined? . . .

A related question: "What is the political, politics?" The mystery of the political, politics. Political relativism and absolute (total) politics (politicization).

2. *The State and the Nation:* From the feudal–military State to the Nation–State in Europe. From personal (so-called "absolute") power to the impersonal and "relative" political power defined by institutions and constitutions.

The relation and interaction between these two terms: the Nation and the State. Ideologies concerning this relation. The State, the child of the Nation or the consciousness of a nationality? Inversion of this apparent (ideological or even mystifying-mystified) relation.

First glimpses of the genesis of the modern State in France, England, the USA, the USSR, Japan, etc. (beginning with the feudal–military State, characterized by an economic activity subordinated to military activity; by "transparent" relations from the base to the summit of these strict hierarchies, etc.). The modern State as a (disparate) sum of historically specific institutions, which appeared during the course of its genesis. Critical examination of the concept of "State apparatus."

3. *The planetary extension of the State:* Its astonishing and recent "Catholicism." The universality of State power as a problem. Examination of the process by which this Western invention has conquered the world. Enumeration of hypotheses. Does the *mondialisation* of the State derive from capitalism?[1] From imperialism? From the generalization of national phenomena? From the inherent rationality of the State? From the universalism of productive industrial labor and the problem of its management? From the role of enterprise as a European model? etc.

Errors of interpretation. The paradoxes of the universality of State power. Fiction and/or reality?

Statement of a general (formal) principal of equivalence (between States in the United Nations). How it masks on all levels and on all scales the contradictions and relations of forces. Strategies in world space. The "developed" and the "undeveloped." The "aligned" and the "non-aligned," etc.

4. *The world system of the State (of States):* Is it a system? Its coherence and its failures. Analogies and differences between modern States. The (growing) inequalities in (fictitious) equivalence. Typological indications: political regimes, the various types of States.

Political stakes and objectives, both from "on high" and from "down below." Alternations and alternatives between authoritarianism and liberalism, between conservatism and the revolutionary overthrow. Retroactive clarification of the formation of Nation–States through the *mondialisation* of the State.

5. *Relations at the heart of each State* (and of each type of State)—Between the "body politic" and the "social body," or "civil society." Immediate relations and mediations. Vertical and horizontal dimensions of the "social body."

The State and the government. "Power." Myths and phantasms concerning Power. The movement of Power. Decision. Apparently rational phantasms: political causality. Irrational phantasms: magical power. How phantasms and images of power obscure reality and political changes. The political function of phantasms.

Economic interests and political power. Irreducibility of the political, politics.

The role of the will to power, which is to say of virtual and actual violence. The language of power and political discourse. How the (destructive) domination of nature and things does not distract from the domination of men. The role of *ressentiment*, identification with the Master (through the phantasms of power). The role of contempt (for the foreign and the foreigner), likewise hatred and *ressentiment* in national sentiment and the identification with "Power." State power as a force of separation and confusion. Tendency toward the absorption of "civil society" and the "social body" by the "body politic" and the State. The relations of dependence at the heart of State power and the social pyramid.

The State as a political form.

The State as a "monopoly of violence." The state and the police. The State and the army. The State and death. Polymorphism, polyvalence, and suprafunctionality of State power: management and violence, (limited) rationality and constraint, peace and war, etc. How State power abolishes the distinction between the animate and the inanimate, the inert and the living, the before and after. The flight of State power before understanding [*connaissance*] (which defines its mode of existence).

6. *The modern State and economic growth:* With industry and nascent (competitive) capitalism, a tendency toward the autonomy of the economic (in relation to religion, to ethics and art, likewise in relation to existing State power). Difficulties of this relative autonomy: crises, stagnation.

How the economically strong (bourgeois) class establishes its political hegemony from this initial situation. The disappearance of autonomy from industrial production. Substitution of State control over the economy for (relative) autonomy. The appearance of new, relatively "autonomous" factors: technology, demography. The (unequal) control of markets by States.

The State of growth and the growth of the State. Research into the articulation between the economic, the social, and the political, during the course of the State's assumption of responsibility for growth—initially into continuous, supposedly limitless growth, then into endangered growth. From the sectoral to the spatial. Space (organization and planning) under the control of State power. From the ideology of progress to that of growth to pessimism (nihilism, millenarianism, etc.), the utopia of limitless growth.

The role of technocrats (the technostructure of State power) in growth. Growth as a "positive" determination of State power in the modern world.

7. *The State and the extraction of social overproduction:* How to effectuate this extraction (through taxes and fiscal revenues, loans, State enterprises, the arms trade, etc.). Global overproduction and surplus value.

On the State as the "accursed share [*part maudite*]" of society.[2]

On the modern State as "political Being." The theatricality and monumentality of State power.

Economic growth and the growth of overproduction.

8. *The great threat: terricide:* From the (bounded) rationality of State power to the irrationality of the State system. Indications on interstate markets

(arms, energy, technology, etc.) and on their relations with the world market, with national markets, etc. Inherent violence. Interstate contracts.

The role of the military and the army in the modern State (in the USA, etc.). State delegations and political treaties. The technostructure of State power.

9. *The mystery of the State:* State secrets and *raison d'État.* The State and mystification. The State and manipulations. Alienation and alterity. The State as "the other of the other" and the "always elsewhere."

The trilogy of State power: occultism-fetishism-mystification. A study of several great modern mystifications: modernity itself, unlimited growth, absolute politics, the "unconscious," and "culture," etc. The role of misrecognition. Representations (continued).

On the State as an ideological force, taking over previous ideologies (religion, philosophy, nature and biology, the consciousness of towns and regions, etc.) to take them to a higher level: political deception, mystifications, and representations.

The conflict between representations (ideology, myths and mystifications, stereotypes and norms) and practice, notable in the course of (planned or semi-planned) growth. The State as the place where representations (occultism and fetishism, myths and ideologies) are born and spread. The State as the place where these same representations are destroyed by the trials of practice. Several conflicts: rationality/phantasms, occultism/positivism, prohibitions/transgressions, disinvestments/overinvestments, identifications/separations, security/risks, passivity/participation, freedom/efficiency, immediacy/mediation, etc.

How the State brings about and manages a mixture of ideology and knowledge. Ideologies of the ghetto and ideological ghettos (managed by the State). Examination of several recent "ideologies," in which representation and mystification are conveyed by the knowledge with which they are indiscernibly mixed: the discourse of the Third World, functionalism and structuralism, scientism and positivism, etc.

The State and knowledge [*savoir*] (first sketch). The State's stranglehold on knowledge. Conflicts between institutionalized knowledge and critical understanding [*connaissance*] (thorough dialectical objectivity).

Part 2: From Hegel to Mao via Stalin (The Marxist Theory
of the State and the Aporias—the Difficulties—
of so-called Marxist Thought)

1a. *Recap of historical sequences:* The distant (religious, magical, sacred) sources
of power. The *ancien régime* in France, its tactics and its strategies: the
centralization, the "enclosure" of urban "elements" that were seen in a
negative light, partitioning and isolation of the premodern [*ancienne*]
communitarian and agro-pastoral society, the accumulation of fiscal stock
as well as sacralizations, sacrifices, etc.

How, since the *ancien régime,* the new society (bourgeois hegemony) prepares itself. The end of the separation between the "orders" and the "Estates"
(including the third estate). Dislocation of the *ancien* social pyramid. The
role of "jurists" and "intellectuals," etc.

The historical production of "the people," "the nation," and "the national."
The French Revolution and Jacobinism. Jacobin rationality, centralism, the
concentration of political power. The Jacobin dictatorship. The new heights
of State power [*sommet étatique*]. The State as measure and creator of
measure. (The "metric system." Impact and meaning of this system.) The
Revolution as total phenomenon, its internal/external contradictions.

Comparison between changes in the social body and the body politic in
France, with analogous and different phenomena in England. Continental Caesaro-Papism and the English compromise.[3] The USA (from the war
of independence to the civil war and the world wars). The Meiji era in
Japan (the revolution from "on high"), etc.

In France, the pursuit and realization of the edifice of the State [*l'edifice
étatique*] by Napoleon (the Code, the prefectures, etc.); the new "partitioning" [*maillage*] of French space after these transformations. The State
and labor. (How the State and Western Logos mirror the laboring people.)
The centralized State in France as the first model of the State (initially
imitated, then superseded in experimental form [*dans le rôle de pilote*], in
the twentieth century by the Soviet State, which was erected on the ruins
of the soviets and the workers' and peasants' movement).

1b. *Note on Saint-Simon and Fourier:* "Precursors" of and inspirational for
Marx. The critique of the State in both. The importance of their relation.

Their shortcomings. Disillusionment at the results of the (so-called bourgeois and democratic) revolution of 1789–93.

2. *The concept of the State:* Expression and theorization of the "historical" results of the French Revolution and Bonapartism.

Relation of the concept of the State to the European Logos, to the concept in general (the concept of the concept and conceptual reflection). Hegel and Hegelianism.

Hegel as theorist (philosopher) of the French Revolution, of Jacobinism and Bonapartism (Napoleon I, world spirit . . .).

In Hegelianism: the central place of the concept of the State (immanent/transcendent to civil society). How Hegel grounds and legitimates a philosophy (methodology) of the concept and conceptual understanding.

Hegel against the Romantic and mystical interpretation of the (French) Revolution. Against Schelling. Hegel against legalistic and abstract interpretation (Fichte).

The political frankness and cynicism of the Hegelian theory. Against the false world, against the world of appearances and illusions (individual, Romantic, etc.), the moral, philosophical, and scientific truth of the State. From philosophy as a "specialist area" to political philosophy. Theory of the State. From comprehension (dissections) to the rational.

3. *The Hegelian State as "system of systems" (totality),* as object–subject. How Hegel discovers and/or establishes connections between all the elements and aspects of social life and spirit (culture).

Relations between the subordinate systems (subsystems) and the State as a total system. How, for Hegel, the State alone exceeds the individual and groups, anthropomorphism, and (subjective) idiosyncrasies. Hegelian thought as the prototype of "systemic analysis." The decadence of this method in modernity.

Partial systems and their relations with one another (reciprocity–reflexivity), needs and labor, public and private life, moral and legal, corporations and the family, etc. Agreements and conflicts. Transitivity and reflexivity in Hegelianism and the Hegelian State.

4. *The structure of the classes of the Hegelian State:* Vertical integration and lateral (horizontal) relations in the global system. Place and role of the middle class, of the political class, of producers, etc. Civil society and political society according to Hegel. Rational *consensus* and (internal–external) conflicts. The State and government.

Hegel and the political absolute (not absolute politics).

The final victory of logic (that of identity) over dialectics in the Hegelian State. In the State, knowledge [*savoir*] (Logos) understands [*connait*] and resolves the contradictions in civil society, contradictions between subordinate systems. The statification [*étatisation*] of society. The State as agency and as referent. The Hegelian State as response to the "loss of being," to the "lack-in-being" [*au "manque d'être," au "manque à l'être"*] of all its elements.

5. *State rationality according to Hegel:* Satisfaction in the State. The philosophical-political system as theodicy and secularized theology. How it is the end, meaning, and realization of history, of knowledge, of Spirit. The State as solution to conflict between specialized philosophy and the universality of Logos.

The State and war according Hegelianism. The philosophical illusion in Hegel: the absolute Spirit that totalizes and absorbs the "whole"; the subtle passage from rationalization to the justification of the "real."

6. *The Hegelian concept as method and theory* (of an absolute truth): The *category* in Marx, a reworking and modification (relativization) of the Hegelian concept. The *categories* in Marx's economic theory, which is to say in the critique of political economy (as an autonomous and specialized science). The linking of categories: exchange value and use value, social labor, average workforce, surplus value, and the organic composition of capital. How this "conceptual" linking defines the *relations of production* in capitalism and not the (capitalist) mode of production as such (as a totality). How it defines a "moment" when the economic tends to become autonomous. The place and role of other moments in the mode of production (including that of the political and the State). The problem of the "mode of production" in all its magnitude.

7. *The total revolution according to Marx:* The first moment of the Marxist project: to restore (to reintegrate) to the social the alienating/alienated factors and elements that tend to become autonomous, namely the economic and the political, technology and even knowledge, etc. The second moment, which implies the first: the dictatorship of the proletariat, with its corollary, the withering away of the State "from its foundations." The third moment, which implies the first two: the *sequence of ends,* which is to say the end of the bourgeoisie, of capitalism, of the working class and of classes; the end of scarcity (in abundance); the end of religion, of the family, of the nation and the State; the end of labor (mechanization of production); the end of history, of philosophy, of politics, etc. Political alienation and its end.

The Marxist calendar of *ends,* a supposedly concrete (practical) inversion of prophetism, of utopianism, of millenarianism, of catastrophism. Marxism as an active (practical) method for making and bringing an end to history. The ends (final causes) as the *meaning* of knowledge, the categories, history, of the State itself. The ends as *supersession* (in the Hegelian sense: conservation of the essential, mastery over nature, wealth of social relations, in short, development). Ends without a decisive ending and/or a decisive ending without ends. Revolution and negativity.

8. *The aporias* (difficulties, problems that are unposed, or badly posed or unresolved, uncertainties, etc.) of theoretical thought in Marx and Engels. Nature in so-called "Marxist" thought.

The problem of the accumulation of capital (expanded accumulation): Possibility and impossibility of the growth of productive forces at the heart of the mode and relations of capitalist production. Rosa Luxemburg and the problems of accumulation (the production of surplus value, the limits of capitalism, etc.).

The problems of nature and space as productive forces, as sources of real wealth (use value). Relations between the *three* terms at which Marx arrives in his analysis: Land–Labor–Capital (rents from the ground and the underground, wages, profits and surplus value, and moreover: owners–workers–capitalists).

The problem of the State (genesis, peak, decline). Outline of a theory (the State and the dictatorship or hegemony of the dominant class, the State and irreconcilable [antagonistic] class contradictions. The State, the stakes and prey of political struggles, the State above society and classes, the managerial and administrative State, etc.). The constant aim: the decline (withering away) of the State, its disappearance, the moment of total revolution. Toward the non-State and/or toward the nonpolitical State (in the "Critique of the Gotha Program").

Connection between the theoretical problem of accumulation and that of the State. The "transition" from capitalism to socialism. Uncertainties surrounding the concept. Jacobin dictatorship and dictatorship of the proletariat.

Ambiguity of the concept of *production* in Marx. Its virtual wealth: the production of things and goods, the production of social relations, the production of works [*œuvres*]. Its impoverishment in economism.

The theoretico-methodological aporia: the relations between logic and dialectic. Contradiction, difference, antagonism. Contradictions of varying depth.

9. *The impasse:* The fragmentation of Marxist thought stemming from a dual problem (accumulation—State). The communard tradition and the Lassallian tradition. The oppositions: "revisionism–orthodoxy–dogmatism" and also "left–center–right" in unrelated theory and practice. Engelsism and Marxism.

The economy and its explosion. The thesis of the catastrophic "end" (Rosa Luxemburg). Contradictions in the "real" (workers') movement and in so-called Marxist thought (Lassalle, R. Luxemburg, Bernstein, Kautsky, Lenin, Stalin, Trotsky).[4] World magnitude and weaknesses of both the movement and its theoretical thought.

Lassalle and Lassallism, the outline and seeds of "State socialism."

The State as stumbling block and buffer of Marxist thought. Oscillation between economism (spontaneity) and politicization (voluntarism), between (theoretical and supposedly scientific) knowledge [*connaissance*] and empiricism, political pragmatism. The ideologization of Marxism. From voluntarism and scientism (economism) to absolute politics.

The predominance of the principle of nation–state power over the principle of class. The conflict at the very heart of Marxism. Cleavage between ideologized (mystifying) Marxism and "purely" scientific Marxism.

The revolutionary solution (according to Marx) and the construction of a world economy. Failure.

The drift of "proletarian" revolution toward predominantly agrarian countries. Questions related to this redirection. Marxism as an ideology of primitive accumulation under the control of a State that does not wither away.

10. *Lenin, Leninism, and the State:* From the Marxism of Marx to that of Lenin. The role of Kautsky. The concept of the Party. Critical analysis of Leninism. The law of inequality. The withering away of the State according to *The State and Revolution.* The polemic between Rosa Luxemburg and Lenin (on accumulation, democracy, etc.).

Stalin. From the Marxism of Lenin to that of Stalin. The five-year plan. Stalinist revisionism. The theory of the reinforcement of the State during the "transition." The Party and the State. The Stalinist State as the successor of the Jacobin–Bonapartist State, as a prototype of the modern State (taking responsibility for growth and putting the whole of society in the service of growth).

Hegel and Stalin. The former as founder of the State Mode of Production (SMP), a concept quite different from that of the "totalitarian State." Fascism and the State mode of production.

11. *Attempts to exit the impasse:* The Frankfurt School (Korsch, Adorno, etc.), Lukács, Gramsci.

Fluctuations between economism (the ideology of growth controlled by the State, which is to say of the SMP), on one hand, and, on the other: philosophism (Korsch), historicism (Lukács, Gramsci), culturalism (Adorno), sociologism (Marcuse).

Reductions and evacuation of State power and the political in these endeavors. Anarchism (Bakunin, etc.).

12. *Trotsky,* Trotskyism and the problem of the State. The contradiction between "productive forces" and "national barriers."

13. *The Yugoslav experience: Autogestion* and its problems. The Yugoslav critique of Russian "State socialism" and Stalinism. Does Yugoslavia escape the SMP? The tenth congress of the Communist League of Yugoslavia and the Yugoslav constitution.[5]

14. *Mao and the problem of the State:* Maoism and Stalinism. The Chinese "Cultural Revolution" and the State.

15. *The worldwide experience* (theoretical and practical) of the revolutionary movement, the working class, and Marxist thought. Attempt to draw up a balance sheet.

The conflict between freedom and efficiency. Libertarian (anarchizing) and authoritarian tendencies. The propensity of each tendency to reduce conflict by denying the other, by expelling it from the movement, by physically destroying it.

Failures. The historical defeat of the working class—or a defensive strategy?

Polemic against the journalistic, pseudoscientific, and ideological ways of treating "Marxism" (the death of Marx, etc.) instead of examining the question in its whole: aporias, internal contradictions, errors, new problems, etc.

The crisis of theory: Where is it heading? (Critique of the "crisis." Impact and meaning of the "critical movement".)

PART 3: THE STATE MODE OF PRODUCTION (SMP)

This part of the work continues from the two preceding parts, notably the first, in drawing out the impact and meaning of propositions, the interrelation of concepts (categories), etc.

1. *The Marxist concept (category) of the "mode of production":* Its necessity and its difficulties. Relations of production and the mode of production. The mode of production and totality. Where and how does the "capitalist mode of production" appear? At what date? The place of the State in the totality. Rosa Luxemburg's theses on the rupture of "totality." Totality or totalization? Discussion of Luxemburg's theses.

The *transition,* according to Marx and Engels, between the capitalist mode of production and possible (socialist, then communist) society. The obscurity of the "transition," as Marx and Engels have sought to define it. Interpretations. Question: can the transition be rendered autonomous, fixed, through the creation of a specific formation, a "mode of production" that would be neither capitalist nor socialist? *The Mühlmann effect.*[6] The State and the revolutionary imaginary.

2. *The foundations of the modern State:* Resumption of the question. Rejection of an evolutionary and continuist conception (genesis of the modern State from "power" that has existed since archaic societies). Critique of Engels's book on private property, the family, and the State. Refutation of the idealist theory of "specific foundations"—juridical, social, legislative—that can be isolated from the economic as such and the social. Research into the conditions of possibility of the modern State, into the hypothesis of *political rupture,* between the modern State and preceding political formations (the monarchic State, the feudal–military State, the City–State, etc.). The "historical transitions" (from competitive and national capitalism to the SMP—first glimpse).

3. *Material exchange:* The commodity and its unfurling. The world of the commodity since the beginnings of commerce up until the world market. From the immediately and initially concrete (production, so-called primary materials, labor and the motions of labor, the tool and the machine) to abstract mediation (the commodity as such, exchange value) to the concrete that spatially incorporates the commodity (channels of exchange, commercial networks, acts of buying and selling according to revealed and stimulated "needs," acts of consumption). Relations between the abstract and the concrete thus defined in space.

The chains of equivalence and gold as a universal equivalent. Circulation (of labor, values and prices, profits, etc.). The formation of *social averages* according to Marx, (average social labor, average productivity, average organic composition of capital, etc.). Contradictions and tendencies inherent to these averages. How Marx conceived these averages. The self-regulation of so-called competitive capitalism. Its end.

The phases of capitalism and capitalist growth. An initially blind (quasi-autonomous) process subsequently controlled by the State. Generalized equivalence. Spatial equivalences, temporal equivalences.

The *continuous aspect* of growth, of productive forces: the unfurling of the world of the commodity, accumulation (of understandings, of technology, of resources and wealth, then of capital, properly speaking). The *discontinuous aspect:* initially, commercial channels and commercial capital, then the difficult passage from commercial capital to industrial capital, from profit on net income to surplus value, and finally the world market, the accumulation described as "growth," etc.

From competitive capitalism to State capitalism, and from the latter to the State Mode of Production (SMP).

The increasingly accentuated, homogenizing role of these phases: the commodity, capital, the State.

4. *Foundations of the modern State:* The (forced) equivalence of non-equivalents: the (forced) equalization of the unequal, the identification of the non-identical. Precisions on the "principle of equivalence" as the foundation of the modern State, as the principal of unity, of identity, of political integration.

The logic of homogenization and identity as the logic and strategy of State power. The State as *reducer* (of diversities, autonomies, multiplicities, differences) and as *integrator* of the so-called national whole.

5. *Law,* as an application and illustration of the principle of equivalence. Law and Right. Law and the "order of the Father." Law and the symbolic order. Law and transgression, deviation, perversion. The relations between the "body politic" of the Nation–State and the "social body," or "civil society." How the Law redirects energies against the outside, the exterior, the foreign, the Other (who does not accept this law).

From custom and customary relations to contractual (stipulated, written) relations in the modern (industrial) world. Relations of production and property relations. The "contractual system" of civil society. To what extent is it a "system"? Its contradictions, its coverage, its phases. Its logic and its incoherences. Its variants. The Codes: from the civil code to the codes of labor, the family, the city, health, etc. Contracts and (ethical) "values."

Rites and contracts. Pseudocontracts, quasi-contracts. Fictions of equivalence and reciprocity.

Verticality and horizontality in civil society. Frontality and laterality. Immediacy and mediation (media). The paradigm of State power.

Inherence of political constraint to so-called "economic" and "social" relations. How all equivalence is forced. How the equalization of the unequal functions on all scales. State power, the functional, the institutional, the directional, the informational, the situational, etc.

The (juridical, contractual, bureaucratic, State) forces of abstraction. The differences and limits of contractual "systems," or quasi-systems, and codes. Their explosion. The theoretical liaison between: logic, right, morality. How the State engenders the "lack of being" that (according to the Hegelian schema) it completes.

6. *On the State considered as a concrete abstraction:* Abstraction considered as "denaturing" in its economic form (the commodity, money, coinage); in its social form (contracts, law, codes); in its ethical form (moral principles, "values," norms and imperatives); in its "cultural" form (quantity, calculus, concepts, the decline of immediacy, of sense and the body, etc.) and finally in its political form (as the form of State power).

The capacities of abstraction that becomes concrete: the relation of dependence through identification, hierarchization, etc.

How abstraction is embodied: through permanent (latent and confirmed) violence. Reification and/or derealization of the social.

The real/fictitious in the State. Abstraction realized through political power: call to the "affects" of historical, religious, and moral origin—military and police force.

Political abstractions (sovereignty, legitimacy, authority, legality) considered as ideologies and as expressions of latent violence.

From the latent to the evident. Perceived evidence, unperceived evidence, imaginary evidence.

7. *The cumulative process:* Its diversity: resources, wealth, knowledge, technologies, capital, population, towns. Toward hypergrowth [*gigantisme*].

Surplus value and social overproduction. The extraction of overproduction by the State. Its means: fiscal measures, State corporations, private–public partnerships and corporatism, public investments, etc. Other means of the State: prohibitions and injunctions, various forms of manipulation, and finally, *space*.

The employment of overproduction by the State. Monumentality and theatricality. Symbols and signs. The State and the Carnival [*la Fête*]. The State and Sacrifice (inverted vitality and self-destruction).

Political accumulation: Of institutions, of means of action. The State as (apparent) means and (concrete, real) end.

The State as the "accursed share" of society. The accentuation of this role through growth. The State and war (resumption of the theme). The Army.

8. *The division of political labor.* The bureaucracy. "State apparatuses." Parties. Political production (of institutional, contractual, legal relations). The administration. Territorial management and managed space. Spatial and social concentration–hierarchization–integration as (strategic) stakes and objectives.

9. *Growth and development:* The difference between these terms. Possibilities and contradictions that are born of this difference. The general choice of States, statesmen, and political apparatuses for (quantitative) growth without the (qualitative) development of civil society.

From the State that clears the way for growth to the State that manages the space of growth. Planning (of production, of space) and semi-planning.

Initially vague and subsequently increasingly precise interventions, motivated by political need (for the growth of global surplus production, fiscal resources, the population).

The State and capital turnover (acceleration). State action against the tendency of the average rate of profit to fall. The generalization of the principle of profit and its contradictions.

How the modern State goes so far as to seek complete responsibility for growth. Cooperation of the "public" and "private." Plans and programs. Role of "public" investments, centrally made decisions, information and scheduling. The struggle for "full employment" and against inflation (the depreciation of fixed capital). Problems and what they hide.

Influences, micropowers, (global) political power. Political power as permanent "conspiracy."

10. *State capitalism and state socialism as species of a single genus:* The State Mode of Production (the fixed form of "transition" foreseen by Marx).

The SMP as autonomized product of a so-called "historical" movement. The blocking of transition (on a national level).

From competitive to monopolistic capitalism—from monopolistic capitalism to organized capitalism, and from the latter to the SMP. Archeo-capitalism and neo-capitalism in Western countries. Neo-capitalism, the neo-bourgeoisie and the SMP.

The control of markets and space through the SMP.

Consensus over growth. Consumption, models of consumption, and State authority.

Variants of the SMP, according to the country, according to the survival and resurgence of preceding modes of production, of agro-pastoral production, and of the corresponding social relations.

Parties and the SMP. Right-wing conservatism and left-wing conservatism.

Inequalities. The generality of Leninist law. Inequalities in the growth of political apparatuses and States at the heart of the SMP. The SMP as the extreme case of the modern State. Strategy, prospects, futurology.

11. *Worldwide expansion of the State, that is, of the SMP.* Resumption and extension of critical analysis. Typology: the planned State, the "regulatory" State, etc.

The State in the USSR (employer and owner); the State in China and Japan; the State in the USA; the State in the countries of northern and southern (Mediterranean) Europe; the State in Chile, in Portugal, etc. The USA as world power. Its influence on "culture" and the way of life.

12. *The State and the reproduction of the (social) relations of production:* Strategies and the political absolute (politicization, voluntarism). Alternations between authoritarianism—liberalism—will spontaneity, etc.

Inertias and resistances. The "liberation" of signifiers and language, the senses, dream, the symbol, as alibis of the State.

13. *Toward an omniscient, omnipresent, omnipotent* (totalizing and systematized) *State:* The indefinite extension of the competence and performance of political power. Toward a society of pure circulation, controlled politically and without remainder, without recourse.

Possibility and/or impossibility (across various scales, from the national to the worldwide).

PART 4: THE CONTRADICTIONS OF THE STATE (THE DIALECTIC AND/OF THE STATE). INSUFFICIENCIES OF THE "STATIST CRITIQUE OF THE STATE," OF LIBERALISM, OF POLITICAL PROTESTANTISM

1. *Logic and strategy:* The logic of the State and State power as logic (pursuit of identity, homogeneity, equilibrium, reproduction, repetition: evacuation of the contradictory, search for cohesion/coherence, etc.). The logic of production in and through the State (writing and bureaucracy).

The principle of equivalence as a logical principle (in theory) and a principle of integration (in practice). The State and the pregnancy of Logic.

The theory of contradictions and conflicts. Dialectic as a political question. The crushing of the dialectic. Resistance, rebellions, revolts, revolutions as reintroductions of the dialectic (through action and practice).

Political production (resumption of the theme). The emission of symbols, signs, "flows of meaning" (on the recurring themes of religion, ethnicity, patriotism, etc.) by the State. The production of political discourse and language. Separations (space and the representations of space, etc.). Confusions (the fatherland and the state, etc.). Political investment. That which is refused and that which is assimilated by the State. The State as third party in "social games" of two actors, etc.

The State as the above and beyond of binary oppositions. The paradigm of State power (continued). Critique of the semiology of the State.

The State as site of the "logical–dialectical" relation, which is to say of the link between identity and difference, between the homogeneous and the heterogeneous, between the homo-logical and the heterological.

2. *The State as reducer of conflicts* (including social, spatial, intellectual, and "cultural," among others): The politico-ideological system, which is to say perfect coherence/cohesion as an objective of men of the State. "Consensus" and resistances. The fissures of the pseudosystem.

    The state as the site of the relation of forces. The conflictual relation between "summit" and "base," between commands and decisions taken on high and the demands coming from below.

3. *The first problem and the essential contradiction:* "How can the centralized State submit millions and often hundreds of millions of people, their 'private' affairs, and their everyday lives to the management and homogeneity of the State?"

    Effective decentralization or repressive brutality. Through variously skillful degrees of repression, the State *equalizes* the normal and (so-called) "abnormal," but in recuperating, where possible, the exceptional and the anomic.

    The production of individuals who are all the same (identical, identified, identifiable). Infantilism and cynicism as generic traits of these "individuals." Indifference and differences in State power. Magico-religious identification and logical identity.

4. *The State as knot of contradictions* (and not as *knowledge* of contradictions in the economic and the social, in accordance with the Hegelian model consciously or unconsciously adopted by the majority of ideologues of the State and the SMP. Neither understanding nor simple "reflection" on the contradictions in the social and economic . . .). Second essential contradiction: between growth and development. Therefore, between the political and the social, between the production of things and that of relations, between the control of "subjects" and their free existence (the *lived*). Even if the State considers itself liberal, protective, reassuring, and "insuring" . . .

    The technical, economic, political, financial *potential* (an ideologico-scientific name for the possible) of the State. Social demand and political command. The potential of State power focuses on growth and ignores demand. Political economy and economic politics. The "subsystems" at the heart of the State. How "equilibria" and "coherences" constitute revolving doors, vicious circles.

5. *Ungrounding of the so-called "social" and human sciences:* On account of the general evacuation of State power (notably political economy, political science, etc.). Critique of sociologism, of economism, of historicism (resumption of the theme).

The reductive separation, through knowledge and power, of what is properly called the social (the diversity and complexity of social relations) into the economic and the political. The ills of high-growth society (Japan, USA, etc.).

Reduction of social relations to consumption, to "private life," to hierarchical relations of dependence. Impoverishment of "culture" and the "crisis of civilization."

The revolt of the "lived" against abstractions, of the everyday against economism, of the social and civil society against the "high rate of growth," whose demands are upheld by the State.

The consciousness of government, which is to say of the fact of members of a society being "governed" and the ability to accept or refuse government, hence the State. Political naivety. Its role and its end.

6. *Knowledge and (political) power:* The role of knowledge in the control of "civil society" by State power. The modern State and information. The monopoly of information. The filtering and overabundance of information. The reduction of knowledge to snippets of information in the "information society."

The contradiction between the fetishized and mystificatory State, on one hand, and on the other, the empirical action of the State for growth. The effects of this contradiction. Conflicts between representations (signs and symbols, fantasies of power, monumentality, and theatricality) of the State and critical understanding (of the *lived* as such). From Marx to contemporaries.

The status of the University in modern countries. The State and selection (exam systems, competitions, filtering processes, etc.).

The State's stranglehold on knowledge. The difficulties of this. The circulation of a mixture of "ideology-knowledge" that is reductive of critical understanding. Institutionalized, officialized (politically useful) knowledge, a mixture of representations and mystifications.

The political profitability of ideologized knowledge (of Marxism among others).

The revolt of (critical, concrete) understanding [*connaissance*] against established knowledge [*savoir*]. Elitism as a myth of the State. The myth of "recuperation."

The State and Death (resumption of the theme). The stakes of repression. The State and the body, the instituted body.

Philosophy (the withering away thereof) as a game of representations or public service. The demystifying role of the natural sciences (Einstein and "relativism," etc.).

7. *The nation–state grasped between (regional, local, peripheral) differences and extra-national pressures* (the world market, so-called supranational companies, planetary strategies). The rupture of national, frontier, and territorial spaces.

8. *The repetitive and State power:* The importance of the repetitive, from the movements of labor and everyday life to bureaucratic stipulations, to "cultural" stereotypes. Capitalism and the repetitive in production and consumption. The repetitive and the combinatorial. The reduction of the unforeseen and the residual.

The State and the everyday (resumption of the theme). How the State extends its grasp over everdayness, how it controls it. The repetitive and identical ensure total reproduction, including: biological (demographical) reproduction, material production, and the reproduction of (social) relations. Advertising (publicity messages) and propaganda (political messages).

The repetitive as the limit of homogeneity, the absolute logic (of the identical) and of in-difference, therefore the destruction of differences. The systematization of the repetitive (through bureaucracy) as an objective of State power in regard to the content of information, etc.

9. *Exchange value and use value:* Their original relationship (in Marx's *Capital*): a relevant opposition.

How this logical relation becomes a relationship of conflict in the modern world, notably in space. The supremacy of exchange over use, the degradation of use. How exchange value erodes use value. Nature as a source of use value and its destruction. How usage takes refuge in the past (the historical, the folkloric) and in undeveloped countries and regions. The transformation of these refuges into exchange value (through tourism, art, etc.). The State and (the uses of) pleasure [*jouissance*]. Needs and demand.

The notion of a *user.* The counterpart of use, but a weakened, restrictive, narrow notion. The "quality of life," the "framework of life"—metaphors, reductions. (Social) demand and use.

The movements of users and inhabitants (considered as *analyzers* of the spatial-social ruled over by the State as a reintroduction of dialectical contradiction). The revolt of the lived and the everyday.

Their importance. Their strength and their weaknesses. Their relationship with the "base" and the sociopolitical pyramid. The shaking of this hierarchical order. How harassed use finds its ultimate refuge in violence.

The State guarantees exchange, communication, general homogeneity.

The State, the family (and relations of hierarchical dependence: father-children, husband-wife, etc.). Exploitation, oppression, humiliation, and *ressentiment.*

The crisis of identification between the social, the collective, and State power. The illusion of identity under the SMP (identity between the State and the "people." The alleged disappearance of the State.).

10. *The durable and the ephemeral:* The tendency of modernity toward the ephemeral. The fluidity of space (indispensable for accelerating capital turn-over). Ephemeral businesses and towns. The new nomadism. The delocalization or deterritorialization of the social. The speed of superficial (social and spatial) changes. The circulation of intelligibility and the circulation of ambiguity. Circulations and stabilities.

Conflicts between change and homogeneity. The tendency of the State toward stability, toward the instantiation of fixed centers of decision making, toward controlled repetition. The society of communication (without remainder) as the utopia of the State.

Flows and the problem of mastering flows. Surfaces and flows. Stockpiles and flows. The uprooting and putting down of roots. The fluidity and rigidity of space. The growing difficulties of State control. Problematic of the relation between the State and social times (linear and cyclical rhythms).

11. *The State and space:* The spatial structure. Its levels. Its genesis. The politicization of social space. The State management and control of space as an essential element of the SMP. The social hierarchy and the spatial hierarchy (of places). The relation of spaces and relations of dependence. The state and urbanization. Ghetto society. The division of space.

The role of the State in the reciprocal separation and occultation of mental space and social (political) space. Which is to say, of imaginary space and real space.

The "partitioning" [*maillages*] and rectangular division [*quadrillages*] of space in France, the USA, Japan, etc. Spatial planning.

The contradictions of space at the heart of the State and in the territory managed by the State. Historical space, planetary space (that of the world market and the world division of labor). Dominant spaces, dominated spaces. Strong points and weak points. Centers and peripheries. Spaces and counter-spaces. The scrambling [*brouillage*] of space.

From the space of productive labor to the global production and management of space. Conflict between the production of a rationalized space by the State (regulator) and the production of space by "private" capitalism and institutions that escape the control of the center (localities, regions, peripheries). Conflicts between so-called productive investment and so-called social investment (the framework of life, etc.).

The State and urban problems. Conflicts between *integration* and *segregation*. Integration and disintegration. Disintegration. Social relations. Violence and fear.

The explosion of borders and frontiers (continued). Cf. the questions posed by territorial waters and fishing, by the exploitation of ocean floors, by congestion and pollution, by the movement of tides. (The study, for example, of Mediterranean space.)

How the end of classical colonialism and neocolonialism (the exploitation of foreign laborers, of peripheries) have brought about an explosion in metropolitan space. Distortions between economic space, social space (that of "users"), politicized space, planetary space. Conflicts in the space between "public services," "business services," and "State services."

Global [*global*] space (fragmented and homogenized—broken and seized by the State). Conditioning through the spatial.

12. *The State as hierarchical, (spatially) stratified morphology.* Rules for the analysis of hierarchical, stratified morphologies.

The space of catastrophe, following the definition of René Thom (in *The Mathematics of Morphogenesis*).[7]

The space of catastrophes, in, through, and for the State. State power as the space of catastrophe: wars, violence, economic and political crises, convulsions, the abrupt passage from the liberal democratic State to the authoritarian State and vice versa, the pseudostability and unreliability of State power, etc. The haunting of catastrophe.

The implications on a worldwide scale, of the "states-system."

13. *The State and classes:* Complexities of this relationship. The State is not only the *effect* (of class relations, of the hegemony of a dominant class); it is also the *cause* and the *reason*. The political is productive of (social) relations. Which ones?

Social distances. The social-spatial hierarchy and classes. Vertical and horizontal cleavages. The functionality, multifunctionality, and suprafunctionality of classes.

The integration of the working class into the State and by the State (political pressure). Successes and failures. Pseudo-integration through the economic in so-called "industrial," "technical," "consumer" society, etc.

Discontent and revolts. The State, prohibitions, and transgressions (permissiveness and repressiveness).

The middle classes as supports of the State, and vice versa. State production of the middle classes: functionaries, executives, technicians, etc. Political support for this "production" (in businesses and institutions) of individuals and groups belonging to the middle classes.

The pseudorevolution of the middle classes in the USA and elsewhere in the big industrial countries. The bureaucratic middle class and the working class in the USSR. Cleavages and contradictions in the middle classes. Ideologies and models of consumption produced by the middle classes. The critique of these same models and representations by "representatives" of the middle classes. Suprafunctionality of the middle classes.

The army and the middle classes.

The working class (resumption of the analysis). A defensive strategy for the last half-century, or a "historical" defeat? Possibility of an offensive. Qualitative and quantitative demands.

14. *The structural and the conjunctural in the State:* Convergences and divergences on both the same level (in the social body, civil society: in lateral relations), and on the various levels of culture, economy and political economy, organizations and institutions, etc. Conjunctures resulting from these movements.

The nascent conflict between differential, selective growth oriented toward development and absolute (so-called: exponential) growth. The options.

Political Beings on the world stage. The reciprocal actions and reactions of every "member" of the world system or pseudosystem. The multiplicity of strategies. Interferences. Effects.

The dialectical movement at the heart of the State; social forces acting from "the bottom up" and political forces exerting their action from "the top down." Differences and homogeneity: diversities against identification. Pluralism (capitalist and socialist). The State and parties.

Autogestion (of material and intellectual production, of territories, which is to say of the entirety of space). How and why, no more than any nation–state, the "State system" has the possibility of *systematizing* itself (of purging itself of contradictions).

The occupation of space as an offensive strategy of the working class. Objective: the collective management and social appropriation of the space of production and the space of everyday life. The stakes: the primacy of the political, the priority of State power (over the social). Disaggregation of social bonds and qualitative demands. (Conjunctural) breakthroughs.

Nostalgias (the past, the historical, societies without a State, etc.)

The flight forward (toward an imaginary future, toward the possible/impossible). Utopias (of capitalism, of the State, of socialism, etc. Utopians and utopists. From the ideology of desire to the end of political representations. New "values": those that come from demand and from the base: use, appropriation, the laying down of roots, localization, the life of the body, the life of the community, etc. New forms of Liberty ("civil disobedience," etc). The development of Rights (the right to difference, etc.).[8]

CONCLUSIONS

A return to taking seriously theoretical games and conceptual discourses. Toward a conceptual and ideological deflation.

The course of the modern State: from revolution (democratic revolution, led astray by the bourgeoisie) to counterrevolution, through the state mode of production, its variations, contradictions, and its extension into the "world system" of States.

The dangers of this situation. Terricide (a reminder). The State monopoly of the "affects" of behavior, conditioning, and motivation (through the mass media), in addition to the flow of information. The harnessing of symbolism. The State control of "culture."

The battle of "logic–dialectic" as a theoretical expression of the struggle (encompassing class struggle) of the base against the summit. Political activity. The possible and the impossible in political action. Absolute politics and relativism.

The State as parody and simulation of the "Overman." Civilization, society, the State. The relations between these terms.

The cumulative character of contradictions, on all levels (that of the State, of the world system). With regard to the State and worldliness, what future scenario has the best prospects? . . .

The possibilities for each State (authoritarian consolidation, liberal relaxation, upsets and catastrophes, disrepair and putrefaction), and likewise for the world system.

Neoimperialism and the hierarchical order of States (relations of dependence on the world stage). Consolidation or weakening of the SMP. From the dialectic of labor and nature in Marx to the dialectic of the State . . .

Crises and critical moments. Critique of the "crisis." Impossibility of a unified world State (philosophical utopia and its prophecies disavowed by the worldwide process). Confrontations and strategies in planetary space. Is there still a "destiny," a destiny of the State?

The perishable State. The loss of identity and the discrediting of the political as precursory phenomena of the "critical moment." The State and State power, "dead values" still functioning as reference points.

Does this work endeavor to elaborate a theory of the State? No. An antitheory? No. A political science? No. It supplies the theory of a practice: action and social forces going from "the bottom up," from the base to the summit (the anti-State forces that are preparing not for the dislocation of society, but the organization of the social as such, above the economic and the political, according to the project of Marx).

Definition of the site of the encounter between the thought and the action that hail from Marx, and which are accordingly revolutionary—so-called "an-archic"—or subversive—thought and action; so-called "reformist" thought and action. Convergences and difficulties. What to think of Hegelian and Marxist "supersession" [*Aufhebung*]?

The overflowing of existing political formations "by the Left," which is to say by the base; "historical compromises" and their strategic excesses. The withering away of political parties, the announcement of the decline of the State.

Attempt at the redefinition of socialism (through the appropriation, the production, the management of space). Democracy in and through space: the "places" of individuals and collectives in space.

Return to the problem of *transition*. The production of a "second nature." From the oldest community to the State and from the State to a "society of citizens," reinstating a definable territoriality appropriate to social life. Through rebellions and revolts, the refusal of hierarchies and norms, litigations and contestations, slow or sudden revolutions, etc. How time changes "through the dark side . . . ," where we find the State and State power.

Postscript

The fourth volume will end with a polemical section directed in part against some of the authors cited in the course of the work, in part against other authors.

N.B. It goes without saying that the project outlined above will change during the course of its writing.

Translation by Gerald Moore, Neil Brenner, and Stuart Elden

Notes

This text constitutes the introduction to a work that will appear in four volumes in the series 10/18. [See Lefebvre, *De l'État*).—*Eds.*]

1. [On the meaning of *mondialisation*, see the introduction.—*Eds.*]

2. [Lefebvre is referring to Georges Bataille's book *La part maudite* (Paris: Les Éditions de Minuit, 1949); translated by Robert Hurley as *The Accursed Share* (New York: Zone, 1991).—*Eds.*]

3. [Caesaro-Papism entails the subordination of secular government to religious authority. The English compromise, also known as the Concordat of London, refers to an agreement between King Henry I of England and Pope Paschal II in 1107 regarding investiture and the power to appoint church officials.—*Eds.*]

4. [Eduard Bernstein (1850–1932) was one of the leading figures in the German Social Democratic Party during the late nineteenth and early twentieth centuries; he was a member of the German Reichstag from 1902 to 1918. Bernstein advocated an "evolutionary" or reformist route to socialism that involved active participation in liberal-parliamentary systems.—*Eds.*]

5. [The tenth congress and the Yugoslav constitution elaborated a variety of positions concerning *autogestion.*—*Eds.*]

6. [According to René Lourau (*Le gai savoir des sociologues* [Paris: UGE, 1977], 55), a French sociologist who Lefebvre cites frequently in *De l'État* (see also chap. 11 n.1), *L'effet Mühlmann* occurs when "the institutionalization of a social movement is made possible by the failure of the prophecy that enabled the movement." It is named after Wilhelm E. Mühlmann, following ideas elaborated in *Chiliasmus und Nativismus: Studien zur Psychologie, Soziologie und historischen Kasuistik der Umsturzbewegungen* (Berlin: Reimer, 1961), translated into French by Jean Baudrillard as *Messianismes révolutionnaires du tiers-monde* (Paris: Gallimard, 1968).—*Eds.*]

7. [René Thom, *Modèles mathématiques de la morphogenèse*, Collection 10/18 (Paris: Union Générale d'Éditions, 1974). English translation published as *Mathematical Models of Morphogenesis*, trans. W. M. Brookes and D. Rand (New York: Halsted Press, 1983). On Thom, see chap. 11 n.7.—*Eds.*]

8. [Lefebvre elaborates the right to difference most fully in *Le manifeste différentialiste* (Paris: Gallimard, 1970).—*Eds.*]

4 Comments on a New State Form

This article, published in a now-defunct Parisian New Left academic journal, is framed simultaneously around the critique of Stalinism and the critique of French and European social democracy. Lefebvre proposes that a new state form—which he labels the "state mode of production"—is being consolidated, in both Eastern and Western Europe, and he devotes the bulk of the essay to analyzing its main empirical features. This discussion thus provides a concise summary of some essential chapters of *De l'État*, volume 3, in which the notion of the state mode of production is elaborated at considerable length (see also chapters 11 and 14 in this book). Key issues include the state's intervention in the regulation of energy and natural resources; the state's attempt to control information flows; and the state's relation to the world market. Finally, Lefebvre turns passionately to the theme of *autogestion*, or radical democracy, suggesting that it provides a viable grassroots alternative to both Stalinist and social-democratic orthodoxies (see also chapters 5, 6, 8, 11, and 14). While the conceptualization of the state elaborated in this essay is only implicitly spatial, it draws on the key elements of the more spatialized analyses Lefebvre developed elsewhere, some of which appear in part II of this volume.—*Eds.*

Without beating around the bush, I implicate myself at the outset of this article, locating it and myself by declaring that it contains and advances a number of theses. While this procedure—which opens with my conclusions—raises certain pedagogical objections, it also has certain political and theoretical advantages: the reader knows immediately what is at stake, and with whom he is dealing. Scientifically, the theses thus presented may pass for hypotheses, as the orientation for an inquiry. Here, then, are the propositions:

1. Today more than ever, a political action is defined through the type or form of State that it tends to realize. Such an action must thus be conceived more in terms of the potentialities that it cultivates than in terms of its analyses of the extant, analyses that are often tainted by ideology and always risk justifying a dogmatic position. In political thought and in political theory, the category (or concept) of the "real" should not be permitted to obscure that of the possible. Rather, it is the possible that should serve as the theoretical instrument for exploring the real. This methodological principle permits the clarification of the serious contradictions between the texts of Marx, Engels, and Lenin regarding the withering away of the State and its strengthening after the October Revolution.

2. The right-wing critique of institutions and of the State (cf. A. Peyrefitte)[1] collapses into platitudes, endlessly repeated in the name of neoliberalism, regarding bureaucracy, administrative inertia, and so forth. Only a critique "from the left" can grasp that which is essential. But even such a critique must break away from certain "leftist" presuppositions, that is to say, from apoliticism, from a peevish negation of politics, and from the tendency toward nihilism and hypercritique. These latter presuppositions characterize the conjuncture that has given rise to this article.

3. The historical and worldwide importance of Stalin is derived from his construction of a type of State. Stalin's importance extends far beyond the question of his "errors," of his "mistakes," and even of his "crimes." But, oddly enough, accusations and apologies alike miss the fundamental question. Why? I will only say here, in order to move along quickly, that this is a different matter.

4. Even if a large number of countries took their inspiration from it and bear its imprint, the Stalinist State can no longer be considered as a model, at least not explicitly. A new state form [*forme étatique*] is in the course of being established in certain so-called "advanced" capitalist countries, notably in Northern Europe, as an apparent alternative to this apparently discredited model. Personally, I deplore the fact that this new state form should be the only one to distinguish itself from the Stalinist "prototype." It is of utmost importance that a new political thought elaborate both objectives and a strategy. The existence of theoretical thought depends upon it.

5. Political practice bearing the imprint of social democracy can be observed in the countries of Northern Europe. It is, nonetheless, not there that a theory of social democracy is being elaborated; it is in France. Yet once again, political practice is detached from theory while preceding it. I am claiming that this "theorization" bears the imprint of social democracy, that is to say of the Socialist International, which is itself subordinate to German social democracy—I am not speaking of the French Socialist Party, which we know is not homogeneous. (As an aside, is there not perhaps in this diversity the reflection of the particular situation of Southern Europe?)

6. How can we fail to recall the political situation in 1930 in Western Europe? For the communist parties and for the Communist International, social democracy was Enemy Number 1, the principal social support of capital. We know the consequences of such a political position. What should we think of such a position today? Certainly, in terms of strategy and theory, we must push the critique of the "socialist" model to its limits, but tactically, we must accept compromises in order to divert socialists and those that they influence from such a type of State. Now, until the present time, as has been confirmed by the documents prepared for the Twenty-third Congress[2] and by the practical struggles of recent months, the French Communist Party (PCF) seems to have adopted exactly the opposite strategy: it is imposing very strict tactical measures on its militants while at the same time leaving unclarified its theoretical objectives and in particular the question of the State. With some justification, the PCF is posing the question: "Which socialism do we want?" Now, to attempt to respond to this question is inevitably also to ask oneself: "Which State do we want?" Nonetheless, the PCF has at its disposal an essential element of a theoretical and practical response—namely, *autogestion*. Why not make better use of this element by developing a genuine strategy of *autogestion*? To move in this direction it would be necessary to dialecticize the concept of strategy—in other words, to risk seeing tactics and strategy become disarticulated rather than being locked into the formal coherence of an implacable logic.

7. The new state form [*modèle d'État*] that is currently emerging has characteristics that crystallize forcefully, if slowly, through what some have termed "experience" or "social experimentation." Almost every day, a

trait or an aspect of this state form becomes perceptible. For example— and to situate the problematic from this point on—the Nora-Minc report "The Computerization of Society" was very enlightening, even if it only confirmed what was already known about Japan, the Federal Republic of Germany, the USA, and so forth.[3]

Thus we have formulated our theses. One can compile arguments and facts in their favor. This article contains only the outline of a more thorough study, which will be accomplished elsewhere, doubtless with the help of a research team. Will we be able to prove or "demonstrate" these propositions? Such a requirement stems from the remnants of an underlying dogmatism. As far as strategy is concerned, a "demonstration" is supposed to eliminate the risks associated with all long-term action; no action is won in advance. A strategy is deployed against an adversary or adversaries (on several fronts) who themselves have a strategy, and who consequently have ways of winning. The theoretically important point is to specify clearly the settings and the resources, and to disguise the stakes well.

What is it that seems new in the social-democratic model of the State? The strengthening of civil society. In his book *La nouvelle économie française,* Jacques Attali makes repeated calls for the autonomy of the various elements of society;[4] he introduces a project for a relational society and for a "relational socialism"[5] that would constitute, according to him, a "new model for the production of society."[6] Attali proposes "to create relational jobs" by increasing the number of nonprofit organizations in central and local government.[7]

Let us note at once that in the same text, Attali affirms that "the State must be the geometric location at which these transformations are enacted, the site at which the aspirations of new lobbying organizations are brought together. It must remain the essential institution" by controlling the organizational logic. "An excessive decentralization that prematurely weakened the State apparatus would only replace it, in fact, with a multitude of feudalities." For these diverse reasons, Attali arrives at the conclusion "that certain State functions would need to be performed at a European scale." Which functions? Those which "concern energy policy and computer/information policy." It is in this manner that, for Attali, a considerable gamble is embodied in the State in the transition to socialism. The State must "facilitate" massive upheavals and above all "maintain cohesion."[8]

Nonetheless, this project of strengthening civil society is not particularly new. During the course of the second half of the twentieth century, in France as elsewhere, the State has taken charge of—and overburdened itself with—multiple tasks. The accomplishment of these tasks hinges on innumerable, well-timed interventions on the part of state organisms and institutions, ministries, prefectures, and so forth. These interventions become more and more complex to the extent that the units on which they are exercised encounter increasing difficulties due to the interaction of diverse crises. A typical example: the university! It is from here that a tendency emerges which is termed, in official vocabulary, "loosening" or "deconcentration."[9] The notion of "decentralization" goes even further. How to obtain a result in this direction? There is, in fact, only one way and one means: the strengthening of the social—civil society, groups, cities, and local administrations—rather than crushing the social between the economic and the political.

I have noticed that the PCF, building on the momentum of the Italian and Spanish parties, is embarking on this route, but in a timid and dangerously empirical manner. It goes without saying that the economic and the political are not disappearing but no longer have absolute priority over "civil society." It should be mentioned, in passing, that these terms and this concept are frequently attributed to Gramsci, yet they stem from Hegel via Marx. For Hegel, civil society is nothing other than bourgeois society—not because it is bourgeois in the Marxist sense, but because it is differentiated from religious society as well as from the monarchy of divine right and from feudal military power.[10] In this manner, Hegel articulates the political consequences of the French Revolution. Law replaced the king, and decisions are subsequently carried out "in the name of the law." This society promulgated the *civil* code and *civil* law. Hegel inherits from the French eighteenth century the strict link between "civil" and civilization," namely "civility." This is a connection of major importance that is consistent with the rights of man as well as with an important fact in western legal history: confession does not count as proof, because it can be obtained by "questioning," that is, by torture. This is compromised to such an extent today that the demand for a strengthening of civil society is not just a political question.

Nevertheless the experience of the last ten or fifteen last years should make us suspicious. Since De Gaulle, political elites and state officials have attempted a simulacrum of decentralization; this consists, in fact, of transferring the problems, but not the privileges, of the central power to grassroots organizations and associations. All the important decisions remain with the State [*restent étatiques*]. One pretends to redistribute power while in fact only tasks are actually dealt out. A strongly constituted State does not easily give up its diverse powers, which are in turn guaranteed by the institutions that it coordinates and dominates. Isn't it here, and not only in the economic domain, that a radical break is needed?

No one would deny that the relations between the economy and state power [*l'Étatique*] have changed during the course of the twentieth century, notably during the last few decades. In volume 4 of my book *De l'État*,[11] I attempted to illuminate this general tendency in the contemporary world, which has been actualized only in a very uneven manner, and its materialization—the state mode of production [*le Mode de production Étatique*]. A qualitative transformation occurs from the moment in which the State takes charge of growth, whether directly or indirectly. From this moment forward, economic failures are attributed to the State. It has often been objected to me that the interventions of the State in the economic domain date back further in history and that the difference between this new period and the preceding period is merely quantitative and not qualitative. In response, I will limit myself here to recalling the recent characteristics of a cluster of state institutions—the Economic Council, the National Accounting Service in the Ministry of Finance, and the diverse plans and planning instruments, including both financial planning and spatial planning.[12]

But the essential features of the state mode of production are as follows. By various means, the State appropriates some portion, or even the entirety, of the social surplus—without taking into consideration Marx's remarks in his notes on the Gotha program.[13] Such a State raises itself above society and penetrates it to its depths, all the way into everyday life and behavior. It has several dimensions: (a) managerial [*gestionnaire*] and administrative; (b) the power to secure; and (c) the power to kill—by means of repression, the monopoly of violence, the army and military spending, strategies implying the possibility of war, and so forth.

A division of political labor is thus established between: technocrats, the military, and professional politicians.[14] This leads, in turn, to a bitter power struggle in the very interior of the State. In this manner, civil society finds itself threatened with obliteration and an infernal cycle of generalized violence ensues, grounded in violent repression and violent resistance against repression. The dimension of death superimposes itself on the trouble without suppressing it. The State unifies all forms, that of exchange and of the commodity, that of contracts, that of laws. Homogenizing, identitarian, the State crushes that which resists it; it makes differences disappear. Agents of the State [*les gens de l'État*] invent new instruments, for example a space which is at one and the same time quantified, homogenized, and controlled—crumbled and broken—hierarchized into "strata" that cover and mask social classes. The middle classes? They represent at once the reason for the social base of and the product of such a State. It engenders them as much as it is their result. Once constituted, this State functions as a system. It reproduces itself in reproducing the relations of domination; it has at its disposal an unlimited power to constrain its citizens; it can therefore paralyze all their initiatives.

Such is the danger that menaces the modern world and against which it is necessary to struggle at all costs. There is no "good State"; today there is no State that can avoid moving toward this logical outcome: the state mode of production; that's why the only criterion of democracy is the prevention of such an occurrence. No party has yet taken a clear stance on this matter—neither the Communist Party, due to its difficulty in radically distancing itself from the Stalinist model; nor the Socialist Party, due to its attempt to reconcile itself with the social-democratic model as it is to be found in the Federal Republic of Germany. The social-democratic model can be analyzed as a variation and possibly as an improvement of the state mode of production, but the critical analysis of the state mode of production is not limited to this model. It will suffice here to outline the specific features of the state mode of production.

THE STATE AND THE REGULATION OF ENERGY

First feature: the State takes control of energy. It supervises its flow and its distribution—more so with electricity than with coal, a localized form of energy; more so with oil than with electricity; and much more still with nuclear energy than with oil. This state control [*contrôle étatique*] of energy has been progressively institutionalized, that is to say in the guise of progress, and this has been the case for approximately half a century, dating from the first measures regarding the importation and processing of oil. The environmental disadvantages of nuclear energy have been stressed time and again; its political implications have been less forcefully emphasized: that is, the control [*contrôle*]—indeed the repressive partitioning—of space. Aren't these political consequences of even greater importance than the others? In any case, the current State alone seems capable of directing and financing enormous operations, of managing the deployment of technologies and raw materials, of choosing contractors for their distribution and so forth. All of this is accomplished through appropriated institutions, but it obviously consolidates the techno-structure of the State. Wouldn't a total "nationalization" of nuclear energy risk fortifying this consolidation of the state? Only a democratic form of control could oppose this tendency toward consolidation, but its blueprint has yet to be found.

THE STATE AND INFORMATION TECHNOLOGY

The Nora-Minc report revealed to a broad public a very delicate industrial sector, bristling with danger, that of computer science or telematics. If one is to believe the authors, with their accumulation of "sound" arguments, we are moving toward a transparent society in which everything that arises and occurs, is born or dies, reveals itself or attempts to hide, will have already been detected, transmitted, recorded, incorporated into an inventory or memory bank, and all this definitively, inexorably. According to the authors, micro-computers will be introduced everywhere, in every nook and cranny, emitting and receiving. The market for information (computers and programs, otherwise known as "hardware" and "software") is imposing itself, with its own particular logic, on commercial and capital markets. By consolidating these markets? Without any doubt, they suggest. Information marketers are already "selling" entire networks of recorded relations, to public agencies and institutions, as well as to companies and firms. For several years, "firmware" has been gaining ground, replacing the old "packages" that were mere disconnected components within a larger information network. As a consequence of these extraordinarily rapid and immediately commercialized technological innovations, Nora and Minc argue, computer programs, hard drives, and tiny microprocessors will soon extend their performance capacities throughout society. Data banks are becoming the official institutions to which the various social sciences make their contributions. In whose service? That of the "consumers"—individuals, businesses, and bureaucracies—say the authors of the Nora-Minc report.

Let us set aside the ethical, aesthetic, and "cultural" questions that are bound up with this strategy of transparency. Not without reason, they disturb Nora and Minc, who nevertheless do not confront a single one of these problems. Let us pose here only the political question. For whom, from whose point of view, will society become transparent? Who will benefit from this transparency? Who will thus hold together the totality of society? The answer is obvious: the State. Not only will the State manage information, and encourage or discourage this or that application, but it alone can negotiate with IBM and the other global corporations. The State, say the authors of the report, can help the small against the large, light information against the heavy, the small-scale manufacturers against IBM. Perhaps, but won't the miniaturization of physical stock, the multiplication of circuits and terminals, of infrastructure and services, render the activities of the State still more efficient? Particularly since the State possesses satellites, among other technical means. In the eyes of the state (by which I also mean state officials), the transparent society will behave like an "object," not like a spectacle or a receptacle of signs. The telephone and even the television provide only an incomplete image of this information society, even if they do demarcate the field and sketch the template of such a society.

The danger is so great that the authors themselves articulate an appeal for counterpowers. They hope for a society and a State that are democratic enough to secrete these counterpowers, but they are singularly discreet on this matter. Of course, they make allusions neither to workers' struggles nor to urban struggles nor to *autogestion,* which alone could effectively upset the functioning of the informational domain. They write from an idealist perspective in which public powers promote precisely what they are combating. Here the old liberal and reformist dream of a good State—of a rational State situated beyond contradictions—reappears. This State, at once strong and benevolent, would supposedly arbitrate conflicts impartially, as if the power elite could manipulate the counterpowers and provoke them at will. The authors of this plan are ignorant of, and wish to remain ignorant of, active politics, the fact that the State transforms its "subjects" into "objects," into dependents, into passive and manipulated entities, and into self-reproducing functionaries. Here we are at the heart of the real problem. The issue is not liberty in general—often mentioned in this work—but the concrete forms of liberty. If Nora and Minc appeal to decentralization, it is not in order to weaken the State; it is, on the contrary, to preserve it. A grain of sand can derail an immense machine. It is therefore, for the authors, always a matter of throwing the difficulties and dysfunctionalities of the center back onto the peripheries without granting them real decision-making powers.

THE STATE AND THE WORLD MARKET

Another aspect of the State is silhouetted against the horizon: it holds and manages the relations of the interior with the exterior, that is to say of the national market with the world market as well as with multinational firms. This third aspect of the State includes the preceding aspects: insofar as they are commodities, energy and information technology are in effect negotiated on the world market, and this fact implies the prominent participation of States.

Is the national State inevitably an instrument of multinationals for the exploitation of a territory, as well as an instrument of the relations of production prior to the ascendancy of these multinationals themselves? Must we always label such a State "ISM," Imperialist State of the Multinationals (Stato imperialista delle multinazionale), as do the Red Brigades in Italy?[15] Beware! Certainly it has happened, but the opposite has also happened. The pressures that are exercised on the national states are such that the risk of a State in the service of the multinationals always exists. Nonetheless, States can resist imperialisms and can negotiate with global firms. The world is at once the arena and the stake of bitter struggles at all scales; its situation is not the preordained result of a single dominant project. But a State can resist pressures only by having the active support of an entire people who take part in the affairs of State (which presumes the definitive abolition of the secrets of the Prince) and who are constantly ready for mass actions. Without such a foundation the State sells itself and sells the country on the world market. Here we have one of the criteria of democracy and of socialism. Paradoxically, the "State" that is capable of acting thus, which is put under the protection of the people and not the reverse, is already no longer a State in the Hegelian and bourgeois meaning of the term but a State that is withering away in the Marxist sense: a "dictatorship of the proletariat," or whatever name it may be given. This is because such a State allows the contradictions of an entire society to unfurl themselves, including those that threaten the State itself. What I have just described is exactly the opposite of what I know about the social-democratic States of Northern Europe, notably Germany.

The advocates of the continuity of the traditional State, or of its modification in the sense of a new model, insist on the risks of any rupture on this scale. It is claimed that the collapsing State would drag society into chaos. Now, the problem cannot be posed thus. Does (civil) society have in itself sufficient resources and organizational capacities to replace and reabsorb the

State? That is the question. The project for a transformation of society from within—through the strengthening of the civil against the statist [*étatique*]—cannot and should not take this risk into account. To invoke such a risk, and to instrumentalize it ideologically, is to exercise terrorism and to fetishize the State by declaring it to be beyond contradictions. In any case, these contradictions, with the problems that they pose, are transferred from the State as such toward the social.

If the State occupies these three dominant sectors (energy, information technology, and links with the worldwide), if it holds these key positions, it can loosen the reins somewhat toward subordinate units, regions, and cities as well as businesses. As we have said, the State can control everything without needing to monitor everything. This is the crucial point, the trap. Everything depends on the degree of liberty accorded, or rather conquered by, these units that, taken together, constitute the country, that is, the nation and civil society. As with all democratic liberties and as with the rights of man and citizen, the space for initiative granted from above and by a sort of charter to the subordinate units may correspond more to ideology than to practice, more to illusions than to possibilities. In other words, this space for initiative is at once the site and the stake of struggles.

There is one path and one practice that may be opposed to the omnipotence of the State, that of *autogestion*. It is first necessary to define this notion theoretically in all its power, with the full range of its possibilities, before the definition of a strategy may be extracted.

Autogestion is often taken to be a recipe that can be put into action immediately. A business "puts itself under *autogestion*." *Autogestion* is also understood as a magic formula; *autogestion* will solve all the workers' problems.

Now—a first remark—*autogestion* never presents itself with the clarity and the obviousness of a technical and purely rational operation. Practice has a difficult time escaping from a certain ambiguity. In our society, what is there that cannot be assimilated? Nothing. We have seen exchange and the commodity, capitalism, and statism "assimilate" actions and ideas that seemed essentially subversive. The best example is that of the organization of productive labor and of planning, projects, and practices that were derived from Marxism and initiated by the Left, but then more or less completely assimilated by economists and politicians of the right. *Autogestion*, far from being established once and for all, is itself the site and the stake of struggle. It can degenerate, for example, toward co-management [*co-gestion*]. The strategy of *autogestion* can and should permit itself to escape this degraded fate. Each time a social group (generally the productive workers) refuses to accept passively its conditions of existence, of life, or of survival, each time such a group forces itself not only to understand but to master its own conditions of existence, *autogestion* is occurring. This broad but precise definition shows *autogestion* to be a highly diversified practice that concerns businesses as well as territorial units, cities, and regions. This definition also includes all aspects of social life; it implies the strengthening of all associative ties, that is to say, of civil society. This theoretical definition points toward a practical struggle that is always reborn with failures and setbacks. Above all, this definition points to the fundamentally antistatist tendency of *autogestion*, the only efficient and active form of the famous "counterpowers." Certain Yugoslavs committed the error of seeing in *autogestion* a system, and therefore a model, that could be established juridically and that could function without clashes and contradictions, in a sort of social and political harmony. Instead, *autogestion* reveals contradictions in the State because it is the very trigger of those contradictions. The democratic nature of a State or any other apparatus can be evaluated in terms of its capacity to avoid snuffing out contradictions by restrictions or by formalism; it should not only allow their expression and allow them to take shape but should also directly provoke them. This does not happen without real struggles. *Autogestion* must continually be enacted. The same is true of democracy, which is never a "condition" but a struggle.

The concept of *autogestion* does not provide a model, does not trace a line. It points to a way, and thus to a strategy. This strategy must exclude maneuvers and manipulations that render practice illusory; this strategy must therefore prevent the monopolization of the word and the concept by institutions that transform them into fiction. In addition, the strategy must concretize *autogestion* and extend it to all levels and sectors. This perpetual struggle for *autogestion* is the class struggle.

The problematic of *autogestion* in a developed country has still been little explored. Nevertheless all the theoretical and practical elements are combined therein.

Who can guarantee the profoundly dialectical character that is inscribed by *autogestion* into social and political relations? What party can limit the activities of the State and its own activities, instead of imposing decisions from above and exercising constraint? Only a party that has truly assimilated and actualized the thought of Marx in integrating into its political action the critique of the past and that of politics itself, only such a party can accept *autogestion* and stimulate it. Indeed *autogestion* carries within itself, along with the withering away of the State, the decline of the Party as a centralized institution that monopolizes decision making.

How can we break not only with dogmatism and with the absence of theory, but also with the thesis, explicit or not, that transforms political activity into a sort of absolute?

Translation by Victoria S. Johnson and Neil Brenner

NOTES

1. [Alain Peyrefitte was an extreme right-wing disciple of De Gaulle whose policies as minister of education played an important role in triggering the student revolt of 1968. He subsequently served as minister of justice under Giscard d'Estaing, worked as an editor for *Le Figaro,* and wrote a number of best-selling books.—*Eds.*]

2. [The Twenty-third Congress of the PCF was held in Saint-Ouen in May 1979. In contrast to the Twenty-second Congress of 1976, in which the notion of a dictatorship of the proletariat had been rejected in favor of that of a "democratic road to socialism," the Twenty-third Congress approved a motion stating that the Socialist countries "had a generally positive balance sheet" (*bilan globalement positif*) and thus signaled the end of the PCF's participation in the Eurocommunist experiment. By 1980 the PCF had returned to its traditional pro-Soviet stance and—in marked contrast, for instance, to the Italian and Spanish Communist Parties—expressed open support for the Soviet invasion of Afghanistan.—*Eds.*]

3. [This report, which became a best seller in France after its appearance in 1978, had been commissioned in 1976 by French President Valéry Giscard d'Estaing to investigate the ramifications of computer and information technology for social and political life (see Simon Nora and Alain Minc, *L'Informatisation de la société* [Paris: La Documentation Française, 1978]; an English translation of the report appeared in 1980 with an introduction by Daniel Bell: *The Computerization of Society* [Cambridge, Mass.: MIT Press, 1980]). Nora and Minc were both *inspecteurs des finances,* elite technical and political advisors appointed by the French national government to address major policy issues. The Nora-Minc report was particularly controversial due to its suggestion that the development of computer technologies might require a decentralization of political power within the French state. Lefebvre returns to a discussion of the Nora-Minc report in "Information Technology and Everyday Life," in *Critique of Everyday Life,* vol. 3, *From Modernity to Modernism (Towards a Metaphilosophy of Daily Life),* trans. Gregory Elliott (London: Verso, 2006), 136–54, esp. 138.—*Eds.*]

4. [Jacques Attali, *La nouvelle économie française* (Paris: Flammarion, 1978). An economist by training, Jacques Attali was a prominent academic, social-democratic

theoretician and best-selling author during the 1970s. In the work cited by Lefebvre, Attali proposed to construct a cybernetic model of socialism in which relations among producers, consumers, and the state would be coordinated entirely through computers. In the 1980s Attali became one of François Mitterand's closest advisors on matters of economic and cultural policy.—*Eds.*]

5. See Attali, *La nouvelle économie française*, 248.

6. Attali, *La nouvelle économie française*, 244.

7. Attali, *La nouvelle économie française*, 242.

8. Attali, *La nouvelle économie française*, 232–33.

9. [Lefebvre analyzed the role of the university as a site for crisis formation in his commentary on the French student movements of 1968, *The Explosion: Marxism and the French Upheaval*, trans. Alfred Ehrenfeld (New York: Monthly Review Press, 1969).—*Eds.*]

10. [The German term that both Marx and Hegel use for "civil society" is *bürgerliche Gesellschaft.—Eds.*]

11. Lefebvre, *De l'État*, vol. 4, *Les contradictions de l'état moderne: La dialectique et/de l'état* (Union Générale d'Éditions: Paris, 1978).

12. [Lefebvre discusses the consolidation of these new techno-administrative structures within the postwar French state at greater length in *Survival of Capitalism.—Eds.*]

13. [In his 1875 notes, subsequently published as *Critique of the Gotha Program*, Marx criticized the Lassallian socialists' proposal to redistribute the social surplus through the introduction of a progressive income tax. In particular, Marx criticized the purely distributional focus of the Gotha Program: in the Lassallians' vision, the surplus was to be redistributed more equitably by the state, but the underlying capitalist property relations were to be left intact. Lefebvre discusses Marx's state theory—including *Critique of the Gotha Program*—in *Sociology of Marx*, chap. 5, esp. 176–83. Lefebvre discusses the two aforementioned features of the state mode of production—its role in promoting capitalist growth; and its role in redistributing the surplus—at greater length in *De l'Etat*, vol. 3, *Le mode de production étatique* (Paris: Union générale d'éditions, 1977). On this theme, see also chaps. 10 and 11 in this volume.—*Eds.*]

14. [Lefebvre discusses the notion of the "technocrat" at length in his *Position: Contre les technocrates en finir avec l'humanité-fiction* (Paris: Gonthier, 1967), revised as *Vers le cybernanthrope* (Paris: Denoël/Gonthier, 1971). For Lefebvre, a technocrat is a particular kind of bureaucrat who utilized, not always successfully, the power of technology in managing modern society. They had particular dominance in urban planning.—*Eds.*]

15. [Lefebvre uses the original Italian acronym and terminology. This phrase was used in the Red Brigades' infamous Communication No. 9, their final message to the Italian government in May 1978 before killing Aldo Moro, who had been taken hostage nearly three months earlier: "The state of the multinationals has revealed its true face, without the grotesque mask of formal democracy; it is that of the armed imperialist counterrevolution, of the terrorism of mercenaries in uniform, of the political genocide of communist forces" (quoted in Richard Drake, *The Revolutionary Mystique and Terrorism in Contemporary Italy* [Bloomington: Indiana University Press, 1989], 75).—*Eds.*]

5 Theoretical Problems of *Autogestion*

This essay was published prior to Lefebvre's state-theoretical writings of the 1970s, but it represents one of his core statements on the notion of *autogestion* (on this untranslatable term, see the introduction to this volume) and, more generally, on revolutionary political transformation. It builds on the discussion of the withering away of the state that was elaborated in chapter 2 and also represents an interesting counterpoint to the piece "Revolutions" in chapter 15. Lefebvre frames the analysis around the consolidation of industrial capitalism during the nineteenth century and the efforts of theorists such as Marx, Lassalle, and Proudhon to grasp its implications for anticapitalist political mobilization. Lefebvre surveys several paradigmatic struggles, from the Paris Commune of 1871 and the Soviet revolution of 1917 to anticolonial resistance in Algeria in the 1950s, before posing the basic question: how to ignite the basic forces of *autogestion*, or self-management, under modern capitalist conditions? In a remarkable excursus, Lefebvre provides one of his most focused theoretical discussions of this issue, concluding with a series of four succinct theses regarding the basic features, conditions of possibility, contradictions, and possible implications of *autogestion*. Here Lefebvre also reiterates a key aspect of the Leninist concept of the withering away of the state, as discussed in chapter 2. For Lefebvre, this notion refers not to the disappearance of the state as an institutional apparatus, but rather to its subsumption under popular-democratic control as "the state of *autogestion*."—*Eds*.

On the Unity of the Workers' Revolutionary Movement

Who would contest that the problem of unity, which is to say of the reunification of the movement, is essential? It is not worth adding the words "workers" and "revolutionary" to the word "movement" on every occasion. In fact, without the active intervention of the revolutionary working class, there is no movement. Contemporary experience shows us only too well that there can be economic and technological *growth* without real social *development,* without the enrichment of social relations. In social practice, this gives rise to only a mutilated movement, which leaves stagnant numerous sectors of social reality: the life of politics, ideology, culture, and aesthetics. The quantitative growth of production and technical machinery can, up to a point, be separated from qualitative development. Will the gap between these two aspects of the movement be filled by a new period of history? We can hope so. This questioning forms part of the "problematic" of unity.

This fundamental problem is generally posed by official organs and theoreticians in a narrow way that renders it unsolvable. Among institutions and apparatuses, it is treated at best by way of negotiations that end in compromise or bring inconsistencies back to the surface. Specialists in ideology assert themselves as specialists in unity, always ready to seize it. As the props of political bureaucracy, they justify and sustain it. They bring to the investigation of unity the conditions, circumstances, and themes of a division that essentially they could not submit to a radical critique.

These specialists have spread a thesis according to which the workers' movement has split into two tendencies: the reformist current and the revolutionary current.

Let us leave aside the exact definition of the word "current," and likewise the historical study of this "split." In itself, the thesis is false and tendentious. The movement has divided into three: anarchist spontaneity, the skillful and intelligent pragmatism of those who are fearful of reform, and the revolutionary will.

Let us examine these more closely. On the theoretical level, when divergences came to light at the time Marx and Lenin were elaborating their doctrinal positions, the disagreements essentially rested on the famous *transitional period.* For both Marx and Lenin, three indissoluble and inseparable aspects had to mark or rather constitute the movement during this period: the expansion and deepening of democracy, the withering away of the State, and the dictatorship of the proletariat. For Marx, his own objective was not opposed to that of the anarchists: the end of the State, the end of hierarchies and political authorities, accompanied by the abolition of private ownership of the means of production. However, the (Bakunian) anarchists intended to foreshorten the transitional period and even to skip it. The revolutionaries subsequently emphasized the dictatorship of the proletariat, separating it from

the deepening of democracy and the withering away of the State. The reformists, too, emphasized democracy, leaving aside the dictatorship of the
proletariat and, of course, the withering away of the State. Reformists and
revolutionaries engaged in violent and endless controversies, setting continuous evolution and discontinuity in opposition to each other. In tacit agreement over the non-withering away of the State, the former acknowledge the
permanence of the nationally constituted State, with the latter energetically
lauding the transformation of the bourgeois State into a so-called workers'
(or rather "workers" and peasants") State. Political division accompanies the
breakdown of the theoretical unity in Marx's conception of the movement.

Reformism asserted itself as a realist ideology and as a so-called evolutionary strategy against the radical transformation of social relations. There is no
doubt that this was wrong. Reformism has obtained no "structural reform."
The pressure it has applied in the great industrial countries through the
organization of the working class in unions has only obtained measures that
are compatible with capitalist relations of production and, likewise, with
bourgeois ownership and management of the means of production. A reformism without reforms, it has allowed relative surplus value to increase, even
when the working class has scarcely benefited from the growth in productivity.

And yet reformism has not been completely wrong. If it made no sense,
it would have disappeared. Its permanence cannot be baseless. An absolute
rupture, a leap from necessity into freedom, a total revolution, and a simultaneous end to all human alienation, this doubtless naïve image can no longer
be maintained, though it held strong for a long time. The transformation of
society is initially defined as a set of reforms, ranging from agrarian reforms
to a planning implying the control of investments. But, though necessary, this
set of reforms does not suffice; something essential must be added. The transformation of society is a series of reforms *plus* the elimination of the bourgeoisie as the class that manages [*classe gestionnaire*] the means of production.

Was the revolutionary "current" correct? More precisely, has it been proved
correct through history? Yes. It was necessary to seize power by exploiting the
lacunae and holes in the imperialist *system*. It was necessary to deliver the
assault by provoking the greatest possible discontinuity. That said, it is all too
obvious that our era suffers the consequences of a certain failure of world
revolution. The latter shook and even pushed back capitalism and its political expression, imperialism. It did not abolish them, and even stimulated the
bourgeoisie, bringing a jolt of vitality to capitalism. A dialectical movement—

the conflict of two "systems" and their mutual challenge implies multiple consequences—substituted itself for a process that could have followed either
"system" considered in itself. The extension of the revolutionary movement
to countries dominated by questions of agriculture and the problems of
industrial growth can only pass for a partial victory of the revolution. The
movement that aimed for social transformation has itself been transformed
in a way that is not always what one would call "positive." It has fallen into
contradictions (between the Soviets and the Chinese) whose exact significance we cannot yet fathom.

We must return to the evidence. Between 1860 and his death, Marx fought
against the tendency toward State socialism embodied by F. Lassalle.[1] A particularly important and misunderstood text, *The Critique of the Gotha Programme* (1875), is eloquent in this respect. The text gave shape to a specific
ideology, which is rarely studied as such: Lassallism. We can confirm today
that, after a century of fierce struggle, Lassallism has won out over Marxism.
The so-called revolutionary tendency and the so-called reformist tendency
are, in fact, nothing other than variants of State socialism, which is to say
Lassallism.

The anarchist current was the first to be refuted, repudiated, rejected from
the path of revolution. It was savaged (the history of the Spanish Civil War is
still never far away!).

This is the current of spontaneous revolt. It affirms it, it presupposes it, it
seeks to see it through to the end. Under the pretext of historical and theoretical errors, spontaneity has been fought, inhibited. Now its absence is cru-
elly felt. Even if one accepts that it is not sufficient, the anarchist element is
still necessary. If it is the nature of a spontaneous movement that it cannot
be completely foreseen, cannot be fit into a fixed framework, cannot be "structured," that one cannot say in advance where it begins and where it ends, in
such a way that it always contains an element of the unforeseen, it is no less
true that where there is no spontaneity, nothing happens. Lenin, who heavily
criticized the spontaneous, nonetheless used to affirm the existence of a "revolutionary instinct." He saw in spontaneity a first degree of the first level of
intervention by the agitating masses, an energy to orientate, to submit to the
demands of political knowledge, but without destroying its spontaneity. The
Soviets were an invention of spontaneity. Likewise the Paris Commune.[2]
Shouldn't the first task of theory today be to rehabilitate spontaneity? This
restitution cannot proceed without the in-depth analysis that, by sticking

more closely to the conditions, the manifestations and the appearances of spontaneity, would doubtless transform this embryonic and confused concept. If it is true that sociology provides an understanding of freedom, and that sociology takes as its object the creative force of society (which is what Gurvitch thought, like Marx, though somewhat differently), then this task is incumbent on sociology.[3]

The practical and theoretical movement today calls out for a unitary conception that results from neither the constraint nor the pressure of one "tendency" on the others. Will the basis and cement of this unity not come from the current that is most contested, repressed, and humiliated?

Now, the form taken today by revolutionary spontaneity is no longer anarcho-syndicalism, it is *autogestion*.

Elements for a Sociology of *Autogestion*

We can readily trace "management" theory back to Proudhon and Proudhonism. In fact, according to Proudhon, an economic society is constituted spontaneously, and it can and should become society as a whole.

Essentially opposed to political society, to the State, this economic society has its "own reality, its own individuality, its own essence, its own life, its own inherent reason."[4] The producer and the shop floor contradict the governor. The State is only the abstract representative of consumers, while real society is a concrete set of labors and productions. Beyond the state apparatus, in the shadow of political institutions, society slowly and silently produces its own organism, the economic or rather sociopolitical constitution. There are therefore two constitutions that are inherently incompatible. The socioeconomic constitution tends to be subordinated to, and to absorb, the political system.

On this essential point, Proudhon's thought wavers. In his courses on Proudhon,[5] Georges Gurvitch brought this vacillation to light: "The State, as property, is in full metamorphosis; industrial democracy does not so much exclude as complete and reinforce political democracy."[6] Industrial democracy has workers' associations, the seats of the social constitution, as constitutive elements and reference points. This industrial democracy will eliminate the role of employers in factories and in the State. It will make all workers co-owners by entrusting power to their representatives. It will organize the mutual, or federative, ownership of the means of production. Industrial democracy is thus revealed as "the silent partner of labor, through labor or universal mutuality."[7]

There is therefore harmony between the political State and organized economic society.

It does not fall within our remit to resume the discussion of Proudhon and Proudhonism. Justice was served to them only a few years ago by Georges Gurvitch, and more recently by Daniel Guérin.[8] We can affirm that three relatively undifferentiated orientations coexist in Proudhon; they would later necessarily be distinguished and opposed to one another. Some of the author's texts have the revolutionary audacity of Marx, before Marx. Others slide toward what would become reformism. The question of the State is fundamental. The theses are distinguished in terms of their stance toward the State and the problem of the State. This is the criterion. When Proudhon, albeit without designating as such, anticipates the withering away of the State, he comes singularly close to the thought of Marxism. It is, however, a theoretical and methodological error to pose questions of Proudhon that only make sense within a later context. His own relativism prohibits this. Ideas are false, he writes, "if one takes them as having an exclusive and absolute significance, or if one allows oneself to get carried away with this significance . . ."[9] From a philosophical point of view, he certainly oscillated between determinism, pragmatism, and voluntarism. The criticism that accuses Proudhon of contradicting himself invokes the absence of a coherence that he did not seek, and thus risks missing the richness of his arguments and the complexity of his thought.

He doubtless thought that management associations [*associations gestionaires*] were only installed at privileged, hence strong, points of the existing society, in economic and social sectors that were well positioned with reference to the market and competition. Banks, for instance. On this point, the views of Proudhon have not been confirmed by experience, which is to say by social practice. The management associations that were established by workers, and which sought to install themselves in the "strong points" of bourgeois society, turned out badly. Either they went bankrupt, or, with rare exceptions (which still need to be examined more closely), they have been absorbed by capitalism; they have functioned as capitalist enterprises under a "communitarian" or "cooperative" label.

Serge Mallet has very recently proposed a theorization that is linked to the same hypothesis, albeit (whether rightly or wrongly) without explicitly stating its Proudhonism.

Serge Mallet has very perceptively studied the "new working class," from the technical industries to the avant-garde. He believed it possible to draw political conclusions from this socioeconomic study. For Mallet, the new working class turns away from "old ideologies" that are incapable of expressing the needs experienced by workers. He discerned the advent of "a new and superior kind of politicization, derived from a positive assertion of the responsibilities of the working class." And this is said to emerge from the syndicalist movement. "We are making headway here on the problem of participation, of responsibility in management itself, whatever forms this management might assume." From the workers' point of view, the questions discussed between the employers and the unions tend to be focused "on the blueprint for control over administration and over the organization of production."[10]

It is still too soon to condemn this hypothesis decisively. We can, however, suppose that these views have not been confirmed in the meantime. Hasn't Serge Mallet succumbed to the temptation of extrapolating ideological and political consequences from his brilliant analyses of the socioeconomic?

Our hypothesis here will be wholly different. Experience (social practice) shows, in our opinion, that management associations—in their simplest and most interesting form, namely *autogestion*—appear in the *weak points* of existing society. In every society, we can perceive the strong points, the whole of which constitutes its framework or, if you prefer, its structure. We know that the social whole has a cohesion, a coherence. The existing State is grounded upon these strong points. Men of the State busy themselves with sealing up the cracks by every means available to them.[11] Once they are consolidated, nothing happens around these reinforced places. Between them are found zones of weakness or even lacunae. This is where things happen. Initiatives and social forces act on and intervene in these lacunae, occupying and transforming them into strong points or, on the contrary, into "something other" than what has a stable existence. Weak parts, voids, are revealed only in practice, through the initiative of individuals who have the capacity for the latter, or through the haphazard investigations of groups that have the capacity to intervene. If weak points can thus be changed into strong points across the whole of a social structure, they can equally result from a straining or a collapse of the whole (destructuration).[12]

In 1870 Paris is the weak point of the Bonapartist Empire. At the beginning of 1871 the capital is the weak point of France. Due to industrialization and the growth of the proletariat, on account of political activity, the opposition to Badinguet.[13] Because of the war, the defeat, the proclamation of the Republic, the siege, the armistice. Certainly. But also because of the social segregation performed by Haussmann, the relocation of workers to peripheral neighborhoods, the gentrification [*l'embourgeoisement*] and ensuing deterioration in the city center. After March 18, the people took hold of the management of their own neighborhood affairs and also in the City Hall [Hôtel de Ville]. Under the Commune, the workers sought to put under *autogestion* businesses that had been abandoned by the Versailles bourgeoisie, a project that would not have time to reach fruition. In the PTT, the post office and communications network, Theisz anticipated *autogestion* or *co-management* [*cogestion*], which were not yet distinct from one another.[14] Unfortunately, the bourgeoisie, its State, and the capitalist relations of production remained strong outside Paris. At Versailles, Thiers could rapidly rebuild the State apparatus and the army under the benevolent watch of Bismarck.

In 1917, during the collapse of tsarism, the traditional strong points of its sociopolitical framework, namely the army and the village, were transformed into weak points. They were joined in this situation by capitalist enterprises that an ill-established bourgeoisie had not succeeded in consolidating. The weak sectors connected with one another. Soviets of soldiers, peasants, and workers united in the immense movement of revolution. Need we recall that Lenin, in proclaiming the slogan—"all power to the Soviets"—did not see them as representative bodies or as bodies intended to elect representatives, but rather as groups of associated workers, freely managing and directing their interests? A surprising conjuncture. Never before had generalized *autogestion* been possible to such an extent. Never again would it be so difficult to realize. Today we have a somewhat better understanding of the causes and historical reasons for this.

The recent example of Algeria confirms this attempt at analysis. Where is *autogestion* being set up? In the domains abandoned by the colonists. *Autogestion* throws into question society as a whole and the apparatuses that were inherited from the colonial era, or that were established at the time of independence.

It would be of great theoretical and practical interest to discover the weak points of the current French State and society. Where are they situated? In the universities, with the students? In the rural life of the regions located to the south of the Loire? In the new urban housing projects? In the (State-controlled) public sector of the economy? Such claims can only be articulated with extreme care. A two-fold analysis is necessary: an analysis of the attempts at *autogestion* that arise here and there, and an analysis of French society in its totality.

The theoretical implications of this two-fold analysis are as follows: Every society has a framework or structure, which is to say a global cohesion or coherence. However, it is impossible to attribute a definitive character to this cohesion: it neither presents nor represents itself on a single level, on a single plane. A unitary representation would strip the situation of the characteristics of precariousness and momentary equilibrium on which Georges Gurvitch so forcefully and rightly used to insist. It would presuppose that the work of integration for which institutions are employed were realized and complete. At the heart of these structures, forces and deconstructive tendencies are at work. Alongside strong sectors, or even at the heart of these strong sectors, every society has its failures and deficiencies, its lacunae. Without these it would remain forever solid. It would have no more problems, no more history. Juridical relations give form to the relations of production, signaling their difficulties and attempting to iron them out. Likewise, political institutions would shore up the strong points as part of a global strategy of the dominant class, or of those class fractions which are in power. The same goes for ideologies. But circumstance intervenes in structure, and the latter can bend or be bent toward a reorganization.

How do efforts at *autogestion* emerge? Is it a question of the intervention of creative freedom, as Jean-Paul Sartre would say? Or of an effervescence in social consciousness, as Georges Gurvitch suggests? Or is it a matter of human efforts, where it is objectively possible, to harness the organization of everydayness, to *appropriate for themselves* their own proper social life, by abolishing the discrepancy between the technical control of the outside world and the stagnation of practical relations, between the power over material nature and the misery of the "human condition"? Terminology is of little import here. It will be swept aside by a terminology that is most consistent with the facts and that permits their anticipation.

The Problematic of *Autogestion*

We know that *autogestion* is born spontaneously, but that it is not born just anywhere and any way. On the contrary. We have perhaps succeeded in localizing this birth, in defining some of its conditions. *Autogestion* requires a set of circumstances, a privileged place.

Yet it is not adequate to envision a royal route, a path traced out in advance, leading toward *autogestion*. In any place and moment in which *autogestion* is spontaneously manifested, it carries within itself the *possibility* of its generalization and radicalization; but at the same time it reveals and crystallizes the contradictions of society before it. Once opened, this optimal and maximal perspective entails the disruption of society as a whole, the metamorphosis of life. But for *autogestion* to be consolidated and expanded, it has to occupy the strong points of a social structure that constantly bridle against it. From a privileged sector, it must become the whole, the globality, a "system." A difficult transition, during the course of which it can happen that *autogestion* comes into conflict with itself. To manage a division or a business, or even more so a branch of industry, is there not need for expertise, for experts, accountants, and technicians? Thus, internal to *autogestion,* a bureaucracy tends to a form that constitutively negates it, and that, at the risk of being undermined, *autogestion* must absorb.

The principal contradiction that *autogestion* introduces and stimulates is its own contradiction with the State. In essence, *autogestion* calls the State into question as a constraining force erected above society as a whole, capturing and demanding the rationality that is inherent to social relations (to social practice). Once aimed at ground level, in a fissure, this humble plant comes to threaten the huge state edifice. It is well known to Men of the State; *autogestion* tends to reorganize the State as a function of its development, which is to say it tends to engender the State's withering away. *Autogestion* revives all the contradictions at the heart of the State, and notably the supreme contradiction, which can be expressed only in general, philosophical, terms, between the reason of the State and human reason, which is to say, liberty.

In being generalized, in being transformed into a "system" on the scale of society as a whole—units of production, territorial units, including supposedly higher, encompassing levels and authorities—*autogestion* cannot avoid a collision with the "stato-political system" [*système étato-politique*]. No matter what the "system" might be, and from the moment that a state and political system even exists. *Autogestion* cannot escape this brutal obligation: to constitute itself as a power which is not that of the State.

It has to confront a State that, even weakened, even shaken, even withering away in the sense declared by Marx, will always be able to attempt to reassert itself, to consolidate its own apparatus, to turn *autogestion* into an ideology of the State and thereby to repress it in practice. Whether bourgeois or not, the State in essence opposes a centralizing principle to the decentralizing principle of *autogestion,* which moves from the base to the summit, from the component to the totality. In essence, the principle of the State tends to limit the principle of *autogestion,* to reduce its applications. Is this not one of the principal contradictions of our history, a new and barely begun dialectical moment?

Autogestion must also confront and resolve the problems of the organization of the market. Neither in its theory, nor in its practice, does it deny the law of value. One cannot claim in its name to "transcend" the market, the profitability of businesses, the laws of exchange value. Only centralized statism has had this excessive ambition.

It is only in its narrow, doomed conception that *autogestion* tends to dissolve society into distinct units, communes, businesses, services. In a broader conception the modalities of *autogestion* may be proposed and imposed at all levels of social practice, including the agencies of coordination. The principle of *autogestion* revives the contradiction between use value and exchange value. It tends to restore primacy to use value. It "is" the use value of human beings in their practical relations. It valorizes them against the world of the commodity, without, however, denying that this world has laws that must be mastered and not neglected. Limiting the world of commodities does not mean that we purport to free ourselves from it through magic. This would enable us to give content to the projects of democratic planning, prioritizing the social needs that are formulated, controlled, and managed by those who have a stake in them.

The organization of the market and democratic planning cannot proceed without risk. The principle of *autogestion* entails the refusal of "co-management" [*co-gestion*] through an economic apparatus, a planning bureaucracy. It is incompatible with the relapse into capitalism that occurs when the "workers" are accorded a share that is then quickly denied to them.[15]

In itself and through itself the concept of *autogestion* consequently has *critical import.* This critical import is crucial and decisive. Once someone conceives of *autogestion,* once one thinks its generalization, one radically contests the existing order, from the world of the commodity and the power of money to the power of the State.

The true character of institutions and also of the world of the commodity is revealed in this reflection. Conversely, when one contests the institutions of bureaucracy and the State, or the generalized world of the commodity, how can one not evoke that which would replace them? Once *autogestion* appears spontaneously, once it is conceived in thought, its principle weakens the entire system, or systems, of the established order. But this principle is itself immediately called into question and everything seeks to overturn it. If we now attempt to codify these reflections, the following formulae can be proposed:

a) *Autogestion* is born and reborn at the heart of a contradictory society, but one that tends, through various actions (those of the State, those of technologies, of bureaucracies and technocracies), toward a global integration and a highly structured cohesiveness. *Autogestion* introduces and reintroduces the only form of movement, of efficacious contestation, of effective development, in such a society. Without it, there is only growth without development (the quantitative accumulation of production, the qualitative stagnation of practice and social relations). In this sense, the idea of *autogestion* coincides with that of freedom. *Autogestion* is the theoretical essence of freedom, today compressed into and identified with a practical and political notion.

b) *Autogestion* is born of these contradictions, as a tendency to resolve them and overcome them. It is born as the current and universal form of class struggle (although is not exclusive of other forms). It adds to the contradictions of the society in which there is born a new—essential, principal, higher—contradiction with the existing State apparatus, which still asserts itself as the sole organizational, the sole rational, and the sole unifying moment of society.

c) *Autogestion* therefore tends to resolve the totality of various contradictions by sublating them into a new totality, but by means of a theoretical and practical paroxysm in which the sum of these contradictions is pushed to the limit, to its dialectical end point. This presupposes a historical moment, a favorable conjuncture.

d) *Autogestion* must be studied in two different ways: as a means of struggle, which clears the way; and as a means for the reorganization of society, which transforms it from bottom to top, from everyday life to the State.

Its principle implies its extension to all echelons of society. Difficulties and obstacles will run counter to this process, and are all the greater in that they call into question the authorities, the upper echelons of society.

We must never forget that society constitutes a whole and does not consist of a sum of elementary units. Even radicalized, an *autogestion* that only organized itself into partial unities, without achieving globality [*le global*], would be destined to failure. Yet the global incorporates the level of strategic decisions, of politics, of political parties.

It is worth revisiting the concepts and practices of representation, election, the delegation of powers, and the "grassroots" control of democracy, in relation to radicalized and generalized *autogestion*.

With the State unable to coexist peacefully alongside radicalized and generalized *autogestion*, the latter must submit the former to "grassroots" democratic control. The State of *autogestion*, which is to say the State at whose core *autogestion* is raised to power, can only be a State that is withering away. Consequently, the party of *autogestion* can only be the party that leads politics toward its termination and the end of politics, beyond political democracy.

(Provisional) Conclusions

Is the principal of *autogestion* an ideal whose rational core and content is ultimately clearly derived from the democratic ideal? Of course, but *autogestion* is not merely an ideal. That at every moment, at every favorable opportunity, it enters into practice, is a fundamental experience of our age.

Is the project of generalized *autogestion* an ideology? We would rather see in it a theoretical understanding, as removed from ideology as possible, though such an "extrication" would only be a limit. We might see in it the current form of the science of freedom.

Could *autogestion* be a utopia? No, in that this idea does not evoke the image of spontaneous explosion, an effervescence inflaming the whole of society, so much as that of a long sequence, a long process. *Autogestion* can be only one element of a political strategy, but it will be the essential element, giving value to the rest, and without which the rest would be worth nothing. The concept of *autogestion*, today, is the *opening* toward the *possible*. It is both the way forward and the endpoint, the force that can bear the colossal load weighing on society, and which can overcome it. It shows the practical way *to change life*, which remains the watchword, the goal, and the meaning of a revolution.

Only through *autogestion* can the members of a free association take control over their own life, in such a way that it becomes their work [*œuvre*]. This is also called appropriation, de-alienation.

Would it therefore be a particular instance of what Henri Desroche subtly calls "ucoopia," which is to say of a socializing and practicing, or practiced, utopia? Yes, if by this sacred name we mean that theory and practice, at any given moment and in any given conjuncture, attempt the impossible in order to prepare, through concerted thought and action, for the disconcerting moment, the conjuncture that would change this impossible into possibility. No, if Henri Desroche means by this ingenious term a simple, modern version of utopia and uchronia. Moreover, Desroche has firmly grasped how the socialist perspective and its view of the future are connected through the concept of radicalized and generalized *autogestion*. In the conclusion of his study, despite some reservations, does he not return to and accept the programmatic definition of socialism with reference to a dense network of grassroots agencies *plus* electronic devices? The network of agencies of *autogestion* within units of production and within territorial units would ensure the expression of social needs and the social control of production. Without this network, the electronic and cybernetic methods that are applied to economic management would transfer power to the technocrats, machine programmers, serving them as means for manipulating people. Without machines, democracy risks being confused with economic and social disorganization; it risks not surpassing political democracy, not realizing the possibilities of *autogestion*.[16]

Translation by Gerald Moore, Neil Brenner, and Stuart Elden

NOTES

1. [On Lassalle, see chap. 1 n.8.—*Eds.*]
2. Among recent studies on the Paris Commune, see the article by A. Decouflé in *Cahiers de l'ISEA* 9 (August 1965): 173–207. [The title of the article in question is "La spontanéité révolutionnaire dans une révolution populaire: L'exemple de la Commune de Paris" ("Revolutionary spontaneity in a popular revolution: The example of the Paris Commune").—*Eds.*]
3. [Georges Gurvitch (1894–1965) was a Russian-born, naturalized French sociologist.—*Eds.*]
4. [Pierre-Joseph Proudhon, *Idée générale de la révolution au XIXe siècle*, translated by John Beverly Robinson as *General Idea of the Revolution in the Nineteenth Century* (London: Freedom Press, 1923), 147: "The People is not only a *creature of the mind, a personification of thought,* as Rousseau said, but a true personality, which has its own reality, its own individuality, its own essence, its own life, its own reasoning power."—*Eds.*]
5. *Cours de 1952–3*, 2:54–55. [Georges Gurvitch, *Les fondateurs français de la sociologie contemporaine: Saint-Simon et Pierre Joseph Proudhon* (Paris: Les cours de Sorbonne, 1955).—*Eds.*]
6. *Information au Manuel d'une Spéculateur*, 1853. [This is a reference to Proudhon, *Manuel du spéculateur à la Bourse* (Paris: Garnier Frères, 1853).—*Eds.*]

7. [See Proudhon, *Manuel du spéculateur à la Bourse*, 477. Lefebvre misquotes the passage.—*Eds.*]

8. *L'Anarchisme* (Paris: Gallimard, 1965). [This was translated by Mary Klopper as *Anarchism: From Theory to Practice* (New York: Monthly Review Press, 1970).—*Eds.*]

9. *Philosophie du progrès*, 1946 edition, 51. [This is a reprint of the original: Proudhon, *Philosophie du progrès: Programme* (Brussels: Alphonse Lebègue, 1860), 27. There does not appear to be an English translation.—*Eds.*]

10. See *Les Nouveaux comportements politiques de la classe ouvrière* (Paris: PUF, 1962), 52–55, a text where the theoretical position of Serge Mallet is articulated with great clarity. [Serge Mallet was a former member of the PCF who, during the course of the 1960s, became one of the leading theoreticians of the PSU, a dissident socialist organization that promoted factory *autogestion* and supported the student revolts of May 1968. An advocate and theorist of *autogestion*, Mallet became well known within the French and European Left for his ideas about the transformation of working-class politics under advanced, "technocratic" capitalism. Lefebvre's reference is to a collection of interviews edited by Léo Hamon. Mallet's more detailed and widely discussed study was *La nouvelle class ouvrière* (Paris: Seuil, 1963); translated by A. Shepherd and B. Shepherd as *The New Working Class* (Nottingham: Spokesman, 1975).—*Eds.*]

11. [On the distinction between men of the State and Statesmen, see chap. 1.—*Eds.*]

12. This conception could be generalized without, however, pretending that it accounts for all sociological and cultural facts. Are not the "anomic groups"—which either erode or help transform society—are not such groups constituted in these vacuoles of the social fabric? Could it not be argued that ideas, representations, images, and even myths, all these phenomena of social consciousness, arise to fill in or attempt to fill these voids, instead of being the result of a fullness or because they represent the framework of a well-organized society?

13. [Badinguet was a satirical name for Napoleon III. It apparently referred to the name of a man whose identity he used during an escape from captivity in 1846.—*Eds.*]

14. [Albert Theisz (1839–81), French revolutionary in the Commune. PTT—Postes, Télécommunications et Télédiffusion—is the modern name for this public utility.—*Eds.*]

15. On *co-gestion* in Germany, see the interesting suggestions in the new series of "Allemagne d'Aujourd'hui" [Germany today], no. 1, 1966. The co-management agenda of the "Gaullists of the Left" is expressed in the amendment introduced into the finance law of July 12, 1965, at the request of Louis Vaillon, which is intended to bestow financial advantages on businesses which distribute stocks to their employees.

16. See H[enri] Desroche, ["Voyages en ucoopies . . . ,"] *Esprit*, February 1966, 222–45, which contains a reference to an article by Henri Lefebvre that appeared in *Le Monde*, January 29, 1964. [This piece of Lefebvre's was entitled "S'agit-il de penser," 8. The part quoted by Desroche concerns Lenin's famous suggestion that socialism was Soviets plus electrification. Lefebvre's 1964 updating emphasized grassroots organizations rather than Soviets, modern electronic devices rather than electrification, and territories as well as sites of production.—*Eds.*]

6   "It Is the World That Has Changed"

Interview with *Autogestion et socialisme*

This interview was conducted by Yvon Bourdet and Olivier Corpet on February 16, 1976, while Lefebvre was immersed in work on *De l'État*, and addresses the same issues as the previous chapter. It was simply titled "Interview with Henri Lefebvre" in the section of the journal *Autogestion et socialisme* titled "Leninism–Stalinism or *autogestion?*"; the title of this chapter comes from a phrase within the interview. In this wide-ranging discussion with Bourdet and Corpet, two leading theorists of *autogestion* and the editors of the journal in which it was published, Lefebvre surveys key issues related to his understanding of Marxism, politics, state restructuring, and radical democracy. Key themes of the interview include the continued centrality of Marxian and Leninist theoretical ideas to the critical understanding of contemporary global conditions; the relationship between Marx, Lenin, Kautsky, and Stalin as theorists and political strategists; the development of the "state mode of production" and its implications for sociopolitical strategies and struggles; the critique of the PCF and other European communist parties for their hyperstatist, authoritarian tendencies; and the spatial dimensions of *autogestion*—with specific reference to urban movements and peasant struggles.

The piece therefore provides an accessible summary of the political stakes of Lefebvre's theoretical work on the state in the 1970s. Through its concluding discussion of the worldwide and the planetary, this interview also provides a segue into part II of this volume, in which the major themes of the preceding chapters are spatialized and resituated in relation to a broader analysis of worldwide trends, processes, developments, and transformations.

It is also worth noting that one of Lefebvre's interlocutors in this interview, Yvon Bourdet, was a significant contributor to the debate on *autogestion* in France. Bourdet wrote the important text *L'autogestion* with Alain Guillerm (Paris: Éditions Segheurs, 1977), and *L'espace de l'autogestion: Le Capital, la*

Capitale (Paris: Galilée, 1978). The latter analyzes the close relation between capital and the capital city, arguing for the extension of the notion of *autogestion* from the firm (capital) to space (the capital city and center-periphery relations). It is thus an argument for what Lefebvre calls territorial *autogestion*, as well as a Heideggerian and Marxist inspired account of the alienation resulting from the modern crisis of dwelling.—*Eds.*

The current situation of Marxism is too vast an issue to be dealt with in an interview, so we will ask you to clarify your thinking on a few points. Do you see continuity or a break between Marxism and Leninism, between Leninism and Stalinism?

I would like first to say a few words on the current situation of Marxism, which has recently given rise to a number of discussions and polemics in which I have participated very little, because they began when I left for Mexico, where I spent some time. I will say two or three things: there are people who strive fiercely to demonstrate that Marxism is over, that Marxism is dead—for example, Jean-Marie Benoist, in his book, *Marx Is Dead,*[1] the same Jean-Marie Benoist who has since written a book on the structuralist revolution: we get the revolutions we deserve.[2] There are people who speak of Marx the anti-Semite, etc. . . . But the question is not only that of Marx but of Marxism. I personally believe that Marxism is particularly alive but under paradoxical conditions: Marxism has served as a stimulant and an element of neo-capitalism; it is at the heart of capitalism that Marxism is living because statesmen—I do not mean the State as an impersonal entity, but statesmen and their informants—have been able to draw many elements from the thought of Marx, for instance the thesis of planning. Barely perceptible in Marx, though it is hinted at (contrary to what Raymond Aron says), the thesis of rational planning is implicit, referred to, in the thought of Marx and it has since trod a strange path; not only through centralized, bureaucratic, and prescriptive planning of the Soviet variety, but through all sorts of financial and other techniques; indicative planning, planning through financial balance sheets, spatial planning, to which I give a lot of weight, and which I have studied a good deal, are forms derived from the thought of Marx. We therefore come to this idea, which might seem paradoxical, that Marx's thought is dead in the socialist countries where Marx is cited as one might cite the Bible in Church Councils, or the Gospels or the Sermon on the Mount in a gathering of priests. In capitalist countries, Marxism is extraordinarily alive, but on two levels: first on the level of stimulating capitalism itself, which has succeeded in transforming wars, resistance, struggles and even critique itself into factors of growth, if not development. The oft-employed term "cooptation" [*"recuperation"*] is a weak one. There is more than one cooptation of all these negative elements by capitalism. Capitalism has absorbed them; it has used them as stimulants. And then there is the second level: Marxism as critical theory, as more than a dissenting analysis, the analysis of contradictions, the analysis of conflicts that are internal to capitalism. I support the idea of a profound vitality of Marxism in capitalist countries. In socialist countries, it is dead. Let us put to one side the case of China, where the role that Marxism can play has been quite poorly understood: given its theoretical basis, the concepts must be completely different from all that is familiar to us. For my part, I ask myself how Marxist concepts can penetrate a way of thinking, into a brain that has been formed by ideogrammatic thinking; I would like to know. I have posed these questions a few times; no one has replied to me. I thus put the case of China to one side, but in Russia, Marxism is dead, transformed into an ideology, transformed into its opposite: from a critique of the State to an ideology of the State. It is dead but the body is stuffed, solid, and well utilized like poor Lenin in his mausoleum. Marxism is like the corpse of Lenin: it serves as publicity. That is what I wanted to say on a general level.

I believe that the association of Marxism with Leninism is fictitious. It is a political welding, the opposite of a political rupture. There is a profound difference between the thought of Marx and that of Lenin. The thought of Lenin is that of a political strategist, whereas the thought of Marx is that of a theorist who developed and linked together a series of concepts on the plane of theory, who did not finish his work, not by a long shot, since *Capital* is an incomplete work in which we do not see the functioning of bourgeois society. We have glimpses of a few elements of its functioning but we do not see it function. It is an unfinished work on a certain theoretical level, with hypotheses and postulates that now appear quite clearly to us—postulates of a certain historicity—and also highly naturalistic metaphors, according to which a society is born, grows, matures, and declines like the beings of nature. Some underlying postulates have enabled us to constitute concepts, which as concepts and in their interconnection have something thoroughly solid about them. This is what persists today through a problematic that we have to tease out. And that is Marxism.

With regard to Leninism, it is essentially a political strategy adapted to the conditions of a country with a majority of peasants and an autocratic government, the Tsar, tsarism, etc. . . . From his earliest works, Lenin works out a strategy appropriate to this country. In reality, what I call the great drift, which is to say the fact that revolution leaves industrial countries for the shores of predominantly peasant countries, has already begun. Lenin just didn't see things like that, or at least he left them in the dark. But in fact he succeeded in adapting Marxism—which is a theory of revolution in developed industrial countries, where there exists a quantitatively and qualitatively dominant proletariat, capable of hegemony—to revolution in undeveloped countries where agrarian problems are essential, urgent, and decisive. There is therefore a break. This is not at all intended to suggest that Lenin's thought should today be discounted. I think that in the thought of Lenin there are elements of extraordinary importance: for example, the law of unequal development, a significant law that has been verified throughout the modern world, and it is of course Lenin who outlined it. But this is already something totally different from Marx. The most explicit reservations may be articulated regarding Lenin's notion of imperialism and his notion of the party. And in the polemics between Lenin and Rosa Luxemburg there is room for thinking that he was not always right despite the dogmatics of Marxism–Leninism. I therefore believe that Marxism must be detached from Leninism, just as much as Leninism from Stalinism.

So you stress two breaks, that between Marx and Lenin, and that between Lenin and Stalin?

I believe in the importance of political breaks. Breaks are political, they are not epistemological.[3] The breaks between Hegel and Marx are political, Hegel being an apologist for the State and Marx a critic of the State. Likewise, between Marx and Lenin there is a political break: we have passed from the theory of revolution in Germany, in Europe, to the theory of revolution in Russia. I forgot to say, with regard to Lenin, and having worked a lot with his texts on questions of agriculture, that there is, here, a contribution of the highest order, of which little has been said, and it is here that we find the cleavage, the pushing of revolution toward something that was not foreseen at the outset. There is also a political break between Lenin and Stalin. There is no doubt that in Lenin's time and even under his guidance, there were harsh measures, terroristic measures, the foundation of the Cheka,[4] but all the documents show that Lenin did not want what happened, and that he had even taken several precautions against it as his famous testimony shows. At the end of his life, Lenin had certainly abandoned the theory of the immediate and rapid withering away of the State, but I believe that he would never have admitted that the construction of socialism might be accomplished through the strengthening of the State, the consolidation of the State, which is the fundamental thesis of Stalinism. In every respect the contradiction is glaring in the pages of *The State and Revolution.*

To this end, I would very much like to say a few words about the dictatorship of the proletariat, because if I go back to the texts of Marx, Engels, and Lenin (in *The State and Revolution*), I notice that the theory of the dictatorship of the proletariat is connected, tightly connected, with another theory: that of the withering away of the State.[5] The dictatorship of the proletariat is the way to the withering away of the State, and for these authors, the revolutionary process has three aspects, one that might be called the deepening of democracy, another called the dictatorship of the proletariat, which is to say the dictatorship of the majority over a tiny minority, and the third is the withering away of the State.

It is striking to see that Kautsky, who did not want the dictatorship of the proletariat, was a statist . . .

Kautsky has written something on the dictatorship of the proletariat that isn't so bad; he was vilified by Lenin, and I agree with rehabilitating him.[6] In this abandonment of the dictatorship of the proletariat, what has struck me of late is the extraordinary poverty of the discussion. It is miserable, it is absolutely pathetic, lower than anything. The expression "dictatorship of the proletariat" had been contaminated by Stalinism, which made it look like a bloody and brutal crude police-state dictatorship, and the concept has been abandoned as if the dictatorship of the proletariat of Marx and Lenin were that of Stalin. I haven't even seen the idea of the withering away of the State appear in important articles in *Le Monde,* or elsewhere, by Balibar in *L'Humanité.*[7] This shows both the theoretical poverty of the discussion and its characteristic intellectual, theoretical, and ideological underdevelopment. However, I do not think that the people who have led this operation are underdeveloped. I do not think that Jean Kanapa, whom I knew well, is underdeveloped; he

knows very well what he is doing in abandoning the dictatorship of the proletariat: he is abandoning the withering away of the State, without even having to say it.[8] What this means is that the State becomes immortal, eternal,
and we rediscover the Hegelian vision with which Marx had broken. It is an
operation that is full of hidden undersides. I do not at all believe that this
passed unnoticed before the eyes of Jean Kanapa, who knows the texts of
Marx, Engels, and Lenin very well. It is a political ruse, a pretty crudely managed political operation, but with hidden stakes and distant objectives. This
seems to me thoroughly important, and it is moreover one of the themes of
a book that I am preparing on the State.[9]

*You have in fact already touched on what was going to be our second question:
what is your conception of the State?*

One of the fundamental theses that I now embrace is that there is a state
mode of production, which is not the capitalist mode of production, and which
is also not the socialist mode of production, such as it had been defined by
those who espoused this idea, this concept, which is to say Marx, Engels, and
Lenin. We can anticipate the state mode of production in the history of the
Asiatic mode of production. Our mode of production is no longer exactly capitalism, it is just as certainly no longer competitive capitalism; it is no longer
even monopolistic capitalism since the State has taken charge of growth. This
taking charge of growth by the State was realized more or less simultaneously
in socialist countries and in capitalist countries, with a slight head start in the
so-called socialist ones. I have occasion to think that there are two general
types among those countries in which what I call the state mode of production reigns: State capitalism and State socialism, which are quite different but
which fall under the same concept of an economy that is managed, directed,
and oriented by the State, an economy that is entirely dependent on strategic
variables—strategic in the broad sense of the term, in the military sense, and
also in the economic sense—that are decided at the level of the State. I consider it possible to show the importance of strategic variables in economic
matters. The idea of a business that seeks out its own small market is valid
only for small- and medium-sized businesses. Everything that is important
today comes under a general strategy. This is no longer a global society, it is
something else; this is no longer the totality, it is something else: it is a strategy in which all the resources a State has at its disposal are integrated, and

which it directs toward specific objectives. I believe that this defines a new mode of production that is no longer exactly capitalism, which is not socialism: a state mode of production.

How, then, do you interpret the critique of the French Communist Party, saying that capitalist countries are under the regime of State monopoly capitalism?[10]

State monopoly capitalism is old hat. In the era of supranational firms, in the period in which the pressure of world market capitalism is exorbitant, and when there are serious problems on supranational scales—problems of energy, among others—it is no longer possible to speak of State monopoly capitalism.

Yes we quite agree, but why do the directors of the French Communist Party do so?

Because they remain thinkers of the State. This is how I interpret the abandonment of the dictatorship of the proletariat: a clever and indirect way of saying that the State is durable, eternal even. I think that they are preparing themselves to hold on to the State; they are thus preserving its importance. This is Hegelian thinking: the State is an unconditional political existence, an absolute. We can neither envisage its supersession by the supranational, nor its withering or its rotting away, nor its fragmentation by regions. To maintain the State as an absolute, this is the skill of Stalinism. It is Stalin who introduced the fetishization of the State into Marxism, the idea of the State as an unconditional, total, absolute, political existence. That is Stalinism. The crimes, the mistakes, are certainly not stripped of their importance, but they do not constitute the most essential issue. The essential matter is the idea that revolution implies the limitless reinforcement of the State.

It was the idea of Hilferding[11] *and Kautsky that capitalism would prepare the way for socialism by being rationalized and statized [s'étatisant]. We don't really understand why the communists, instead of saying that capitalism prepares the way for socialism, launch the most polemical attacks at State capitalism in the West, which is nearly an imperfect form of what they want to accomplish.*

In my opinion, if they launch polemical attacks it is because they think they will succeed, which is perfectly possible, and in this case there is no other mode of production since, as you know, the schema of the Common Program is simply a schema for accelerated growth, and (beyond the fact that accelerated growth is nowadays barely credible) it is the same mode of production.[12] There are no qualitative changes, at the scale of the nation–State there is nothing really new, just a revival of the quantitative through a wage policy and an allocation of revenues, done better than under current capitalism. It perpetuates the trajectory of the capitalist mode of production but by reinforcing the State; which is to say that preparations are being made to construct a magnificent State socialism in France in which the State will be all-powerful. The same trajectory will thus be shared both by national monopoly capitalism and the police State, a prospect that does not amuse me in the least . . .

Since we are posing these questions to you for the journal Autogestion et socialisme, *do you see a relationship between the thought of Marx and the* autogestion *movement?*

I do not believe that the idea of *autogestion* can be found in Marx. There is no doubt that there is an idea of grassroots democracy, of a bottom-up democracy that rises from the base to the summit. Nor is there any doubt that he had a notion of workers' and producers' associations, but I think that Marx barely defined this idea of association, which has remained somewhat ideal, not idealist but ideal. We should perhaps look at this extremely closely.

And the Paris Commune . . . ?

Perhaps there are a few brief glimmers in the Paris Commune, that does not justify saying that Marx discovered the concept. No, but you are familiar with both the impact and the difficulties of this concept. I personally believe that the problematic of *autogestion* is transposed more and more from enterprises toward the organization of space. I have found some extraordinary examples, like in a Mexican shantytown, where two hundred thousand inhabitants are under complete *autogestion.*

We know that in Oporto and in Lisbon, the socialists have proposed to construct houses through public housing schemes, and the inhabitants of the shantytowns have said: "we do not want these houses."

That doesn't surprise me.

A final, subjective question: you haven't always thought about these questions as you think about them today. So, without returning to your previous works, may we ask you to specify the essential reasons for your shift, for your intellectual itinerary?

Your question is not at all a subjective one because in fact it is the world that has changed. I am not saying that it has changed completely—unfortunately not; there are some constants, notably some of the relations of production that we encounter, but even so there is much that has changed. The world as a bundle of contradictions has obviously changed. I have therefore modified my perspective. For example, I spent ten or fifteen years on the agrarian question, which amounted to nothing; no one was interested in that research in this era.[13] Then one fine day—during the 1960s—I noticed that the peasant question was no longer decisive, that revolutions had been fundamentally peasant-based for several decades, but that this was now over. It was necessary to study the urban questions that were emerging. Up until the middle of the century, the revolutions are peasant-based, including aborted revolutions in Indonesia and elsewhere, including the agrarian reforms that were basically accomplished through peasant revolutions, as in Mexico. After this I began to focus my attention on urban questions, because they were mounting; the great movement of urbanization following all the economic transformations began right around the years between 1955 and 1960. It is the world that is changing. So naturally, since I am not a systematic or dogmatic spirit, I do not cling to the past. Given the number of questions, it would almost be necessary to publish continuously, a sort of continuous bulletin that would follow the transformations of everyday life, the transformations of the State in a world that is paradoxical because there are some things that have remained fixed and others that have entirely changed. Your question has a subjective and biographical feel to it, but in reality I think that I have followed the transformations of the modern world, from before the First World War, through the polemics on fascism and subsequently the polemics against Stalinism and finally against dogmatism in general. There, too, we find a sequence of polemical positions, of discussions that were and continue to be fierce.

Let's say then that what is subjective is the fact that, contrary to others, you embrace change.

I try, but you know, it's not easy, especially not at the present time. Currently my guiding idea is that there is a worldwide experience. The worldwide and the planetary are in the process of forming, but we are at great pains to discover what lies on the horizon, and we are therefore still required to produce an accounting, an inventory. I believe there is a worldwide experience that is the first occurrence of worldness [*mondialité*]. Beyond this formulation of a worldwide experience, we risk launching ourselves into speculation, like Kostas Axelos, for example, who is a very great thinker, but who is very speculative in what he says about the play of the world; it is almost metaphysical.[14] My work is to try comparatively to bring together the elements of the worldwide experience, within which I include the Soviet centralization of the State, the type of state mode of production realized in Russia, centralized planning, etc. . . . , the failures and also the difficulties that all these experiences run up against. This was a part of the worldwide experience: we don't really know the extent to which the State apparatus has been called into question, but even so, the political hierarchy has been called into question, seriously weakened; one must exercise caution here, but even if it has not achieved its goals, the idea of cultural revolution is to weaken the apparatus of politics, hierarchy, sclerotic bureaucracy, and this is also a part of the worldwide experience. Likewise Yugoslavian *autogestion;* and also the regionalization of space in Italy, which the Italian communists are counting on. I think that 1968 was also a part of the worldwide experience, through the simultaneous calling into question of the State, State socialism, and State capitalism; the fact that in Paris and France the working class occupied space, its own space—yes, I believe that this is a part of the worldwide experience whose concepts must today be formulated, dealt out to be drawn on, which is not exactly easy. This worldwide experience has a very eclectic feel to it, and the people who live it are massively at odds with one another: the Chinese haven't had moderate insults for the Yugoslavs, but quite overwhelming contempt . . .

You thus see a kind of link between regionalization, the destruction of the State and autogestion.

Yes, I believe so. A territorial *autogestion* that includes an *autogestion* of production appears to me to presuppose restricted units, more concrete than
countries. I believe that we have done well to gamble on the Occitan region,
even if the whole world does not agree and if that hardly pleases the centralizing parties that nonetheless try to profit from it.[15] I believe that *autogestion*
initiatives are rooted, embedded within the soil, but ultimately it is still only
a question of potentialities.

Translation by Gerald Moore, Neil Brenner, and Stuart Elden

NOTES

1. Jean-Marie Benoist, *Marx est mort* (Paris: Gallimard, 1970). French editors' note:
See also a critique of this book: "Quand l'arraignée structuraliste croit voit en sa toile
que Marx est mort [When the Spider of Structuralism Believes It Sees in Its Web that
Marx Is Dead]," in *L'Homme et la société* 17 (1970): 297–307.

2. [Benoist, *La révolution structuraliste* (Paris: Grasset, 1975); translated by A. Pomer-
ans as *The Structural Revolution* (New York: St. Martin's, 1978).—*Eds.*]

3. [The notion of an "epistemological break" between the writings of the early and
late Marx is found in Louis Althusser's book *For Marx*, trans. Ben Brewster (London:
Verso, 1996 [1965]).—*Eds.*]

4. [The Cheka was a state security organization and secret police established by
Lenin in 1917. It is commonly seen as a forerunner of the KGB.—*Eds.*]

5. [Lefebvre's elaboration of his interpretation of this notion appears in chap. 2 of
this volume.—*Eds.*]

6. [Karl Kautsky, *The Dictatorship of the Proletariat*, trans. H. J. Stenning (Man-
chester: National Labor Press, 1919; original German in 1918).—*Eds.*]

7. [Étienne Balibar (1942–) was, at that time, a close associate of the structuralist
Marxist Louis Althusser, having been part of the team that wrote *Reading Capital*. Balibar's book *Sur la dictature du proletariat* appeared in 1976 (Paris: François Maspéro),
and extracts appeared in *L'Humanité*, January 22, 1976, 178–84.—*Eds.*]

8. [Jean Kanapa (1921–78) was a leading member of the PCF.—*Eds.*]

9. French editors' note: See the detailed plan of this work in *L'homme et la société*,
no. 37–38 (1975), 3–23. [This piece is translated as chap. 3 of the current volume.—*Eds.*]

10. [This theory, which originated with Lenin and was further developed among
Soviet, East German, French, and American communists after the Second World War,
contended that the state and large capital were being fused together into a single institu-
tional ensemble. In *De l'Etat*, 3:129, Lefebvre refers to the work of PCF theoretician Paul
Boccara, *Études sur le capitalisme monopoliste d'État, sa crise et son issue* (Paris: Édition
Sociales, 1973).—*Eds.*]

11. [Rudolf Hilferding was a leading member of the German Socialist Party in the

Weimar Republic and its key theoretician. He was the author of *Das Finanzkapital,* originally published in Vienna in 1910 (English version published as *Finance Capital,* trans. Morris Watnick and Sam Gordon [London: Routledge and Kegan Paul, 1981]).—*Eds.*]

12. [The Programme commun or Common Program was a political alliance formed in 1972 by the PCF and various factions of the noncommunist Left, including François Mitterand's newly formed Socialist Party (PS).—*Eds.*]

13. [Lefebvre wrote a number of books on the French countryside. The most detailed study is *La vallée de Campan: Étude de sociologie rurale* (Paris: PUF, 1963), but the best general sampling of the transition can be found in *Du rural à l'urbain,* 3rd ed. (Paris: Anthropos, 2001 [1970]). At one point, Lefebvre planned a comprehensive *Manuel de sociologie rurale,* but he reports that this was stolen from a car in a late draft. It was never rewritten.—*Eds.*]

14. [Axelos, *Jeu du monde.* See chaps. 12, 13, and 14.—*Eds.*]

15. [The Occitan (or Provençal) is the linguistic region adjoining and encompassing the Pyrenees Mountains in southern France, in which langue d'Oc is spoken, and where Lefebvre was born. During the 1970s Lefebvre supported initiatives for self-government in this region. His own views on territorial *autogestion* were strongly influenced by an Occitan activist, intellectual, and poet, Robert Lafont, whose writings he cites frequently in volume 4 of *De l'État,* especially *Autonomie: De la région à l'autogestion* (Paris: Gallimard, 1976). See also Lefebvre's book *Pyrénées,* 2nd ed. (Pau: Cairn, 2000 [1965]).—*Eds.*]

Part II

Space, State Spatiality, World

7   Reflections on the Politics of Space

The following chapter, which originated in a presentation Lefebvre gave at a conference at the Institut d'Urbanisme—the Institute of Urbanism or "Town Planning"—in Paris in January of 1970, was published that same year as the first essay in the first issue of *Espaces et sociétés*, a journal Lefebvre had established with the urban architectural historian Anatole Kopp. The article was later reprinted by Lefebvre in his book *Espace et politique* (Paris: Anthropos, 1972), the second volume of his classic text *The Right to the City* (the first volume was originally published in 1968 and is now available in English translation in *Writings on Cities* [Oxford: Blackwell, 1996]).

The French title of this essay is "Réflexions sur la politique de l'espace," which could also be translated as "Reflections on Spatial Policy." Indeed, much of the essay is focused on *la politique de l'espace* in a narrow, specific sense, which we have rendered as "spatial policy." This aspect of the piece illustrates Lefebvre's move from questions of the urban to the more general study of spatial policy, and it sets out a research agenda on state theory that Lefebvre would pursue subsequently over a number of years. The essay is focused most explicitly on the politics of spatial planning, regional development policy, and the ideology of urbanism within the French Fifth Republic, particularly those organized and implemented by DATAR, the Delegation for Regional Development and Territorial Planning (Délégation pour l'Aménagement du Territoire et l'Action Régionale), a central government agency for territorial planning and development that had been newly created in 1963. In a series of polemical, if at times empirically imprecise, references to the postwar policies, plans, and planners of DATAR, Lefebvre interprets the French state's strategies to reorganize the geographies of population settlement, infrastructure investment, and capitalist expansion, both within and beyond the Parisian metropolitan core, during a period that is today often described as the "golden age" of Fordist–Keynesian capitalism.

However, the essay also transcends this immediate historical context in order to offer a number of classic formulations regarding the interplay between spatiality, state strategies, and politics. In this he is clearly concerned with a broader focus on the "politics of space," and this piece certainly serves as an overture to his broader reflections on that topic in *The Production of Space* and *De l'État*. Where the French phrasing is significant, we have provided it in parentheses in the text. Lefebvre outlines differential aspects of spatiality—its role as ideology, historical product, and stake of political struggle. Concomitantly, he underscores the central, if deeply contradictory, role of state institutions in producing and transforming the sociospatial landscapes of modern capitalism. Although some of his formulations are rather preliminary, this is a powerful opening account of Lefebvre's work on this topic, which leads to his oft-quoted aphorism that "there is a politics of space because space is political."—*Eds.*

It is now possible to step back and assess what was said and done [in the urban planning profession] during the last decade. This step back allows a balance sheet. However, at the beginning of 1970 something changed: a shift of perspective has begun to occur in the higher ranks of the profession, which needs to be understood and assessed. . . . Until very recently, the field of urban planning [*en matière urbanistique*] was dominated by a theory, or rather an ideology, that was never clearly expressed. This ideology, to my mind, comprised three propositions:

1. There exists a coherent practice [*action*] called *urban planning* [*urbanisme*]. Although it is sometimes empirical and often applies the concepts and methods of a predetermined *science* (demography, political economy, geography, etc. . . .), sometimes it stems from an overall assessment and interdisciplinary givens, but approaches these various procedures of scientific and technical practice as does a previously constituted science, such as political economy.

2. Urban planners, or at least some of them, engage in a methodical examination of their professional practice, an examination of a theoretical order with the implicit or explicit aim of constituting an epistemology, that is to say, a field of knowledge [*savoir*]. This would contain a core of acquired knowledge, in short, what is indicated by the term epistemology.

3. This examination is capable of being expressed in the theoretical language and concepts of urban planning practice; this theoretical reflection consists of a science of space, either global [*globale*] (on the scale of society as a whole) or local (on the scale of the dwelling [*habitat*]).

More generally, it should be remembered that during the previous decade it was only partly understood, or rather misunderstood, that the object par excellence of this science was space, not time. The space of knowledge and the knowledge of space, scientificity, and spatiality went hand in hand, in both intellectual and social designs, within a general structure. Through the notion of a science of space, the urban planning practice and technique were raised to a general level of scientificity. This situation was implicit in the writings of many theorists—I need only cite the remarkable works of Robert Auzelle and Ionel Schein.[1] In these works, urban space, which was formerly discussed either in connection with ad hoc land utilization or the general culture of a society, was isolated from the context; it appeared as a given, as a specific dimension of social organization; and it was first discussed in connection with jointly undertaken action at a higher scale; and second, with highly localized social needs. Such was the underlying postulate in urban planning theory and instruction. A more hidden postulate was the following: the objectivity and "purity" of the space of urban planning an object of science gave it a neutral character. Space passes as being innocent or, in other words, as not being political.

This container only had existence through its contents, only had value through this content, thus formed as the objectivity and neutrality of mathematics, of technology, and without doubt a logic of space. The science of space therefore became the crown and the content itself of urban planning theory. But this is where the problems begin. Effectively, if this science is a science of formal space, of a spatial form, it implies a rigid logistics, and this science would consist of nothing but the constraints placed on the contents (the people)! By contrast, if one engages in the study of what populates this form, either the needs of people or their demands; if the focus is on the content and not the "pure" form, what guarantees that the contents are going to go into this form without being subject to privations? What guarantees that the people and their needs can be inserted into this logistics without resistance? This explains, it seems, that in spite of attempts, there is still no epistemology of urban planning.

This has therefore resulted in peculiar divergencies in the elaboration and interpretation of facts. One approach sought a basic component, a constitutive element, such as the family unit. In this approach, one is preoccupied with knowing how to provide the optimal satisfaction of certain needs. This produced some interesting studies: to those basic human needs already classified in the Charter of Athens have been added other needs such as the needs for freedom,[2] creativity, independence, the needs of rhythm, harmony, dignity, even of hierarchy—I cite these at random. These studies neither succeeded in developing an internal structure of these highly diverse needs, nor in discovering a spatial form capable of imposing a structure on so-called "functional" needs.

Another approach attempted to determine, at a much larger scale, "vitalizing poles" that could restore an organic unity to urban phenomena, a unity either internal to the urban community, or external, namely, active in the environment. Occasionally, some studies limited themselves to an examination of the formal properties of space, its role as the vehicle for the provision of material goods and information, for example by studying interconnections at the scale of global space [*l'espace global*] or even at the local scale.

In these approaches, it was not exactly denied that there was a politics, but this was conceived in a peculiar manner. In the past, the not-so-distant past, the political [*le politique*] was viewed as an obstacle to rationality and scientific procedure, as a perturbation, a kind of irrationality. Politicians, it was thought, operated either by chance conjecture or according to the special interests they represented, but that they usually concealed. Having a self-serving and, moreover, constantly changing viewpoint, seeing neither the options nor the objectives clearly, these politicians distorted the rationality of the urban planning process and the effectiveness of its science. At best, politicians were seen as being in the process of forming a science of strategy; using this explanation, one allowed the politicians to operate, saying that the day would arrive when they too would be guided by a similarly disengaged scientific method.

In these approaches toward the political and its intervention in urban planning, the postulate of space as objective and neutral was retained. But now it appears that space *is* political. Space is not a *scientific object* removed [*détourné*] from ideology or politics; it has always been political and strategic. If space has an air of neutrality and indifference with regard to its contents and thus seems to be "purely" formal, the essence of rational abstraction, it is precisely because this space has already been occupied and planned, already the focus of past strategies, of which we cannot always find traces. Space has been fashioned and molded from historical and natural elements, but in a

political way. Space is political and ideological. It is a product literally populated with ideologies. There is an ideology of space. Why? Because space, which
seems homogeneous, which appears given as a whole in its objectivity, in its
pure form, such as we determine it, is a social product. The production of
space cannot be likened to the production of any particular object or commodity. Nonetheless, there are relations between the production of things
and that of space. The latter accrues to private groups who appropriate space
in order to manage and exploit it. Space is a historical product—like anything
else—but, moreover, is historical in the classical sense of the term. The science
of space, therefore, must be assessed at several levels. It can be taken as a science of formal space, that is to say, close to mathematics; a science that employs
such concepts as sets, networks, branches, lattices. However the science cannot be situated at this level; it cannot remain formal. Critical analysis defines
how and according to what strategy a given space has been produced; finally,
there is the study and science of the contents, that is, of the contents which
may resist the form or the strategy: namely, the users.

It can be asserted that planning [*planification*] at the highest level has three
dimensions. The first dimension is *material* planning, which is quantifiable
and measurable in tons of wheat, cement, or steel. This dimension originates
from the contemporary concept of political economy and from precise analytical tools: matrices. The second dimension is financial planning, which uses
financial balance sheets and involves the study of production costs at the highest level. This is still political economy, but a more refined version. The third
dimension has to be spatiotemporal. It assumes the establishment of local-
izations, the knowledge of networks of commerce, flows, the study of centers
of production and consumption, on the terrain. The first dimension permits
a crude type of planning based on material inventories [*bilans-matière*]. The
second dimension, being much more flexible, could permit, at least in some
countries, the use of electronic computers. In France and certain other countries, this is the method of financial balance sheets, of the banks, which is
known as "indicative" planning. In the USSR, however, authoritarian and centralized planning is still dictated through the use of material inventories.

As for spatiotemporal programming, it should be carried out theoretically,
at the same time as the others, simultaneously; it should coordinate the other
dimensions to the global simultaneity of space. In fact *it continues separately.*

Moreover, one wonders to what degree a complete, simultaneous programming of these dimensions would be desirable. Only the technocrat seems to

want it.[3] This could chain the entire society to the leash of cybernetics. Would this not prevent any kind of democratic planning, by giving those who are currently in power, and who understand how to use these tools, a terrifying effectiveness?

At the moment, democratic planning is only able to slip through the holes in the total plan. It would not seem that, at the moment, the total plan is a very immediate danger. One has the impression that the spatiotemporal dimension is not yet linked to the two other dimensions, which furthermore are not in themselves really linked together or harmonized. The former dimension still remains independent.

The spatial therefore has formal properties. There are special techniques that permit a certain amount of programming, notably calculus, or forecasting. And then there are also the contents. What does this prove? We already know that the science of space, being divided into several levels, is not a unified and comprehensive science, that it does not have a logistics of space as its culmination. Now, let us go a bit further. This proves that there are contradictions concerning the use of space. The method for approaching spatial problems cannot consist of one formal method, logical or logistical; it can only be, and must be, a *dialectical method* that analyzes the contradictions of space in society and social practice.

If the idea that space is political is abandoned, a double critique, itself political, arises (both in theory and in practice): the critique of the right and the critique of the left. The right-wing critique is largely a critique of bureaucracy and of state intervention [*interventions étatiques*], insofar as these interventions constrain "private" initiative, that is to say, capital. The left-wing critique is likewise aimed at the bureaucracy and state intervention, but this intervention does not take into account the users or social practice, that is, urban practice—or does so poorly.

I would like to dwell for a moment on the distinction between the critique of the left and that of the right. This distinction entails and assumes that there are conflicts and contradictions in space, without which the conflicts associated with the "critique" cannot be understood. This distinction was abandoned in the period when everything seemed to be simply an epistemological formulation of a technical operation. Let us look a bit at the extent of this double concept and let us apply it to an example that at first glance seems even more paradoxical than that of space: that of nature.

During the entire period that is ending, nature was a kind of poetic symbol.

It was ignored or relegated to the background, we don't know how much, as some sort of residue, as something that appears here and there, escaping rationally organized operations. Now it is known that nature too is created, modeled, transformed, that it is to a large degree a product of action, that the face of the earth itself (in other words, the landscape) is a human creation [*œuvre*]. Within a certain ideology, nature is today still understood as a simple matter of knowledge and as an object of technology, as an easily understood concept and as a technical problem. It is dominated and mastered. To the extent that it is dominated and mastered, it disappears. Now, suddenly, it is realized that in the process of being mastered, nature was ravaged and threatened with annihilation, which in turn threatened the human realm which, although still bound to nature, caused its annihilation. From this came the necessity of a strategy of intervention. Nature becomes politicized. And this problem does not give rise to a simply technical, epistemological, or philosophical reflection, but to a double critique, the critique of the Right and the critique of the Left.

The critique of the Right? This critique is lost in sorrow over the vanished beauty of the landscape, and over the purity and virginity of disappearing nature; a seemingly obsolete Rousseauism becomes topical once again. One grieves for simple and wholesome pleasures; one remembers the era before suburbanization when the Île de France still offered an admirable landscape to appreciative sightseers. There already have been numerous campaigns in favor of protecting nature. One of these, led by a respected academician, Georges Duhamel, against noise, remains celebrated.[4] Recently Bernard Charbonneau has just published a beautiful, eloquent book on this theme, *Le Jardin de Babylone*.[5]

Where is this going to lead? To a great nostalgia for the past, to a complaint about lost nature. It is impossible to return to the past. The left-wing critique tries to understand the implications and consequences of the ravaging and destruction of nature. Yes, nature is involved in a process of self-destruction in the sense that "man," who is born of nature, now turns against it, to eradicate it.

It is the "elements," as they were called in classical philosophy—water, air, and light—that are threatened with destruction. We are now at the brink of a terrifying day of reckoning, the gravity of which we are only now beginning to realize. We must anticipate a time when we will have to recreate nature. To produce particular objects will no longer be sufficient; we will have to reproduce what was the basic condition for production, namely, nature. With space.

In space. The question thus can be posed: how and why is this a critique of the left? It is not a critique made in the name of a left-wing group, political party, or club. It is not a critique made in the name of an ideology that is classified as more or less leftist. We must get to the root of things. It can be envisioned that within the next thirty years, perhaps sooner, there will be (or at any rate the possibility will exist for—let us be prudent!), collective ownership and management [*gestion collectives*] of: (1) the remaining natural areas; and (2) the reproduction of nature—space, air, water, light, and, still more broadly, new *scarcities*. The old scarcities were bread, the means of subsistence, etc. In the great industrial nations there is already a concealed overproduction of those necessities of life that were formerly scarce, and whose scarcity produced horrific struggles. Now, not in every country, but virtually on a planetary scale, there is an abundant production of these things; however, new scarcities emerge—such as water, air, light, and space, over which there is an intense struggle.

Urban planning must be understood in terms of this struggle. Despite its defects and shortcomings, to a certain extent this justifies its research, inquiries, and investigations. One can, therefore, forecast the collective management and ownership of the means of production and the social management of production as a function of social needs. Thus, one can foresee, around the year 2000 or so, a worldwide socialism that will no longer have much in common with what Marx called socialism, but which, however, will have originated from it or will have a more or less distant relation to it. This discounts the recuperative capacity of capitalism and the possibility of irreparable catastrophes! It is in this sense that the critique of the policies concerning space and nature is a critique from the left. This does not permit "predictive" analyses—but no matter. Here and now, like space, nature is politicized because it is embedded within direct or indirect strategies. The planning of national parks, etc., is already a strategy, albeit a minor strategy, or rather a tactic. But it is necessary to look much further.

At this point I hear the realists: "You speak to us of tomorrow, of the day after tomorrow, but speak to us about today." Agreed, we must be realists. But sometimes it happens that tomorrow becomes today and your reality hits you in the face. For example, from one day to the next, an extraordinary outbreak of pollution can suddenly occur. . . .

I repeat that there is a politics of space because space is political [*il y a politique de l'espace, parce que l'espace est politique*].

Concerning current urban planning, the right-wing critique emphasizes the individual house and private initiative. In the great pendulum that swings in French society between state power [*l'étatique*] (curiously labeled "social" or "collective") and the "individual" or "private," the balance clearly lies today on the side of the individual, that is to say, on that of "private" initiative and capital. The objective of this critique evidently is to clear the way for private capital that is looking for the most profitable investments. This capital is looking for a secondary circuit, an appendage in relation to the usual primary circuit of production and consumption, in case of fluctuations in the latter. The objective is to admit land and housing completely within exchange and the marketplace. The strategy is to normalize the secondary circuit, the real estate market, perhaps preserving it as a compensatory sector. As for the left-wing critique, its starting point is the user, the inhabitant, considered not quantitatively (which is the usual resolution to the housing problem), but also qualitatively, in relation to urban practice.

In the contemporary situation, what is interesting is not only the official presentation of the right-wing critique, but also, and I say this loudly, the end of a certain type of terrorism. I am speaking of a long-established intellectual terrorism. The pressure of techniques, technicians, technocrats, epistemology, and the research of a purely technical or epistemological order resulted in an intellectual terrorism. The bureaucracy still allows this terrorism to dominate. There are things that can be spoken of and things that cannot be spoken of. In the decade of the 1960s there were topics that were considered as matters of gravitas and those that were lacking gravitas. This spirit of gravity was, and still is, in many places the expression of a latent terrorism tied, moreover, to the sense of responsibility, to the respect of competence, incontestable qualities of the techno-bureaucracy. But it was impossible to be heard if one said, for example, that the people were bored. Where? In Sweden, in the United States? Perhaps. Certainly not in France! The boredom of the people was not measurable, it did not have to be taken into consideration except as a journalistic theme or in humor. Repressive space could also not be spoken of; that was not a "serious" topic; since space, possessing an objective character and being a scientific object, was neutral, politically. . . .

The at least temporary improvement must not allow one to forget the perils of this situation. For example, the Fifth French National Plan was able to consider urban centrality—that precious historical heritage and essential characteristic of the European and western city—as untouchable.[6] Urban centrality had to be maintained in urban planning projects, even in the absence of an adequate analysis of it. Nonetheless, for quite some time, there has been talk of a crisis of urban centrality, of a decline of the urban cores. It is obvious that centralization results in saturation, the least example of which is automobile congestion. Thus, the right-wing critique announces the end of urban centers, the dispersal of activities and population, and hence, eventually, an intensified segregation of the population.

In my opinion, the left-wing critique must demonstrate that centrality is constitutive of urban life, that if there is not centrality there is no longer urban life, that the dislocation of centrality threatens the very heart of urban practice. This form of critique must illustrate ever more profoundly that urban centers are multifunctional. Furthermore, it must not hide the problems. If there are contradictions in the use of space, they also appear at this level, and urban centrality cannot be presented, supported, or propounded without recognizing the problems. There are dialectical disturbances, displacements of centrality; there is saturation, the self-destruction of centrality, from which perhaps will come the need for polycentrality, for a polycentric conception of urban space. I mention this only to show a certain trend.

Today, the Sixth French National Plan proposes to eliminate centrality from official urban planning.[7] First observation: enormous commercial centers are presently forming, containing service annexes of all varieties and producing a new conception and practice of space; in reality, these new commercial centers are not isolated, but form networks. Secondly, what is going to persist is the centrality of decisions, that is to say the urban center containing power, wealth, information, and influence. Consequently, the right-wing critique of urban centrality can be dealt with not in terms of the actual dissolution of centrality, but with reference to the reinforcement of a double centrality composed of two aspects: the networks of commercial centers; and the centrality of decisions, decision-making centers, veritable fortresses of the State that neoliberal ideology attempts to conceal.

Let us have the courage to go right to the bitter end. What was urban planning during the last decade? A vast and polyvalent operation. An uncertain science searching for its object and its objectivity, but finding them not where it looked for them. A practice, certainly, but not necessarily a scientific one. It was certainly a mixture of institutions and ideology, a means of masking the urban problematic in its totality. Urban planning also involved a socialization of waste disposal and public safety functions, thus transferring to the

State and the public sector an underdeveloped economic sector that was still using artisanal techniques at the beginning of the decade; the sector was deficiently developed, yet it was crucial to society. On the other hand, since the underdeveloped features of these industries—that is to say, housing and urban space, the artisanal and deficient characteristics—had disappeared, perspectives evolved, and this now-profitable economic sector could be entrusted to private capital.

Let's not forget a historical detail of extreme importance. The ownership of land, whether or not it has been built on, is of feudal origin. To properly understand what has occurred, it should be recalled that the landowner, whether he owns land or buildings, is initially someone other than the industrial capitalist. Mobile capital and fixed capital are not the same; they are not managed in the same way. An indication and proof of this is that during the two world wars there was a moratorium on rents, which was a way of causing the landowner some difficulties. I do not believe that a moratorium on the dividends of industrial capital has ever been mentioned. The mobilization of rent and real estate wealth must be understood as one of the great extensions of financial capital within recent years; the entry of the construction sector into the industrial, banking, and financial circuit has been one of the strategic objectives of the last decade. This is entirely logical and coherent in a society such as ours. More precisely, the real estate circuit has long been a subordinate, subsidiary economic sector. Even though it is normally a compensatory investment sector when the production–consumption cycle slackens or when there are recessions, it is gradually becoming a parallel sector heading toward integration into the normal production–consumption circuit. Capital investment thus finds a place of refuge, a supplementary and complementary territory for exploitation. Usually this situation does not last for long time; it is an "unhealthy" phenomenon. In Spain, during the rapid growth period of the 1960s, Spanish capitalism became bogged down in the real estate sector and constructed a huge modern façade in front of the country's underdevelopment. In certain countries, such as Spain and Greece, the real estate sector has become an essential part of an economy that consists of an all-too-familiar type of governmental intervention. In other countries, such as Japan, recourse to the real estate sector to compensate for difficulties in the normal production–consumption cycle and to increase profits is quite common: even being forecasted and planned in advance.

The paradox, the comedy, is that the right-wing critique, which completely conceals a whole series of operations (the customary role of ideology), presents itself as being revolutionary. What did Albin Chalandon say? That the spread of the residential subdivision [*la banlieue pavillonnaire*] is a revolution?[8] In reality, official neoliberalism conceals a sectoral conception of economic management, a diversified strategy. It appears that the government wants to vary its policies according to the economic sectors of agriculture, industry, and real estate. One can clearly see within agriculture the form of a quasi-socialist reorganization, whereas private capitalism dominates in the real estate sector.

The question regarding the success or failure of such a policy is pretty much the following. In industry there has unquestionably been established what Galbraith calls a technostructure (a group of highly competent technicians capable of effectively intervening in management).[9] Has a technostructure also been established, during the last decade, in the urban planning sector that could remain in place under the guise of neoliberal ideology?

In short, without quarreling over, avoiding, or minimizing the dangers, we have alluded to a type of comprehensive spatial policy [*politique de l'espace*], a prospective planning that would predict the future—that is to say, the disappearance, destruction, and self-destruction of nature—without questioning, recoiling from, or minimizing the dangers. Such a spatial policy would not simply proceed by enumerating the constraints; it would attempt to unite the appropriation of time and space by the users, the individuals, and the groups. It would attempt to unite the appropriation of space at the highest scale with socioeconomic organization, taking into account a factor of prime importance that was ignored by the futurologists, namely the complexification of society, the fact the society is becoming increasingly complex and diverse. In my opinion, this would be the project or program of a leftist who would finally take an interest in these problems.

What I say is perfectly utopian because it not only presupposes the existence of an intelligent leftist, but also profound economic and sociopolitical modifications. I recall a thesis that I have had occasion to defend here and elsewhere: it is that, today more than ever, there is no theory without utopia. Otherwise, a person is content to record what he sees before his eyes; he doesn't go too far—he keeps his eyes fixed on so-called reality: he is a *realist* ... but he doesn't think! There is no theory that neither explores a possibility nor tries to discover an orientation. Of course, as soon as one eschews the overpowering philosophy of positivism (which is nothing more than the absence of thought), it becomes rather difficult to distinguish between the possible and the impossible. Nevertheless, there is today, especially in the domain that concerns us, no theory without utopia. The architects, like the urban planners, know this perfectly well.

With regard to the space of France, we have, as elsewhere, three layers of phenomena: first, nature, that which still remains of the works [*œuvres*] and artifacts [*travaux*] of the period where agriculture predominated, in other words, landscapes, districts, and regions; second, a layer of historical transformations, notably from the industrial period; and, finally, the contemporary processes that disrupt or weaken, in terms of time and space, the earlier phenomena. The result, as one knows, is perfectly contradictory and incoherent. On the one hand, there is the "French desert," the underdevelopment of a whole series of regions, and not only south of the Loire, since one must also include Brittany and, to a certain degree Alsace, within the uneven development of French regions.[10] On the other hand, there is an unbelievable and unsustainable centralization of French society as a whole in the Parisian region. Hence the famous demand for decentralization that is today directed toward spatial policy. Decentralization? How can the centralized State take responsibility for decentralization? This is a façade, a caricature. In projects of decentralization, local and regional communities do not have true autonomy nor do they have real capacity for management; at the most, they can continue to paralyze, to a certain degree, the initiatives of the central government, and the national government is even trying to take this capacity away from them. Whether one likes it or not, French spatial policy is subjected to demands for decentralization, or rather, it is caught in a huge conflict between the imperatives of state centralization [*centralization étatique*] and concrete demands for decentralization. *Space is political!*

During the decade of 1950–60, spatial policy was conceived of as a function of a European strategy. There were heavily promoted studies proposing a decentralization related to the major European transportation corridors (the PADOG).[11] For ten years, some very competent people worked on these projects; but now one no longer even knows what these projects were about. This is the bureaucracy and the self-criticism of the bureaucracy, its self-destruction!

Thus, for example, ten years ago there was the matter of constructing a large international-scale airport at Strasbourg that would have put it in a good position to effectively become the capital of Europe. One day we learned that this airport would not be constructed. It has never been well known how, and by whom, this decision was made. But what was known was the political nature of this decision, that is to say, the abandonment of a policy. The major Mediterranean–North Sea corridor, the spatial policy oriented toward Europe, was abandoned. If I remember correctly, there was a high-level decision made at the beginning of the 1960s concerning spatial strategy; not European, not European space, but a French space. In other words, it represented centralization, and Parisian centralization. It was necessary that Paris become an urban core as rich and as powerful as the Ruhr or the English megalopolis.[12] This was a political decision concerning spatial policy. Furthermore, this policy was maintained throughout the decade. It is only now that studies based on the Regions of France have begun; and as spatial policy no longer requires that Paris become the single and only center of France, this famous redistribution to the so-called "counterweight metropolises" [*métropoles dites d'équilibres*] has occurred, a mechanical method to balance on paper the influence of Paris in France, even though the earlier strategy was completely different.[13]

Today one may ask: what will become of this spatial strategy? Will the centrality of Paris be further reinforced? Nonetheless, a partial decentralization, cleverly configured in order not to compromise the privileges of central government, had to be deployed.

If one now considers the existence of those persons called, by a rather curious neologism, *decision-makers* [*décideurs*], another problem is posed. What is their capacity for change? Are their orientations fixed? What is their ideology? What is their degree of autonomy? In other words, let's repeat the question: has a technostructure been set up during the past decade in those agencies concerned with the urban structure and spatial policy of France?

Whatever they are, these "decision-makers" have options before them. They have to choose between contradictory solutions. All the contradictions of space are magnified. They can either attempt to plan an equilibrium pattern by following a policy encouraging the development of provincial metropolises—but equilibrium presupposes stability—or, otherwise, they can engage in forecasting and produce ephemeral outcomes. One can devise houses and public infrastructure that are discarded after a given period of time, in the same manner as paper napkins and cardboard plates are thrown away. Why not? It certainly has been necessary for the companies and steelworkers of the Moselle area to comply with production changes; they had to be relocated to Dunkirk.[14] Given rapid changes in the methods and conditions of production, one can either manage the ephemeral, or one can retain the maximum amount of equilibrium and stability. This is an option in the spatial policy that is the order of the day, a choice in the midst of contradictions.

Thus, there is a choice between equilibrium and the ephemeral, an option between effective decentralization and the neoliberal laissez-faire policy with regard to the trend toward political centralization in France. Here are several elements of this problematic.

The issues are intertwined. On the one hand, if one promotes laissez-faire, there will be centers of decision making, influence, power, wealth, and information, i.e., useless "quaternary" formations. From the viewpoint of these decision-making centers, which could be strengthened to the advantage of the neoliberal critique of centrality, spatial policy risks exacerbating inequalities of growth and development even more than in the past. In theory, these inequalities of growth and development had been fought and more or less corrected, but there might come a day when these inequalities could be aggravated in a coordinated way, that is to say, used by the central government. In this case, several extremely grave events will occur: the introduction of colonialism into the metropole,[15] a semi-colonization of the underdeveloped regions and zones by the decision-making centers, especially the Parisian center. There are no longer colonies in the old sense of the word, but there is already a metropolitan semi-colonization that subjects rural populations, large numbers of foreign workers, and also many French workers and intellectuals, to a concentrated exploitation through the methods and maintaining the elements of a state of spatial segregation. What justifies and confirms this evaluation, as far as I am concerned, is an ongoing study of the Lacq-Mourenx complex in the Pyrenees, plus a series of studies in other places, particularly the Parisian region.[16] Needless to say, the situation is becoming explosive. Here I beg that those who would criticize my position do not confuse the storm with meteorology. I am the meteorologist, but I do not cause the storm.

On the other hand, the pendulum-swing between the private and the collective, between the individual and the governmental [*l'étatique*], can continue for a long time. Each time the pendulum swings, it brings a transformation of French society as a whole, whether toward neoliberalism, neo-statism—the pendulum has swung to one side and now it is swinging to the other side. This is ludicrously illustrated on the landscape through the contrast between the *grands ensembles* and the residential suburb [*la banlieue pavillonaire*].[17]

On the "public," collective, governmental [*l'étatique*] side, the *grands ensembles* are promoted. On the "private" side, the residential suburb is promoted. Other examples could be given.

Through the presentation of these contradictions, the critical analysis of political space and the politics of space illustrates the trends, and also the dangers and threats, contained in the present situation.

Translation by Neil Brenner and Stuart Elden

NOTES

1. [Robert Auzelle (1913–83) and Ionel Schein (1927–2004) were French architects and town planners. With Ivan Jankovic, Auzelle edited the multivolume *Encyclopédie de l'Urbanisme* (Paris: Vincent Fréal, 1947). Schein was the author of *Paris construit: Guide de l'architecture contemporaine* (Paris: Vincent Fréal, 1961).—*Eds.*]

2. [The Charter of Athens was the product of an international architectural conference organized by the Congrès International d'Architecture Moderne (CIAM) on the theme "The Functional City" in 1933, which was subsequently published in 1942 by Le Corbusier. It looked at the way in which a city could be rationally structured to address functional needs, including zoning, infrastructure, and transportation. Although influential in postwar planning and reconstruction it was heavily criticized for its rigidity, sterility, and inhumanity.—*Eds.*]

3. [See chap. 4 n.14 for further references on Lefebvre's view of the "technocrat."—*Eds.*]

4. [Georges Duhamel (1884–1966), novelist and poet, wrote about the problems of mechanized civilization and modern life in a number of books, notably *America the Menace: Scenes from the Life of the Future*, trans. Charles Miner Thompson (Boston: Houghton Mifflin, 1931).—*Eds.*]

5. [Bernard Charbonneau (1910–96) was a French philosopher. This book, *Le jardin de Babylon: Encyclopédie des nuisances* (Paris: Gallimard, 1969), criticizes the dehumanizing effects of the metropolis.—*Eds.*]

6. [While the Fifth National Plan (1966–70) continued the decentralization policies associated with the Fourth National Plan, it also devoted extensive attention to the physical planning problems and economic development of the Parisian metropolitan region.—*Eds.*]

7. [The Sixth National Plan (1971–75), which was being prepared as Lefebvre wrote this article, continued to promote nationwide industrial decentralization while also devoting extensive attention to the situation of medium-sized French cities. Additionally, in anticipation of trade liberalization in the European Common Market, the authors of the plan suggested that further industrial concentration in powerful urban centers such as Paris was likely to ensue.—*Eds.*]

8. [Albin Chalandon (1920–) was a banker who served as French Minister for Public Infrastructure and Housing between 1968 and 1972; he later served as director of ELF-

Aquitaine, the French petroleum company. In contrast to earlier policies designed to provide public housing in large projects known as Grands Ensembles (see n.17), Chalandon introduced various financial schemes to promote private home ownership. Lefebvre discusses the notion of the "pavillon" at length in "Preface to the Study of the Habitat of the 'Pavillon,'" in Lefebvre, *Key Writings*, 121–35.—*Eds.*]

9. [Lefebvre is referring to a book by Canadian American economist John Kenneth Galbraith (1908–2006), *The New Industrial State* (Boston: Houghton Mifflin, 1967). Lefebvre's most extensive discussion of Galbraith's work can be found in *De l'État*, 3:301–5. Whereas Galbraith understood the technostructure to be composed of highly skilled technicians and scientists working for large capitalist enterprises, Lefebvre appropriates the concept in volume 4 of *De l'État* to examine the role of such scientific experts in large-scale projects of state spatial planning (see chap. 11 in this book). In such contexts, Lefebvre speaks of a *technostructure étatique*, a "state technostructure."—*Eds.*]

10. [Lefebvre's mention of the "French desert" is a reference to Jean-François Gravier's postwar classic *Paris et le desert français: Décentralisation, équipement, population* (Paris: Portulan, 1947), which famously criticized the overwhelming dominance of Paris over the French space-economy. The "French desert" referred to the "underdeveloped" regions beyond the Parisian core. Due to its emphasis on intranational spatial disparities within France, Gravier's book became an essential ideological and intellectual reference point in the development of French spatial and regional policy during the subsequent three decades.—*Eds.*]

11. [The PADOG (Plan d'Aménagement et d'Organisation de la Région Parisienne) was a spatial development plan for the Paris region issued in 1960. It promoted the construction of decentralized new towns in a second suburban ring beyond the urban core and its previously sacrosanct "urbanized perimeter."—*Eds.*]

12. [Lefebvre is here presumably referring once again to the PADOG (see n.11) and possibly also to its successor, the 1965 Schéma Directeur d'Aménagement Urbain de la Région Parisienne (SDAU). He may also be alluding, more generally, to the formation of DATAR, the French agency responsible for national spatial planning, which was founded in the early 1960s.—*Eds.*]

13. [The *métropoles d'équilibres* were one of the cornerstones of the Fourth National Plan mobilized by the French national government and the newly created national spatial planning agency, DATAR, beginning in 1962. Through this policy, population growth, economic activity, and infrastructural investment were to be dispersed away from the core Parisian metropolis. Eight provincial cities—Lyon, Marseille, Bordeaux, Lille, Strasbourg, Toulouse, Nantes, and Nancy—were delineated as target zones for this publicly funded decentralization of national spatial development.—*Eds.*]

14. [Lefebvre is referring to the organizational and spatial restructuring of the French steel and iron industries during the late 1960s and early 1970s, which entailed the closing of large plants in the northeastern *département* of Moselle (which overlapped with the Lorraine industrial region) and the opening of newly modernized factories in the northwestern Dunkirk port region, where they could receive cheaper raw materials supplies from abroad. A prominent example of this tendency was the Usinor steel sheets

factory, a huge infrastructural complex in Dunkirk, which had been conceived in the late 1950s and was nearing completion around the time Lefebvre wrote this article.—*Eds.*]

15. [While *métropole* means metropole or metropolis, Lefebvre is here playing with its original Ancient Greek meaning of *matron-polis*, the mother city from which people left to form a new *polis*. It thus also connotes a colonial power.—*Eds.*]

16. [Lacq-Mourenx is an industrial new town, based largely on petroleum, gas, and sulfur extraction industries, located near Pau in the Atlantic Pyrenees region. Lefebvre's most extensive discussion of Lacq-Moureux in English can be found in *Introduction to Modernity*, trans. John Moore (London: Verso, 1995), 118–20. He also discusses it in *Pyrénées*, and in various chapters of *Du rural à l'urbain.*—*Eds.*]

17. [The *Grands ensembles* are large-scale public housing projects from the 1958 to 1973 period located on the fringes of major French cities, known as *banlieue*. They were intended to provide workers with modern living conveniences at relatively low cost. They typically used variants of the high-rise architectural style popularized by Le Corbusier and his followers in the CIAM movement.—*Eds.*]

8 Space

Social Product and Use Value

In the early 1970s J. W. Freiberg, a young and radical professor at Boston University, invited Lefebvre to discuss his work in a colloquium series in his department. This essay served as the basis for his presentation and the subsequent discussion. Although in part the essay lucidly summarizes—and at times directly quotes—key theses of Lefebvre's *The Production of Space*, its importance here is that it develops several crucial claims that particularly underscore the essentially political nature of his analysis of spatiality. Lefebvre argues that an epochal shift has occurred within capitalism: production no longer occurs merely *in* space; instead, space is itself now being produced in and through the process of capitalist development. On this basis, Lefebvre examines the social relations that are involved in, and produced through, the sociospatial configurations of capitalism. The bulk of the essay is devoted to elaborating these claims in detail, with specific reference to several key aspects of "capitalist spatiality"—the abstract character of capital flows and the material underpinnings of transport and information infrastructures. Lefebvre looks at the role of the state in the control of space, but also at the question of class struggle, spatially understood, and the transformative potential invested in the contradictions of capitalist space. This piece is also notable because it illustrates Lefebvre's concern to relate studies of social space to the key agendas of political economy. Lefebvre relates several core Marxian concepts, such as exchange and use value, to the *problematique* of space, and he reflects on the possibility of establishing a "socialist space" as a "space of differences." This leads Lefebvre, in the final pages of the essay, to link these ideas back to the notion of *autogestion,* as discussed in several essays in part I of this book, but now understood in an explicitly spatialized manner.—*Eds.*

"To change life," "to change society," these phrases mean nothing if there is no production of an appropriated space.

"To produce space," these are surprising words: the production of space, in concept and in reality, has only recently appeared, mainly, in the explosion of the historical city, the general urbanization of society, the problems of spatial organization, and so forth. Today, the analysis of production shows that we have passed from the production of things in space to the production of space itself.

This passage from production in space to production of space occurred because of the growth of the productive forces themselves and because of the direct intervention of knowledge in material production. This knowledge eventually becomes knowledge about space, information on the totality of space. Production in space is not disappearing, but it is oriented differently. One can speak of an economy of flow: the flow of energy, the flow of raw materials, the flow of labor, the flow of information, and so forth. The units of industrial and agricultural production are no longer independent and isolated.

From this follows an important consequence: the planning of the modern economy tends to become spatial planning. Urbanism and territorial management are only elements of this spatial planning, the effects of it are felt everywhere, although this has been particularly the case in France.

Space is social: it involves assigning more or less appropriated places to the social relations of reproduction, namely, the biophysiological relations between the sexes, the ages, the specified organization of the family, and to the relations of production, namely, the division of labor and its organization.

The past has left its marks, its inscriptions, but space is always a present space, a current totality, with its links and connections to action. In fact, the production and the product are inseparable sides of one process.

Social space is explained by neither nature (the climate and the topology), history, nor "culture." Furthermore, productive forces do not constitute a space or a time. Mediations and mediators interpose themselves: with their reasons derived from knowledge, from ideology, from meaning systems.

Is space a social relation? Yes, certainly, but it is inherent in the relation of property (the ownership of land, in particular), it is also linked to the productive forces that fashion this land. Space is permeated with social relations; it is not only supported by social relations, but it also is producing and produced by social relations.

Space has its own reality in the current mode of production and society, with the same claims and in the same global process as commodities, money, and capital.

Natural space is irreversibly gone. And although it of course remains as the origin of the social process, nature is now reduced to materials on which society's productive forces operate.

Each society is born within the framework of a given mode of production, with the inherent peculiarities to this framework molding its space. Spatial practice defines its space, it poses it and presupposes it in a dialectical interaction.

Social space has thus always been a social product, but this was not recognized. Societies thought that they received and transmitted natural space.

All social space has a history that begins from this natural base: indeed, nature is always and everywhere characterized by particularities (climates, topologies, etc.).

But if there is a history of space, if there is a specificity to space according to periods, societies, modes and relations of production, then there is a space of capitalism, that is, of the society managed and dominated by the bourgeoisie.

Capitalist Space

Capitalism and neo-capitalism have produced an *abstract space* that is a reflection of the world of business on both a national and international level, as well as the power of money and the *politique* of the state. This abstract space depends on vast networks of banks, businesses, and great centers of production. There also is the spatial intervention of highways, airports, and information networks. In this space, the cradle of accumulation, the place of richness, the subject of history, the center of historical space—in other words, the city—has exploded.

Space as a whole enters into the modernized mode of capitalist production: it is utilized to produce surplus value. The ground, the underground, the air, and even the light enter into both the productive forces and the products. The urban fabric, with its multiple networks of communication and exchange, is part of the means of production. The city and its various installations (ports, train stations, etc.) are part of capital.

Abstract space reveals its oppressive and repressive capacities in relation to time. It rejects time as an abstraction—except when it concerns work, the producer of things and of surplus value. Time is reduced to constraints of space: schedules, runs, crossings, loads.

The Different Functions of Capitalist Space

Means of Production

Space is a means of production: the network of exchanges and the flow of raw materials and energy that make up space also are determined by space. The means of production, themselves a product, cannot be separated from the forces of production, techniques, and knowledge; from the international division of social labor; from nature; or from the state and other superstructures.

The city, the urban space, and the urban reality cannot be conceived simply as the sum of the places of the consumption of goods (commodities) and the places of production (enterprises).

The spatial arrangement of a city, a region, a nation, or a continent increases productive forces, just as do the equipment and machines in a factory or in a business, but at another level. One uses space just as one uses a machine.

An Object of Consumption

Space as a whole is consumed for production just as are industrial buildings and sites, machines, raw materials, and labor power.

When we go to the mountains or to the beach, we consume a space. When the inhabitants of industrialized Europe descend to the Mediterranean, which has become their space for leisure, they pass from the space of production to the consumption of space.

A Political Instrument

Space has become for the state a political instrument of primary importance. The state uses space in such a way that it ensures its control of places, its strict hierarchy, the homogeneity of the whole, and the segregation of the parts. It is thus an administratively controlled and even a policed space. The hierarchy of spaces corresponds to that of social classes, and if there exist ghettos for all classes, those of the working class are merely more isolated than those of the others.

The Intervention of Class Struggle

Class struggle intervenes in the production of space, today more than ever. Only class conflict can prevent abstract space from spreading itself across the planet and therefore erasing all spatial differences. Only class action can produce differences that oppose what is internal to economic growth, namely, strategy, logic, and system.

Thus, in the current mode of production, social space is considered among the *productive forces and the means of production, among the social relations of production and, especially, their reproduction.*

History emerges on a world level, and it therefore produces a space at this level: the formation of a world market, an international generalization of the state and its problems, new relations between society and space. World space is the *field* in which our epoch is created.

With this world space, and with new contradictions effacing old contradictions, new aggravations will appear; for example, the international relations between states and their confrontational strategies.

The Contradictions of Capitalist Space

This space, produced by capitalism and by its state, has its own contradictions.

A Major Contradiction

The major contradiction of space arises from *the pulverization of space* by private property, the demand for interchangeable fragments, and *the scientific and technical (informational) capacity to treat space on ever more vast levels.* The contradiction "center/periphery" results from the contradiction of "global/partial" since all global constructs lead to the establishment of a concentrated centrality.

A Space Oriented toward the Reproducible ...

Oriented toward the reproduction of the social relations of production, the production of space enacts a logic of homogeneity and a strategy of the repetitive. But this bureaucratic space conflicts with its own conditions and with its own results. When space is of this nature, occupied, controlled, and oriented toward the reproducible, it soon sees itself surrounded by the nonreproducible: nature, the site, the locality, the regional, the national, even the world level.

The activity of the base, discontinuous, multiple, soon proposes a return to precapitalist space. Sometimes proposing a counter-space, it pushes toward the explosion of all spaces organized by the state-bureaucratic rationality.

... and Negating the Differences

This formal and quantified abstract space negates all differences, those that come from nature and history as well as those that come from the body, ages, sexes, and ethnicities. The significance of such factors dissimulates and explodes the very functioning of capitalism. The dominant space, that of the centers of richness and power, is forced to fashion the dominated spaces, those of the periphery.

In the space of neo-capitalism, the economic and the political tend to converge, without, however, the political mastering the economic. Conflicts are therefore manifested between the hegemonic state—which is still not the master of things—and the owners of these things.

The Generalized Explosion of Spaces

Because of these contradictions, we find ourselves faced with an extraordinary but little-noticed phenomenon: *the explosion of spaces.* Neither capitalism nor the state can maintain the chaotic, contradictory space they have produced. We can witness, at all levels, this explosion of space:

- At the level of the immediate and the lived, space is exploding on all sides, whether this be living space, personal space, scholastic space, prison space, army space, or hospital space. Everywhere, people are realizing that spatial relations also are social relations.
- At the level of cities, we see not only the explosion of the historical city but also that of all the administrative frameworks in which they had wanted to enclose the urban phenomenon.
- At the level of regions, the peripheries are fighting for their autonomy or for a certain degree of independence. They undertake actions that challenge their subordination to the state, economic, and political centralization.
- Finally, at the international level, not only the actions of the so-called supranational companies, but also those of the great world strategies, prepare for and render inevitable new explosions of space. The Mediterranean is an excellent example because if it has become a strategic space it is only after the accumulation of many factors. This network, which contained the oldest commercial relations of the world, which gave us our great cities and ports, recently has been completely transformed into a space of leisure for industrial Europe. Still more recently, this space has been crossed by the flow of energy and raw materials. Finally, it has become a nearly over-industrialized space with enormous complexes installed on its periphery, not only at Fos, but also at Sagunto and at Taranto.[1] These phenomena represent extraordinary alterations of the space and enable us to study the problems already posed by the transformations of contemporary space.

Social Movements that Question the Use of Space

In all the industrialized countries, a very old movement exists that comes from demands concerning work, businesses, and workplaces; however, it seems that current movements are arising on a world level that, while still divided, incomplete, and largely unconscious of themselves, call for a reorganization of space other than the places of work.

These are *consumer movements*. In the United States, they are very frequent, numerous, and more or less question the use of space. They reveal that:

- Space is not merely economic, in which all the parts are interchangeable and have exchange value.
- Space is not merely a political instrument for homogenizing all parts of society.

On the contrary, they show that:

- Space remains a model, a perpetual prototype of use value resisting the generalizations of exchange and exchange value in a capitalist economy under the authority of a homogenizing state.
- Space is a use value, but even more so is *time* to which it is intimately linked because time is our life, our fundamental use value. Time has disappeared in the social space of modernity. Lived time loses form and social interest except for the time of work. Economic space subordinates time, whereas political space eradicates it, because it is threatening to existing power relations. The primacy of the economic, and still more, of the political, leads to the supremacy of space over time.

One of the most important points for the power of the left is to support consumer movements that have not yet found their voice and that are very often enclosed in such narrow frameworks that the political significance of their actions escapes them.

One of the political roles for the left, then, is to use the class struggle in space.

Toward a Socialist Space

Like the societies that preceded it, socialist society must produce its space, but in full consciousness of its concepts and potential problems.

It is currently popular to say that Marxism is old-fashioned, that it is less relevant for history. However, it is precisely today, more than ever, that we cannot analyze world phenomena except in the light of the fundamental categories of Marxism, being ready to modify them to specific situations.

Although space is not analyzed in *Capital*, certain concepts, such as exchange value and use value, today apply to space. At present, we must use the distinction, which Marx did not introduce, between the domination and the appropriation of nature. This conflict unfolds in space: in dominated spaces and appropriated spaces. Even more than in Marx's time, nature is the source of all use value.

Should we socialize space? Certainly not: it is already socialized in the framework of the existing society and mode of production. A society that is transforming itself into socialism cannot accept (even during the transitional period) space as it is produced by capitalism. To do so means accepting the existing political and social structures; it leads only to a dead end. It accepts the reproduction of the relations of production: thus, in the end, it is the same, and however it would be hierarchialized and controlled, it would still reflect the former social hierarchy.

A "different" society invents, creates, produces new forms of space, but the relations of property and production now block these possibilities. Some want socialism in the industrialized countries to continue with growth and accumulation, that is, with the production of things in space. Others want to break this mode of production. But the productive forces have changed enormously, passing from the production of things in space to the production of space; it is necessary then to proceed to the ultimate consequences of this qualitative leap. This involves the process of quantitative growth, not to break it, but to unleash its full potential.

The production of socialist space means the end of the private property and the state's political domination of space, *which implies the passage from domination to appropriation and the primacy of use over exchange.*

Furthermore, capitalist and neo-capitalist space is a space of quantification and growing homogeneity, a commodified space where all the elements are exchangeable and thus interchangeable; a police space in which the state tolerates no resistance and no obstacles. Economic space and political space thus converge toward the elimination of all differences.

Insofar as we can conceive it, given certain current tendencies, socialist space will be a *space of differences.*

The Determining Role of Social Movements

There is reason to believe that only the convergence and the conjunction of the worker and peasant movements, linked to the production of things and material work and those who use space, will enable the world to change. Relative to the possession and management of space, urban social movements do not have the continuous character and institutional promise of those that come from the factories, units, and branches of production. Yet if the pressure from the base (the consumers) occurs with enough force, it will influence production in general toward space and toward the social needs of this base. The action of those interested parties would determine the social needs, which would then no longer be determined by the "experts." The notions of equipment and environment would thus break free from their technocratic and capitalistic context. However, the spontaneous explosion of the social "base," although revolutionary and profound, would not be sufficient to produce an adequate, operational definition of space in socialist society. It would, however, be an integral part of these determinations. But the management of social space, like that of nature, can only be collective and practical, controlled by the base, that is, democratic. The "interested" parties, the ones "concerned," would intervene, manage, and control it. But first, they would lead to the end—the explosion—of all imposed space.

A General Autogestion

The reconstruction of the "low to high" of social space, previously produced from "high to low," implies general *autogestion,* that is, at the various levels, complementing that of the units and instances of production. Only in this way can the socialization of the means of production include the issue of space. To do otherwise, to define "socialist space" as natural space or as communes living on a privileged space or by "conviviality," is to confuse the end with the means, the goal with the stages; it is, in other words, abstract utopianism.[2]

Production in a socialist society is defined by Marx as production for social needs. These social needs, in great part, concern space: housing, equipment, transportation, reorganization of urban space, and so forth. These extend the capitalist tendency to produce space while radically modifying the product. This is what contributes to the transformation of daily life, to the definition of development more in social than in individual terms, without the exclusion of the latter. The individual in a socialist society *has the right to a space,* as well as the right to urban life as the center of social life and of so-called cultural activities, and so forth.

The beginning of this transformation has to wait for the thought, the imagination, the creativity, which in turn depend on surmounting the separation between "public" and "private," by dissipating the illusions about the social and the collective confounded with "public charity," and so forth.

Socialist politics of space can resolve the contradictions of space only by adding them to the other economic and social contradictions. Of course, the pressure from the base and the *autogestion* of space cannot restrict themselves to a reformism.

Turning the world "back on its feet," according to Marx, implies overturning dominant spaces, placing appropriation over domination, demand over command, and use over exchange. *Autogestion* reveals itself to be both the means and the end, a phase of the fight and its objective. In the transformed space, there can and must be a redefinition of the relations between productive activities and the return to the internal market, oriented deliberately toward issues of space. It is space as a whole that would be redefined, that would bring about a conversion and subversion.

A Redefinition of Space as a Function of Use Value—How Are These Revolutionary Processes Foreseen?

If the current situation does not reduce itself to an economic crisis, but instead calls for a profound modification of the society and the civilization, it still offers a point of reference from which the transformation can begin. The modification can be thus defined: space produced from the perspective of the priority of the means of exchange and transportation will be produced from the perspective of the priority of use value. The revolution of space implies and amplifies the concept of revolution, defined as a change in the ownership of the means of production. It gives a new dimension to it, starting from the suppression of a particularly dangerous form of private property, that of space: underground space, ground space, aerial space, planetary space, and even interplanetary space.

The so-called transitional formulas—state control of land, nationalizations, municipalizations—have not succeeded. But how can we limit and suppress the ownership of space? Perhaps by remembering the writings of Marx and Engels: one day, which will indeed come, the private ownership of land, of nature and its resources, will seem as absurd, as odious, as ridiculous as the possession of one human by another.

The problems relating to the "pollution of the environment," which are seen by ecologists as primary, are indeed important, but they are secondary. In this perspective, the real problems of society and its transformation are diverted toward naturalism: take, for example, the biologism involved in treating human space as animal space.

In conclusion, a transformation of society presupposes the possession and collective management of space by a permanent intervention of "interested parties," even with their multiple and sometimes contradictory interests. This orientation tends to overcome the separations and disassociations in space between a work (unique) and a commodity (repeated).

This is an orientation. Nothing more and nothing less. But it does point out a meaning. Namely, something is perceived, a direction is conceived, a living movement makes its way toward the horizon. But it is nothing that yet resembles a system.

Translation by J. W. Freiberg

Notes

1. [These port cities on the Mediterranean coasts of southern France, southeastern Spain, and southern Italy, respectively, were the sites for large-scale investments in the steel and petrochemicals industries during the late 1960s and early 1970s.—*Eds.*]

2. [Lefebvre is apparently referring critically to the work of Ivan Illich (1926–2002), an Austrian social philosopher whose book *Tools for Conviviality* (Berkeley, Calif.: Heyday Books, 1974) was widely discussed among the global New Left. Illich argued that the modern educational, transportation, and medical systems were enslaving rather than liberating, because they reduced people to mere "accessories" of large-scale bureaucratic institutions and industrial machines. Against this, Illich advocated the creation of "convivial" institutions and tools based on creative, autonomous interactions among individuals.—*Eds.*]

9 The Worldwide and the Planetary

Like the previous selection, this essay develops the arguments of *The Production of Space* in a more explicitly political register, in this case through the introduction of a conceptual vocabulary for analyzing the increasing expansion of social processes onto the world scale. Lefebvre suggests that the consolidation of the world market, and the state's increasingly active role in managing capitalist accumulation at a planetary level, leads to a fundamental transformation in the capitalist mode of production. Lefebvre reflects on the implications of such transformations for the interpretation of sociospatiality and, more generally, for transformative political action. This essay rather remarkably anticipates key strands of contemporary discussions of globalization, particularly through its emphasis on the tension between mobile flows and fixed places and territories. Lefebvre also distinguishes three key concepts—the global, the total, and the world—that subsequently play essential roles in his analysis of the contemporary worldwide condition (see chapters 12–15).—*Eds.*

Pre-Text and Outside-the-Text

These propositions present a project,[1] that of a simultaneously descriptive, analytical, and global understanding that would positively and negatively be linked to social practice. This understanding would be called "spatio-logy," or "spatio-analysis," were we to label it.[2]

Some *propositions* do more than enunciate: they pose and propose. They pose an actual "object" and propose an "objective." This implies the use of classical deduction and induction, but also of *transduction,* which targets a virtual "object" and its realization on a path heading toward a "pro-posed" horizon.

These propositions are abstract, but in the sense of conceptual abstraction, which, more and better than signaling the concrete, incorporates it.

Proposing does not amount to *producing,* but *propositions* open the way for those who will produce. These are *theoretical* assertions that in this respect entail certain so-called "methodological" approaches; these approaches will become apparent *along the way,* without there being room here to follow the banal procedure of detailing them.

If someone asks: "why start here and in this way?," here is a response: "Start, if you will, by rereading Marx, (Marx and not Lenin, Rosa Luxemburg, Trotsky, etc. . . .), some of whose concepts are reprised here, albeit with modifications whose impact will also become apparent *along the way.*"

1—The first proposition will seem anodyne and even banal. Its implications may not be. Here it is: *social space, the practice of social space* (in short: spatial practice), *the ensemble of questions and the project relating to (social) space have assumed a paramount importance in modern societies.* In fact, each society, the product of history, with its particularities, once molded its space through violence, through subterfuge and through labor. Its space, its work [*œuvre*]! Today, the issue is space on the world scale (planetary and even beyond that). The causes of and reasons for this new situation are themselves coming to light, emerging from the shadows of history: the world market, technology and the sciences, demographic pressure, etc. These causes and reasons coexist in space alongside their effects and their consequences—for example, the all-too famous pollution, the exhaustion of resources, and the destruction of nature. It is worth gathering them together under a unitary conception. Such a gathering will constitute a theory, on the condition, of course, of not conflating (of discerning) reasons and consequences, causes and effects in their spatial simultaneity. The theoretical conception thus set out does not claim to determine a realized "totality," much less to erect itself as a "system" or a "synthesis."

2—In our societies, there is a "problematic" of space (conceptual and theoretical), and an empirically observable practice. This "problematic," to employ the language of philosophy, is composed of interrogations of mental and social space, their connections, their link with nature and logic, etc. Observable in architecture, in "town planning" [*urbanisme*] (to employ the official language), in the effective planning of thoroughfares and places, in everyday life—in short, in urban reality, spatial practice is distinct from this problematic but cannot obviously be separated from it.

3—The predominance of space requires the reconsideration of a great deal of knowledge, notably in sociology, political economy, anthropology, and also history. This knowledge has been conceived through global schemas, be they *atemporal* (in the manner of classical philosophy up until Hegel), or *temporal*, in the sense of *historicity*, by asserting the priority and primacy of time over space. Are these sciences not already caught up in the confrontation between the spatial and the temporal? There are grounds for thinking this! This inevitable, painful, and perilous confrontation cannot avoid giving rise to a crisis of knowledge in both theoretical thought and in practice. Both individually and in general, languages are spoken and written in a mental space-time; they articulate social time and practical space poorly, and they do so even worse with world space and its inherent time. They have to be deconstructed and reconstructed. How could it be otherwise, if it is accurate that popular languages (lexicons and syntaxes) have a peasant and artisan origin and that the more elaborate, established languages have a theologico-philosophical origin. With regard to industry and its technologies, they have only begun to influence vocabulary and syntax.

Wouldn't a methodically pursued reconsideration of knowledge be the only way to save it—by unifying critical knowledge with the critique of knowledge (instead of fixing knowledge in epistemology)? Without such a reconstruction, knowledge collapses under the blows of non-knowledge and anti-knowledge: into nihilism. It is not, for the time being, necessary to insist on the question, which thus posed presupposes its own answer. Just one point: the question of space, taken outside of practice, and on the plane of a "pure" knowledge that imagines itself "productive," even this highly philosophical question can degenerate. Into what? Into a consideration of intellectual space, of "writing" as the spiritual space of a people, as the mental space of an epoch, etc.

The trial by space cannot be separated from another trial: that of the body (the relation of theoretical knowledge to the body, the foundation of practice).

4—The connections between mental space (that of mathematicians, that of philosophers, that of epistemology, which is to say the refined representation of space, but also the space of commonplace perception, the space of representations and everyday discourse), and *social* space (that of the accumulations invested in the planet and the investor, that of spatial practices), these connections form part of the problematic. Whether clearly or poorly articulated, they constitute a methodologically essential link in the sequence that goes from the elementary and the partial to the global. Only their careful examination will enable us to avoid two pitfalls: the confusion of mental and social space (which reduces one to the other, generally the social to the mental), and their separation (which makes the elucidation of practice impossible). We should not carelessly *objectify* the schemas developed in a mental space, even if this space is epistemologically rationalized. This is accomplished unscrupulously in the dangerous operation known as "operationalism" (the handling and manipulation of so-called "operative" concepts). But conversely, we cannot realize the "real," which is to say (actual and virtual, present or possible) practice, without beginning from mental space, without accounting for the trajectory that moves from the abstract places of this mental space to the space of social practice and social practice in space. A work like that of Heidegger (see *What Is Philosophy?*) attempts an *aggiornamento* of philosophical thought—without succeeding in this, due to his maintenance of the supremacy of time over space; this in turn prevents him from resolving the conflict he uncovers between Dwelling and Errancy.[3]

5—The *problematic* and (if one prefers, yet again, to employ the language of philosophers) the *thematic* of space, in addition to elaborating *suitable categories,* suppresses neither concepts and categories, nor the questionings derived from the past, in the time of the origin, the reflexive attempt to be present at the births, in a word, of history. If there is "suppression," it is in the well-known sense of a supersession [*dépassement*] that transforms but does not abolish in an instantaneous effacement. The new problematic displaces the old one, substituting itself for it by modifying it. Meaning is no longer disclosed in the origin (the beginning)—despite what recent philosophers (Heidegger) suggest—but before that, over the course and length of a journey, toward the horizon, into the possible and impossible (and their relations). The *contradictions of space,* yet to be discovered in their vastness, conceal those of time by displacing them, though not without adding new conflicts to them. The concept of *strategy* being deployed in worldwide-social space [*l'espace social-mondial*] is gradually replacing those of historicity, historical time, historical determinations, and determinism. These latter concepts refer back to a surpassed past; they have a truth only within this past. In any case, in the name of the present, it is not worth either decrying the historical, or collapsing back into historicism—nor refusing memory, nor fetishizing its images, symbols, and icons. That which arises from time is at this moment undergoing a trial: the "loss of identity" of cultures, of peoples, groups, and even individuals. The references and frames of reference that are derived from history are collapsing. Whether or not established as systems, values are crumbling as they confront and conflict with one another. The most cultivated of people find themselves in the situation of peoples who have been dispossessed (alienated) through conquest and colonization. By inventing (producing) a morphology, whatever is not reinscribed in space shrivels into signs, dissolves into abstract narratives, and only avoids contentless formalism by inflating itself with myths and fantasies. When, like rivers to the sea, historical formations reach (worldwide) space, some spread out like a swampy delta, others imitate the turbulence of estuaries. Some gamble democratically on surviving through inertia, others gamble on military and political violence. There always comes a dramatic moment of skepticism, whether concerning capitalism or socialism, philosophy or religion. *Moment.* The word designates an *epoch* here.

This formidable trial and confrontation unfurl in a highly unequal manner among social formations, depending on their strength, their rootedness in nature, and their modalities of collision with the historical. None of these formations—"cultures," nations and nation–States, languages, oral traditions, and writings—nothing can escape having multiple confrontations in space with the others (other cultures, languages, nations). Not even philosophy and knowledge. Especially not "historical materialism" (the core of which is starting to be delinked from the classical rationalism, metaphysics, and finalism—the taken for granted sense of becoming, of history, etc.—that persists in Marx). What we call ideology, which always has several objectives, serves here as a disguise, a defense. The trial has already begun. The "time-space" relation evades the philosopher. It is produced in social practice.

Information technology and cybernetics, which is to say the quasi-instantaneous transmission of information and its almost punctual concentration into a place, transform knowledge while covering space. They introduce specific contradictions between knowledge as such and its utilization by power (strategies).

6—At the planetary scale, within the "framework" [*cadre*] (as it were) of the world market, political economy is being transformed. The world market is not a sovereign entity, mastered by imperialisms: it does not coincide with a single one of them. It is complex: solid and imposing from some angles, fragile and threatened from others. It includes the commodity and capital markets:

this doubling prohibits us from speaking about it in logical terms, from un-
critically applying the Marxian notion of a logic and a language of the commodity. It assumes and imposes a *division of labor* (a distribution of productive
labors and investments in space). We know that the *technical* division of labor
introduces *complementarities* (productive operations that rationally entail
one another), whereas the *social* division of labor introduces blind and, as we
say, "irrational" *inequalities and conflicts*. The relations of production do not
disappear in the framework of "worldness" [*mondialité*] any more than they
do within the framework of the "mode of production" considered as a totality. They remain the key, that which is essential in reality, in the *concrete*—
and thus, in interactions and exchanges. Through these interactions, the world
market outlines configurations that are inscribed on the terrestrial surface of
changing spaces. Hence the contradictions in space and of space, between
countries, peoples, classes. The critical analysis of the double division of labor
(technical and social) which was already undertaken by Marx on the level of
industrial enterprises, national markets and, in sketch form, worldness, must
today be resumed at the level of the (world) space of multinational firms, etc.

Old-style political economy is transformed into a political economy of
space. It has been transformed since several thinkers (including François Perroux and subsequently Samir Amin)[4] expounded on the already spatial concepts of the (growth) *pole, center,* and *periphery*. Everything in the economy
is "mobilized," spatialized, and made dialectical. The abstract models of growth
and harmonization are discredited, rendered obsolescent. The procedures of
planning and semi-planning (the empiricism of administrators, the pragmatism of politicians, balance sheets for inventory and finances) give way to
spatial planning. Spatial planning deals with *flows*: of energy, raw materials,
money, the labor force, various goods, mixtures of people and things, signs,
information and understanding, symbols, capital, etc. It endeavors to connect
and coordinate these multiple flows in space. In which space? In great geopolitical units (Europe, etc.) that are inscribed in the worldwide. The science of
political economy, including its now classic formalization in Marx (where it
was rigorously unified with his critique and self-critique), cannot avoid a
reassessment. What will remain of it? After reconstruction, will it bring about
unity between formalization and content, between scientific "positivism" and
critical negativity? Perhaps. Since Marx, new evidence has appeared on the
horizon; *social bodies* (including classes, institutions, etc.) occupy space and
make (produce) space, with occupied space and produced space not coinciding.

Social bodies and their relations act, "express" themselves and, as we say, "reflect" on themselves pretty adequately in space. Occupied and produced, the urban fabric invades the entirety of space. This space participates in the production of goods, things, and commodities; it consumes productively; but at the same time it is totally covered by exploitation and domination. Having completely ceased to be a "neutral," passive, and empty milieu, space becomes a social and political instrument. In whose service? To what end? Who uses it and why? This is the central question. The answer: it becomes a site [*lieu*] and a context for the *reproduction of the (social) relations of production*, and primarily for the (social) relations of capitalist production.

A new contradiction appears on the horizon: that between *flows* (the moving, the ephemeral) and *fixities* (established centers, decision-making positions, institutions, various "properties," etc.). Will this disjointed sum of realities allow itself to be grasped and understood? Will this understanding bear a familiar name, like political economy or sociology? Nothing is less certain. What is certain is that, in space that is thus created, distances are no longer confused with proximities, the production of space detaches the far order from the near order, that of "natural" neighborhoods, and the geo-political is distinguished from the geo-graphical.[5]

7—*The producers of space* emerge from an analysis that will define their current role as distinct (but not separable) from the role of the producers of things in space. There are numerous agents of the production of space. Some situate their interventions at the level of "macro-decisions," and others on that of "micro-decisions." These "agents" engage in interventions that are simultaneously connected and unconnected and that occur within a space that is both homogeneous and broken. Such "agents" are referred to as politicians, technocrats and planners, military and financial officials, local authorities, construction workers, "users" and "urban struggles," etc. The architect and the town planner contribute more straightforwardly to these producers of space than do painters and sculptors, etc. They are inserted into the process of production and reproduction and consequently into the spatial practice of the capitalist mode of production. To what extent can they break free from these constraints and from instrumental space? That depends on the *grassroots* democratic movement, that of local communities, unions (when they attend to the question), "users," construction workers—in short, on the network of social relations that more or less clearly and intensively targets the quality of space.

The spatial practice of the capitalist mode of production attempts to utilize *instrumental space* (space as a tool) and to institutionalize it, in order to introduce a coherence into exploitation and oppression, that is to say into the relations of production and class such as they are concretized "on the ground." Spatial practice cannot realize this objective except through a confluence of circumstances and opportunities, because it elicits new contradictions, the contradictions of space. Since the space that was once "neutral" (in appearance) is transformed into an instrument and an institution, a set of questions is formulated with reference to each space and each intervention in space: "Who? For whom? For what?" Do we thus return to the old philosophical question of the Subject? Yes and no. The questions and answers have changed.

The critical analysis of the production of space acquires a practical interest, implying the study and the understanding of the role of (private and public) construction as a decreasingly subsidiary branch of industry—the understanding of "responsible" institutions and the relations between "agents." The role of construction, of "real estate," as we call it, is no longer limited to an economic function; it goes as far as the elaboration of a space that removes from all (its users) the control of their everyday lives, redistributing the workforce according to the (changing) demands of neo-capitalist production, treating the labor force as a "reserve" of energy, a flow of objects.

To grasp these changes in the mode of production, here is a point of departure: the worldwide market, the conquest of planetary space by the market, the strategy of the capitalist mode of production, the (technical and social) division of labor on a planetary scale, and consequently, the current level of productive forces, their link to the sciences and information, the capacity for dealing with space and producing space on a worldwide level. Despite the fragmentation of the space for exchange—despite the disintegration of knowledge in the fragmentary sciences—and for all the diversity of words and concepts, this point of departure constitutes a unity from first to last.

From the occupation of space that has been attempted and to some extent achieved by the capitalist mode of production, there results a new type of theoretical and practical crisis that has only just begun. Violence is inherent to political space, not only as an expression of (political) will to power, but due to a permanent reign of terror separating that which seeks to be unified (from sexes to peoples) and fusing together, without analysis, that which is differentiated (for instance, the spatial inscription of history from historical time; or yet again, constructed, second nature—the city, the urban, designed space—from immediate nature). A formidable force of homogenization exerts itself on a worldwide scale, producing a space whose every part is interchangeable (quantified, without qualities).

This force is in no way mysterious or deceptive; the car is as much a part of it as is money and the worldwide market. There are forces and opposing tendencies that resist this force, albeit very unequally: more energetically in the so-called "socialist" countries (especially in China), and less forcefully but efficiently in so-called "underdeveloped" countries and regions. Resistance to these pressures is itself twofold; sometimes passive, stagnant, and therefore "reactionary," sometimes active, dynamic, creative (hence subversive). These tendencies toward *differences* generate conflicts with the brutal tendency toward quantified uniformity. The violence inherent to these forces that deny differences, which are thus reduced and shrunk, elicits another violence, that of "counter-cultures," that of *specificities* (as they are often called with an obscure, metaphorical, and often dangerously used word), and, consequently, that of other (still uncertain) procedures for the production of space. These oppositions, these contrasts, these conflicts, these contradictions can be observed in space and can only be conceived in relation to space.

The matter may be articulated in more classical terms. A long accumulation of quantitative data will engender (and already has engendered, through historical and contemporary conflicts) not only a *qualitative leap,* but a *leap into the qualitative.* What is classically termed "class struggle" today assumes a thousand forms, more complex than ever before. Urban demands and struggles are a part of this. The struggle implies qualitative demands concerning space (transportation, "habitat," everyday life). One of the principal contradictions of space is that it appears to be the milieu par excellence of quantification, that it is the most efficient instrument of quantification, while in reality and truth it conveys (practical) qualities, places, sites and situations, "topias," and the relations between these elements.

The fronts on which these (theoretical and practical) battles are fought out can no longer be delineated as they once were, with an abstract line separating the camp of the exploited class from the camp of the dominant class (holding power). The demarcations traverse all social formations, including those claiming to be *extrapolitical* (cultural, scientific, trade union, etc.), and those that claim to be *political* (parties and "movements"). The strategic objective of this struggle is the gathering together of separated elements. Joined to this is the operation of differentiating what had been fused together.

Differences borne of generalized confrontation are only discovered through this trial. Who separates? Who mixes the dominant thought and action in the capitalist mode of production? Why? On account of the extreme (material and intellectual) division of labor; on account of the parcelization of knowledge (under the sign of a fictitious unity, one with the veneer of encyclopedism or containing an outdated philosophy of the political State); on account of the functioning of a nondialectical intellect, which can only, and only knows how, to separate, to disperse, to disseminate that which it has caught in its machinery. The separation of quality and quantity, among others, and the attribution to space of a quantity (without qualities) originates in the outmoded philosophy that is withering away, de-dialecticized. To separation and scattering is opposed grouping, as the comprehension of differences and their realization is opposed to conflation and enforced unification. The struggle unfurls on multiple, violent, diverse, and shared fronts, against that which separates and that which conflates. The "Total" [*Total*] and the "Global" [*Global*], otherwise and better termed the worldwide [*mondial*] and the planetary [*planétaire*], are conceived by producing themselves in social practice (in the time of spatial practice, its conflicts and its confrontations).

In the absence of growth, would the zones and regions that are resisting quantitative totalization and systematization be consigned to nondevelopment? Certainly not: they *can* experience a true development, another growth.

8—One more point: "What is the relation of this theory of space to the actually existing revolutionary movement?"
Answer:
a) The practical application of this theory contributes to the dissolution of existing society; it intervenes at the heart of this society's prosperity in order to eat away at it and decompose it, for in its expansion, this society produces only spatial chaos. If it was able to resolve some of the contradictions that are derived from history, only unexpectedly will it be able to resolve the contradictions of space (of *its* space).

b) Existing political formations misrecognize questions about space. They extend history; and yet, their leaders know that space—its problematic—already supersedes or will supersede them. Now what is misrecognised [*méconnu*] today will be understood [*connu*] tomorrow, and thus will become the politics of tomorrow and the beyond of the political. The ensemble of populations (excluding people in power, who only understand obstacles to their strategies) is already living through the painful trial by space and by confrontation.

c) With regard to the treatment of space, the "model" of (Soviet) State socialism offers only a buttressed and worsened version of the capitalist "model"; accelerated in accordance with the model, planned growth accentuates the privileges of "implantations," those of industries and the decision-making centers; the other places remain passive (peripheral).[6] It seems that only the Chinese way entails the effort to secure the (active) participation of an entire people in a dual process: the creation of wealth and of social life— and the production, in space, of space as a whole.

d) It was once considered necessary and sufficient to define revolution with reference to a political change, or to collective (state) ownership of the means of production (of the units of production: industrial and—to a lesser degree—agricultural enterprises). This appeared to imply the rational organization of production and of society as a whole. Revolutionary thought has thus degenerated into an ideology of growth. Today, this definition is no longer adequate. The revolutionary process implies the end of all private property, and primarily of all private (or rather, privative) ownership of the soil. A society thus transformed presupposes the collective ownership and management of space. With regard to the orientation of a process that begins in this way, passing through this opening, it will tend to overcome the contradiction between the work [œuvre] and the product: between the repeated and reproducible product—its reproduction entailing that of social relations—and the work, the unique, which bears the mark of a "subject," of a moment that can never be restored. It will be a question of producing planetary space as the work of the human species, in the manner of what has been and is still called *art*. Terrestrial space is thus created as the social support for a transformed everyday life: containing multiple possibilities. This is what the great utopians Fourier, Marx, and Engels promised and, stimulated by imagination, understanding, and dreams, their thought could be realized. A concrete and limitless work, with space avoiding the temporal alternative between the finite and the infinite (between the beginning and the end).

9—This "point of view," these "perspectives" will appear equally as simplifications, abstractions, and utopias. In response to this objection: these propositions imply, on the contrary, the refusal of reductive methods. They entail a nonreductive unity. They appear as simplifying only to those who prefer chaos (that of spatial, social, and other phenomena) to putting these phenomena into a nonreductive perspective that renders intelligible. And which appeals to all forces: poetry and the imaginary, the body and knowledge. This perspective brings an *orientation*. Nothing more and nothing less: what might be called a *sense*, that is to say, an organ that perceives, a movement that forges its path, a direction toward a specific horizon. Nothing that resembles a "system." The old philosophical abstractions retain a meaning only in being concretized; they become concrete only in being transformed: the "total" into "the worldwide," the "system" into the "planetary," another way of confronting temporality with spatiality.

Long filled by the "being" of philosophers, then by time, history, and the State, the category of "totality" would remain empty without "the worldwide," which receives a double determination: the "planetary" and the "mode of production" into a unity that is rich with virtualities: the production of space.

A revolution wanting to change life and transform the world other than by understanding them and by fulfilling them would be both impossible and irrational (voluntaristic and nihilistic). It would not be "utopian" [*utopienne*] (understanding the possible and the impossible, gambling on the transformation of the currently impossible into possibility), but *utopistic* [*utopique*].

So-called communist parties at the worldwide scale have shown that they renounce not only economico-political transformation (for which Trotskyists and Maoists quite rightly reproach them), but also the transformation of life. They are thus resolutely (strategically) opposed to the qualitative demands that the qualitative brings to the horizon, and into the order of the century. The "users" in urban struggles are demanding certain "qualities of space," thereby producing the qualitative. And also wars (shelters, underground bunkers).

From what has just been said, it follows that the command to "change life" has an impact only in conjunction with a very high level of productive forces: after the long and difficult period of so-called growth. Prior to such a level, it is *utopistic*. It acquires another meaning only from the moment in which the quantitative tends (conflictually) to be changed into the qualitative; where growth without development appears absurd; where techniques and science permit the production of space; where automation paves the way for non-work. And yet, as an aspiration and a demand, whether it is anarchizing, individualist, or elitist, this injunction to "change life" serves as a symptom of the future. It announces a shifting of meaning, an inflection of time and space: a (total) revolution.

If only understanding could declare itself subversive but not nihilistic; necessary but not sufficient. Above all, if only it didn't give up on itself, under the pretext of negating the "real" in the name of Desire or "panic philosophy."[7]

Translation by Gerald Moore, Neil Brenner, and Stuart Elden

NOTES

1. Seminar given in Lima, Peru, at the Faculty of Architecture and Town Planning, December 2, 1972.

2. See also *Le droit à la Ville* (Paris: Anthropos, 1968); *La révolution urbaine* (Paris: Gallimard, 1970); *La pensée marxiste et la ville* (Tournai: Casterman [1972]); *Espace et politique* and *La production de l'espace* (Paris: Anthropos 1974), etc. On transduction, see *Le droit à la ville*, 121f. [English versions of these texts include "The Right to the City," in *Writings on Cities* (the reference to transduction is found on 151–52); *The Urban Revolution*; and *The Production of Space*. *La pensée marxiste et la ville* (Marxist Thought and the City) is not yet translated into English, nor is *Espace et politique* (Space and Politics), although some excerpts from the latter appear in *Writings on Cities.—Eds.*]

3. [Martin Heidegger, *What Is Philosophy?/Was ist das—die Philosophie?* English-German edition, trans. William Kluback and Jean T. Wilde (London: Vision Press, 1963). This text was a lecture given in France, for which Kostas Axelos (on whom see chaps. 12, 13, and 14) served as Heidegger's interpreter. *Aggiornamento* is an Italian term meaning updating, and connotes theological modernization.—*Eds.*]

4. [François Perroux (1903–87) was a French economist and regional development theorist who is generally credited with the development of the term "growth pole." Samir Amin (1931–) is a radical political economist; he was born in Cairo, educated in Paris, and is currently based in Dakar, Senegal. Amin is best known for his contributions to Marxist theories of underdevelopment, neoimperialism, and global inequality.—*Eds.*]

5. [The original numbering for this article jumps from point 6 to point 9. There seems to be no good reason for this, and there are no obvious missing numbers or text, so we have renumbered from this point on.—*Eds.*]

6. [The term "implantation" is occasionally used in industrial geography to refer to a planned settlement—whether for industrial production, housing, military, or governmental purposes. In the state socialist contexts to which Lefebvre is referring here, it refers to the large-scale factory centers and housing estates that were constructed as concentration points for accelerated industrial development. In referring to these installations, Lefebvre's point is to suggest that uneven spatial development has been intensified, not alleviated, under Soviet-style state socialism.—*Eds.*]

7. [The relation of the real to desire is one of the themes in Gilles Deleuze and Félix Guattari's book *Capitalisme et schizophrénie,* vol. 1, *L'anti-œdipe* (Paris: Éditions de Minuit, 1972; translated by Robert Hurley, Mark Seem, and Helen Lane as *Anti-Oedipus: Capitalism and Schizophrenia* [New York: Viking, 1977]). "Panic philosophy" is likely a reference to Fernando Arrabal's book *Le panique* (Paris: UGE, 1973).—*Eds.*]

10 Space and Mode of Production

These excerpts are taken from two chapters of Lefebvre's 1980 book *Une pensée devenue monde: Faut-il abandonner Marx?* [A Thought Become World: Must We Abandon Marx?]. This book is a study of the contemporary relevance and limitations of Marxist theory; these excerpts deepen and extend the preceding discussion of sociospatial theory, state theory, and globalization. The first selection focuses on the problem of spatial inequality—specifically, the relation between the city and the countryside. Lefebvre emphasizes the key role of state institutions in managing and exploiting these spatial oppositions. Lefebvre then proposes a threefold schema for understanding spatial relations: homogeneity, in which space is reduced to equivalency; fragmentation, in which social relations are divided and differentiated; and hierarchization, in which discrete spaces are distinguished and delineated from one another as part of a broader system of domination and exploitation. The latter aspect of sociospatiality includes the problematic of spatial inequality, as expressed, for instance, in processes of ghettoization and in the core/periphery opposition. It also enables Lefebvre to reintroduce his earlier notion of the right to the city, initially developed in the late 1960s but now broadened into the concept of a "right to space." The second selection below provides an overview of arguments concerning the relation between the economic mode of production and spatial relations. It elaborates a sweeping historical survey of this relationship, from the Greek city–state through feudalism to modern capitalism and the consolidation of the world market. The third selection explores the world system of states, with a specific emphasis on the restructuring of state spatial strategies in geohistorical context. Taken together, the latter two selections, in particular, provide useful, accessible summaries of key chapters in volume 3 of *De l'État*, in which these arguments are elaborated at greater length.—*Eds.*

SPACE

The schema under consideration must not only be drawn out from Marx—and especially from his analyses of labor—but we must also envisage its generalization. We shall see how and why. Let us first consider (social) space.

It is possible to study Marx's work in texts, and there are several ways of doing this, such as *by thematizing,* which is to say by gathering together the sparse texts concerning, for example, philosophy. This procedure has been kept at a distance here for several reasons, notably because of its trivialization due to the multiplicity of "Marxological" works. Moreover, in order to justify the attempt pursued here through texts, with the aim of situating, reinstating, and reconstituting Marx's approach, its implications and consequences, it would be necessary to wade through a mountain of texts (not just those of Marx and Engels, but those of "Marxists"). In any case, no thematic exposition could produce a chain of concepts like that of *Capital,* which we know proceeds from exchange value and social labor to the organic composition of capital and the (incomplete) theory of production via surplus value.

Even if he approaches Marx with a new synchronic, and not diachronic, way of reading,[1] the reader of Marx will not find a systematic exposition of social space. The theme appears here and there, but it is not treated in detail. Why? Because capitalism (enterprises, networks of communications, and exchange) set itself up in natural space, the geographical space of first nature. It has not yet substantially changed it, let alone integrated it through a process of modification. Space appears to Marx only as the sum of the sites of production, as the territory of various markets. The city does not yet pose big major problems, except for the problem of housing (dealt with by Engels). It lives in symbiosis with its surrounding environment, the countryside/nature, which is stressed by Marx. The relation between town and country appears above all as an instance of the division of labor. In Marx—and above all in Engels—there is, therefore, a tendency to neglect the large city, to imagine restricted communities established associatively around businesses that are themselves managed associatively. The utopia of Fourier's community? Marx admires it but neither adopts it nor rejects it. He leaves the trouble of collective decision and organization to the (post-revolutionary) men of the future. In his calendar of ends, he does not explicitly mark the end of the city. However, the units of production remain essential and central for him, and the hypergrowth [*gigantisme*] does not seem to scare him. The growth of productive forces implies it.

Is there any need here to repeat that it is only in the second half of the twentieth century that these massive interrogations of space, the city, hypergrowth and excess, and the organization of space, take shape? Why? Because capitalism integrated the historical city with agriculture, themselves long precapitalist.

The State has presided over this integration. Spaces that were once unoccupied—mountains, the sea—enter into exchange, become commodities, are occupied by the enormous new industries of leisure and culture. In the functioning of the economic and the political, in the reduction of the distance that separates these "instances" or "levels" (a reduction that implies the breakdown of the *social*), space plays a major role. It partakes in the recent conquest of the mode of production in a way that has yet to be determined; in fact, space plays a role at all levels: the relations of production and property, the organization of labor and productive forces, "superstructures" and representations (ideologies). It is certainly not, as scholastic "Marxism" claims, a simple and thus superficial result of the superstructure, of existing society. As much as the planning of space—through space—tends to replace the other modes of planning and intervention. Social and political space today is both real and operational, both a given and an instrument, a necessity and a virtuality. It is produced, a product, but also producer and reproducer (in the maintenance of relations of domination). To study it, we must call simultaneously on philosophy and philosophers (who have explored space and time), on the fragmented sciences (political economy, geography, etc.), and finally—especially—on practice.

Now this space produced by the current relations of production, reproduction, and domination, this space falls under the schema of "homogeneity–fragmentation–hierarchization."[2] The importance of its analysis is found simultaneously in the conception of this schema (which is virtual and not expressed as such in Marx and in general).[3] It is this analysis that, through a retroactive effect already hinted at on a number of occasions, has allowed us to draw out the schema in Marx, by bringing together—as already underlined—philosophy, science, and practice in a reciprocal critique.

1. Homogeneity

It is on the worldwide scale that the space born in the second half of the twentieth century is reproduced: airports, highways, vertical cities of concrete, horizontal cities of detached houses [*pavillons*].[4] The sameness need not be underlined, and only the details differ among the ugly buildings, functional edifices, and even monuments. We enter into a world of combinations whose every element is known and recognized. The resemblances border on (abstract, self-evident) identity and visible equivalence. Systems of equivalence take on a sensible existence and are inscribed in space. Futile effects of difference, understood scornfully as aesthetic (variations in color and form), do not interrupt the monotony. This repetitive consumption of things in space and of space filled with things gives rise to an indelible boredom. The curious coupling of malaise and satisfaction operates at full effect. Produced space contains, or rather envelops, all products, like the wrappings of indestructible plastic stuff that serve as packaging for so many things.

This type of second nature escapes every analogy with the creative force of first nature; it is its negative neuter. The creative force of primary nature still shows through in historical towns, whose diversity, much like that of ancient monuments and buildings and unspoiled landscapes, astonishes. The simulation of second nature that is nowadays possible reduces it to the homogeneous. Thus there grows a distance that becomes a chasm between the product (which is multiplied in homogeneity) and the work (which is rarefied in difference). Everywhere, the acquisition of snippets of information accentuates homogeneity, a reductive product that does not negate but informs us about things that are similar (but not identical, since information excludes the redundant but not similarity) to the ones you have before your eyes, by enlarging the minimal details that "differentiate" (the simulation of difference). This space, with its optico-geometrical sheen of apparent indifference, in political truth, this space makes itself visible. As it fills itself with signals and signs, it makes itself a spectacle, but this spectacle is monotonous. Revealing a boredom that risks both definition and the definitive, the homogeneous determines social existence in this society. A profound boredom that, within these strange and dominant couplings of "satisfaction and malaise," "abundance and rarity," only particular worries and preoccupations cause to vary.

Through organization and information, there is produced a kind of unification of world space, with strong points (the centers) and weaker and dominated bases (the peripheries). In these latter zones are perpetuated differences that, for better and for worse, resist but do not paralyze the process as a whole. The latter is translated through efficient apparatuses [*dispositifs*] of control and surveillance, linked to informational machines: satellites, radars, beacons, and grids. In this respect, space has a much stronger connection with the

State than territory once had with the nation. It is not only produced by the forces and relations of production and property; it is also a political product, a product of administrative and repressive controls, a product of relations of domination and strategies decided at the summit of the State. And this not only at the scale of every State, but also at the international and worldwide scale, the scale of the planetary state system. Hence the harmony and cooperation that is manifested in inspection and surveillance procedures.

2. Fragmentation

Space is broken down into separate spaces, occupied by functions that are exercised within these distinct spaces: labor, housing, leisure, transit and transportation, production, consumption. If we consider what is established outside the historical towns and their varyingly preserved centers, we see a *specter* in the double sense of the term; that which was given as a unity, like the bright light of the sun, projects itself over the terrain and in so doing separates out into component parts; and we have before us a phantom—that of the urban. This metaphor, already used elsewhere,[5] is, of course, not found in Marx, who did not acknowledge such phenomena as the explosion of big cities and the separation of centers and peripheries, though Engels may have anticipated them. However, the descriptions and analyses of fragmentation are only too applicable to this crumbling of urban space. The separation of elements and components is at once both *fictive,* because we cannot completely separate out these functions and "amenities" [*équipements*] (though each localized function is represented and even effectuated in itself and through itself, as philosophers would say), and in another sense *real* (because all fragments of space and their functions, divided up in the manner of tasks within a business, thus acquire and retain an autonomy). Space—like labor—becomes parcelized: the juxtaposition of parcels fixed to a partial activity whose whole, and the process of inhabiting it, escapes its participants. Strictly quantified, measured in square meters as well as money, this compartmentalized space is delivered over precisely to exchange (buying and selling), often in very small parcels. Once sacred and even inalienable as a patrimonial and collective good, space becomes a commodity like any other, with no particular privilege other than being subjected to formalities that are meant to protect property (notary deeds, mortgage agreements). It is not only the atomization of the social into unconnected individuals, into hostile and disdainful individualities, but the quasi-limitless division of that which "contains" society, a container that is not indifferent to the content that is contained, but that is on the contrary the *support of social relations,* linked to their mode of exis- tence, a mode that is singular, since it is simultaneously abstract-concrete, mental-social, fictive-real (none of which places this mode of existence under the sign of the general and crude entities that escape analysis: the unconscious, the imaginary, culture, etc.). In social space, the simultaneously "material" and "immaterial" support of social relations, fragmentation is an instrument of political power; it divides and separates in order to rule. The rupture of the form and formers of society (of the urban), the spectral separation of ele- ments, matters little to this power, even though the results, misfortunes, and actions of discontent, can disrupt it and compel "reforms."

3. Hierarchization

Spaces broken down in the homogeneous are placed in a hierarchy: noble and crude spaces; residential spaces; the functional spaces of so-called "ameni- ties," themselves classed according to their importance; various ghettos termed "public housing projects" [*ensembles*] by a obscurantist bureaucracy, luxury housing projects, housing projects for immigrants and natives, those for the middle classes, spaces populated by detached houses [*pavillons*] of greater or lesser quality, etc. In short, segregation: the specter of the urban. Hierarchi- zation takes general and specific forms: the distinction between the strong points of space and the *centers*—of power, wealth, material and spiritual ex- change, leisure, and information, which are likewise multiplied and hierar- chized—and the *peripheries,* which are also hierarchized, at varying degrees of distance from some principal or secondary center, to the point of some- times appearing deserted, abandoned by gods and men.

   The opposition of center and periphery goes a long way, since it stretches from the great capitals and world cities to the most miserable, so-called "undeveloped" regions and countries. It includes a no less pertinent and hier- archizing opposition between activity and passivity. The domination of centers over dominated spaces guarantees the homogeneous character of space. It ex- ercises its control at all (organizational, administrative, juridical, fiscal, police, etc.) points of view over peripheries that are both dominated and broken apart. Unless unexpected, the informational accentuates this domination. The centers also have machines and processors at their disposal. The centers link up the peripheries, coordinate them, submit them to the global strategy of the State. Hicrarchization is linked to stratification in that, in being realized only on the hierarchical scale that goes from places to the general and spatial ordinance of society, these changes do not compromise the totality.

A curious thing: the discovery and analysis of this social and mental spatial structure have accompanied or followed its production very closely. It is in fact over the 1960–70 period that the technocracy in power produced this space, in a way that institutional (university) knowledge has misrecognized, though some bearers of this knowledge (geographers, economists, sociologists) collaborated in its production, and though in another "unconscious" sense, the great revolt of May 1968 rose up against this reworking of society in France, by believing itself to be fighting against something else and for something else. The privileged example, the production of space, enables us *simultaneously* to grasp the analyses of Marx better, despite their earlier lineage, to complete some of his concepts by transforming them, and finally to generalize the schema drawn out in this way.

SPACE AND MODE OF PRODUCTION

Undertaken in accordance with the approach of Marx, continually combining critique with self-critique, dialectical research relentlessly develops a concept that dogmatism treats statically as received knowledge: *the mode of production.* Dialectical research refines and enriches this concept. Among "Marxists" and even in Marx, there used to be a void between the *relations of production* and the *mode of production.* Many bring them together to the point of conflating them. Capitalism as a mode of production was already there from the moment that its characteristic relations of production—the sale of labor power and the wage system—come into being. Now, according to Marx himself, these relations initially existed sporadically in medieval towns and in armies (day laborers, paid at the time of their work, without means of production and employed for dirty work—earthworks, for example).

At times, "Marxists" used to insist on the mode of production as a totality, but they made an audacious leap from relations (which is to say, from the "base") to superstructures, always considered with some disdain, as mere consequences (instead of considering them in social practice as that which enables collective life to live, and thus to be perpetuated: institutions, "values," activities like medicine, teaching, art, etc.). A naïve representation of dictatorship (of the ruling class) has paralyzed the understanding of social practice. Only Gramsci, albeit in a stumbling and incomplete manner, has understood how the ruling class gradually marked, modeled, and built a society, the economic being necessary but insufficient. The conquest and production of a society presupposes that one takes possession of the existing institutions (the University, the judiciary, taxation), and that one creates other institutions (thus schools and prefectural administration in France, for example).

The study of social space and its organization (and likewise the study of social time and its organization, which is linked to that of space) has enabled the demonstration that there exist not only abstract mediations, like law, but also concrete and practical mediations, such as space, between the relations of production and the mode of production (base and superstructure). Space has a history that is linked to that of modes of production, in Marx's sense, though Marx may only have glimpsed this link.

A mode of production is only affirmed as such and only merits this name if it has given rise to a space (and a social time). This genesis depends on the relations of production, but also on the constitution and political power. So-called "primitive" societies, which have been defined at times by the absence of writing, at others by the absence of a State (Pierre Clastres),[6] move within primary nature, a space that is empty yet full of dangers. The so-called slave era gives birth to the City–State, Athens or Rome, the imperial centers of a maritime or continental space organized by its force. The Asiatic mode of production gives rise to vast organized spaces, on the one hand in relation to water (embankments and irrigation systems, thus large projects coordinated by the State) and, on the other hand in relation to an administrative and military power ruling over peasant communities that are subjugated to a central town. All this is found, suggested, and often developed in Marx. Feudalism is founded on a strong organization of agrarian space, at least in the territorial manors [*seigneuries*] of Europe. With regard to the medieval town, which partakes in the mode of production through artisanry and modest trading, it was the place, the germ, of the implosion of feudalism, but on account of complications that were unforeseeable at the outset: the constitution of a royal power that played on the class struggle between the bourgeois (inhabitants of the towns) and the lay and ecclesiastical feudal barons. In any case, as a society or entity, feudalism is decomposed by the analysis of modern historians. It emerges in an extreme diversity, as a hodgepodge [*bigarrure*] of components and relations, varying according to the country and even the place. Some constants (the existence of peasants, sometimes free but more often indentured) scarcely justify the formulation of a medieval or feudal mode of production.

To tell the truth, giving the words a precise and full meaning, capitalism reveals itself as the "mode of production" par excellence. And yet it must be understood in its historical context, which is in no way straightforward. The commercial bourgeoisie of the early years, thriving at the dawn of what we have come to call the modern age, ruling over towns from Italy to Flanders and the North Sea, has nothing in common with the manufacturing, and later the industrial, bourgeoisie. The mode of production is transformed but consolidated. It integrates itself with the historical town over a very long period of time, which is still ongoing. It incorporates spaces that once seemed unproductive. It invents new sectors: not only new techniques and industries, but entire domains: the culture industry (which has become a huge industry, though the "Marxists" of the Frankfurt School timidly only saw in it an elite artisanry and a small industry), and also the enormous leisure industry, with its hotel chains and air transport on a world scale.

Capitalism, which is to say the mode of production, becomes worldwide [se mondialise], while the previous modes of production designated by Marx remain local and diversified. With its prodigious complexity—its convergence of and interference with multiple flows—the world market bears down heavily on so-called socialist countries, which thus lose out on what they demand: Marx and his definition of socialism.

In short, the mode of production has not only given rise to local and national spaces, molding the space of nature through networks and productions of exchange and communication. It in fact gives rise to a worldwide space, a political space superimposed on the characteristics of the economy, encompassing them, integrating them. This concretizes the terms of superstructure and ideology employed by "Marxists" in ways that differ from their common usage. Social and political space on a world scale reproduces and accentuates the local and national links to the productive forces, to advanced technologies (notably information technologies), to property relations (notably those of States and their territories), to forms of organization (notably transnational firms), to ideologies (notably the representations of airspace, information, etc.). It encompasses the totality that separates current distinctions into "instances" (the economic, the social, the political). It constitutes on a planetary scale this still unrealized totality, which is still at stake through a confrontation between colossal forces, which were already spelled out precisely in and through space.

The capitalist mode of production realizes itself. It constitutes itself as a totality that circumscribes, destroys, and absorbs obstacles (the countries that escape or seek to escape it). Those who have seen it "in reality" and "in total" since its beginnings, or since competitive capitalism or monopolistic, national-scale archeo-capitalism, have grasped it erroneously through the difficult concept of *totality*. They have misrecognized worldness [*mondialité*]. Now, the thought of Marx understood in all its magnitude, with the concept of the *total* that it inherits from philosophy but does not apply according to the rules of philosophers, this thought opens toward the worldwide, if only through the (incomplete) analysis of the world market. But for it to attain worldness, it should be considered neither as a dogma nor as a system, but adjoined with other concepts, like that of space.

Through a retroactive effect that we have now come to understand, the critical analysis of current space discloses not only that which happens today; this effect unveils certain misunderstood aspects of historical time; but also and above all, following a term that has already been used, it serves to *highlight* a schema that is itself misunderstood, restricted in Marx to the analysis of labor under pressure from the relations of production: "Homogeneity–fragmentation–hierarchization." In the same moment, it reveals the role of both labor and space in the realization of the mode of production; as we shall observe, it ultimately illustrates the schema's generality.

Before generalizing this schema, let us recall that, on the worldwide scale, that of space reworked or rather produced by the mode of production (which also implies a new kind of State), a contradiction resurfaces between private ownership—meaning, here, that of space—and the productive forces—meaning, here, those of the techniques applied to space and capable of changing it on a grand scale.

[...]

THE STATE AND THE WORLDWIDE SYSTEM OF STATES

To speak as a philosopher, or like Marx himself in some of his writings: due to its role as both supreme "subject" and supreme "object," and yet also due to its role as something other than "subject" and "object," the State does not fall under the schema. It produces it. It acts in accordance with the schema: it homogenizes, it fragments and hierarchizes. It superimposes itself in this way for other reasons and causes that proceed in this way: the reign of exchange value, the market of knowledge, etc. A paradox: the State operates in the same way on itself. It homogenizes itself, but it fragments itself and, as it fragments itself, hierarchizes itself from bottom to top, if one dares to put it this way.[7]

What discloses itself here is not the entire interrogation and its problematic, but the node, the center. And it is here and now that the schema, which does not encapsulate the whole of Marx's thought, but which is an important aspect or moment thereof, will appear in its *worldness*. A paradox that is neither the first nor the last, but one of the most surprising: this thought of Marx is realized, but in that which it has fought, in that which it defined in order to prevent it from coming into existence. In such a way that, in realizing itself, it undermines and perhaps even contradicts itself. Which is what it expected of the proletariat!

An ensemble, and not a *sum* of institutions, the State cannot be reduced to any one of them (neither the system of taxation, the army, or the judiciary, for example). However, each one refers back to some other, for example, the university to culture, and the judiciary to various (civil, criminal) codes, in such a way that the State seems ungraspable, as if it only existed through the Parliament, the Presidency, the Council of Ministers, etc., which are, however, only aspects and moments of it. The fact that, once we seek to define it, each institution refers back to something else, does not mean that these institutions have no autonomous existence. On the contrary. Each administration fights to persevere in being, to affirm and perfect itself, to gain more reality.

Even if it is difficult to grasp the existence and functioning of the modern State in general and each State in particular, even if reflection on politics only grasps its manifestations,[8] and even if classical concepts (sovereignty, legitimacy) take us no further in their analysis, it is difficult to deny that the State fits perfectly into the general schema. Homogeneity? It is incarnated, as it were, in the world system of States (the so-called United Nations). It is a well-known fact that homogeneity is also incarnated in a bureaucracy that is everywhere endowed with similar features. Everywhere, the broadly compact and coherent "reality" of technocrats dominates a mass of bureaucrats who fill the capitals and major cities (the centers of decision making).

Whether quantitative (number, wealth) or qualitative (social origin, competence, skill, manipulation, or brutality), the slight differences between State bureaucracies are not an adequate basis for defining the differences between States. This is a type of State that has instituted itself and quickly become worldwide [*mondialisé*]. It is not a question here of describing and analyzing this State and its modalities of intervention into the economic and social.

What matters, here, is to underline the homogeneity of the system of contemporary States. This homogeneity does not exclude fragmentation. The existence of over 150 States in the UN already implies this fragmentation—with classic rationality that, like Hegel, believed in the rational nature of the State, permitting the hope of the constitution of a unitary world State managing the planet. An abstract utopia! The state becomes worldwide as it fragments itself [*L'État se mondialise en se fragmentant*]. In its own, each State is undergoing an analogous process. The fragments of bureaucracy have common traits, but bureaucracy divides into . . . offices [*bureaux*]! Partial and often rival centers of decision making are established: (several) police forces, armies (insatiable for loans), electoral organizations, judiciaries, systems of taxation, etc. These partial bureaucracies quarrel with one another over status and especially over money. Each in turn takes the glory and the subsidies, but the system of taxation (finances) remains enduringly predominant. It holds the resources—in other words, the massive extraction of national revenue (overproduction or global surplus value) taken by the State.

There is thus a double fragmentation: internal to each State, and external, which is to say the worldwide system. The latter includes the juridical equality of States; in discussions, each State may make itself heard and vote. From the small and weak States without resources (the fourth world) to the two superpowers, the hierarchy is no less strict. The schema can be found both in the works and operations of the State and in the State as a work [*œuvre*], as well as in the state-political ensemble [*ensemble étatico-politique*] that nowadays covers the planet.

If we recall that Marx and Engels, and Lenin after them, foresaw the withering away of the State, we can measure the distance between practice and theory. What a failure of thought and the Revolution, in Marx's sense! And yet, what a victory of this thought up to and including its defeat, since it is *the schema of the worst*, implicit in this thought, that is realized, and every day recalls all those who contemplate the immensity of the disaster, the bloody results of this disaster.

Translation by Gerald Moore, Neil Brenner, and Stuart Elden

NOTES

1. [Lefebvre is apparently referring critically to the reading of Marx developed by Louis Althusser and his colleagues in the 1970s. This was partially translated by Ben Brewster as Althusser and Balibar, *Reading Capital.*—Eds.]

2. [See also the discussion of these terms in chap. 11.—*Eds.*]

3. See *La production de l'espace* (Paris: Anthropos, 1974). [Translated by Donald Nicolson-Smith as *The Production of Space.—Eds.*]

4. [On the notion of a *pavillon* see chap. 7 n.8.—*Eds.*]

5. [Lefebvre is probably referring to his use of this idea in *La droit à la ville,* 109; translated by Eleonore Kofman and Elizabeth Lebas as "The Right to the City," in *Writings on Cities,* 142.—*Eds.*]

6. [Pierre Clastres (1934–77) was a French political anthropologist whose works *La société contre l'État: Recherches d'anthropologie politique* (Paris: Éditions de Minuit, 1974; translated by Robert Hurley and Abe Stein as *Society against the State: Essays in Political Anthropology* [New York: Zone Books, 1989]) and *Archéologie du violence: La guerre dans les sociétés primitives* (Paris: Payot, 1977; translated by Jeanine Herman as *Archeology of Violence* [New York: Semiotext(e), 1994]) offer a Nietzsche-inspired anarchistic analysis of tribal societies.—*Eds.*]

7. [The French is as complicated as the English: "Il s'homogénéise mais il se fragmente et, se fragmentant, se hierarchies des pieds à la tête, si l'on ose dire." The use of reflexive verbs continues throughout this section.—*Eds.*]

8. See in particular the third volume of Lefebvre, *De l'État.*

11 Space and the State

In this key chapter from volume 4 of *De l'État*, Lefebvre presents some of his
most foundational statements on the politico-theoretical questions that concerned him in the 1970s. Lefebvre provides a comprehensive analysis of the
state's relation to space, both in terms of the material spaces of the national
territory and the country/city relation, and also in terms of the state's own
inherent spatiality as a territorial-institutional form. He also explores diverse
strategies through which states attempt to mold and reshape the spaces within
and beyond their territorial jurisdictions. States, Lefebvre suggests, attempt at
once to homogenize, to hierarchize, and to fragment social spaces. Lefebvre
analyzes the resultant political economy of space in some detail. First, he
provides an explicitly spatialized account of the development of modern
capitalism as it follows from earlier forms of spatial organization (analogic,
cosmological, symbolic, and perspectival). Second, he develops an analysis
of the state mode of production as an institutional and territorial basis for
managing the process of capital accumulation, its contradictions and its
crisis tendencies. One of the lynchpins of the chapter is Lefebvre's detailed
analysis of the diverse spatial strategies (including material interventions,
institutional innovations, and new forms of scientific knowledge) through which
states attempt to manage the intensely volatile social relations of capitalism at
once on worldwide, national, and local scales. For Lefebvre, the homogenized,
hierarchized, and fragmented spaces of capitalist modernity are produced not
only through capitalist strategies (as explored in many chapters of *The Production
of Space*), but just as crucially, as he now stresses, through the variegated
regulatory strategies of the state mode of production. Finally, he considers the
challenge of creating a qualitatively different, socialist form of sociospatial
organization based upon what he now terms "the right to space" (a phrase
derived from his earlier book, *The Right to the City* [1968]). Here, Lefebvre

broadens the notion of *autogestion,* suggesting that it has to be applied both
at the level of the unit of production—the firm or enterprise—and at various
territorial levels, including local communities, towns, or regions. This chapter
thus provides a more explicitly state-theoretical route into some of the key
issues Lefebvre had addressed a decade earlier in "Theoretical Problems of
Autogestion" (see chapter 5).—*Eds.*

During the course of its development, the State binds itself to space through
a complex and changing relation that has passed through certain critical points.
Born in and with a space, the state may also perish with it. The moments of
this relation can be described as follows:

a) The production of a space, *the national territory,* a physical space, mapped,
   modified, transformed by the networks, circuits and flows that are
   established within it—roads, canals, railroads, commercial and financial circuits, motorways and air routes, etc. Thus this space is a material—natural—space in which the actions of human generations, of
   classes, and of political forces have left their mark, as producers of durable objects and realities (rather than only of isolated things and products, of tools, and of goods destined for consumption). During the course
   of this process, the city and the country develop a new relationship in
   and through the mediation of a third term—the State that has the city
   as its center. Although the city and the country can no longer be separated, this does not mean that they have somehow been harmoniously
   superseded. They each survive as places assigned to the division of labor
   within a territory. Morphologically, this relationship (in the modern
   State) results in a shapeless mixture, in chaos, despite the administrative order and spatial logistics of the State.

b) The production of a *social space* as such, an (artificial) edifice of hierarchically ordered institutions, of laws and conventions upheld by "values" that are communicated through the national language. This social
   architecture, this political monumentality, is the State itself, a pyramid
   that carries at its apex the political leader—a concrete abstraction, full
   of symbols, the source of an intense circulation of information and messages, "spiritual" exchanges, representations, ideology, knowledge bound
   up with power.

"No institution without a space. . . ."[1] The family, the school, the workplace, the church, and so on—each possesses an "appropriate" space. Appropriate for what? For a use specified within the social division of labor and supporting political domination. In these spaces, a system of "adapted" expectations and responses—rarely articulated as such because they seem obvious—acquire a quasi-natural self-evidence in everyday life and common sense.

Thus, each State *has* its space; the latter belongs first to nature, which the State opposes historically and politically through its entire powerful mass. Moreover, each State *is* a social space, symbolized by the pyramid and the circle of circles (Hegel). In this social space, there is a minimum of *consensus:* just as a dog is commonly labeled a "dog," every French person knows what he's talking about when he refers to the town hall, the post office, the police station, the prefecture, the *département*, a member of the National Assembly, the grocery store, the bus and the train, train stations, and bistros.

c) In this latter sense, comprising a social (but not immediately political) consensus, the State occupies a *mental space* that includes the representations of the State that people construct—confused or clear, directly lived or conceptually elaborated. This mental space must not be confused with physical or social space; nor can it be fully separated from the latter. For it is here that we may discern the space of representations and the representation of space.

As the product, the child, of a space, the so-called national territory, the State turns back toward its own historical conditions and antecedents, and transforms them. Subsequently, the State engenders social relations in space; it reaches still further as it unfurls; it produces a support, its own space, which is itself complex. This space regulates and organizes a disintegrating national space at the heart of a consolidating worldwide space [*l'espace mondial*]. The space produced by the State must be termed *political* due to its specific features and goals. The State provides the *relations* (that is, the social relations of production) with a calibrated spatial *support;* it clashes with the preexistent economic space that it encounters—spontaneous poles of growth, historic towns, commercialized fragments of space that are sold in "lots." It tends to renew not only the social relations inherent in industrial production, but also the relations of domination inherent in the hierarchy of groups and places. In the chaos of relations among individuals, groups, class factions, and classes, the State tends to impose a rationality, its own, that has space as its privileged instrument. The economy is thus recast in spatial terms—flows (of energy, raw materials, labor power, finished goods, trade patterns, etc.) and stocks (of gold and capital, investments, machines, technologies, stable clusters of various jobs, etc.). The State tends to control flows and stocks by ensuring their coordination. In the course of a threefold process (*growth,* i.e., expansion of the productive forces; *urbanization,* or the formation of massive units of production and consumption; and *spatialization*), a qualitative leap occurs: the emergence of the state mode of production [*mode de production étatique*]— SMP. The articulation between the SMP and space is thus crucial. It differs from that between previous modes of production (including capitalism) and their manner of occupying natural space (including modifying it through social practice). Something new appears in civil society and in political society, in production and in state institutions. This must be given a name and conceptualized. We suggest that this rationalization and socialization of society has assumed a specific form, which can be termed politicization or statism.

It is difficult to explicate and prove the above series of arguments. To start with, although we have elaborated them in other works,[2] the reader cannot simply be referred to these texts, nor will it do for us merely to allude to them. We must thus "explicate" these arguments, summarizing their components and claims. Indeed, we must even complete them and update them. For new inventions and discoveries are emerging every day in this domain, which lies at the very crossroads of the political, the social, and the economic. Thus the works cited above have hardly exhausted the topic of the State.

But this is not the only problem: there is also the burden of the recent past. So-called "Marxist" thought, which purports to base itself on Marx, has long neglected precisely what is today most directly in the spotlight—the city and the urban, space, the State itself. Hence, due to a still-underdeveloped vocabulary, we meet further difficulties in constructing and articulating concepts. Knowledge of (social) space is now being established as a science, even though this is still in an early stage. This knowledge appears no less complex than the sciences of abstract space (geometry, topology, etc.) and physical space (from physics to cosmology). For example, the science of (social) space must include a *history of space.* Similarly, many volumes would be needed for a simple analytical study of *monumentality* and the relationship between the monument and the building. Oppression and domination, and thus power—but also splendor and meaning—are inherent in the very word "monument." This is another doubtless inexhaustible trilogy . . . [. . .]

An analysis of western countries reveals, first, the demands of capitalism and neo-capitalism, of developers and investment banks. It reveals, second, that state intervention does not just occur episodically or at specific points but incessantly, by means of diverse organizations and institutions devoted to the management and production of space. This state space [*espace étatique*]— which we analyze below—lacks the same chaotic features as the space generated by "private" interests. On the contrary, the aim is to make it appear homogenous, the *same* throughout, organized according to a rationality of the identical and the repetitive that allows the State to introduce its presence, control, and surveillance in the most isolated corners (which thus cease to be "corners"). The relation between "private" interests and the activities of "public" powers sometimes involves a collusion, sometimes a collision. This creates the paradox of a space that is both homogeneous and broken. This paradox will be self-evident, if hard to express, to all those who pay any attention to their surroundings.

In the third place, "*users*" *movements* (their protests and struggles) have become a worldwide [*mondial*] phenomenon—as have protests related to work and the workplace, albeit in a different manner.

"Users" movements in France cannot be compared to those in Japan, Spain, Italy, or even the USA. In these countries, users and even consumers seem more conscious of their interests and their goal—namely, to appropriate, for the first time, a space whose use was neglected by those who produced it. How can we explain this weakness in France? It is undoubtedly due to the State, which represents both a constraint and a means of appeal, a form of pressure and, it seems, a form of arbitration. Not only is the State's impact stronger in France than elsewhere; it is also reinforced by the Jacobin currents of the Left with their centralizing agenda. This agenda contributes to the weakening of movements that only a certain leftist [*gauchiste*] faction is willing to support regardless of other, hidden political motives. Japan is probably the country where these movements have become most powerful and have voiced the most ambitious objectives. In contemporary Spain [1977] more than four thousand "resident" committees [*comités de "vecinos"*] are undertaking efforts questioning the organization of society at the same time as that of cities and space.[3]

These movements are resurrecting the concept of "*use*" without reducing it merely to the consumption of space. They emphasize the relations between people (individuals, groups, classes) and space with its different levels: the neighborhood and the immediate, the urban and its mediations, the region and the nation, and, finally, the worldwide [*mondial*]. These movements are experimenting with modes of action at diverse scales, always in the light of the participants' experience and knowledge. Their current development suggests a possible convergence between struggles regarding work (the workplace) and those concerning all of space, that its to say, everyday life [. . .]

Is not the secret of the State, hidden because it is so obvious, to be found in space? The State and territory interact in such a way that they can be said to be mutually constitutive. This explains the deceptive activities and image of state officials [*hommes de l'État*].[4] They seem to administer, to manage, and to organize a natural space. In practice, however, they *substitute* another space for it, one that is first economic and social, and then political. They believe they are obeying something in their heads—a representation (of the country, etc.). In fact, they are establishing an order—their own.

To illuminate the junction between the State and space, it is necessary that we stop misrecognizing the spatial, and, correspondingly, that we come to recognize the importance of a theory of (social) space. From this perspective, "users" movements throughout the world are allied with a science of space that can no longer be seen as external to practice.

The understanding of social space is the theoretical aspect of a social process that has, as its practical aspect, the "users" movement. They are the inextricable aspects of the same reality and the same potentialities. This corresponds, to a certain extent, to the situation in which Marx found himself vis-à-vis the workers' movement and its protests over work (and the workplace). In that epoch, the "vulgar" economists (as Marx called them) were preoccupied with products, indexing, and comparing objects, estimating their respective costs. In short, they busied themselves with *things*. Marx inverts this approach. Instead of considering *products*, he examines *production*, that is, the labor process and the relations of production as well as the mode of production. In doing so, he founds a theory. Likewise, today many people are describing spaces, writing discourses about space. So our task is to invert this approach by founding a theory of the production of space. The State becomes more and more clearly the agent, even the guiding hand, of this production.

Does the understanding of space constitute a science? Yes and no. Yes, because it contains concepts and moreover a theoretical series of concepts. No, in the sense that science works in general terms and positions itself within an "objectivity" that abstracts from the "lived," that is, from the body and the "subject" that dwells, and resides in it.

The understanding of space cannot reduce the lived to the conceived, nor the body to a geometric or optical abstraction. On the contrary: this understanding must begin with the lived and the body, that is, from a space occupied by an organic, living, and thinking being. This being has (is) its space, circumscribed in its immediate surroundings, but threatened or favored by that which is distant. Within the reach of the body, that is, of the hands, it is what is useful or harmful to it; beyond this proximity begins a social space that stretches out without well-defined limits into physical and cosmic space. Three indistinct spheres and zones: the mental, the social, the cosmic—the lived body, the close, the distant.

This said, there is a history of space. The *lived* gives rise to *spaces of representations,* imagined, beginning with the body and symbolized by it. The conceived, the distant, gives rise to *representations of space,* established from objective, practical, and scientific elements. Think of medieval space: on one hand, the space of magico-religious representation, with hell below, God in heaven above, and the terrestrial world between the two. But this did not prevent *representations of space:* the construction of the first maps, the knowledge of navigators, merchants, and pirates; the Mediterranean as the center of the world, etc.

The history of space would show how spaces of representation and representations of space diverge and come together, with practice "really" changing the nature of space and the space of nature [*éspace-nature*].

To decipher space, we can propose various tables or schemas and try them out on existing space. This space is characterized by the often-conflictual coexistence of works and products from different periods. Diachronies, interruptions, and imbalances between ancient ruins and the products of modern technology generate tensions that animate space but make it difficult to decipher.

We can analyze the urban (the city) as a *subject* (conscience and consciousness, degrees of consciousness, the activities of groups); as an *object* (the location and the site, flows); as a work (monuments and institutions). We can trace monumentality historically in relation to functional construction (warehouses, office blocks, etc.), demonstrating the contemporary possibility [*événtualité*] of overcoming this classical opposition.

We can also compare space to a language and study its dimensions: the *paradigmatic* (relevant oppositions: inside/outside, above/below, verticality/ horizontality, etc.)—the *syntagmatic* (sequences and linkages: roads, avenues and boulevards, routes, etc.)—the *symbolic* (the meaning of monuments, special places, etc.).

With regard to global space, two kinds of theoretical propositions allow insight into its relation to the state. The first has a historical and genetic character: in an approximate manner, *it puts space into relation with modes of production*. The second, more substantiated and better defined in terms of the synchronic, refers to the concept of hierarchically stratified morphology. It is not clear, from a distance, whether these two propositions are mutually exclusive. The genetic (history) of space can and should be opened onto a *spatio-analysis*, leading in turn to a *rhythmanalysis* (the relation of space to time, with its cycles and rhythms, in the nation, society, and reflective consciousness). This last development bypasses the State and goes beyond it. It cannot therefore be considered here.

Analogic space: the primitive community was more complex than Marx perceived it, with combinations of social forms, priests and sorcerers, warlords, lineages, bloodlines, and overlapping territorialities. We can, in this grouping, characterize the occupation of space—space occupied by societies—as *analogic* space. Precise and convincing examples of analogic spaces are found in the Dogon villages of Africa, following the work of M. Griaule and G. Dieterlen, in their imagining of the human body.[5] The village and its organization is supposed to represent, or rather reproduce, a divine body, itself a projection of the human body. The head, limbs, male and female genital organs, and feet are represented by the grouping of huts: command huts, huts for socializing between men and women, huts for storing work tools, and so on. Space that is appropriated by analogy with the body is a projection of the latter onto or into space.

Cosmological space: the ancient mode of production (city, slaves) is linked to a cosmological space. Monumental objects are grouped in such a way as to suggest an image of the cosmos. The town is an "*imago mundi*" (an image or map of the world). Often a particular monument is intended to represent the most characteristic space: thus the Pantheon, designed to welcome all gods—even the unknown god—by representing the firmament, cosmic space.

The town includes, in the ancient or Asiatic mode of production, a place marked by a monument, an obelisk, or a stone, considered as the navel, the *omphalos,* the center of the world, around which is constructed a representation of dominated space.

Symbolic space: the medieval town is endowed with another form of space, symbolic space. The space of these towns, cathedral towns, is filled with religious symbols. We can thus understand the movement from the cosmological space of Roman churches to the symbolic space of Gothic cathedrals. These latter symbolize the emergence of the city above the earth and the momentum of a whole society toward a clarity which is, at this time, conceived as that of *Logos,* i.e., the Word, Christ. In cryptic space, truth remains hidden in the tombs. Space is transformed during the Gothic period into a space of decryption, an ascent toward the light. This is also the historical moment of the great class struggle: the urban bourgeoisie against the landed gentry. A double-sided symbolism: religious and political.

Perspectival space: although it is not part of the classification of modes of production, perspectival space is worth dwelling on because it is embedded in our custom, our language, though at the dawn of modern times, there is a crisis of all points of reference. It is an error to continue to think in terms of perspectival space, because since 1910 the painting of Kandinsky, Klee, and analytic cubism has shown us that perspectival space has been ruptured. The line of the horizon disappears in these painters like the meeting of parallel lines at infinity.

Perspectival space was born in the Renaissance, in Tuscany, when towns took on more importance: Florence, Siena, Lucca, and Pisa. On the basis of merchant capital (cloth makers processing the wool of the flocks) banking capital established itself in these cities. The bankers of Florence, Siena, and Pisa bought land from feudal lords and transformed it. In place of the exploitation of serfs they substituted the exploitation of sharecroppers who yield a portion of the harvest to the landowners. Sharecropping is thus a progression relative to serfdom; the sharecropper is free and divides the harvest with the landowner, so there is an incentive to produce as much as possible. The bankers, as masters of the Tuscan towns, have a need for increased harvests in order to sustain the town markets and the towns themselves. By virtue of their position, they are thus greater beneficiaries of this progress than are the peasants. These bankers, like the Medici family, build stately homes in the countryside, and around these homes, smallholdings. The roads that link their homes to others are planted with cypress trees, and the countryside takes on a depth and magnitude that it did not have before. The lines toward the horizon are marked out by avenues of cypress, symbols of both property and longevity; and from this moment perspective appears, which, to a certain extent, is derived from the reciprocal influence of towns on the countryside. However, this is not sufficient, as a space cannot be solely explained by economic and social conditions. Alberti's elaboration allowed perspective to take shape.[6] Space remains a symbol of the body and the universe, even in having been measured and made visual. This transformation of space toward visualization and the visual is a phenomenon of crucial importance. According to Alberti, the visual arrangement of the elements of space—lines and curves, light and shadows, male and female elements (that is, angles and rounded forms)—results in optical beauty, a spiritualized sensation creating both admiration and pleasure. Space retains certain qualities of nature, such as luminosity and clarity; while art and innovation bring other qualities, such as convenience, nobility, and adaptation to the laws of society.

This space of perspective takes over nature in measuring it and subordinating it to the requirements of society, under the domination of the eye and no longer of the entire body. In the fifteenth century, we find in painting a perspectival space that provides a common language to inhabitants, users, authorities, and artists, including architects. From then on, the town is organized in a perspectival manner. It is subjected to a dominant characteristic, the façade, which determines perspective and the vanishing point [fuite] of parallel lines, i.e., roads. The crystallization of this system involves multiple consequences: differences are now manifested only in the sequence of façades. Breaks, recesses, and corbelling are reduced to a minimum; they should no longer interrupt the perspective. Since the façade is made to see and to be seen, it is essential and dominating. This did not exist before and especially not in antiquity. To façades themselves, balconies are attached, to enable both seeing and being seen. It is therefore an entire space that is organized, governing the whole of the arts (painting, sculpture, architecture, and town planning), a space that is common to all; the inhabitants situate themselves in this space; the architects and political authorities know how to control it: we are dealing with a code. This is probably the only time in the history of space where there is a unique code for the different stratified levels, that is, the level of the apartment, buildings, the row of buildings, the quarter, the town, and its position in the surrounding space. This is the source of the harmonious and fixed beauty of the towns that adopted this model.

Capitalistic space: for perspectival space, capitalistic space would be the space of catastrophe. Capitalistic space initiated its destruction. The phenomenon is visible since Picasso's analytic cubism and the paintings of Kandinsky. This destruction of perspectival space is characterized by the fact that a monument, a work of architecture, any object, is situated in a homogeneous space and no longer in a qualified (qualitative) space: in a visual space that enables the gaze and suggests the gesture of pivoting around. Picasso, Klee, and the members of the Bauhaus simultaneously discovered that one can represent objects in space such that they no longer have a privileged side or façade. They are no longer oriented toward what they face or what faces them. They are in an indifferent space and are themselves indifferent to this space tending toward complete quantification. The tower block for which Mies van der Rohe designed the prototype is located in a space of the type we can pivot around; it is an object with neither face nor façade. Without the façade, the road falls away. Perspectival space is thus replaced by an entirely new space. An ambiguity follows from what Le Corbusier and the members of the Bauhaus believed to constitute a revolution. We took them for Bolsheviks when actually they inaugurated capitalistic space. Their conception of space has spread alongside neo-capitalism and especially with the triumphal rise of the State.

This capitalistic space is not easy to describe or to define. It is not sufficient to claim that it is only quantitative, or that a quantitative space has been substituted for a qualitative space, that is, perspectival space. This quantitative space is a homogeneous yet fractured space. Pictorial and sculptural art produce genuine models of this space. Art highlights the violence internal to the fracturing of space.

How can a space be simultaneously homogeneous and fractured? Isn't this absurd, impossible? No. On the one hand, this space is homogeneous because within it, all is equivalent, exchangeable, interchangeable; because it is a space that is bought and sold, and exchange can only occur between units that are equivalent, interchangeable. On the other hand, this space is fractured because it is processed in the form of lots and parcels, and sold on this basis; it is thus fragmented. These aspects of capitalistic space are shaped both within the realm of the commodity, in which everything is equivalent, and within the realm of the State, in which everything is controlled. This capitalistic space is fractured because it is processed in the form of parcels that are sometimes minuscule—yet these parcels cannot be made so small that they can no longer be used for constructing buildings; the parcels are sold for as much as the laws or the rules of speculation permit. It is a *logical* space—even though the logical character of the homogeneous whole is contradicted by the fragmentation of the parts.

The classification of spaces proposed here corresponds approximately to Marx's view of the sequence of modes of production. This sequence cannot be taken for granted, nor can the characteristics of each mode of production be viewed as settled. It is a question here of showing, briefly, that there is a production of space inherent to the mode of production, and that this cannot be defined solely by class relations (vulgar Marxism) or by the ideologies and forms of knowledge and culture (Gramsci), but is also defined by this specific production.

Analogical, cosmological, symbolic, and logic or logistical suggest a diachrony (a sequence). Each mode of production has had its space, but the characteristics of space cannot simply be reduced to the general characteristics of the mode of production. Medieval symbolism cannot be defined by the rents peasants surrendered to the lords of the manor, nor by the relations between towns and the countryside. The reduction of aesthetic, social, and mental phenomena to the economic was a disastrous error that some "Marxists" still perpetuate.

The current mode of production is characterized by the space of state control [*contrôle étatique*], which is simultaneously a space of exchange. Through its control, the State tends to accentuate the homogeneous character of space, which is fractured by exchange. This space of state control can also be defined as being optical and visual. The human body has disappeared into a space that is equivalent to a series of images. Perspectival space inaugurates this scotomization of the body, which was preserved, albeit in a changed form, in symbolism.[7] In modern space, the body no longer has a presence; it is only *represented,* in a spatial environment reduced to its optical components. This space is also phallic; towers with their arrogance provide sufficient testament to this. Phallic, optical, visual, logical-logistical, homogeneous and fractured, global and fragmented—these terms enable us to label and conceptualize the features that mark the space of the SMP.

The Bauhaus and Le Corbusier had idealized this space; at the same time, they actualized it. Their idealization followed from the visual and optical character of this space, from which it derives its specular and spectacular allure.

An analysis of Le Corbusier's works shows that he envisioned this space in a manner that produced and reproduced the exultant image of a strong man, joyfully contemplating light, nature, green spaces, and the figures of other humans moving about in the glorious brightness of the sun. This space implies not only that everyday life is programmed and idealized through manipulated consumption but also that spatiality is hierarchized to distinguish noble spaces from vulgar ones, residential spaces from other spaces. It also implies a bureaucratic centrality, termed "civic" but occupied by the decision-making powers. It is a space organized in such a way that, unless they revolt, "users" are reduced to passivity and silence. Their revolt can and must start from the presentation of counter-projects, of counter-spaces, leading to sometimes-violent protests, and culminating in a radical revolt that calls into question the entirety of interchangeable, spectacular space, with its implication of everydayness, centrality, and spatial hierarchization.

These contradictions of space are added to and superimposed on the entrenched contradictions of the capitalist mode of production. Knowledge that is directly invested in the production of space can process it in vast expanses (highway construction); but this space is fragmented, pulverized by private property. Thus appears a modern form of the contradiction noted by Marx between the productive forces and the relations of production and of property. Private property (that is, its social relations) prohibits knowledge from being deployed. It paralyzes the intentions and inventions of architects as well as urbanists; it annihilates their critical and creative capacities. The impact of the relations of production and of the social relations (of property) becomes more pronounced. The actions of property developers embody this impact.

The concept of a *hierarchical stratified morphology* (and its corollary—the "space of catastrophe") stems from the research of R. Thom.[8] It can be generalized and applied to social space. Synchronic analysis (of the present) does not prohibit a diachronic analysis (a history of space). On the contrary, the latter leads to the former. Morphological analysis presupposes genetic analysis.

One can speak of a stratified morphology whenever definite forms composed of discrete units are embedded within one another in a definite order. In linguistics, for example: the *phoneme* (a sound or syllable without meaning); the *word* (an articulation of connected phonemes into a signifying unit); the *clause* or sentence; the series of sentences and the unfolding of meanings. An analogous morphology exists in social space—from the "room" or hut to the house and the building; from the building to the group of houses, to the village and the neighborhood; from the neighborhood to the city, the region, the nation, and the State.

The figure below presents some observable morphologies that have been formalized to reveal the hierarchical embedding of levels. Contrary to the abuse of this term within technocratic ideology, the articulation between the levels is not simply a "positive," unchanging fact. It also entails negative effects: ruptures, catastrophes.

When studying a hierarchized morphology, one has to define its "space of catastrophe," i.e., the conditions under which the space might explode.

Theory shows that, from a genetic perspective, the conditions for stability and the conditions for a rupture are produced simultaneously. Perspectival space was produced historically through economic, social, and political factors, but it cannot be reduced to these factors; it has its space of catastrophe: logistical space. This possesses the character of a space of catastrophe: *homogeneous/fractured* and *total/fragmentary,* resulting in the explosion of previous spaces; it is opposed to possible (differential) space, but at the same time, it tends toward the latter.

These concepts enable us to delineate and define the junction (the articulation) between space and the modern State from the "outside." This articulation may also be captured from the "inside."

Linguistics	Physics	Biology	(Social) Space
• phonemes	• particles	• molecules	• room (hut, shack)
• syllables	• molecules	• groups of molecules	• building (house)
(morphemes)	• bodies	• organelle	• neighborhood
• words	• planets	• cells	• city
• clauses	• solar system	• organs	• district (country)
• sentences	• galaxies	• individuals (of a	• nation (state)
• sequence of		species)	• continent
sentences		• ecological system	• planet

Hierarchized morphologies.

1. The close cooperation between the State and the automobile industry in reshaping preexistent spaces, including the historical city, is well known. While varying from country to country, certain effects are evident to some degree everywhere—highways, parking lots, but also factories, garages, hotels and motels, gas stations, etc. In the large modern countries, some 20 percent of production and the working population are devoted to the automobile and its use. Everything is being sacrificed to this form of growth: the historical past, convenience, amusement, "culture." The historical city is rebuilt according to the demands of growth "impelled" by the automobile. Automobile and construction lobbies join forces with the state technostructure [*technostructure étatique*].[9] Working together, they eventually circumvent popular opposition to traffic, pollution, the withdrawal of public transport, etc. However, a "critical point" (critical state) is being reached more or less everywhere as the automobile's predominance is called into question and this questioning becomes political. Resistance is becoming more intense, and its sources multiply, ranging from dispossessed, deskilled "landowners" to "users" of all classes. From this critical point on, a new conception of space is sought, with new functions and new forms that cannot be reduced simply to traffic circulation. "Quality of space," "qualitative space"—these concepts impose themselves gradually during a period of utopianism, dreams, nostalgia, efforts to go back in time or to live "as if things were different" (elite neo-anarchism).

2. When the State, in any given country, took control of energy production (electricity, oil), some people assumed it would be transferred to "private" companies at low prices, while others assumed that the State was taking responsibility for investments that the "private" sector could not manage. Few people perceived that the State was continuing to install a dominant space, extending the space demarcated by motorways, canals, and railroads. This would only be confirmed for certain later on through the State's creation of networks of highways and air traffic routes, and the production of nuclear energy (everywhere controlled by the State). With its technostructure controlling energy questions, the State gradually becomes the master of them, not only because it controls the units of production, but because it partitions space under the double surveillance of its technicians and the police. The production of energy is

closely tied to the production of political space, i.e., state space [*l'espace étatique*].

3. The techniques permitting the management of space on a large scale, ownership relations, and the needs defined by residency—these all circumscribe the conditions for the small-scale management of space. But only the State is capable of taking charge of the management of space "on a grand scale"—highways, air traffic routes—because only the State has at its disposal the appropriate resources, techniques, and "conceptual" capacity.

The sale and management of space in parcels, often very small (co-op apartments), has brought about a catastrophic situation of urban chaos. In several countries, the State attempts to impose an order on this chaos through diverse institutions (in France, research bureaus such as OREAM, etc.).[10] What kind of order? That of a homogeneous, logistical, optico-geometrical, quantitative space.

State initiatives in France and elsewhere are often described as "failures" because there seems to be a lack of harmony in their results. Such judgments, whether aesthetic or ethical, mask the real situation. For the measures taken by the relevant institutions and administrations are not without effect. However, rather than resolving the contradictions of space, state action makes them worse. The space produced in this process is not entirely new; instead, state action engenders a specific product of the collision between the public and the private. The State's rational and organizational capacity works to the extent that flows are made to circulate rather than being lost in the chaos of spaces abandoned to "private" and local interests. The apparent result is no less chaotic. Wherever the state abolishes chaos, it establishes itself within spaces made fascinating by their social emptiness: a highway interchange or an airport runway, for example, both of which are places of transit and only of transit. This is what clarifies the apparent absurdity of this space with its double characteristic of being both homogeneous (the same) and fractured (not by difference but by a rupture in homogeneity). This result arises from the collision between two practices and two conceptions of space, one *logistical* (global [*globale*], rational, homogenous), the other *local* (based on private interests and particular goals). In so-called capitalist countries, the contradiction can be intensified significantly between, on the one hand, the specific goals of individual property developers, speculators, and investors (the agents through which this space is produced) and, on the other hand, the general (strategic) goals of the State, as represented in the state technostructure. In these cases, the State prevails. Although the conflict does not always become so intense, its effects are felt more or less everywhere. Hence the discomfort and uneasiness we experience when confronted with these spaces in which one sees at work, simultaneously, operations at specific points in time and space that correspond to particular interests, as well as a rationalizing, generic [*globale*] thought that is completely indifferent to its "users" (that is, to the "living bodies" as opposed to the "functions").

4. The rational and scientific space produced and administered by the State encounters not only the commodified space that is marketed and sold in parcels. It also encounters spontaneous, almost blind growth poles that generally date back to the previous epoch (archeo-capitalism, paleo-technology, etc.). These growth poles include, first, the large corporations that developed near natural sources of energy (coal), raw materials (ore), and supplies of labor (masses of workers previously trained through traditional craft or farm work); second, they include the large cities that used to function as accelerators of growth. The collision between these spontaneous modalities of growth that predate the flows of the modern economy, on the one hand, and state space, on the other hand, does not occur without causing damage. State rationality prevails. Only the State can control the flows and harmonize them with the fixed elements of the economy (stocks), because the State integrates them into the dominant space it produces. The huge investments that accompany the disintegration of the spontaneous growth poles and the many resultant displacements (of equipment, of energy, of the labor force, and of raw materials) can only be properly accomplished with the agreement and support of political power. No one denies this. What is often less well understood, however, is the consolidation—at a national and even at a supranational scale—of this new space, superimposed on the previous spaces, and thoroughly reordering them. One need only consider, for example, the relocation of French heavy industry from Lorraine to Dunkirk and Fos-sur-Mer. One could also mention the colossal installations by Italsider in Taranto, the automobile factories in Sagunto, Spain, etc.[11]

5. The modern State is confronted with open spaces, or rather, spaces that have burst open on all sides: from apartments to buildings to the national territory by way of institutions (the school, the neighborhood, the city, the region). As historical products of previous epochs, carrying within themselves the various remnants of those periods (analogical, symbolic, etc.), these spaces are devastated, disintegrated, and ripped apart; at the same time, they overflow their borders. This is just one part of the catastrophic picture being sketched here. Apartments and buildings form open links with collective infrastructure, neighborhoods with the city and the urban. The nation itself no longer has any borders—not for capital or technology, for workers and the workforce, for expertise, or for commodities. Flows traverse borders with the impetuosity of rivers.

If regulating flows, coordinating the blind forces of growth, and imposing its law onto the chaos of "private" and "local" interests is the primary function of state-political space [*l'espace étatico-politique*], it also has another, contrary function that is no less important for being so. This is its role in holding together spaces that have been ripped apart and in maintaining their multiple functions. The dominant space is characterized by the following two elements: it imposes itself on those who threaten to pulverize the conditions for social life, and it forbids the transgressions that tend to produce a different space (whatever that might be). These two functions are correlated and yet conflictual. How can both atomization (pulverization) and transgression (supersession [*dépassement*]) be prevented?

The State tends, once again, to establish chains of equivalence, in this case of interchangeable surfaces and masses. It pushes this tendency to the point of identifying the dominated spaces within the homogeneity of the dominant space. At the same time, it controls certain effects that tend to dissolve the extant space and thus to constitute a new space defined in a different way—namely, by the differences between places and between the activities linked to these places. State action is thus not limited to the management of the social and "private" life of millions of people (the "citizens," the political "subjects") by institutional and administrative means. It proceeds in a more indirect but no less effective way by making use of this privileged instrument—space.

The capitalist mode of production (hereafter CMP) is defined by the relations of production, but not by them alone. The concept of "relations of production" is necessary, but not sufficient. The CMP is constituted neither by an *interaction of "subjects"* (individual or collective, including classes) nor as a "system" endowed with an internal coherence. This latter interpretation, despite its bold claims, implicitly glorifies what it pretends to critique.

The CMP can be defined, first of all, by a chain of concepts, from exchange value to the organic composition of capital, emphasizing the production of surplus value and the accumulation of capital with its associated theoretical problems. In contrast to the analysis of production in general, the analysis of the production of surplus value involves considering how surplus value is *realized* (trade patterns) and how it is *allocated* (investment patterns). The production of surplus value occurs within companies—that is, workplaces. The realization and allocation of surplus value occurs in cities, a fact that by no means exhausts the concept of the *urban*.

This is not all. The CMP is also defined by the production of social and political relations, including the State and state power [*l'étatique*]. It is defined, finally, by the production of a spatial *support* (a foundation for the relations of production and for their renewal or reproduction). This spatial support is not particularly mysterious. It is shaped out of preexisting space—the (geophysical) "nation-space," historical spaces. In this sense it is also shaped by definite agents—developers, bankers, urbanists, architects, landowners, political authorities (local or national), and sometimes by "users."

As this vast process unfolds, something new appears. The CMP is transformed. The *socialization* of the productive forces, of production, of society, of the product, is accomplished, as foreseen by Marx. The space thus engendered is "social" in the sense that it is not a thing among things, but the system of links, connections, networks, and circuits. Nevertheless "socialization" and "nationalization" took the form—unforeseen by Marx—of statification, of political space (or better: of logico-political space).

Let us continue, condensing and summarizing these arguments. As it develops, the CMP produces its space, and thus a *social product*. Once a certain level (of the growth of the productive forces) is reached, it utilizes preexistent spaces, but it does not stop there. First, it *integrates* older spaces (nature, the countryside, historical cities) while destroying them; then it invests knowledge more and more deeply in the management of space (the soil, the subterranean and its resources, airspace). The CMP produces its own space; in so doing, it is transformed, and this is the advent of the state mode of production (hereafter SMP). During the course of this process, space enters simultaneously into:

a) *the productive forces* (for example, from an empirical and descriptive point of view, into what economists term "agglomeration economies");

b) *the relations of production and of property* (since space can be sold and bought; and since it includes all flows, circuits and networks, etc.);

c) *ideology* and the instruments of political power (since space becomes the basis for rationality, the technostructure and state control);

d) *the production of surplus value* (investments in urbanization, in airspace, in the tourism industry with its exploitation of mountains and the sea, i.e., of the empty spaces beyond industrial production, etc.); *the realization of surplus value* (the organization of urban consumption and everyday life, of the "bureaucratic society of controlled consumption"); *the allocation of surplus value* (ground rents and underground rents, banks specialized in real estate, speculation, etc.)

The moment at which space becomes predominant, i.e., when a dominant (political) space is constituted, is also the moment when production no longer spontaneously and blindly guarantees the reproduction of social relations. Although necessary, reproduction inside the corporation (investments and amortizations) and beyond (reproduction of the labor force in and by the working-class family) is no longer sufficient. The primary role of the modern State is to prevent the collapse of the edifice that extends from the labor force to the political caste—to maintain a hierarchized system of places, functions, and institutions. The process of reproduction does not become functionally autonomous; it is actualized in a space, political space, the condition for generalized reproduction. The latter entails:

a) biological (demographic) reproduction;

b) the reproduction of the labor force (families grouped in "housing projects" or in working-class quarters, suburbs, etc.);

c) the reproduction of the means of production (equipment, technology, resources);

d) the reproduction of the relations of production (which the company is no longer able to ensure or guarantee) and the relations of domination.

From a certain point on, as capital investment expands, the task of ensuring the conditions for the reproduction of the relations of domination is left to the State. Strategically, the modern State organizes space in order to:

a) break up oppositions by redistributing groups of people, including opposing groups, into ghettos;

b) hierarchize places on the basis of power relations; and

c) control the entire system.

The space that thereby ensures this generalized reproduction has the following familiar characteristics:

a) *Homogeneous:* it is the same throughout, implying the interchangeability of places and even of moments (time), organizing the set of places for everydayness (work—family and private life—planned leisure). This requires a powerful centralization, and thus a center–periphery relation. Exchangeability and interchangeability take on the appearance of the identical and of the repetitive.

b) *Fractured.* A homogeneous, optico-geometrical, quantifiable, and quantified and thus abstract space, can only become concrete by being embodied in a practical use, in building activities that unfold in and through "parcels." The contradiction is exacerbated between the *functionality* that state control is supposed to ensure and the *absurdity* of the results, which is more or less perceptible, if not obvious, everywhere.

c) *Hierarchized.* Inequalities are a necessary outcome of the exchange of spaces, since use does not disappear, but reappears in the scheduling of time. Places are arranged unequally in relation to the centers, which are themselves unequal—from commercial centers to administrative centers. State action exacerbates this situation: spaces form extreme hierarchies, from the centers of domination to the peripheries that are impoverished but still all the more strongly controlled. Hence the paradoxical aspect of the space that is constituted in this way. It is difficult to locate (social) *classes* within it; however, *segregation* continues. Habitats are closely entangled, yet nonetheless the "residential" spaces of the elite, the bourgeoisie and the middle classes are distinguished perfectly from those reserved for blue-collar and service workers (small houses or tenements in fragmented cities [*villes éclatées*] and in suburbs).

Social space then assumes the form of a *collection of ghettos:* for the elite, for the bourgeoisie, for the intellectuals, for foreign workers, etc. These ghettos are not simply juxtaposed; they are hierarchized in a way that represents spatially the economic and social hierarchy, dominant sectors, and subordinate sectors.

The State coordinates. It prevents "properly" capitalistic space—i.e., space broken into fragments [*en miettes*]—from breaking society itself apart. But the State can do no more than substitute the homogeneity of the identical–repetitive for this situation of pulverization. The State makes use of logic but cannot impose either an abstract coherence or a spatial cohesion on the diverse moments of the process leading from the production of surplus value to its realization. While bound within and by the dominant space, this process remains fragmented: commercial capital, finance capital, industrial capital, and real estate capital fall under the control of groups whose interests often diverge and sometimes clash. The State prevents speculation from paralyzing the general functioning of civil society and the economy. It organizes, it plans directly or indirectly, on occasion even closing some spaces, or controlling some flows by means of computers. But the space that is thus created, which is meant to be both political and regulatory, proves to be both bureaucratizing and bureaucratized, i.e., administered by "bureaus." It thus complements the primary form of the repetitive by a secondary form, whose repetitiveness originates in exchangeability/interchangeability. Last but not least, this space—which is made repressive by the mere fact that it is hierarchized—imposes *the reproduction of the relations of domination* (which in turn completes the reproduction of the relations of production).

The regulatory character of political space (and state space) can therefore be analyzed in three dimensions:

the ideological—the technocratic representation of the social;

the practical—instrumental, a means of action;

the tactical-strategic—consisting principally in the subordination of a territory's resources to political ends.

The ideology is that of a coherence–cohesion, of a neutral, and thus all the more effective logic, of a homogeneity that is optico-geometric, and thus both quantifying and quantified. This ideology also entails the representation of a certain transparency—of a space in which the elements of society would be made transparent and would coexist peacefully. But shouldn't certainties be questioned? The Cartesian spirit will rule as long as this proposition is not admitted as a certainty (counter-certainty). Among all certainties, aren't those concerning space the most suspect?

The rationality of this space is stripped off like a veil when one realizes that, in reality, it "regulates" and perpetuates the relations of domination. It accomplishes this by subordinating simple reproduction (of the labor force) to the more complex reproduction of the relations of production, and by subordinating the latter to the relations of domination, incorporated into space. These modalities of reproduction include and imply one another, constituting in turn a hierarchical morphology that guarantees their intelligibility but also threatens them: for there can be no such morphology without a rupture (catastrophe). This is how the relation of the dominant to the dominated can be explained. This relation must be reduced neither to the empirical nor to mere representation. A space that is dominated may itself be dominant over another space. We know that the spatial hierarchy presents itself as an entwining or imbrication of dominant/dominated spaces. This relation of inclusion/exclusion has a logical (logistical) character.

Here one may add that the following elements include and imply one another morphologically—*everydayness* (time programmed in and by space); *spatiality* (center–periphery relations); and the *repetitive* (the identical is reproduced under conditions in which natural differences and particularities are abolished). The social hierarchy thus presents itself, more evidently today than ever, as a *spatial hierarchy.*

We thus arrive at an expanded conception of the *mode of production.* Capitalism is defined not on the basis of production in general, but by the production of surplus value, by the accumulation of capital (R. Luxemburg),[12] as well as by the reproduction of determinate social relations. Starting from a certain critical point, the latter result is gradually accomplished through and in space, as well as through the identification–repetition of gestures, of actions, of everydayness, of the inscribed–prescribed. Fragments of spaces and of social activities are coordinated, but not without conflicts. Space: how practical [*Quelle aubaine, l'espace*]! It may be sold and bought. It expands the realm of the commodity. At the same time, it permits the social forces that would otherwise resist established political power to be controlled. And so the state mode of production is inaugurated.

All sorts of obstacles and conflictual situations resist this comprehensive process. The repetitive must made to appear new; the identical must be made to appear dynamic. Hence the incredible mixture of the neo, the retro, and the archaic in modern life. The repetitive fits poorly with the realm of the lived, for its dependence on logic and identity implies the abolition of lived experience [du vécu]. Thus ensues sickness, boredom, rejection: the massive disgust that follows the establishment of the SMP. At this critical point, violence enters onto the scene. Hence the strange (alienating/alienated) climate of the modern world: on the one hand, a repetitive and identitarian rationality; on the other hand, violence, whether as a means to affirm lived experience and use, or as a means to extend them. Violence smolders everywhere as this rational world is reduced to the principle of interchangeability. Violence and the tranquility of "regulatory" space strangely intermingle. Can't we today consider social space to be the very incarnation of violence, whether virtual or actual? This in turn calls for a global project [un projet global], that of another society in another space.

But let us not skip ahead. In what sense is contemporary space a "space of catastrophe"? The point of Thom's arguments[13] is to show how and why the logical character of morphological embedding [des implications morphologiques] generates ruptures rather than stability (contrary to the technocratic thesis). In other words, logic and violence belong together.

The agents of the state [gens de l'État] conceive and construct dominant spaces ruling over dominated spaces (for example, through the planning of airspace, airlines, airports, runways, etc.). They subject space to a logistics, believing thereby that they can either suppress conflicts and contradictions, or at least understand them in order to combat them. Against this, however, the intrinsic connection between logic and violence suggests that these agents in fact revive conflicts and aggravate contradictions.

Today a mondialisation of production and of production cycles is occurring. Doesn't the word "internationalization" [internationalisation] limit the scope of the phenomena that are contingent on the growth of the productive forces? The accumulation of investments and productive capital is occurring on a world scale. The so-called supranational corporations reflect this growth, while the relations of production (and of property) remain fastened to the national scale. A mondialisation of labor flows, of technology, of expertise, is also taking place. The so-called developed countries, the "centers," purchase massive quantities of labor power (generally low skilled) in the peripheries. Moreover, capital and investments have begun to seek on site the labor power they set into movement. The relation between capital and the labor force has thus changed scale. This implies a *mondialisation of capital markets* (and thus of surplus value transfers) in which the so-called "socialist" countries are also included, for they too are sites of investments but also of accumulation (of the means of production), technology markets, enormous reserves of labor power, etc.

A *mondialisation* and diversification of the class struggle ensues which penetrates physical, social and mental space, creating new cleavages. The production of a planetary space likewise ensues, whose frontiers oscillate between visibility and invisibility, and in which national states have until now maintained their functions—control and hierarchization (of dominant/dominated spaces), regulation. Even the space of the corporation can and must today be reconsidered in the light of global [*globales*] perspectives. An article in the journal *Place* states: "Due to its general character, the strategic importance of wages has already been sufficiently demonstrated, but there are other broadly significant factors that would require a comparable analysis. Space is one such factor. . . ."[14] The employers, the article continues, have not neglected the impact of space as a variable, either inside or outside the factory. This is made clear, for example, by the organizational charts that delineate "the distribution of jobs and positions within a spatial apparatus," including the functions of surveillance, which are the pivot of smooth operations. Yet, the typical or traditional space inspired by Taylorism—with its double perspective of enclosure (narrowed for the machine and the worker; but widened for purposes of surveillance)—is no longer sufficient. It disintegrates. According to official texts, the relationship between the worker and the machine will be superseded [*dépasser*] by a complex system that is organized by three relations: worker–production process; process–building; building–environment. (This nonetheless leaves aside the relations among the workers themselves).

The disintegration of a space that juxtaposes locations and the possible establishment of a space that articulates and hierarchizes them—the contours of these developments are clear enough. This reveals a new field of protest within the factory, but it also begins to transcend the division between work and non-work (that is to say, between everyday life and the environment, and thus between housing, collective services, and landscape). A new right emerges—*the right to space* (in and beyond the workplace), or *the right to control investment insofar as it manages and operationalizes space.*[15]

The new mode of production (let us label it "socialist" once again) must produce its own space, which can no longer be a capitalist space. Any transformation of the world that remains caught in the preexistent morphology will do no more than reproduce the relations of domination in a more or less disguised form. Capitalistic space is in the process of disintegrating; will it be reconstituted in the name of socialism? A new space must be created that builds on the tendencies that are already perceptible in the capitalist mode of production. In the context of capitalistic space, what does this destructive space—the "space of catastrophe"—look like, and how should we describe it? It is a space of differences or a *differential space,* which represents for capitalism an antagonistic and ruinous tendency.

The fact that a new space, which is formed on one or another level of the stratified morphology, devastates this or that inherited space—this event-emergence can no longer come as a surprise to us. Doesn't perspectival space catastrophically devastate symbolic space? Doesn't logistical space devastate perspectival space? These phenomena can be recognized insofar as they can be deciphered in our cities (as long as we do not accept what is before our eyes as a straightforwardly obvious proof!).

The history of space would emphasize destruction—be it on the scale of architecture and the house (the building), on the scale of the urban or on that of a country. Such a history would extricate the meaning of these destructions—not as the will of a particular agent, but as the substitution of one space by another, including the destruction of antecedent spaces by subsequent spaces (catastrophe).

The same history of space would emphasize reappropriations (modifications of the purpose and meaning of buildings) through which the destruction of what exists is avoided.

Such destructions and reappropriations are accomplished around *critical points,* during a *critical situation* of a society or a State, when such a situation obtains (transition).

In order to define the link between the SMP and space, in order to demonstrate that logico-political space is a "space of catastrophe," we must also recall that the formation of this space is accompanied by convulsions, crises, and wars—which a fallacious analysis attributes to purely economic or political factors, thus eliminating the spatial dimension. Yet the transformation of space cannot be conceived as an accidental result of such convulsions. Nor can this transformation be represented as the effect of conscious reasoning, as the intended goal of crises and wars. The convulsions of the modern world were provoked by the displacements of settlements (colonization) and resources (raw materials) across space. This resulted, following each large war, in a redistribution of space, including its resources, and in changes in how space was settled (the transition from early forms of colonialism to contemporary neocolonialism). These changes could be foreseen from the onset of crises and tragic events; however, they were neither expected nor planned as such.

These considerations concerning space as a field of (non-abstract) possibilities permit a conception of *virtual causality* that does not lead into teleological assumptions about "final causes" or into mystical-metaphysical visions of a "causality of absence" (that is to say, of the future) or of a "metonymic" or "structural causality."[16] The political conception of space makes possible an understanding of how history and its by-products enter into the worldwide process [*le mondial en marche*] and are thus transformed.

This same process through which historicity is transformed into "something else"—worldliness [*mondialité*]—may explain why war and peace are not "declared" clearly, if at all. Conventional history and historicity presuppose a distinction between these *two states of affairs* that tend to become identical within the modern state. The new modality for settling space seems today to have entailed the most extreme strategic consequences: occupation of the oceans, unbridled threats to planetary space as a whole and even beyond. One might contend that the space of property—which reaches from the underground to the earth's surface and beyond—in itself represents a "space of catastrophe": it unsettles, atomizes, and pulverizes preexisting space, tearing it into pieces. But the space of property cannot be established without its corollary: state space [*l'espace étatique*], which corrects and supports it. What is it exactly that has *disintegrated?* All specialized spaces that have been subsumed within an institution, and which are thus enclosed, functionalized. The *uses* of space persist nonetheless: spaces for sports, the body, children, transportation, education, sleep, etc. Pulverized space tends to be reconstituted in spaces that are *differentiated according to use* (time, the scheduling of time, cycles of time). Armed with its instrument of logistical space, the State inserts itself between pulverized spaces and spaces that have been reconstructed differentially. The State's pressure prevents both a chaotic pulverization and the formation of a new space produced through a new mode of production. It prevents disintegrated spaces from being reshaped according to a Reason that has been rendered more flexible and open (dialecticized) through the relation of time (cycles and rhythms) to space. The catastrophe consists in the fact that state space hinders the transformation that would lead to the production of a differential space. State space subordinates both chaos and difference to its implacable logistics. It does not eliminate the chaos, but manages it. On the other hand, it does capture differences at the moment of their emergence and abolishes them. It rules an empty order animated only by that which it negates, defined by chaos and dissolution on the one side, the differential and the concrete on the other. The logic of this space coincides with the State's strategy, and thus with the objectives and the stakes of power. We know too well that this logic is empty only in appearance; it serves as the pivot and the axis for the political forces that seek to maintain the equilibrium between the levels of the morphology (the infra-national and the supra-national) and that contravene the rupture of that equilibrium. But the logic of state space *is* already this rupture, since it interrupts the movement.

At this level of state logic [*la logique étatique*], the risk implied in the trilogy of representation–participation–institution comes into play. The real and concrete movements, those of the "users," their protests and struggles, fall into the trap set for them by the State (especially when it possesses the full power of centralization). The study of urban movements shows this. To the triad or trilogy mentioned above corresponds the triple trap of *substitution* (of authority for grassroots action), *transfer* (of responsibility from the activists to the "leaders"), and *displacement* (of the objectives and the stakes of social protests to the goals set by the "bosses" who are attached to established order. The previously mentioned study by Katharine Coit[17] is confirmed by the recent book of Michel Ragon, *L'architecte, le prince, la démocratie*.[18] Only control by the base and *territorial autogestion*—exerting pressure against the summits of state power and leading a concrete struggle for concrete objectives—can oppose an actualized democracy to administrative rationality, i.e., can subdue state logic through a spatialized dialectic (concretized in space without neglecting time—on the contrary, integrating space with time and time with space).

Here, and in this framework, one may return to Marx's *Critique of the Gotha Program* and Lenin's *State and Revolution*. On the way to its depoliticization, the declining State should first take charge of space in order to repair the damage inflicted during the current period: the ruins, the chaos, the waste, the pollution (which eventually causes the death of the seas, the Mediterranean, for example, and even the Atlantic Ocean!). This work [*œuvre*] cannot be accomplished without conceiving a new *texture* of space. The declining State will be dissolved not so much into "society" in an abstract sense as into a reorganized social space. At this stage, the State would be able to maintain certain functions, including that of representation. The control of flows, the harmony between flows internal and external to a territory, will require that they be oriented *against* the global firms and, by implication, will also require a general management [*une gestion globale*] of a statist type during a certain period. This can only lead toward the *end* (goal and conclusion) by means of the activity of the base: spatial (territorial) *autogestion*, direct democracy and democratic control, affirmation of the differences produced in and through that struggle.

Translation by Alexandra Kowalski, Neil Brenner, Aaron Passell, Bob Jessop, Stuart Elden, and Gerald Moore

NOTES

1. René Lourau, *L'analyseur Lip* (Paris: Union Générale d'Éditions, 1974), 131. [The passage cited by Lefebvre actually reads "No institution without a *space of legitimation*" (italics in original), but the final two words are excluded in Lefebvre's citation. René Lourau was a colleague of Lefebvre's at the University of Paris–Nanterre, and his *Lip* book is cited frequently by Lefebvre in *De l'État*. This book is a study of the Lip watch factory, which was taken over by its workers when threatened with closure—a classic instance of *autogestion*. Another influential volume from this period by Lourau was *L'analyse institutionnelle* (Paris: Éditions de Minuit, 1970).—*Eds.*]

2. See, in particular, *La production de l'espace* (Paris: Anthropos, 1974) [*The Production of Space*]; *Le droit à la ville* (Paris: Anthropos, 1968) ["The Right to the City," in *Writings on Cities*] and the film that bears that title, one that already has quite a history. Practically banned in France, it created a scandal right until the "truths" that it proposed became obvious and trivial, i.e., rehearsed by politicians (without the least form of acknowledgment, it goes without saying). See also *La revolution urbaine* (Paris: Gallimard, 1970) [*The Urban Revolution*], where the word "revolution" designates a multifaceted, global [*globale*] transformation and not simply a violent political operation.

3. [The Comunidad de Vecinos and Comunidad de Propietarios are committees made up of the occupants of a shared housing community, such as an apartment block or a community with shared amenities. They are responsible for costs of communal services and rules for behavior and maintenance.—*Eds.*]

4. [On this term, see chap. 1.—*Eds.*]

5. See the work of M. Griaule and G. Dieterlen, summarized in D. Forcle, *African Worlds* (London, 1954); and A. Tzonis, *Towards a Non-repressive Environment* (New York,

1974), chap. 2, pp. 22ff. [The references are Marcel Griaule and Germaine Dieterlen, "The Dogon of the French Sudan," in *African Worlds: Studies in the Cosmological Ideas and Social Values of African Peoples,* ed. Darryl Forde, 83–110 (London: International African Institute and Oxford University Press, 1954); and Alexander Tzonis, *Towards a Nonoppressive Environment* (Boston: i Press, 1974), 23ff.—*Eds.*]

6. [Leon Battista Alberti (1404–72) published *Della Pittura (On Painting)* in 1435–36, a treatise that explained how artists could apply mathematical principles to their work. In particular, the book presented geometrical techniques—including the horizon line and the vanishing point mentioned by Lefebvre in the preceding passage—through which a three-dimensional world could be represented on the two dimensional surface of paintings.—*Eds.*]

7. ["Scotomization" is a somewhat obscure psychological term developed by French researchers in the 1920s to describe the phenomenon of "negative hallucination," a denial of, or blindness to, an object, perception, or memory. While the term was rejected by Freud, it was later reintroduced by Lacan in his discussion of foreclosure.—*Eds.*]

8. René Thom, *Modèles mathématiques de la morphogénèse: Recueil de textes sur la theorie des catastrophes et ses applications* (Paris: Union Générale d'Éditions, 1974) [*Mathematical models of morphogenesis,* trans. W. M. Brookes and D. Rand (New York: Halsted Press, 1983)]. [Thom (1923–2002) was a French mathematician whose work on catastrophe theory during the 1970s was later taken up in work on chaos theory. He was interested in how discontinuous, abrupt change could occur within apparently stable systems. Lefebvre engages with Thom's work elsewhere in *De l'État,* 4:256–58, in the context of a discussion of Rosa Luxemburg's approach to crisis theory.—*Eds.*]

9. On the concept of "technostructure," which Lefebvre critically appropriates from John Kenneth Galbraith, see chap. 7 n.9.

10. [OREAM is the Organization d'études d'aménagement des aires métropolitaines—the Organization for Research on the Management of Metropolitan Areas. Established in 1966, OREAM was tasked with overseeing the broader infrastructural requirements of several newly introduced urban plans.—*Eds.*]

11. [During the 1960s and early 1970s, France and other major European states actively subsidized industrial development in strategic logistics hubs and "growth poles" located away from the heartlands of Fordist industrial development. Lefebvre refers here to several major European industrial zones that grew extensively during this period in conjunction with such political strategies.—*Eds.*]

12. [Although he does not provide a citation, Lefebvre is referring here to Luxemburg's book, *The Accumulation of Capital,* trans. Agnes Schwarzschild (New York: Monthly Review Press, 1964). Lefebvre discusses Luxemburg's work at length in *De L'État,* 2: chap. 11, pp. 305–28.—*Eds.*]

13. Thom, *Modèles mathématiques.*

14. [Lefebvre's citation is incomplete. He is referring to an article published in the journal *Place: Peuple, Espace, Pouvoir* no. 6 (1977): 27–28, titled "Espaces de travail: Une revendication des travailleurs." While no specific author is listed in the original publication, the journal editors indicate that the essay was written by "several militants of the

CFDT." The CFDT (Confédération Française Démocratique du Travail) served as the main noncommunist trade union federation during this period in France. It actively opposed the political programs of both the PCF and the Socialist Party (PS) in favor a workplace-based form of *autogestion.—Eds.*]

15. "Espaces de travail," 27–29.

16. Louis Althusser, Etienne Balibar, and Roger Establet, *Lire le capital* (Paris: François Maspéro, 1965), 2:165–66. [The passage in question can be found in Althusser's essay "Marx's Immense Theoretical Revolution," in *Reading Capital*, 182–93, esp. 186–88.—*Eds.*]

17. [Here, and earlier in volume 4 of *De l'État* (p. 163), Lefebvre refers to Katharine Coit, *Silences et révoltes des usagers: Une comparaison des mouvements sociaux urbains aux Etats-Unis, en France, en Grande-Bretagne et en Italie* (Paris: Université de Paris X, 1975).—*Eds.*]

18. [Michel Ragon, *L'architecte, le prince, la démocratie* (Paris: Albin Michel, 1977), esp. 133ff. In this book, particularly in the pages Lefebvre references, Ragon is concerned with the extension of *autogestion* to spatial issues, especially architecture.—*Eds.*]

12 Review of Kostas Axelos's *Toward Planetary Thought*

Lefebvre's thinking on the question of the world is profoundly influenced not only by political concerns but also by a philosophical lineage that can be traced through Heraclitus, Marx, and Heidegger. One of Lefebvre's contemporaries, the Greek émigré Kostas Axelos, extensively mined that seam, and Lefebvre forged many of his ideas in dialogue with his writings. In this fascinating but neglected text, Lefebvre reflects in detail on Axelos's reformulation of the young Marx's aphorism in his doctoral thesis that the "the world's becoming philosophical is at the same time philosophy's becoming worldly" (see Karl Marx, *Writings of the Young Marx on Philosophy and Society*, ed. L. D. Easton and K. H. Guddat [New York: Doubleday, 1967], 62). This argument, Lefebvre suggests, deserves sustained analysis. In doing so Lefebvre quickly moves beyond a commentary on Axelos's book and begins to discuss the interrelated yet distinct terms of the world, the earth, the globe, and the planetary. These early conceptual explorations serve as an important foundation for his subsequent analysis of *mondialisation* and the world scale in volume 4 of *De l'État* and elsewhere in his writings of the 1970s (see other chapters in part II of this book).—*Eds.*

In his latest book, Kostas Axelos unveils his ambition better and further than in the two other installments in his trilogy on errancy, *Héraclite et la philosophie: La première saisie de l'être en devenir de la totalité* [1962; Heraclitus and Philosophy: The First Understanding of Being Becoming Totality] and *Marx, penseur de la technique: De l'aliénation de l'homme à la conquête du monde* [1961, 1963; Marx, Thinker of Technology: From the Alienation of Man to the Conquest of the World].[1] This ambition is grand and many-faceted. First, he wants to create and impose a language, his own. To this language there corresponds a form of thought that could only be realized through, by, and in language. Illustrious precedents encourage him—these include Heraclitus and Heidegger, of whom it might be said that they allow themselves to be grasped only slowly and to the extent that their language is accepted. This type of thought (that of Heraclitus, among others) insinuates itself across the centuries. It gradually colors the forms of consciousness, ultimately bringing about unexpected victories: Hegel calls on Heraclitus after two millennia. Rightly or wrongly, with his processions of words, turns of phrase, and rhythms (with his syntagms, paradigms, and symbols, as a linguist would say), a thought like that of Heraclitus nowadays seems fundamental, both unique and inexhaustible. It gives us the example of a heroic and victorious endeavor, playing less on vocabulary than on turns and detours, the inflections and figures, the marvelous torments and exquisite tortures inflicted on the phrase, on syntax, on habitual associations, on the "syntagmatic" (the clearest and simplest example of which is nothing other than Logic). If for Axelos the "world" and being today deliver themselves over to us only in the fragments of a shattered totality that loses and refinds itself in its own debris, every one of his phrases symbolizes this conception.

The writings of Kostas Axelos happen to irritate many readers, exasperating some of them. And furthermore, one never knows, in reading his books, exactly where and when we encounter an essential thought or mere wordplay. Axelos knows this. Behind this ambiguity we glimpse his laughter, the laughter of the Sphinx before the young Oedipus (the reader). A demon of dialectics, he uses and abuses this game. Although not exactly Latin, is not a certain rhetoric an integral part of his thought? What right do we have to reproach him for it, in an age where everything is thrown into question, including language? No one can guarantee that word games are always facile, inoffensive, and merely amusing.

Let us therefore seek to establish that a formula of Kostas Axelos has meaning. If one formula has meaning, most if not all have one, though they generally put forward an enigma.

For human beings, "earth" is the fundamental point of stability: soil without a horizon, a sphere. The spherical form is also the immutable figure of perfection. When practical action and understanding are removed, this earth appears as a unity of cycles, self-regulating, stable systems: waters, winds, air, light, soils, and sediments. If we consider the modern world, the whole of the devices [*l'ensemble des dispositifs*] assembled by humans begins to cover the earth. These devices and their arrangement [*Ces dispositifs et leur ensemble*], all constituted on systems of (physical, chemical, economic, etc.) self-regulation, unwittingly imitate these fundamental stabilities by making use of them. This is how a "human world" constructs itself.

Technologies become worldwide [*mondiale*] only in attaining this perfection. Individuals admire technological change and its speed. But on a planetary scale, technologies tend toward a self-sustaining equilibrium. Thus the "earth," the "round machine" becomes for us and through us what it used to be: a giant and minuscule machine bearing giant and minuscule machines that will manage to reclothe it in a suitable cloak. Mastered, captured in concrete and steel, a source of harnessed and trapped energies—does not this machine gradually close in on itself again? Will not space and time take on a new form, delimited in the following way: the infinite around a technologically consolidated "human world"?

Around us and for us, planet earth is the "world." Not the pseudo-world imagined by Teilhard de Chardin.[2] Under new conditions, the world acquires for us some of the meaning it had in myths and mythologies: the mother of life and thought. Will it become the great automaton corresponding to the cosmos in ancient representations of the "world," according to which the cosmos produces, maintains, and moves itself? Everything happens as if the earth and the humans it bears sought out this destiny. And yet we conceive and see the earth because we come from it. Not only have we discovered the errancy of the planet in space (where it turns, the wheel [*roue*] among wheels on which the human is wheeled out [*roué*] alongside a sun that spins aimlessly), but also that for humans this planet is no longer just the terrain of departure for a limitless adventure, with no discernible goal except the conquering of unlimited space.

As "world," the earth conceals the call of a formless future. From a stable model, it changes into a figure of errancy. The wheel [*la roue*]? It is invariance, clockwork [*rouage*]. It is also the wheel of becoming. The circle symbolizes both the perfection of thought and an infernal prison.

The absolutely coherent closure and equilibrium of the sphere symbolizes the equilibrium and realization of that which would be self-sufficient. A cybernetic notion of self-regulation extends this definition of a perfect and disastrous condition across all systems. And humans? It would be a major pleonasm,[3] the supreme tautology, if they came to define themselves in this way. Happily, luckily, unluckily, this definition cannot be upheld. Wandering into outer space, humans have already taken leave of this earth.

Is it not therefore true that the "world" is one and total, and furthermore, that if things were otherwise, the world would be forever incomprehensible and ungraspable? Is it not equally true that the world is not a unity and a totality, that it offers itself to us in differences, incompatibilities, partial truths? How to unite these propositions, if not by suggesting that the totality shatters itself, that it is thus fragmented, that it delivers itself and becomes? The relation between unity and multiplicity, according to Kostas Axelos, is much more dramatic than in philosophy: secretion? differentiation? splitting and the rending of unity? No. Ruptures. Fractures. The planet rises into our horizon only in separation (separation between the East and West, for those who grasp things slowly) and in the threat of (nuclear) annihilation. Technologies unify the terrestrial world only by plunging the people of this earth into angst.

A tragic vision? Yes and no. For this drama of stability, this stability in errancy, is a "game" [*le jeu*]. The tragic contradiction is the contradiction (the antagonistic unity) of seriousness [*gravité*] and play [*le jeu*]. The human is a serious being, but nothing is more serious than the game. The human plays his destiny seriously, and the universe plays with planet earth, with the seriousness [*gravités*] and games of humans. Appearance and apparition play with reality, because reality is only the play of appearances. Being? Nature? The absolute? Let us not speak of these. When we play, we are there without speaking of it. "It" is an eternal child, gathering his dice to throw them into the infinite.[4]

Oh, demon of the dialectic! Divine demon! Eternal childhood! He who would speak clearly becomes as obscure as Heraclitus—and Axelos. Reader, hypocritical reader, it is your turn to play—and to judge.

Translation by Gerald Moore, Neil Brenner, and Stuart Elden

NOTES

1. Kostas Axelos has published all his works in the Arguments series he founded in 1960, which he directs for Éditions de Minuit, and which follows on from the journal *Arguments*, which was closed down. His latest work, *Vers la Pensée planétaire: Le devenir-pensée du monde et le devenir-monde de la pensée* (1964) [Toward Planetary Thought: The Becoming-Thought of the World and the Becoming-World of Thought] already announces the next, *Le Jeu du monde: Fragments de la totalité* [The Play of the World: Fragments of Totality]. [Axelos published the last mentioned book in 1969, without the subtitle listed by Lefebvre. Axelos's book on Marx was translated by Ronald Bruzina as *Alienation, Praxis and Techne in the Thought of Karl Marx.*—Eds.]

2. [Pierre Teilhard de Chardin (1881–1955) was a Jesuit philosopher whose works, such as *Le Phénomène Humaine* (Paris: Les Éditions du Seuil, 1955; translated by Bernard Wall as *The Phenomenon of Man* [New York: Harper and Row, 1959]), attempted to account for the origin and development of the cosmos.—*Eds.*]

3. [A pleonasm entails the use of excessive, repetitive, or redundant words to express an idea.—*Eds.*]

4. [One of the extant fragments of Heraclitus, number 52 in the Diels-Kranz numbering, suggests that "time is like a child playing a game."—*Eds.*]

13 The World according to Kostas Axelos

Explicitly engaging Axelos again, this essay demonstrates Lefebvre's work on the world in its most philosophical form. Although written by Lefebvre in 1986, the essay was not published until 1992, a year after his death; it was more recently republished in a volume celebrating Axelos's philosophy. In addition to Axelos, a range of other philosophical figures feature strongly in the analysis, including Heraclitus, Nietzsche, and Heidegger. Little of Lefebvre's explicitly philosophical work is available in English translation, so this brief piece is important for demonstrating the detailed engagement he had with that tradition. The piece is also notable for a remarkable, extended parenthesis in which Lefebvre discusses his earliest writings of the 1920s. This passage illustrates how crucial the intellectual climate of the period before Stalinism, Trotskyism, and the publication of Heidegger's *Being and Time* was to his intellectual development.—*Eds.*

> The w/World "is" the space–time of opening; more precisely, there is World as the space–time of the Open, the adventure of errancy, the game of itinerance and the reemergence of what is at stake.
>
> —KOSTAS AXELOS, *Systematique ouverte* [Open Systematic][1]

"The terrifying solitude of the last philosopher. Nature petrifies him, vultures circle overhead. He cries to nature: give us forgetfulness! . . . But no, like a Titan he bears sorrow—until reconciliation is granted in tragic great art."[2] These lines of Nietzsche evoke the figure of Kostas Axelos; yet if he is the last philosopher, he is neither the last of men, nor the Oedipus of his final challenge, who resolves the enigma of man only at the end of this failed species. On the contrary: Kostas Axelos is also the first or one of the first of a species that supersedes the derisory human, though without, for all that, assuming the traits of Nietzsche's Overman.

PHILOSOPHER? OF WHAT? THE LAST? HOW AND WHY?

He begins, like philosophers of all ages, with a rupture. He takes distance, a step back. He detaches himself from (social and political) practice. He thus remains within the philosophical tradition of the *epoche*. Of course, his program does not consist in a "reduction" (phenomenological, semantic, or otherwise), and if he leaves the terrain of the everyday, it is in order to return to it, to appreciate it by situating it. From the outset, he has nonetheless not abstained from intervening. Once militant, an activist even, Kostas Axelos only became a philosopher in abandoning action, and because political action disappointed him. An appreciable advantage of the philosophical attitude: it creates a "space of freedom" where thought and its discourse can unfurl, transforming this space into a vast theater of worldness [*mondialité*]. The world puts itself on show [*se théâtrilise*] magnificently, with hidden games becoming visible. The disadvantages of this program? The splendid and solitary unfurling requires a total acceptance, since it comprehends the totality, as we shall see. Kostas Axelos can only have disciples who accept him as he accepts the universe. And yet he does not want disciples. But was this not the situation of the greatest, from the origins (Heraclitus) to the present day? But how can one refrain from introducing something (a seed or poison?) into "reality," into becoming "worldwide and planetary"? How can one not attempt to inflect the course of things, whether directly or otherwise? Can thought not begin otherwise than through this act of renunciation and distanciation, which only recovers the "real" in order to describe it in relation to the totality, and to appreciate it highly and bitterly?

Does not the opposite program target the same goal in another way? The everyday sublates history, ideologies, technology, economics, and politics. It derives from them because it results from them. A fragmentary and fragmented totality, in the process of becoming, is also realized along this path. But such a concern would make Kostas Axelos smile, because, though not without several detours, he proceeds from Marx and what has communally been called "Marxism." It is not in this sense that Kostas Axelos overcomes ancient contemplative philosophy. It is in immediately grasping the principle of immanence–transcendence, which for him is to say that play gives birth to the becoming of the world (the world in becoming).

Kostas Axelos is a philosopher in the sense that he brings to completion the lengthy (re)search of philosophy, its (millennium-) long journey over the course of which thought has sought in vain to define itself, to constitute itself, to establish itself as the mode of a substance. The speculative privilege attributed to some aspect or fragment of the "world" affords us these endeavors and makes the earth promptly draw back under the footsteps of philosophers. Because when the thought that searches for itself and searches for what it thinks *shifts*, slowly but inevitably, it traverses the mediations to which it gives rise and heads toward new horizons. Philosophers first conceived and then explored nature [*physis*]; then they posited and presupposed divine transcendence, stretching theogonies, theologies, and theodicies into metaphysics; after which philosophy put the human and man to the fore, in order finally to open itself to the world.[3]

Who marked out this last line of the long passage of thought toward itself and toward the world? Without wishing to go back further, there was Schelling, then Schopenhauer, then Nietzsche, and finally Heidegger. In the margins, seeking to define man and the human in their relation to a nature also represented as the universe: Marx.

Thus presented, the succession and movement of thought connect together the various aspects of Heidegger's philosophical teaching, phenomenology, historicity, and ontology. They speak, he argues, the history of Being, its sending and concealment. Heidegger realizes the withdrawals and gifts of Being through language and especially through the philosophical vocabulary of different eras. For Kostas Axelos, it is no longer about a history of being, but the becoming-world of thought at the heart of a world in becoming. From the beginning, the world disclosed itself to Heraclitus and Parmenides through the fundamental opposition of the Same and the Other, becoming and repetition, substance and errancy, the true and the not-true (appearance). However, it is only after century upon century of chasing and meditation (and confusion) that the *world* is found and recognizes itself (being becoming a fragmentary and fragmented totality of the multidimensional and open *world*, Axelos writes).[4] From the beginning to the end of philosophy, the world is here, there and up there, present and absent, realized and fleeting. For Axelos, the movement of thought that seeks itself in seeking out the world throws light on its becoming: its rises and falls, its life and death, its history, in short. That which is refused by historians, intent on showing the internal coherence of systems and the reasons for their succession, either through relation to a particular problematic, or through relation to the economic, the social, and the political.

There is a delicate point here, a fine distinction. First, Kostas Axelos extends philosophy through Heidegger, but does so by turning his back on him. The move or approach of Heidegger is typical; he discovers or rather recovers the world; he barely explores it. He perceives the opening and does not engage with it. He goes back, toward the original, the initial, the foundational or the foundation in a pursuit over whose course he strays into (he errs toward) considerations on language and truth (the truth of Being) that he holds onto and maintains in spite of his vision of errancy. Heidegger is thus diametrically opposed to those who orientate themselves toward the final, toward theology and the sense of history revealed by its end. Yet Kostas Axelos opens up another way: the exploration of the eventual, of that which advenes or supervenes, the advent and the event. What is it that advenes and supervenes? Always and everywhere the ordeal [*épreuve*] and the proof [*preuve*] of becoming. All those who engage themselves in a meaning and thereby affirm this meaning, all those who bet on an action, on a goal, they all find themselves *outplayed*. Whether they have won or lost, something other than what they wanted, planned, and projected, emerges from their actions. The outplaying [*déjouement*] testifies to [*prouve*] the game [*jeu*] and shows the stakes [*enjeux*], whether real and/or fictitious, practical and/or imaginary. That which derives from becoming, differs from that which is possibly expected. The game of the world plays out thus; the dialectical thought of Axelos announces itself in terms of the played and the outplayed. Thus begins the exploration of the world and creates itself a still nascent thought. . . .

We should not be afraid of insisting that, and showing by how much, this exploration differs from Western philosophical traditions. For example, in Axelos it is no longer a case of the classical relation between "subject and object." The dialectic (or pseudo-dialectic) of the subject and the object is aborted; it culminates in a tautology: no subject without object and no object without subject. Moreover, the subject has broken down along with its implicit model, the individual, the atom of society. This breakdown has been described several times among philosophers, whether they deplore it or welcome it; they have poorly reinstated and reconstituted the "subject" as the "collective subject" or the "subject of history." And the object? It, too, has broken down into a thing, a product, materiality, objectivity, probabilities, etc. We have speculated interminably over the unity of the subject and the object, whether it be "pre-perceptive" and infra-conscious, be it synthetic and supra-conscious. Kostas Axelos flippantly sweeps aside these questions around which philosophy turns and returns. For him, if there is an "object," it is the planet, the Earth placed in danger during the course of its errancy, by "Man," who thus also calls himself into question. Who will be the planetary man?[5]

Breaking with philosophy in the way he breaks with practice (the empirical), Kostas Axelos has, however, understood what was—once—the soul or the spirit of philosophy. Science goes from the finite (zero and unity, the fixed beginning, the point, the segment, etc.) to the cosmological, spatiotemporal, and mathematical infinite. By contrast, philosophy inverts this program and, since Spinoza, has moved implicitly or explicitly from the infinite to the finite. The definite and the finite create a problem. The analytic of finitude, of its places and moments, of its place in the world, emerges in contemporary thought, which is to say in thought that seeks to be born, and which is aborted, though the impact of this inversion of scientific knowledge—which does not destroy it but rather overcomes it—is not yet fully understood. In the whole of Kostas Axelos's works, the dialectic of the finite and the infinite at the heart of the world comes through in all its magnitude, enveloping the dialectic of the outplayed player who becomes the plaything [le jouet] of becoming. He perceives at the heart of finitude the presence and absence of the infinite (becoming): the space–time that gathers up the finite, fragments it, and fragments itself into it, which multiplies and totalizes itself, the irreversible and irredeemable path of life inseparable from death. In an errancy with neither beginning nor assignable end, with neither truth nor error.

This way of ending and beginning, this inaugural act, this initial and therefore initiating program that properly belongs to Axelos are not the only possibilities today. Through theoretical research we can doubtless also take into account all of political and social practice—and attempt in a critical manner to totalize it through the work of the negative (the "crisis"). Putting things thus into a perspective that is offered rather than imposed, play receives no ontological privilege; it cannot pass for that which reveals the world and becoming. It is one moment among others, always unique and never the same and yet stands in a relation to the Other and other moments: love, creation, action, contemplation and meditative repose, knowledge, etc. Which would tend to overcome the passage, the transition, between philosophy and meta-philosophy. We shall return to this . . .

A philosopher, then, but Kostas Axelos is the last one. Anyone who does not believe that this situation has clearly been shown should consider those who regard themselves "philosophers," or who have been bestowed with the title. What do they do? Either inventories of the knowledge acquired by others, or attempts to make old philosophy fertile through random bits of partial knowledge: historical, sociological (the author of these pages could slip in a little self-critique, here, but is this the place?), biological, psychological, and of course psychoanalytic and even political. Is this still philosophy? No. It is rather a mix of knowledge and abstract speculations. Often agreeable, this mixture certainly responds to a curiosity, an expectation. The philosopher who draws inspiration from such fragmented knowledge along the way encounters the specialist in this knowledge, who would also claim to be a philosopher and a "generalist." Hence some spectacular successes. But these fashionable books only indicate the withering away of philosophy. They no longer realize a philosophical approach and do not generate an innovative approach. Kostas Axelos cannot place himself among the official, superficially critical, and even contestatory gravediggers of philosophy. In any case, he has never had much success, but his stature does not cease to grow.

Certain intellectuals who have read or tried to read the books of Kostas Axelos perpetrate some curious misunderstandings about them. They would doubtless attribute to him the idea that "man" and his planet risk their existence, with "man" being threatened and assailed from all sides by forces that he himself unleashed—technology and arms, spiraling demographics, the exhaustion of resources and the ravaging of Nature, the explosion of venerated entities, namely the town, reason, the nation, the family, the State, history, etc. They would even attribute to him the idea that "man" emerges before his own eyes only due to these threats, which dissolve so-called ideological illusions, including humanism. However, these philosophers attribute to Axelos a representation that is itself ideological. They believe that "man," for Axelos, finds an invisible counterpart in some kind of malevolent demon or a cruel god who toys with him. This absolute player would take part in a contest with "man," either in accordance with strict rules like those of chess, or by leaving the greater part to chance, like in poker. The gamble—what is in play—for "man" is himself.

Yet this representation distorts the thought of Axelos. The play of the world, for him, is time—becoming. Human activities and knowledge in general gamble on repetition: the repetition of movements, actions, signs, situations, experiences. Even reflection gambles on redundancy. Which tries to negate by putting a stop to its becoming. Yet sooner or later, becoming sweeps away that which resists it. It ushers in the unforeseen, the nonrepetitive, like Heraclitus's child who plays without rules, whimsically, but always in a way that upsets the order assumed by the pawns or the pieces of the game. This is neither absurd nor irrational, for becoming plays out through that to which it has itself given rise, and which struggles in vain to live on against it. "Time is a child at play: the kingdom is a child's."[6] This is the Heraclitean aphorism to which Heidegger comes at the end of his course—and it is from this aphorism that Axelos departs in order to take it further.[7]

He knows that neither dialectics nor logic form a part of "superstructures," and that in any case, this latter concept and the problems associated with it—base and superstructure—collapse into the debris left to us by history. The Heraclitean dialectic, we ought to recall, enunciates propositions that derive from immediacy and direct contact with the world: fire, rivers, childhood, etc. In order to traverse these, "man" subsequently gave rise to multiple and powerful mediations between himself and the world. He separated that which was confusing and brought together that which was given separately. It is not only a case of representations—like nature and gods and/or god—but of capacities that belong to "man" and come from him, even if they interpose themselves between man and the world, between man and himself. Our understanding of all these forms of mediation (in science and the sciences, but also works of art and civilization, like the city) has been constituted, traveled, traversed. Last among these: technique and technology, which follow their courses endowed with an autonomy that is both apparent and real. Apparent, in that these are human powers [*puissances*]—real, in that these powers constitute the "real," turning back against "man," threatening him, superseding him, destining him to impotence [*l'impuissance*] before his own powers (which is so well expressed by the philosophical term of alienation).

For Kostas Axelos, we—which is to say "man" and modernity, the thought that reawakens itself or is awoken—enter into a new immediacy, into a new relation with the world that passes over mediations without, in so doing, misrecognizing or rejecting them: on the contrary, by totalizing them. The specificity of each power and the differences (between them)—for example between techniques and art—imply relations among them. These powers are simultaneously relative and absolute. Which implicates/explicates on one hand their capacity for autonomy and on the other their place within the totality. This totality, which has never disappeared and which gives rise to different

powers, albeit powers that are concealed by the way they fragment the totality, now is recovered through its fragments—the totality in becoming, fragmentary and fragmented, open and multidimensional. The intuition of that
which animates becoming—the game of the world—enables it to dominate
ancient philosophy by reactualizing the aphoristic flashes, the philosophies
of Heraclitus and Parmenides, that herald and precede this philosophy. Philosophy tried in vain to overcome the mediations and separations with which
it was contemporaneous, bringing them back together in a system; but the
time had not yet come for the totality present in the relation between "man
and world." Philosophers would consequently accentuate rather than overcome the separations. They took to the absolute a representation of Being,
Truth, Nature, God, the essence of the human. . . . It is thus that the spirit of
Heraclitus traverses the work of Kostas Axelos: poetic lyrics, apodictic formulae, aphorisms, but also expositions succeeding one another in the rigorous order that thought in movement intimates to them.

Hence there where empiricism believed it saw either an objective determinism, either as the result of a free will or just simply the effects of chance
(so much controversy over chance and necessity . . .), the critical analysis of
Axelos shows play and games. Even if the players do not know that they play,
even if there are no explicit rules and the stakes [*enjeux*] only appear in the
endgame [*fin de partie*]. Thus, the politics (the political) that is at times taken
for an art, at times for a science, and at times for a technique boils down to
projects and strategies. And victory? Never certain. Defeat? Never guaranteed.
It is necessary to try, to attempt, to pave the way forward. This flight forward
would seem to be quite frequent. But if there are multiple games, frivolous,
serious, or both at once, the games consisting in sequences of smoothly accomplished actions are inscribed, according to Axelos, in a much more vast
framework or horizon; the world of human games is part of the play in the
world and the game of the world. How to grasp the latter? In a general or
rather universal intuition that falls under common sense but loses itself in
knowledge, in determinist reflections, in rationality—*logos*—as in irrationality. Philosophers have lacked this intuition; they pass over it in the name of
received knowledge, positing the priority of determination or determinism,
opposing necessity to chance and getting lost in this opposition. Kostas Axelos
returns to this fundamental intuition; he brings it to a concept, to language.

Whether badly or well understood, this thesis remains a little bit paradoxical. If becoming implies errancy, if the planet Earth merits this name, how

can the totality encounter itself or be recovered? How can it be understood or recognize itself? Does the totality not include truth? Do error, appearance, illusion, and lies boil down to the concealment of the total by its own works and its own fragments? How can a theoretical and only theoretical act—an act of thought—acquire the ability to reinstate the global that is lost along the way, and to recover the immediate? In short, for the most attentive readers of Kostas Axelos, there remains an aporia: "Errancy, Truth? The true totality?" A prisoner of truth, Axelos remains a philosopher, at the frontier of meta-philosophy. . . .

It is necessary to recognize, however, that Axelos is not short of arguments. Does not the experience of modernity show the most reasonable attempts as the most insane, that the best-laid strategies have failed, turned away from their objective (their *target*, as specialists would say)? In such a way that the result always surprisingly differs from the initial intentions and envisaged goals. In this sense, without there being symmetry or even analogy, the failure of fascism responds to the failure of the revolutions following Marx and Marxism. How can we forget that the heralding of the withering away of the State and of the political in so-called scientific socialism gave rise to an all-powerful State and a worldwide reinforcement of the political? And what is the worldwide if not the market plus strategies? More and more clearly, every action, including political action, appears as a wager with risks and dangers, fortune and misfortune, possibilities of losing or winning (but what? Something other than expected.). The notions of play [*jeu*], stakes [*enjeu*], risk, tactical and strategic operations, are generalized, though without, for all that, making reference to Axelos, who, like Heraclitus, haughtily contemplates this passably unworldly [*immonde*] world—this pile of crap. . . .[8]

But isn't this still a weak point? The philosopher of Play watches the games but does not play them. A weakness that comes close to those of the great names of the philosophy that is withering away. There is a theory of the project in Heidegger, but there is no Heideggerian project. Likewise in Jean-Paul Sartre, though to an attenuated or finer degree. Now it is certain that there is no consciousness without a project, no action without possibilities. No more than there is a subject without an object. The question that comes up is therefore of how to construct an acceptable project, which is to say one with some prospect, and how to gamble on its eventuality. How to play. At the risk of losing.

Axelos would doubtless reply: "I play with the theory of Play; my game possesses a privilege: No one will know how to outplay me . . ." What luck!

(Here I open a parenthesis. A long one. I, Henri Lefebvre, raise my voice here to say that, since the beginning, in reading the books of Kostas Axelos, I have found much more of, and much better elaborated, something from my own first writings. It was around 1925: the end of the postwar, the restoration of capitalism in the West, surrealist protest and contestation, imperialist war in Morocco, the consolidation of the Communist Party, etc. It was therefore before Stalinism and Trotskyism, before *Being and Time,* before the publication of the philosophical works of the so-called "young" Marx—which we would come to know upon their publication in France. We: a group of young philosophers, with a journal, *Philosophies*—which is remembered rather too little—though many texts and authors have been exhumed. I would like to recall that Norbert Guterman, Georges Politzer, Pierre Morhange, a bit later Paul Nizan, and many others were in this group. A curious bunch, rivaling the surrealists, with whom relations were sometimes cordial and sometimes strained. I will pass over the anecdotes and stick to repeating that a good number of the themes that would subsequently excite contemporary reflection were to be found in this journal, either anticipated or explicitly formulated. Including the controversies over psychoanalysis. This group was, and would emerge as, the [or more modestly, a] head peeping out amidst the enigmatic chaos of modernity. For my part, in addition to nature and naturalness, I rejected every substantialization of consciousness and the subject, I also rejected, alongside the transcendence of consciousness and thought, the thesis of a preexisting or given essence of "man." This was not so much and not only to theorize freedom, but also to affirm *adventure.* This term, philosophically freed from its trivial meaning, roughly designated what Kostas Axelos calls *opening,* the initial act of thought opening the way, without preconditional logic or ontologic. Hence the idea, or, if you will, the hypothesis of a time without the guaranteed support of nature or substance, but not without relations. This idea of adventure was in accord with, though not without some distance from, surrealism, even if the preference for philosophy prohibited members of this group from accepting the absolute priority of poetic language, affirmed to the point of revolutionary action by André Breton. This idea or this representation of adventure rested on a kind of existential phenomenology before its time, lengthy extracts of which appeared in the journal. I remember that my friends and I would often embark on a kind of supreme monadology, according to which the forces and moments of human life, Love, Understanding, Poetry, and Action were neither pure and distinct forms, nor substances, nor simple relations, but [without following too closely the philosophy of Leibniz] were defined as "monads," which is to say absolute and yet without transcendence, relative or rather relational: endowed with a sovereign existence but only acting through relations with one another and the universe. Interactions with nothing guaranteed, with each one of the forces referring back to the others. From this perspective, understanding was only a monad, in relation with all other monads and the totality.

(The group of philosophers renounced these hunches, these anticipations, shortly after 1925 in order to adhere to Marxism and, by way of consequence, to the Communist Party. At the same time so too did the majority of surrealists, it should be noted, as well as the intelligentsia of the avant-garde. Hence a series of *misadventures,* to which it is not worth returning here, except to recall the provisional abandonment of philosophy and the huge amount of energy deployed in a struggle on several fronts: against capitalism and its ideologies, against the dogmatic attitude that was already becoming fixed on the inside of the Communist Party, against the unconditional admiration for the USSR, etc. In any case, since the publication of the works of the young Marx, we [soon reduced to two, Norbert Guterman and Henri Lefebvre, the first having furthermore left France for New York] returned, by way of expanding the critical analysis of reality, to a forgotten but transitional notion between philosophy and something else, the notion of alienation. A theme and a concept that, not without controversy, would realize a dizzying trajectory. Here ends the parenthesis, intended not to detract from Kostas Axelos but on the contrary to situate him by justifying the present homage . . .)

Rather than overcome philosophy himself, Kostas Axelos opens the horizon, shows the way. He sketches it out; he lays out the first markers. He "is" nascent and heralding thought. He knows that we have still perilously to advance down this road that ends up somewhere.[9] But where? We still do not think, do not yet know. We are emerging from the stuttering attempts that have lasted more than twenty-five centuries in the West. What does the world hold in store for us? We do not yet know how what the Greeks called *physis* or *hylè,* which is to say nature or matter, operates; we know that they saw in it an immanent, intelligible order, a vision that was unconfirmed and moreover not Heraclitean. All those who have believed they have grasped an ultimate element of nature, living or non-living matter, have thus far found themselves disabused in the same way as all those who sought to define a universal law. The infinite infinity of the world, the spatiotemporal with all the complexities it harbors, with the scarcely extricable intertwining of beginnings and ends and without anthropomorphic final goals, remains to be explored. But this is only one aspect of the emerging problematic: the relation of thought to the world comes to the fore.

Nietzsche glimpsed tragic understanding: he relinquished it for a vertiginous and reassuring vision of absolute repetition, the eternal return. A vertiginous and ultimately reassuring vision, like the clarity of the sun above Zarathustra's cave or the rock of Surlei.[10] For better and for worse, Nietzsche associated the eternal return with a no less vertiginous and reassuring prophecy of the Overman. New and strong, his poetic words spread the news but did not entail the realization of the promise.

Tragic understanding cannot be confused with tragedy, the work of art. Tragedy presupposes the tragic but metamorphosizes it by uprooting it from the everyday and exposing it; it transforms the tragic by putting it on stage. Tragedy moreover cannot be confused with a philosophical consciousness or with a state of consciousness; with the comprehension of any particular past or present situation. Often thought to be identical, the tragic and the dramatic are profoundly distinct from one another.

In the grip of tragedy, which is to say of becoming, Kostas Axelos knows this and knows it magnificently. He captures and attacks "realities" at their weak points, at the links that give way toward the dark side, which optimists of rationality since Hegel have always said is the better side: the side of change for the better, always for the better, the side of the sense of history. Kostas Axelos ruthlessly exposes that which waits for something, and it is rarely favorable, though he does not always exclude this hypothesis. In fact, Axelos is not exactly a systematic pessimist, he does not denigrate. He assumes no fleeting value as either positively or negatively established. Nor, in so doing, does he tend toward the feeling Nietzsche called tragic optimism. But no one up until now has successfully been able to define this perspective on, or rather this assessment of, the world. The two words are to be heard separately; we understand the first better than the second, and their association remains paradoxical. And yet doesn't their link designate the *value* to come? It remains to be seen if "man" can follow the poet and declare: "Deep is the suffering of the world, but deeper still is joy."[11] Isn't this promise also difficult to keep? What a gamble! What a weird game!

Kostas Axelos's critique of modernity has much magnitude and force. It leads him to hate and it fascinates. He has written unforgettable pages on the

City and its deterioration, on Ethics and on Logic and its place in knowledge, on planetary man, on the worldwide today and its derisory aspects.[12] Decline, corruption, withering, and rotting closely follow or accompany formation and ascension, for Axelos. His dialectical critique magisterially realizes the work of the negative at the heart of modernity "such as it is." However, he states the tragic only indirectly, by reducing it to what is for him a privileged aspect, the game. And the Game is without doubt, and certainly only a moment, but one moment among others, without predominance, and is itself swept away by and in becoming.

Three screens mask the tragedy of becoming: the everyday, Logic (the logical), and institutionalized Knowledge, considered as received wisdom; an indispensable and perhaps even beneficial error. It is necessary, it is inevitable that they be *there (Da)*.[13] They constitute and establish "reality," this singular mix of the concrete and the abstract, signs and things, truths and illusions, static appearances and dynamic lies. "Reality" dissimulates the world to us: the *mundane* [*mondain*] serves as a screen. Hence the strange oscillation that ensures that the "real" seems wholly "unreal," like a dream and sometimes even a nightmare. And that the "more real," the world beyond this familiar reality, often seems surreal. "Reality," whose construction begins in the repetitive, resists becoming, and it is thus that it hides from us this becoming, which is to say the tragic. "*Es ist so! . . .* [Thus it is! . . .]" And on the condition of not allowing ourselves to be duped, it is also thus that we open our eyes through and go beyond the mask. Into the world. On the path of metaphilosophy, which is to say of the understanding of the tragic.

And what of tragedy? And its relation to the tragic? Nietzsche tried to break through the enigma. He did not manage it but perceived the questioning: "How and why do the ghastly, the horrible, and the intolerable, represented and given as spectacles, bring much more than agreement, and more than esthetic pleasure, a joy?"[14] By what surprising transfiguration that perhaps anticipates thought? How was Greece, the fatherland of Axelos, able to invent such a work, more than a form and more than an artistic creation, a work that marks our history, in the same way as another Greek invention, Logic, which faces history in a surprising symmetry . . . ? The enigma remains almost complete. Is this the propitious moment, and the place, for untying the umbilical knot?

In the last lines of his *Systematique ouverte*,[15] Kostas Axelos tells us that the world has "received" various names, broadly through the light and scotomizations[16] of *logos: logos, ôn, thèos, cosmos* and *physis, anthropos, history* and *society, technical Gestell* [échaufaudage technicien], *game*.[17] All these names and buzz-words and still many other formulations do not exhaust its game. *Logos* lets itself be named multiply and often decisively in the unity of its fragmentary totality; it is, however, more than all that. It "is" the opening of the time that is past–present–to come.

Translation by Gerald Moore, Neil Brenner, and Stuart Elden

Notes

1. [Kostas Axelos, *Systematique ouverte* (Paris: Éditions de Minuit, 1984), 142; translated by Gerald Moore as "The World: Being Becoming Totality."—*Eds.*]

2. [Friedrich Nietzsche, *Le livre du philosophe*, ed. Angèle Kremer Marietti (Paris: Aubier Flammarion, 1969), 85; see *Philosophy and Truth*, trans. Daniel Breazale (Atlantic Highlands, N.J.: Humanities Press, 1990), 33.—*Eds.*]

3. See Axelos's first two books, *Héraclite et la philosophie* (Paris: Éditions de Minuit, 1962) and *Marx, penseur de la technique* (Paris: Éditions de Minuit, 1961) [*Alienation, Praxis and Technē in the Thought of Karl Marx*].

4. See *Vers la pensée planétaire* (Paris: Éditions de Minuit, 1964), *Le jeu du monde* (Paris: Éditions de Minuit, 1969), and *Horizons du monde* (Paris: Éditions de Minuit, 1974).

5. [This is probably a reference to Wilfrid Desan, *The Planetary Man*, vol. 1, *A Noetic Prelude to a United World*, vol. 2, *An Ethical Prelude to a United World* (London: Macmillan, 1972). Axelos had the first volume translated for his Arguments series, to which he wrote a postface.—*Eds.*]

6. [A standard English translation of this fragment is found in Jonathan Barnes, *Early Greek Philosophy* (Harmondsworth: Penguin, 1987), 102: "Eternity is a child at play, playing drafts: the kingdom is a child's."—*Eds.*]

7. [This is a reference to Heidegger's course published as *The Principle of Reason*, trans. Reginald Lilly (Bloomington: Indiana University Press, 1992).—*Eds.*]

8. See *Problèmes de l'enjeu* (Paris: Éditions de Minuit, 1979), 123, among others.

9. [The French is "ce chemin qui va quelque part," a reversal of the standard French translation of Heidegger's book *Holzwege*—*Chemins qui ne menent nulle part* (Roads That Go Nowhere).—*Eds.*]

10. [In *Ecce Homo*, Nietzsche recounts that he developed the idea of an "eternal return of the same" when he encountered the rock of Surlei—"6,000 feet beyond man and time"—on a hike in the Swiss Alps (trans. Walter Kaufman [New York, 1967], 295). In *Thus Spoke Zarathustra*, the movement of the sun is Zarathustra's first sense of this return.—*Eds.*]

11. [Friedrich Nietzsche, *Thus Spoke Zarathustra*, in *The Portable Nietzsche*, ed. Walter Kaufmann (New York: Viking, 1954), 436, translation modified.—*Eds.*]

12. See the essay "La ville-problème" in *Problèmes de l'enjeu* (Paris: Éditions de Minuit, 1979), and also *Pour une éthique problématique* (Paris: Éditions de Minuit, 1972),

Contributions à la logique (Paris: Éditions de Minuit, 1977), and *Horizons du monde* (Paris: Éditions de Minuit, 1974).

13. [The parenthetical *Da* is Lefebvre's interjection following the French *là.—Eds.*]

14. [This is close to a claim in Friedrich Nietzsche, *The Birth of Tragedy*, sect. 24, although if so Lefebvre's translation is rather liberal.—*Eds.*]

15. Paris: Éditions de Minuit, 1984.

16. [On the meaning of scotomization, see chap. 11 n.7.—*Eds.*]

17. [*Échaufaudage*, or "scaffold" is Axelos's translation of Heidegger's notion of *Gestell*. The standard English translation of this term is "enframing," in *The Question Concerning Technology and Other Essays*, trans. William Lovitt (New York: Harper and Row, 1977).—*Eds.*]

14 The Worldwide Experience

This is the final chapter from the final volume of *De l'État*. Here, Lefebvre briefly analyzes the philosophical roots of his notions of the world, drawing on Heraclitus, Marx, Heidegger, and Axelos. He provides an important, succinct discussion of the world market and the growth of multinational firms, and he distinguishes the agrarian, industrial, and urban phases of capitalist development. Lefebvre also discusses the relation between the concept of the worldwide and history. This chapter thus illustrates how Lefebvre's theoretical work builds on and critiques traditional historical materialism by incorporating a spatial perspective. Through a number of contemporary political examples, Lefebvre explores some of the practical implications of his analyses in *De l'État*. The key concepts here are, again, those of the state mode of production, *mondialisation*, and *autogestion.—Eds.*

The Revolution had been relied upon to create the "world" and "worldness" [*le "monde" et la "mondialité"*]. It was the *worldwide revolution* [*la révolution mondiale*]. Today we have to realize that the worldwide and worldness, with their hazardous and unforeseen features, constitute the "revolution" itself, instead of concluding it.

But what is revolution? What is the worldwide? After an initial look we notice the prodigious complexity of the movement: the worldwide market, generalization of state power, generalized but processed information, unbridled demography and technology, space, the Third World and minorities, ethnic groups, women, peasants, youth, etc. The working-class movement set out by Marx and Marxism as (fundamentally and essentially) privileged, would only be a movement among others, important, or the most important, but the generator of contradictions, and not the only one. Which requires a reconsideration of the "worldwide."

That having been said, the concept of the *worldwide* made itself known. It detaches itself slowly, but not without difficulties, from the historical. Concept rather than metaphor? Of course, but with a new meaning, placing emphasis on the possible and not on the "real."

We do not have to examine here certain important and maybe decisive aspects of the "worldwide," such as the "aero-politics" of information. One only has to mention them. Information reserves more than one surprise.[1] From these elements should now be drawn aspects and moments, the concept of the worldwide, present from the outset in this work: now this concept, this point of departure and anchorage point is far from explanation. It appeared *dialectically* as what is shown, designated, given rise to, *produced* by the whole of present-day forces, and as what they conceal, inhibit, forbid, and thwart. Which poses without resolving it the question of the *worldwide* as possible/impossible, as out-of-reach virtuality. For whom? For those who carry along the movements that engender these very same virtualities.

The worldwide paradoxically appears on the horizon as possibilities already partially (sketchily) realized, induced, and produced, but also resisted and thwarted by the forces in action in modernity. Conversely, the worldwide tends to break obstacles, explode boundaries, and drag along that which opposes it. We already know how the State is becoming worldwide [*se mondialise*] and at the same time opposes the worldwide. Nation–states, attached to a territory, managers of this space, arbitrate and act as the dominant power from and by this space. They manage it as *eminent* owners, almost in the way this word meant under the *ancien régime,* whereby the written rights and powers of the nobles and the king were superimposed on the common rights of the peasants, "commoners," holders of perpetual usufruct.[2] An analogous superimposition governs the modern State and its relationship to its space (territory). Methods (sometimes compelling and sometimes violent) and multiple procedures, the best known of which is "expropriation," give concrete expression to this eminent right, which we know extends itself to under the ground and to airspace, forests, and water sources, rivers, coasts, and maritime territories and to recently extended territorial waters. Productive forces tend to the worldwide. Unfortunately, this tendency of productive forces—the latest worldwide experiences and of primary importance—has engendered "supra" or "multi" firms and companies that, as we know, tend to outclass States and use them to dominate and manage a territory to their profit.

When philosophy has explored worldness, it has established significant propositions. When Heidegger utters "*Die Welt weltet*" (the world worlds [*le monde se mondifie*]),[3] this statement, which is close to a tautology, has great meaning. He means to say that the worldwide conceives itself in and by itself and not by another thing (history, spirit, work, science, etc.). The world becomes world, becoming what virtually it was. It transforms itself by becoming worldwide. In it discovery and creation converge. It does not exist before it creates itself, and yet, it proclaimed itself, possible/impossible, through all the powers, technology, knowledge, art. This "terminus ad quem" has a consistence and an existence in its own right. Are we looking to the "terminus a quo," inaccessible and definitively lost, for the original?[4] That is a mistake of ancient philosophy. The secret, the code of being, is not discovered in the original, but in the possible, without omitting history. The whole process, history (of being in Heidegger) can and must be considered, but does not contain the word of the enigma. The possible and the impossible manifest themselves in the here and now as call or interpellation The worldwide cannot represent itself. The worldly [*mondain*] represents itself: it is composed of representations (is conceived by representative thoughts), according to principles of identity, of difference, of non-contradiction, abstract principles. The being [*l'étant*] is represented, but not Being [*l'Être*]. The worldwide is born from cosmic duration; it is produced as world, "by making luminous, making shine the dispensations taken by the being," it is the dispenser of being. Heidegger adds, along the lines of Heraclitus: "the dispensation of being—a child that plays." Man is engaged in this game and thus sets into motion: play is without why, but it is played and cannot but play. Only play remains, that which is the most elevated and the most profound. It is the One, the Unique. Therefore the Worldwide, the stake of this game [*enjeu de ce jeu*] in which being, no longer hiding itself, will unfold and spread.[5]

In the same vein, K. Axelos defines or rather conceives the world as a "limitless horizon." The play of the world embraces and crushes games and rules, transgressions and calculations, significations and interpretations, all the truths and all the figures of error. The worldwide would not have, according to Axelos, more consistency than the real or the actual. The totality on the move or rather in progress has neither center nor focus, nor source nor core: this non-center, which is play that in this way plays at chasing a center. He who is closest to a center is at the same time he who is furthest from it, whether philosopher or scholar, lover or politician, magician or artist. All great thinkers think (and miss) the meaning of the totality of the world. Thus Nietzsche's thought has a center: the death of God. But his voice says and repeats that there is no answer in the (modern) world to the *why*, as the world of non-total totality (the being inseparable from nothingness and death) has no ground: is play. So that Nietzsche anticipates the crisis of the *future world* (of the possible). After Marx and Nietzsche the death of philosophy has long been celebrated, institutionalized, and ritualized. It no longer counts because it counts for too much, wanting itself to be competent and accountable. The philosopher no longer plays, no longer takes part in the game, while basic forces and their powers continue their game: language and thought, work and struggle, love and death, which leads the game, sometimes by their presence, sometimes by their absence—sometimes by the *said* sometimes by the *done* (the Logos and Praxis). For us the *planetary* is the only figure accessible to the worldwide. Thus goes the world without truce, without end.[6]

Before the transition from philosophy to metaphilosophy, Marx had explored the worldwide by contributing a double proposition, one "realist," the other theoretical. For Marx, in practical terms, the world first takes this form: *the worldwide market*. Marx had outlined history: he began the elaboration of the concept without finishing it. He differentiates between periods of the worldwide market: before capitalism and after capitalism. He knows that commodity and money markets go together but no more coincide with one another than with the labor market (of the labor force). The worldwide market, for Marx, already multiplied and differentiated, always presents itself according to a spatial configuration. The domination of a political power and center (England in Marx's time) entails and governs this configuration that rules over the currents (flows) of goods and investments—but not without giving rise to often-violent interactions and reactions. Marx completed neither this analysis nor the reintegration of the spatial (the ground and underground, the earth and land rent) into his account of reality.

The world and the worldwide are also understood by Marx from the point of departure of philosophy, that is, from its overcoming. Philosophy makes itself world: it makes the world and the world is made through it. The world is produced to the precise extent that philosophy is realized and, realizing, becomes world. Philosophers have interpreted the world: now it must be changed; can this change be accomplished without philosophy?[7] No, because it consists in the practical realization of what philosophers have only thought or represented: freedom, happiness, knowledge, joy. Who can realize philosophy by overcoming it, by realizing it in such a way that it becomes world?

Who carries the becoming-world (the world in becoming and the becoming of the world)? *Total* revolution, which proclaims and executes the order of endings, the end of capitalism, of the bourgeoisie, of the State, of the family and the nation, of work, of the separated individual, of the historical, of the economical, and of the political, etc. So, the working class, the bearer of this capacity, is *universal* as such and only as such.

In the course of the present work, we have proposed the theoretical discourse—a non-contradictory discourse on the contradictions of the modern world—which envisages the worldwide. By *becoming worldwide [en se mondialisant]* on the basis of the worldwide market, the State opens and closes the paths of worldness. This therefore calls for the end of the State (that is, its withering away). This last image of historical time is also the first of worldwide space—an image that will fade and already is becoming blurred before other configurations. The world? It is the planetary, therefore *space* at one and the same time product and work: an ensemble of places, and result of a creative and thus artistic activity, both conscious and unconscious. The worldwide does not define itself by Nature; the latter opens onto the worldwide, but transformed into "second nature," disturbing and poorly defined. The Earth, threatened by terricide,[8] as such the stake of a terrible game, is proposed as the beginning and end of the productive-creative activity. Before that of the galaxy, planetary space gives itself to the human species as theater and scenario, field of the possible, and sudden appearance of the unforeseen.

The State, this unforeseen that political thought could have and should have foreseen, which it glimpsed with Hegel without daring to extend it to the world, by reserving it for Europe and the elected nation—the State has nothing eternal about it. Already the absolute and perfect State, the nation–State according to Hegel and according to the French revolution, this State is moving away. It explodes, caught in contradictions, torn apart between what overwhelms it from the inside and from the outside. In this, the State relates to history and historicity and time. What will carry it away and already is sweeping it away? Worldness. The State has not lost its link with the "real," notably with the spatial. It runs the risk, precisely in this way, of becoming the instrument of multinational firms, or of collapsing under their blows and manipulations. The least of these risks: to consolidate, enrich and become more oppressive and repressive. This State will not let itself wither away or be overcome without resistance. Which announces new events similar but without reproducing them to the older ones (fascism, Stalinism, anarchism, terrorism, etc.). Perhaps the worldwide would take form only in the course of a worldwide crisis? Or after it?

To grasp the worldwide, would it be necessary to interview the CEO of IBM, or an illustrious American expert in the style of Galbraith?[9] Let us find solace in the problems of this approach. These personalities do not perhaps have the global concept or vision that a sympathetic appreciation attributes to them. The CEO is easily persuaded that the interests of the firm might be identified with those of the USA and of the world as a whole. With regard to the illustrious expert, does he, too, not risk conflating the strategy of the U.S. State and of high capitalism with worldness [*mondialité*]?

Let us return, rather, to probe more deeply into the concepts, toward Marx and Marxism. Why? Because the thought of Marx also constitutes the world-wide, and doubly so: in becoming worldwide [*se mondialisant*] on a theoretical level; and in giving practical impetus to the movements that have changed the world and moving in a worldwide direction. It does this by taking account of drifts, diversions, failures; and furthermore by defining theory (including Marxist theory) as an activity that brings practice, which is to say the real transformation of the world, to bear on language and concepts, by rigorously linking them together.

Considered over the "long term," which is to say after some duration (and not short term, after a brief duration), the practical transformation of the world has experienced three phases. Only analysis can distinguish them. This differentiation is deliberate, because theoretical thought must not jumble to-gether these *moments*, even and especially because they interact and obstruct one another. In social practice, these phases have obstructed one another, sometimes violently, their movements gaining strength through combat with one another.

a) *The Agrarian Phase:* the transformation of agriculture, of land ownership, of ground (and underground) rents and revenues;

b) *The Industrial Phase:* introduction of and changes to industrial labor, hence also of technology—initially, at least, under the administration of the bourgeoisie. Modern forms of production and surplus value (com-prehensive [*global*] overproduction);

c) *The Urban Phase:* general urbanization, induced through industrializa-tion—the reorganization of society as a whole around urban centers (of power, of decision making).

It is clear that these phases are intertwined and affect one another. The transformations of world agriculture were accomplished through economic pressure from the industries of "developed" countries and through the political
pressure of imperialism. Industrialization rolls out amid ruptures in the initially primitive accumulation of capital. If we examine the history of Europe
and the countries at the "forefront of progress" at the outset of industrialization, namely England and France, we observe that the transformations of
agriculture and farming precede industrial capitalism but follow merchant
capitalism and the formation of the world market, accompanying the first
symptoms of industrialization (manufacturing, the importance of cloth and
textile production, the initial growth of towns, etc.). As for the urban period,
this flows from industrialization, but also from the transformation of the
countryside: the ruination of part of the peasantry, migratory movements,
the summoning of the labor force into the towns . . .

    The social and political forces that were set into action, and the causes and
effects of the movements and struggles, differ greatly according to the phase
and the moment. The agrarian phase was driven by poor or bankrupt peasants
whose revolts were not easily transformed from peasant uprisings [*jacquerie*]
into revolutions; they required an external input that was both theoretical
(Marxism) and practical (leaders from other strata and classes, notably from
the working class). An essential episode in this phase was agrarian reform.
Leaving aside a historical fact, namely that the French revolution achieved,
without naming it as such, an agrarian reform that was as vast as it was exemplary, these revolutionary reforms continued throughout a good deal of
the twentieth century. Oriented toward a form of primitive accumulation that
was deemed "socialist," these reforms constituted the essential political act of
the Russian and Chinese revolutions. The hypothesis that agrarian problems
and their solutions have blemished "socialism" demands theoretical reflection. It explains the drift from socialism toward statism and the SMP. A proletarian revolution in Marx's sense has not yet occurred: both the political
and the social orientations of the urban "phase" remain indeterminate. Up to
the present, the revolutions of the twentieth century have remained bound to
the soil, to the earth, to national territory; they remain tainted by national-
ism; they obscure the worldwide horizon while simultaneously opening it up.

    Peasant revolutions and agrarian reforms have transformed the surface of
the planet, exhausting their possibilities during the course of the twentieth
century. Everything has happened as if the working class had let the peasants

do as they please, casting a favorable eye over their activities and joining with them, albeit cautiously. Agrarian reforms everywhere favored the extension of the (internal and external) market, hence the unfurling of the world of the commodity and general circulation. And yet, these activities have had a revolutionary impact at the worldwide scale; they defeated a class. They did not completely liquidate the feudal aristocracy and landed (latifundiary) property.[10] There remain traces, even fragments, of them (Spain, Italy, Mexico, etc.), notably in Southern Europe, not to mention in the Arab world. And yet, the landed aristocracy was close to extinction. Long withering away, seeking rebirth in Europe (France, England, etc.), with the rise of capitalism this class lost, at a worldwide scale, its monopoly over private land ownership (the "double monopoly" described by Lenin). If this class reappears, this happens in unforeseen ways: through the possession of the underground and its riches (the oil of the emirates, etc.). Along with the aristocracy, though for different reasons, the village community and the village itself disappears.

The industrial phase has been managed by "representatives" of the bourgeoisie and other classes, representatives aligning themselves with the administration of capitalism but readily bringing about *something else* unforeseen: the state mode of production. The bourgeoisie and the capitalist administration of growth have given rise to the adversarial forces of the working class. This has exerted a continuous pressure during the course of the twentieth century, a push if not a puncture. The revolutionary breakthrough has failed. Where? In Europe, and specifically in Germany, in conditions that have yet to be fully elucidated.[11] The workers' mobilizations have nonetheless obtained significant results in highly industrialized countries, and in several others. These results include the legalization of trade unions and the institution of labor law (union rights, the right to work, workers' rights). Considered not unreasonably as a major victory for workers, the legalization of trade unions has, however, entailed unexpected consequences: their bureaucratization, their association with the play of forces and with "posturing" ["*representations*"], their operation at the heart of existing society, their manipulation. At a worldwide scale, everything has happened as if the working class had exhausted its capacities for transformation (of itself and of social practice). We can ask ourselves whether this class is not declining, following a brief and tragic saga, without having attained the status of "political subject," "hegemonic," or "ruling class." Resurgences are, in any case, not impossible—far from it. The supposed integration of the working class into capitalism is only an illusion (an ideology asserting that illusions and traps have worked successfully). That the working class participates in the operation and general circulation of existing society (the circulation of goods, representations, information, and even enjoyment) is a generalized fact. That there is no longer either resistance or reluctance is a dogmatic assertion. The proof: the fractures within the workers' movement, the "brutal" strikes and revolts, the "grassroots" aspirations. It could be that the period of proletarian revolutions has begun. This is more of a plausible, if not probable, hypothesis than a thesis!

Urban questions and movements do not today have the complex and troubled history of the peasant and workers' movements. They emerge, they appear and disappear pretty much everywhere in the world. The problems posed by the modern city (the exploded historical city and the city of the present, both endowed with peripheries, suburbs, and often immense extensions, the agglomeration situated at the core of a proliferating urban fabric) are worldwide problems. The organization of space is at stake in urban movements of highly variable intensities and objectives. This new phenomenon reaches out, so to speak, toward earlier movements. The peasant movement likewise radically and directly changed the organization of space. Industrialization and the workers' movement changed it, but indirectly and blindly, through the space of business, of productive labor and various scales of the division of labor. *The urban problematic and related movements have obtained a major result: they have generated a language, concepts, and a theory of social space, its organization, its management.* During the course of this transformation, first nature (or primary matter) disappeared, leaving behind many traces and much nostalgia, and were replaced by second nature, the urban, the stake of new struggles.

What we see here is an effect at the worldwide scale that tends to assert itself as the reason and cause of spontaneous movements, and of decisions motivated by knowledge. Despite the restrictive, reductive, and reformist interpretations that accrue from various sources and blossom into manipulative ideology, the phase under consideration has a revolutionary effectiveness. At first, it tends to resurrect earlier phases. The peasants that spill into the cities acquire, without fitting in there, a rather unforeseen capacity for mobilization (in Latin America, for example). Workers, blue collar or not, who have obtained a decent level of compensation on business matters, salaries, and working hours, nonetheless find themselves stalked by space: transportation, urban infrastructures, etc. Their initiatives continue, sometimes multiplied and modulated, so to speak, by the new problems of the everyday. The city and the urban ultimately kindle highly diverse movements, from the most everyday demands to those of the urban guerrilla (who, specifically targeted, endlessly disappears and is reborn). So many science-fiction novels evoke the worldwide city [*la ville mondiale*], the metropolis [*cité*] of fifteen billion inhabitants covering planet Earth, run by computer but harboring tumultuous forces, provoking savage rebellions or great revolutions! . . .

How are such changes enacted? In a way that can be seen and felt, that can be read in the terrifying events described by historians such as invasions and revolutions? Here we glimpse one of the traps of historical thought, which condenses that which unfolds gradually, "over the long term," and summarizes it in a dramatic narrative. The drama? The tragedy? They are real, but they rarely come to the fore. One morning, some peasant family leaves some village; a long time afterward, another leaves too, then another, and the village disappears. In the vicinity of a small village market, a workshop is set up, grows, and one day the newcomer beholds an industrial town.

The everyday cloaks the transformations of the modern world. It conceals them and is revealed. Everydayness is assembled: payroll clocks and alarm clocks, leisure and travel. Nothing is accomplished without a plan, but that which is accomplished usually has nothing in common with plans (hence the philosophical misunderstanding regarding the importance of topics and plans!). With the transformation of the world, everydayness, too, becomes worldwide [*se mondialise*]. It becomes an integrating and integrated part of the world in formation and transformation. And once upon a time, the best and worst of times, it is everydayness, people say, that must be transformed. "Change life," but everyday life has smothered the dramas and the tragedies of modernity with its monotony and its intrusive drabness. Like the State, in consolidating itself, it has experienced wars and revolutions. In each case, it reacts obstinately to the questioning of "Why am I here? What am I doing? What is the meaning of life? What does the future hold?" But the everyday reacts to this questioning only by strangling it, causing it to be reborn perpetually from its dusty ashes . . .

What is becoming worldwide? We can enumerate its implications and consecutions. First, exchange, the market. Then the State, in the system of States, alongside technocracy, the state technostructure,[12] or rather the sharing of political power within each State among the technocrats, the military and the professional politicians (the whole constituting that which has been called, since Hegel, the "political society" above "civil society").

With its chaos drifts, schisms, detours, degeneration, reprisals, and comebacks—with its conflicts and contradictions—"Marxism" is an intrinsic part of the worldwide. But it is worth emphasizing once again here the conflicts and contradictions; "Marxism" includes different schools and tendencies; within it are juxtaposed, superimposed and opposed, received, and even trivialized truths, such as the importance of *productive forces* (techniques, the division of labor) and illusions (ideologized Marxism, the instrument of political manipulation), errors and failures, unforeseen possibilities, notably with respect to the theory of the State and the theory of worldness. Only this ensemble enters into the "worldwide" and merits the title *planetary*. From this perspective, it is therefore through Marxism that philosophy becomes worldwide: is realized in being overcome, and in being diversified. Which leaves the largest opening and the greatest role for works that end classical philosophy (Hegel and his following, up until the present), or which open horizons (Nietzsche and to a lesser extent Heidegger). Which excludes no one but does not include closed systems, all too conjunctural analyses, efforts to rescue classical philosophy, ultimately nihilism.

Has the "historicity–worldness" relation been fully elucidated? No. We have shown its conflictual, hence dialectical, character: unity and contradiction. The old metaphors of universal history and the world-historical have exploded. The historian, as such, does not attain universality. History opens onto something else, and the *Weltgeschichtlich* of Hegel, who posited the State as the end of history, constitutes the final error of a philosophical system that the philosopher decides to close. History has its end neither in the specific State of Prussian Germany, nor in the State in general. This rendering-identical of the historical and the worldwide is an intrinsic part of the logic of the State, which is ultimately victorious in the Hegelian dialectic. Dialectically, and in a contradictory manner, history stretches out into a post-history that, as Marx understood, entails the overcoming [*dépassement*] of the State. However, the solution to the "historicity–worldness" conflict has not, up until now, been fully drawn out, and neither has the movement that cuts across it and elicits the contradiction. How to exit history? (The aporia is glimpsed in *La fin de l'histoire*.) The conflict that is here envisaged, what type of *product* is it? In a sense, we return here to the aporia of Marxism (already mentioned, without explanation, in the chapter on "aporias" in *Métaphilosophie*), namely *transition* (the transitionary period).[13] If there is a passage, a qualitative leap from the historical to the worldwide, how is the transitional period presented and defined? With conflict henceforth recognized as fertile and not as sterilizing, what does it produce? Where is it going? Where and toward what does it lead? Toward the sequence of more or less explosive contradictions and conflicts that, for the moment, constitute modernity?

The questioning, which once again concerns the *possible* considered at one and the same time as founded on reality, and as perspective on the real, finds its answer in the trinity "historicity—worldness—spatiality." The "historicity—worldness" conflict resolves itself in and by the production of worldwide space, the work of a historical time in which it is realized. The contradictions conveyed by historical time go through various fortunes; some worsen, others wane; new contradictions manifest themselves, overloading the previous ones according to the conjuncture. It is through these obstacles, these risks, that the *new way* appears, which the present work has tried to open up. It is through these difficulties that new values are created, among which are those attached to space (work and product) that have been used here as illustration.

Let us include the following to the list of the experience of worldness:

a) *The mondialisation of Marxism,* as already noted with its numerous consequences. Certain "Marxist" concepts tend toward the concrete universal—that of praxis, that of contradiction and conflict, etc. As can be witnessed in the work of Mao Tse-Tung. Which on the contrary does not exclude either the renewed use of certain concepts (surplus product or global surplus value, organic composition of capital, etc.) or the introduction of new concepts (including the everyday, difference, the urban, social space, the SMP, etc.).

b) The *worldwide market,* one and many, understood at its most complex. Which involves the worldwide division of productive labor, knowledge at the worldwide scale and information, space on a worldwide (planetary) scale, gold as supreme equivalent, the problem of transfers of surplus value and monetary exchanges, etc.

c) The *existence,* the growing power, the menacing action of *worldwide firms* manipulating currencies, resources, territories, the States themselves (national or pluri-national).

d) *The nature of the transformation of the world,* made up of various movements, including (characteristically) of the working class.

e) *The failure of authoritarian and centralized planning (USSR).* A relative
failure: it accelerates growth but by directing it (heavy manufacture, arms)
and worsening internal inequalities (poorly developed zones, such as
agriculture). Which leads to an *inversion of the situation.* "Socialism"
and "Marxism" change into their opposites; absolute domination of the
State, ideology of the State, oppressive character of the State, etc.
	This relative failure of the SMP with "socialist" components corre-
sponds to the relative failure of the SMP with "capitalist" components.
The latter functions by also promoting gigantism (enterprises, cities)
and simultaneously by excluding from growth an increasing number of
casualties. The failures of the two forms of the SMP correspond but
should not be conflated. It could be that the future of the State differs
according to its modality of existence; that it degenerates here (without
withering away in the Marxist–Leninist sense) and that it prospers there
(without entering in the "reign of liberty").
	The failure of the SMP with "socialist" components involves the fail-
ure of a society (a "culture," a civilization) founded on labor and the valorization (ethical, aesthetic) of productive material (manual) work. The
corresponding failure of the SMP with capitalist components involves
the failure of a society founded on the formalism of art, discourse, etc.

f) *The mondialisation of the State* as hierarchical morphology conveys with
it *possibilities of rupture* rather than the stabilization of the whole. The
worldwide experience includes that of explosion, collapse, deterioration,
pulverization of state units (recent examples are Portugal, the State established by Salazar shattering [*volant en éclats*] after the death of the Prince,
Portuguese imperialism unable to sustain itself; or Chile).[14] It is one of
the essential elements or moments of the worldwide experience, which
confirms the impermanent nature of the State.

g) *The cultural revolution considered as political revolution:* assault from the
"grassroots" against hierarchical apparatuses (party, administrations,
institutions) erected above society.

h) *Autogestion* (along the lines of the Yugoslav experience) with its problematic: relations of self-managed [*autogérées*] units with the market and

investments; extension of the self-management [*autogestionnaire*] practice to all of social space.

i) *The Spanish and Italian experience of the regions,* of active decentralization, not without risk of a decomposition of the State, which would make it vulnerable to imperial powers and multinational firms, without inasmuch bringing about the rational withering away of the State and the double reabsorption of the State into civil society and of the political into the social. The region as substitute for the State is nonetheless an important stage in the global process.

Along this difficult road *difference,* category (concept) both theoretical and practical, that is to say gathering together long-disunited practice and theory, makes its way.

j) *The experience of 1968 in France and elsewhere:* the State threatened by the extension of the movement from a vulnerable point: the occupation of its space by the working class, etc.

k) Let's add here, pell-mell, disparate, often mentioned aspects: the pressure of worldness on each country and on each national State, the risks of productivism transformed into an absolute ideology, the explosion of spaces derived from history and historical time, the relativity of borders, the decline of political parties, etc.

The various moments of the worldwide experience do not lie outside one another. They form a whole: the acquired assets of theory and practice can in the twentieth century open and illuminate a path yet to be followed.

The outcome is that these times are not without challenges. These are challenging times! But what is being challenged? The products and creations of history. The challenge of the worldwide consists mostly in this, that the transformation of the world that produces the worldwide is accompanied by the most terrifying danger and terror. The planet enters its unitary existence and life at total risk. Which is not to say that destiny declares itself thus and that the final catastrophe will be fatal.

Revolution presents itself as worldness on the move: a transformation with multiple aspects, dominated by peasant, national, state [*étatiques*], and political questions. Turning the world upside down also includes the overturning of this domination. Which leaves room for the combined action of the worldwide working class and of theory reaching the concrete universal.

The theory explores the possible/impossible and declares that "one must" (a theoretical imperative, not an ethical one) want the impossible in order to realize the possible. Nothing closer to and nothing further from the possible. Utopia therefore assumes an urgent character. *Urgent utopia* defines a style of thinking turned toward the possible in all areas. Which tends to redefine "socialism" and "communism" not by the state [*l'étatique*] and the political, but by, on the one hand, a critique of the state [*l'étatique*] and the political, and on the other hand, as production, appropriation, and management [*gestion*] of space. Neither the individual nor the group exist without an appropriated space (produced as such).

Conceptual thought explores ways, ventures on paths. It can precede practice, but cannot separate itself from it. Practice alone, freed from political obsession and released from state pressure [*la pression étatique*], can effectively realize what promises to be the simultaneous use of concept and imagination (utopia). Theory opens the road, clears a new way; practice takes it, it *produces* the route and the space.

Translation by Elizabeth Lebas, Gerald Moore, Neil Brenner, and Stuart Elden

NOTES

1. See the book by A. Mattelart already mentioned and the "Radio-Alice" collective, Bologna, 1976. [Lefebvre is referring here, first, to Armand Mattelart, *Multinationales et systèmes de communications* (Paris: Anthropos, 1976; translated by Michael Chanan as *Multinational Corporations and the Control of Culture: The Ideological Apparatuses of Imperialism* (Brighton: Harvester Press, 1979); and second, to Collective A/Traverso, *Alice è il diavolo: Sulla strada di Majakovskij: Testi per una pratica di comunicazione sovversiva* (Milan: L'Erba Voglio, 1976), translated by Danièle Guillerm and G. Marco Montesano as *Radio Alice, Radio Libre*, preface by Félix Guattari (Paris: Jean-Pierre Delarge, 1977). The Radio Alice collective was a pirate radio station set up in 1976 by members of the Autonomia movement in Bologna. It broadcast a mix of music, left-wing and other radical news, and phone-ins. It was subsequently raided by the *carabinieri* and the organizers were imprisoned. A manifesto appears as "Radio Alice-Free Radio," trans. Richard Gardner and Sybil Walker, in *Italy: Autonomia*, Semiotext(e) vol. 3, no. 3, ed. Sylvère Lotringer and Christian Marazzi, 133–34 (New York: Columbia University, 1980).—*Eds.*]

2. [Usufruct refers to the right to use and profit from property belonging to another.—*Eds.*]

3. [Heidegger actually writes, "Welt *ist* nie, sondern *weltet*"—"world never *is*, but *worlds.*" See "Vom Wesen des Grundes," in *Wegmarken* (Frankfurt am Main: Vittorio Klostermann, 1967), 60; "On the Essence of Ground," in *Pathmarks*, trans. William McNeill (Cambridge: Cambridge University Press, 1998), 126.—*Eds.*]

4. [*Terminus ad quem* is a finishing point or goal; *terminus a quo* a starting point or origin.—*Eds.*]

5. See Martin Heidegger, *Le Principe de raison* [trans. André Preau (Paris: Gallimard, 1962)], last pages. [*Der Satz vom Grund* (Pfullingen: Günther Neske, 1957), 186–88; *The Principle of Reason*, trans. Reginald Lilly (Bloomington: Indiana University Press, 1991), 111–13. The quotes are from 187–88/113 (something of a loose paraphrase for the first). The French *disposition*, which has been translated as "dispensation," is a very limited translation of the German *Geschick*, which is related to *Geschichte*, history, and might be better rendered in English as "destiny" or "sending."—*Eds.*]

6. See Axelos, *Jeu du monde*.

7. [Lefebvre is referring here to Marx's famous 11th thesis on Feuerbach, which states: "The philosophers have only *interpreted* the world, in various ways; the point is to *change* it." See Karl Marx, "Theses on Feuerbach," in *The German Ideology*, ed. C. J. Arthur (London: Lawrence and Wishart, 1970), 123.—*Eds.*]

8. [*Terricide* is Lefebvre's term for the death of the earth.—*Eds.*]

9. [On John Kenneth Galbraith, see chap. 7 n.9.—*Eds.*]

10. [Latifundia are large, consolidated zones of agricultural production, generally controlled by a small number of landowners. They figured crucially within European feudalism.—*Eds.*]

11. See Broué, *L'Allemagne de 1920 à 1923: Spartakisme, bolchevisme, gauchisme* (Paris: Éditions de Minuit, 1972). [Pierre Broué (1926–2005) was a Trotskyite historian. Lefebvre is referring to *Révolution en Allemagne, 1917–1923* (Paris: Éditions de Minuit, 1971), translated by Ian Birchall and Brian Pearce as *The German Revolution, 1917–1923* (Leiden: Brill, 2005).—*Eds.*]

12. [On Lefebvre's notion of a "state technostructure," see chap. 7 n.9.—*Eds.*]

13. [*La fin de l'histoire* (Paris: Éditions de Minuit, 1970); *Métaphilosophie* (Paris: Éditions de Minuit, 1965). There is no complete English translation of either of these works, nor of the cited passage from the latter. However, excerpts from both are translated in Lefebvre, *Key Writings*, 22–30, 177–87.—*Eds.*]

14. [António Salazar (1889–1970) was Portuguese dictator until 1968. When he died, the dictatorship swiftly collapsed, and elections were subsequently held in 1976. The "Prince" is presumably an allusion to Machiavelli. Salvador Allende's democratically elected government in Chile was overthrown in 1973 through a CIA-backed military coup led by General Augusto Pinochet.—*Eds.*]

15 Revolutions

This final chapter is drawn from one of Lefebvre's last major books, *Le Retour de la dialectique* (The Return of the Dialectic), published in 1986 when he was eighty-five years old, just five years before his death. Lefebvre organized his wide-ranging reflections around discussions of twelve "keywords of the modern world": State, history, information/communication, logic/the logical, philosophy/metaphilosophy, politics/the political, production, the everyday, relations/the relative, revolutions, socialism, and the urban. Much like Raymond Williams in his classic *Keywords: A Vocabulary of Culture and Society* (New York: Oxford University Press, 1976), Lefebvre uses an inquiry into the meanings of these terms as a basis for a broader series of reflections regarding the nature of capitalism, modernity, the epistemology of critical thought, and the dynamics of sociopolitical transformation. His chapter on revolutions, which is presented here in full, explores the theory and practice of systemic, large-scale social transformation during the course of modernity. During the course of his discussion, Lefebvre traces the origins of modern revolutionary transformations to diverse types of peasant, worker, and urban movements. The chapter also elaborates an eclectic but remarkable "Table of the Twentieth Century" that lists some of the conjunctural events that Lefebvre considered most fundamental to the evolution of revolutionary theory and practice. He then situates the concept of "world" and related terms in the philosophical tradition, as complements and supplements to notions of universality–rationality–totality, and offers a commentary on the schema that resituates his own version of Marxian thought in contemporary political context. The essay provides a fitting conclusion to this book because it makes a series of linkages—between history and the present, between theory and practice; between cultural movements and political–economic transformations; between underlying structural constraints and the possibility of revolutionary transformation—all in the context of an

abiding interest in harnessing the forces of historical change toward the creation
of a genuinely democratic form of socialism.—*Eds.*

THE TERM "REVOLUTION"

Before we approach the most recent form of this century-long transformation—namely, cultural revolution—we must return to the term *revolution*.
The Marxist tradition distinguishes democratic revolutions (bourgeois revolutions, such as 1789–93) from socialist revolutions (proletarian revolutions,
like that of Russia in 1917). Yet since these dates, the break or fissure between
these two types of revolution has been smoothed over: there are "democratic"
revolutions that are more and less *mature:* the most mature tend to overcome
the qualitative gulf that separates them from "socialism" (which itself needs to
be defined or redefined!). The great revolutions are social and historical convulsions—they have complex consequences; reversals, bifurcations, choices,
and alternatives mean that historical becoming has nothing linear about it;
the "sense of history" no longer appears predetermined.[1] The first example
of a reversal: the Thermidor in France. The most recent example: wasn't the
rebellion that five years ago [1979] toppled the State and the army of the Shah
of Iran a popular revolution? Yet it was the Shiite clergy, who alone had a
countrywide network at their disposal, who were able to seize power and
thereby bring about the most "reactionary" theocratic State! . . .

So-called "modern" times have given rise to three great movements whose
aim is the transformation of society, and which are therefore revolutionary:
peasant movements, workers' movements, and urban movements. The first
type of movement sought the abolition of the feudal (aristocratic) ownership
of land and the redistribution of these lands. The French Revolution was, at
the outset (August 4, 1789), agrarian and peasant-based; after two centuries,
the movement has not yet ended (Nicaragua). The workers' movements targeted the private (bourgeois, capitalist) ownership of the means of production
and aimed for a different organization of industrial society than capitalism.
The third type of movement targeted the absence of urban politics, the "un-
tamed" but profitable character of urbanization, and the impoverishment of
cities and their surrounding areas. The political genius of Lenin and Mao
consisted in their appeal to peasant forces to eliminate the aristocracy and
feudalism, along with the surviving traces of "primitive" community, and in
allying the peasantry with proletarian forces to eliminate "capitalism" and
imperialism.

Lenin and later Mao knew how to provide a clear direction to these allied forces, thus preventing the peasant movements in Russia and China from degenerating into local peasant revolts. Revolutions of the second type are well known. Urban revolutions are less so; because while their emergence seemed to have provided the foundations and reasons for radical protest (culminating in 1968), this has not continued, and they have declined.

Revolution isn't what it used to be and will never be again. This assertion from a couple of years back[2] came as a surprise to those who assume a unique, specified, and unchangeable "model" for the transformation of the world. And yet all sides recognize that today revolutionary situations are always new, specific, and therefore *conjunctural*. If many people nowadays consider that practice can and should be modified, they less readily accept that theory can change. This throws up a quite pressing question: that of the *cultural* revolution (and its relation to political and social revolution).

To understand the interactions between cultural movements and political and social movements in the present epoch, we need to grasp the cultural revolution theoretically, rather than pontificating about it mistakenly or misleadingly, or pointing out some aspect of its supposed "novelty," be it real or apparent. Or worse still: viewing cultural revolution as being localized in the China of Mao, or elsewhere. Thesis: cultural revolution traverses the twentieth century, but through relations of (dialectical) conflict with it. The presentation of the concept of "cultural revolution" calls for a return to the past, a recourse to history. It is impossible to forget that, in France and in Europe, a "cultural revolution" occurred that was not labeled as such. When? In the eighteenth century, when an active and effective avant-garde began to shake up the foundations of social relations, beginning from the surface-layer of "culture" (or, if you prefer, from the superstructure).

A look backwards into history can be useful in order to comprehend a table (see below) that draws parallels between cultural transformations and sociopolitical transformations within the eventual framework of a change in the mode of production. Is it simply by chance that, from the fourteenth century to the "Renaissance," the following appeared almost simultaneously (by historical standards) in Western Europe:

a) beat or measure in music, which frees itself from speech (from the liturgical discourse in Latin) and opens the way, and the tonal system, for harmony and new rhythms;

b) perspective (the horizon line), which separates urban space from natural space, which opens the way for a new architecture and a new urban form;[3]

c) the expansion of exchange, the growth of towns and their political weight;

d) national language and national sentiment, the "cultural" unity of the country (France)—the centralized State and an increasingly strong monarchy;

e) advances in the sciences: mathematics, cosmology, etc., bringing about the slow but definitive collapse of ancient representations of Heaven, Earth, and Hell.

f) the rapid growth of capitalism (first mercantile, then manufacturing), with the invention of the disruptive technologies of the printing press, the telescope, etc.;

g) turmoil and new religious schemas: Protestantism, Jansenism, paracletism. In philosophy, a new rationalism, etc.

We can thus establish a table of these changes, showing that, taken together, they *transform* social life; a table that focuses not only on production, philosophy or the State, but rather upon a *becoming* which proceeds by leaps, or rather through the abundance and creation of forms: *transformations.* "Culture" and the sociopolitical thus interact continually.

Cultural Revolution

The more people speak of cultural revolution, the less they understand what they are talking about. The notion is confused with "vague" representations of "transformation," profound "change," seen as radical, or simply as "crisis." Some people, in fact many people, assert that techniques have a revolutionary impact and transform society, as well as relations and modes of living. The Right hopes that the collapse of traditional themes of the Left (rationalism, humanism, universalism) will give new visibility to its own values, obsessions, and theses. On the Left, each tendency depends on "transformation" in order to valorize its own orientations, which are not always well defined.

Cultural revolution? In Mao's time, we knew (or rather, we thought we knew) what it was: a consequence of, a result of, political revolution. This prestigious representation contributes, in France, to the replacement of the term "civilization" by (the more vague and long suspect term) "culture." In the vast country of China, where the majority of the population are peasants, Mao wanted to establish a way of living, a community of sentiment against traditions and recent hierarchies; in poverty. He did this by destroying, at the same time, a past that was rich and yet too heavy, as well as the ambitions of the apparatus that was already in place; and in such a way as to orient development toward an "egalitarian socialism." In short, the Cultural Revolution was as much against Confucius and the traces of the Mandarin hierarchy as it was against the bureaucracy set up in Mao's own name! The social cost of this operation was enormous. The damage caused was as large as the scale of the task. To recall: barefoot doctors, communes, and the outrageous valorization of the peasant and artisan life. And the exploits of a certain "gang"; the abuses of power in the midst of creative disorder and radical corruption. In the same vein as Lenin, it must be added. The weakening of order spreads to Western countries . . .

Upon its arrival in these countries (Italy, France, the USA, England), the idea of "cultural revolution" would encounter analogous aspirations, appeals, memories, and obstacles. In the history and experience of the West, "cultural revolution" *preceded,* announced, and prepared the political and social revolution—both by legitimating it, and also contributing to it. It begins in the eighteenth century, in France, with the *Encyclopedia,* around 1750. But Diderot and the encyclopedists represented only one faction, one group within a European avant-garde that included "philosophers," scholars, the majority of artists and writers, freemasonry and part of the clergy, the cultivated bourgeoisie, and artisans, in short, all critiques of the feudal–military–ecclesiastical (religious) order. Hence all partisans, more or less coherent, of a *civil society* possessing its own principles, its own self-definition, laws, and codes, instead of taking them from a higher authority, royalty, the Church, military power. From the most idealistic to the most materialistic, all "progressives" have such a *project* in common; however explicitly, *consensus* is constituted around what has quite clearly been defined (by Jean-Jacques Rousseau, among others) as "civil society"; up until the moment Kant formulated it in Germany, though in France it was realized in a revolutionary manner, not conforming to predictions and expectations. Civil society: freed from the order determined by the prioritization of "order," from the religious (hence a "lay" society), but also from the State of divine right. Realized "explosively" in 1789 and subsequently, but full of contradictions both old and new . . .

The project of *civil* society linked the civil to civilization and civility: it implied the disappearance of practices linked to the dominance of privileged "estates" and orders. Torture, for example, applied to the accused, *with confession passing for proof*. Facts? No. Secondary corroboration? Not essential? In *civilized* society, it is up to justice (the judge) to establish guilt, to piece together the crime and find proof . . .

Already two schemas have been presented: according to Mao (and Lenin), cultural revolution *follows* political revolution, which is a prerequisite and a necessary (though not sufficient) condition for global change. In the West, cultural revolution precedes political revolution. Hegel retained this latter schema, but in so doing tried to show that (following the formation of the Napoleonic State), revolution no longer had an essential role. While Marx, who introduces the notion of (the working) *class*, criticizes Hegel and the Hegelian project, its "bourgeois-democratic" realization and the ending of history at this stage. Later, Gramsci retains the role of culture and cultural revolution in the progressive acquisition (conquest) of the deep-seated hegemony of power. Hence new problems! . . . Is it clear that the twentieth century, or its second half, is consistent with one or the other of these now classical schemas? Are there no other possibilities than this process of cause and effect?

But this possibility not only exists, it is realized before our eyes. Is it not enough just to look around? Political and "cultural" changes play out simultaneously, in a complex way, without one preceding the other in a relation of determinism, causation, or final causality. On the contrary there is a conflicting entanglement, where one sometimes induces, accelerates and intensifies, or sometimes obscures, paralyzes and even stops, the other. Isn't this almost clear on a worldwide scale, when we take account not only of France, Italy, and Europe, but also of Iran, Asia, Latin America, the oil-producing countries, Africa, and so on? . . .

It is therefore impossible to establish a complete, worldwide table of these interactions and interferences. We should more modestly be content with a reduced table that sheds light on the simultaneity and *dialectical* reciprocity of these two great movements, the social–political and the cultural–scientific. Obviously they cannot be reduced to classical relations of "truth vs. ideology" or rather "reality vs. its reflections," "rational vs. irrational," etc. (although of course they include them). The table therefore shows that the cultural and the political are not superimposed on one another, but *interlink* in a conflicting world (unity vs. contradiction).

TABLE OF THE TWENTIETH CENTURY

A table with gaps, of course, and incomplete, laid out with an orientation and aiming at this object: the contemporary nature of, and the relations between, *cultural* (ideological, scientific, etc.) and *political* (economic, social, etc.) revolution. This is therefore neither the logical table desired by Wittgenstein—nor the genetic table sought by many historicists. It leaves aside precursors (Hegel, Marx, Nietzsche), but also Stirner,[4] Lassalle, Bernstein, the Paris Commune and other facts and events (colonialism, Empires, etc.).

1900

The beginning of the century—quiet optimism; confidence in progress; the beginning of science, industry, Reason. We enter into a period of stability; of balance (of powers)—into the reign of regulated time and coordinated space—of gold as the supreme value, a guarantee of stability—of law and rights, property and Liberty. The *Universal Exhibition*—(but also the Dreyfus affair and the struggle for secularism as a foundation for the table).

1905

The Russo-Japanese War. Japanese victory. The First Russian Revolution; the appearance of the Soviets (Councils). The rise of Imperialism—the rise of the workers' movement; its division (Bolsheviks–Mensheviks, etc.).—The discovery of *relativity*; the weakening of certitudes regarding space, time, matter, and energy. The onset of a separation between the everyday and knowledge (the everyday persists in clock time—in three-dimensional, optico-geometrical, Euclidian, "absolute" space).

1900–1914

Imperialisms. The International against the War. Regional wars (the Balkans). The impotence of rationalist philosophy and liberal humanism. Naïve conceptions of law, socialism, justice, Liberty. Stagnation of theory in France (except for a few writings, including those of Jaurès,[5] but nothing comparable to the works of Kautsky, Rosa Luxemburg, or Lenin).

Circa 1910

The disintegration in art and knowledge (culture, ideology) of the frames of reference adopted and maintained through common sense: the space of perspective (through analytic cubism)—of the time of watches and clocks (through more precise ways of measuring)—of the family and paternity (the beginnings of psychoanalysis)—of the city (its explosion into suburbs)—of History (which obfuscates), etc. The entry into *modernity* but a silent catastrophe. The work of the Negative. The heightened separation and virtual conflicts between the everyday and knowledge, art. The end of the tonal system in music, like the end of perspectival space in painting and, soon after, in architecture. The figure of the "man without qualities" as a figure of the European.[6] *Hypothesis*: it is thus that the cultural revolution is inaugurated; it announces events (wars, crises, revolutions), without thereby determining them. The epicenters of this shock: Venice, Saint Petersburg, Berlin, Paris.

1914

The defeat of the pacifist, anti-imperialist, and anti-military internationalist workers' movement. The murder of Jaurès. The War! The uncertain beginnings of a radicalization refusing "sacred Union" for the sake of the Fatherland, Civilization, and Law against the "barbarians" . . .

1917

Lenin and Tzara in Zurich.[7] Radical negativity in works: Lenin's *The State and Revolution*—Dada and Tristan Tzara—the October Revolution. The separation of theory from political practice: Lenin and the State (following the seizure of power). Conjuncturally: the alliance in Russia between peasants, workers, soldiers. The soviets.

1920–1921

The Third International against the (socialist-reformist) Second International and against the "libertarians." The Twenty-one Conditions.[8] The success and then failures of the revolutionary movement in Europe (the Battle of Warsaw, lost by the Red Army and Trotsky, etc.).—The foundation of the French Communist Party (PCF). Dominant in France: the "Blue Horizon,"[9] ex-servicemen, the question of reparations, etc. On the Left: the beginning of surrealism, Dadaism, anti-literature, the "Great Refusal" . . .[10]

1925

"The provisional stabilization of capitalism" according to the Third International. But war in Morocco. The unveiling [*dévoilement*] of French imperialism. The avant-garde, constituted by a movement of intellectuals who were sympathetic to the Communist Party (philosophers and poets, artists and scholars). Revolutionary hope and the project of a new optimism. Trotsky removed from power in the USSR by Stalin. The rise of fascism in Italy.

1925–1930

The end of the postwar; order reestablished, but French society is archaic, with economic stagnation and a tendency toward "stockholder capitalism" grounded in the redistribution of influence (in Europe, Africa, Asia) at Versailles. Consolidation of the Communist Party, but with Trotskyism comes upheaval, the onset of an era of suspicion (with every objection being accused of Trotskyism). The attractiveness of Trotskyism on a "cultural" level: Trotskyism and surrealism; surrealism as a project of cultural revolution (beginning with poetry and "culture")—the attractiveness of the Communist Party at the level of action against imperialism, capitalism, and the bourgeoisie. Internal struggles going all the way down to the base, the grassroots. Peasant questions, raised at the founding of the USSR but soon abandoned for being "outside the revolution." The Five Year Plan and economic rationality. The formation of the (Stalinist) apparatus in the PCF and the Third International, against Trotskyism, reformism, and "libertarian" currents and tendencies, etc.

1930–1934

The "crisis" begins in the USA in autumn 1929. With unforeseen consequences. It is recognized (too late) that an economic program does not suffice to support work and workers any better than a political one. The illusions, errors, and mistakes of the Third International. The tactic of "class against class"; its failures (in Germany, in France, etc.). Lack of direction and theoretical orientation of the workers' movement. The lack of a sufficiently broad project. Contradictions: in France and elsewhere, the persistence of antimilitarism alongside admiration for the Red Army and the denunciation of the danger posed by Hitler. The critique of the "anarchy" of finance capitalism but an acceptance of the rationalization of productive labor, etc. The reduction of Marxism to an economic perspective, in praise of (Soviet) planning.—But at the same time, the discovery of Marx's philosophical works and his injunction: realize philosophy. The renewal of humanism and hope—but, against expectations, the rise of nationalisms and Hitlerism. The (long denied) despondency [*accablement*] of the German working class. The contrast between defenses of German culture and magnificence and the political incapacity and impotence of the great German tradition (the Frankfurt School—Brecht—Thomas Mann, etc.) The rediscovery in France of dialectical thought and the formation of a French school with "Marxist" tendencies.

1934–1936

The inversion of the International's injunctions: the abandonment of "class against class"—orientation toward an alliance with "democratic forces," with the "Left," radicalism, and social democracy. The realization of this tactic (or strategy) primarily within the sphere of culture. The hurried dissolution of the AEAR (Association of Revolutionary Writers and Artists). The foundation of the Cultural Institute (the first in France). The establishment of the intellectual avant-garde, controlled by the Communist Party (despite strong ideological and political divergences, but reassembling against fascism, Hitlerism, and their French equivalents). In 1935, the *World Congress of Intellectuals.* Both the fracture and the end (the exploding of the avant-garde). Numerous incidents during the course of this congress. The sidelining of surrealism, psychoanalysis, populism, and even "Marxism" (a domain reserved for the Party). A Congress whose only "cultural" openings and conclusions are confused. However, the momentum given by the "cultural" (a term introduced into France on this occasion) reverberates across the plane of politics. The Popular Front and its electoral success—then the deceptions, the contradictions lived in fleeting euphoria (the Spanish Civil War, etc.).

1939–1945

The Second World War and its terrible events, Hitlerism and Italian fascism, the pro-Hitler "collaboration" in France.—Yalta: the rise of the USA and the USSR (Stalin victorious).—Over the course of the same war, the momentum acquired by knowledge since the start of the century (Einstein, then probabilistic physics, etc.) is intensified. The discovery of operational logic (the organization of sea-borne transportation). The nuclear (the Bomb!) enters the scene. The ensuing possibility of the (nuclear) destruction of a revolutionary, popular insurrectional movement. The possibility of the self-destruction of society and the planet. Extermination camps. After the liberation and the disillusionment that soon followed, there begins the era not only of suspicion, but of terror (which appears at the end of the war).

1945–1950

The restoration of capitalism in the West. The division of the world into two "blocs." The triumph of Stalinism (the fusion and mixing of power–knowledge). The moment of the realization of philosophy is lost. The constitution and discovery of the everyday (established, manipulated, and soon to be programmed). Philosophy views itself as a cultural revolution (with existentialism), though it drifts toward psychologism, sociologism, and historicism; but also toward absurdism, nihilism, and pessimism. The birth of cybernetics and information theory (the engineers at Bell, etc.). In the West, productive labor and discourse become "values" (of substitution). Revolution in China. The formation of the State of Israel. The intensification of conflicts: "planning vs. market," "*dirigiste* state intervention vs. liberalism," "Marxism vs. philosophy," etc. The theory of "proletarian science" versus "bourgeois science," with the latter including information technology, relativity, quantum theory, etc.

Circa 1956

The failure of Stalinism (the "secret" Khrushchev report).—The failure of colonialism (the Algerian War, the Suez Crisis)—the upholding of Stalinism in France. A "cultural" void but the birth of radical protest and revolutions outside communist parties (Algeria, Fidel Castro). China, the nonaligned countries, Yugoslavian *autogestion* enter onto the scene . . . A crucial year. Turning from the postwar period toward a different era, the strengthened yet repressed opposition to Stalinism within the PCF. The beginnings of decline within the PCF, which begins to disassociate itself from "men of culture."

1960–1975

(1968 is covered in the following section.)

The famous "scientific and technical revolution" (accompanied by a rampant demography); its two- or threefold meaning: filling a great void, a substitute for the political and social revolution that did not take place in the West, and which is elsewhere in decline—an attempt to reconcile the everyday, the (applied) sciences, and art—dizzying advances in productive forces, in the precise sense of the term. Accelerated industrialization and urbanization. Growth without development. Automated technologies (poorly controlled and valorized without reference to a standard). The worldwide strengthening of the State, of State logic, and logic or rather logics in general. Reformism returns

to the scene (after the explosion of 1968). Political independence of the former colonies; third-worldism, the expectation of a cultural transformation
through the contribution of peripheral, so-called developing countries.—
Technocractic ideologies: structuralism, positivism, logical empiricism, etc.
An apology for stability and equilibrium. The obfuscation of Marxism and
all critical knowledge, and of theory in general. The *worldwide* as a problem
(worldwide companies, the worldwide market, worldwide strategies, etc.).
The world of the commodity, the general system of equivalencies (and inequalities, hidden and revealed conflicts, unstable equilibria . . .).

1968

After the cultural revolution in China and various local protest movements,
in 1968, the high point of protest and critical understanding. Contradiction:
"prosperity vs. protest." The retort of students, the "working class," the entire people, to "capitalist prosperity." An almost revolutionary situation (in
France). A general strike, unique in history. Exasperation. No project. Confusion between the cultural and the political. The weakened State; promptly
reestablished. The failure of (subversive) "movements," their consequences
and defects. The injunction: "change life . . ."

1975 and After

The crisis gradually spreads, becomes worldwide [*se mondialise*]: moving
from the economic to the political, to the "cultural," to (ethical and aesthetic)
values. The totalizing negative, the accumulated but veiled contradictions. The
decline of protest and the workers' movement. Historical compromises and
the projects of societies. Revolution in Iran (against the Shah and Western-
ization): a people emerging into political existence, but not into civil society.
The return of religions, in force. Movements in Latin America. Religion as
popular "culture" or counterculture? . . . Tendencies toward depoliticization
as a global problematic. The human species called into question from all points
of view (nature—war—religion—the passage from the era of labor to the era
of non-work, from scarcity to abundance, etc.). Bets and stakes. Philosophy,
the cultural, and the possible as problems. The dialectical conflict of the
"positive" and the "negative" (of *production vs. creation* and of *self-destruction*).
Tendencies opposing the reconstitution of civil society and the invention of
self-determination, *auto*-gestion, and *auto*nomy [*auto-détermination, -gestion,
-nomie*] in the guise of (apparent) disorder. What will come of it?

SUPPLEMENT TO THE TABLE OF THE TWENTIETH CENTURY

World and the Worldwide, Mondialisation and Worldness [Mondialité]

Complements and supplements to the concepts of classical philosophy, namely: universality–rationality–totality. It is a question of the Terrestrial and the Planetary, not of the Cosmos (which can also be called: world). In the "modern" era, the worldwide and *mondialisation* present themselves as a becoming that is full of contradictions and highly unequal, with regressions, displacements, and leaps, from the market and production to so-called "cultural" creation. For two to three centuries, by expanding channels outward from Western Europe, each country has *conjuncturally* become a bearer (support) of the worldwide. Which is not to imply that other countries fall behind, are rendered infertile, are "provincialized."

In the eighteenth and the first part of the nineteenth century, England then France and Germany enter onto the scene, inaugurating worldness beyond their (aspired) nationality. Then "Mitteleuropa" and Russia (Nietzsche left Germany, but innovation persisted there into the twentieth century, with Thomas and Heinrich Mann, Brecht, the Frankfurt School, Musil, etc.). Subsequently the USSR and the USA, which quickly opposed each other, then quite remarkably Latin America (including Liberation theology), etc.

This movement incorporates the well-known thesis of uneven development. But the countries bearing worldness are not necessarily the most industrial or the most politically advanced ones. The *negative* enters into action as well.

COMMENTARY ON THE TABLE

Where does the current effacement, the weakening, of "Marxism" come from, even though it is apparent that the difficulties and the problems, but also the possibilities, of the modern world stem from the growth of productive forces (the applied sciences and technologies); this entails innovations and changes in labor, and in the division and organization of this labor. This confirms the most "classical" theses of "Marxism." As long as these theses are completed . . . The present work (following several others) proposes this objective. There are numerous reasons for this obfuscation; they cannot be conceived by referring just to the works of Marx and Engels. Or to dogmatism, Stalinism, or intellectual terrorism. Let us try here to grasp, enumerate, and define some of these reasons. And foremost, where does this growth come from, with its (ideological and institutional) outgrowths? How has this expansion of the (capitalist)

mode of production been *possible?* After the simultaneous collapses of colonialism and Stalinism, the "scientific and technical revolution" introduced a
replacement product, the effects of which exceeded its causes and reasons . . .

Now the theorists and researchers inspired by Marx were ill prepared to
suffer these shocks (except for a tiny minority); having been influenced by
short-term political decisions, arbitrarily generalized as knowledge, they assimilate scientific notions poorly (though they assert themselves as partisans of
"scientific" socialism and "scientific" society!). Let us pass over their surprise
at the elasticity and "creativity" of the capitalist mode of production. Their
surprise is well justified: wars and crises have not defeated capitalism; they
have stimulated it. The theorists and researchers believe not only in the objectivity (of representations and understandings) but also in essentiality and in
the absolute substantiality (of the "real," of the "material"). By a great majority, they remained tied to a cursory materialism, only discovering the contradictions of others: the bourgeoisie and capitalism. Materialists, "realists,"
"mechanists," they cling to the *thing*, to the elementary "object"; here, in front
of us, this pebble, this metal object, this hammer "really," "objectively," practically, exist, with proof, such as our seeing, touching, and handling them.
"The proof of the pudding is in the eating . . ." Test: the sad polemic over
genetics and Mendel's hybrids, where stability and immobility were taken as
benchmarks of species. Simultaneously disdainful of practice, the dialectic,
and becoming, and proclaiming "proletarian science" as opposed to bourgeois
science, "Marxists" impose this cursory ideology in the name of Stalin. And
Stalinism? This was a crude and imposed dogmatism, a fusion and confusion
of limited knowledge with unlimited power.

One cause of boredom for Marxists was and remains the fate of the work
[*œuvre*] and the concepts inherited from Marx and Engels. They are imported
into ideology (shielding a practice that distances itself from theory); furthermore, in the West they are imported into "the cultural" but also into the specialized sciences (history, economics, and sociology, etc.). Losing the privilege
of ideology and the prestige of theoretical totality, "Marxism" finds itself increasingly discarded, cut off, and relegated to the realm of disparaged protests.

And materialism? Like Marx's other concepts concerning the economic,
the political, and revolution, materialism is simultaneously right and wrong.
If it is correct to say that productive activity shifts from the production of
objects (things) toward that of images, signs, and texts, attempts to defend
the "non-material" dimension are no less demagogic. Just as with the "real"

use and operation of technological equipment, as with elements that are removed from the sensible and from practice, the "non-material" (images, signs,
and texts) can likewise only proceed through a "material" base. The opposing of "creativity" to material "productivity" reveals a "cultural" degradation
that could rank alongside the opposition of fetishism and culture! Without
returning to the old concepts of *nature* (Romantic and naturalist concepts,
etc.), the sensible and practical "real" could and should be conceived as such.
Maintaining some primary truths about production, work, workers, while
simultaneously prohibiting changes and modifications, this attitude also reveals a theoretical incapacity; the degradation of knowledge gives rise to the
degradation of culture (which can be separated neither from "pure" understanding, nor from technically applied knowledge).

"Crisis"? This word, now trivialized, has long since lost all well-defined
meaning. To whom or to what does it refer? To French society? Of course, the
latter is in crisis and even in a critical state; but the point of theory is not to
adopt a confused point of view on a partial reality. The world? Well, we must
uncover *all the contradictions,* including and especially the most hidden, those
that accomplish what is most dear to "us"! An essential, if not principal, contradiction concerns the always surprising relation between the *positive* and
the *negative,* which was already signaled above. Extending across all areas, the
ambivalent and conflicting effects of technological acquisitions, the elements
of *another positivism,* are accumulated but remain fragmentary, broken up.
The *negative* has deep effects within the transformation. It has nothing in
common with the individual negation described by a series of writers (since
Sade). It is no longer about the "subject," in that this "subject" and subjectiv-
ity are swept away by the torrent. "Crisis"? Yes; it is *total;* the negative totalizes it! The general weakening of ideas, representations, and "culture," in short
the *cultural revolution* that proceeds through "crisis," entails the discrediting
of the State as a form of domination–exploitation–alienation. Which sometimes entails the obfuscation of what seemed the simplest, the most traditional, the most easily acquired: the practices of language, reading, and writing. But which does not entail the deconstruction of the State, let alone its
reconstruction in a profoundly changed society. The criterion for a revolution is that it *destroys* a historically produced form of politics and produces
or creates another. The State cannot be abolished immediately, on command;
it must be reconstructed—differently. Thus the voices of Marx and Lenin
reach into our era.

Using the words and the concepts of their own time, they announce several profound *transformations* of the human being during the course of its *becoming*, a course that is partially foreseeable (determinism) but partly unforeseen: innovation, creations—and also accidents, encounters, and even catastrophes.

It nonetheless remains the case that Marx and many "Marxists" after him have underestimated, without having completely ignored:

a) Questions of land, the ground and underground, rents and agricultural production, peasants and the agro-food industry;

b) cities, urbanization, and the urban.

They have focused on industry and industrialization. This has also played several (bad) tricks on "socialism."

Autogestion? Of course, but we need to say how to put it into place, how to make it function (in the State; in relation to the market, which has its own laws that nobody can abolish by decree). The mastery and control of the conditions of existence stretches from the achievements of the work of Marx, through the experiences of the Soviet Union, Yugoslavia, and China, and not without reason. This mastery and control enter into the definition of socialism. Which leads to the idea of direct democracy. But where and how to realize it? Is it "self-instituted"? Does it emerge from a constitution? Or from practice, from a way of living?

To try to see clearly, shouldn't we begin again with Marx, thus moving more deeply into the history of socialism: from its conception—and its realization during the course of the twentieth century? This history, which appears, in contemporary works, to have ended a century ago, can and should be rewritten precisely in order to serve contemporary history. It happens that this experience—this ordeal—throws another light over the work of Marx himself. Through a retroactive effect that forms a part of the dialectical approach.

Another eventual interrogation: can the alliance between the *national* and the *worldwide* be conceived through a circumvention of the transnational, since the latter seems to have the failings of the international? But how? Through what procedure—or what transformation?

Translation by Gerald Moore, Neil Brenner, and Stuart Elden

Notes

1. [*Le sens de l'histoire* has an ambiguity in it, as it can mean "the meaning of history," "the sense of history," or even "the direction of history." Lefebvre plays with these meanings in his book *Le fin de l'histoire.*—*Eds.*]

2. [Lefebvre is referring to Lefebvre and Régulier, *La révolution n'est plus ce qu'elle était*, 21. The title of this book translates as "The revolution isn't what it used to be."—*Eds.*]

3. [See Lefebvre's discussion of this issue in chapter 11, in the context of an analysis of the development of capitalism and the modern state.—*Eds.*]

4. [Max Stirner (1805–56) was a German philosopher, best known for his book *The Ego and Its Own*, which was criticized by Marx and Engels in *The German Ideology.*—*Eds.*]

5. [Jean Jaurès (1859–1914) was a French socialist and antimilitarist politician and writer.—*Eds.*]

6. [This is a reference to Robert Musil's unfinished modernist novel *Der Mann ohne Eigenschaften*; English version published as *The Man without Qualities*, trans. Eithne Wilkins and Ernst Kaiser (London: Secker and Warburg, 1979).—*Eds.*]

7. [Tristan Tzara (1896–1963) was a Romanian poet and one of the founders of the Dada movement.—*Eds.*]

8. [These were the conditions set out by Lenin for membership of the Third International, also known as the Comintern.—*Eds.*]

9. [The "Blue Horizon" derives from the color of the uniforms of the French army, and refers to a right-wing tendency in interwar France.—*Eds.*]

10. [The "Great Refusal" was coined by André Breton as a rejection of all the associations of bourgeois society. It was picked up by Herbert Marcuse, among others.—*Eds.*]

Further Readings

Henri Lefebvre discusses themes related to those explored in this book in a number of other texts, and we offer here suggestions for readers interested in following up on them. This list is necessarily incomplete, because many of Lefebvre's central writings, particularly of a philosophical nature, have yet to be translated into English and because the political concerns on display in his work run as continuous threads throughout his career.

Fundamental to almost all the issues discussed here is *The Production of Space,* translated by Donald Nicolson-Smith (Oxford: Blackwell, 1991): cross-references could be given on almost every page. The specifically urban aspects of the question of politics and space are explored in detail in *Writings on Cities,* translated and edited by Eleonore Kofman and Elizabeth Lebas (Oxford: Blackwell, 1996), and *The Urban Revolution,* translated by Robert Bononno (Minneapolis: University of Minnesota Press, 2003).

Lefebvre's analysis of capitalism and its particular forms in the late 1960s and early 1970s can be found in *The Survival of Capitalism,* translated by Frank Bryant (London: Allison and Busby, 1976), and *The Explosion: Marxism and the French Upheaval,* translated by Alfred Ehrenfeld (New York: Modern Reader, 1969); the French version of *The Survival of Capitalism* reprints much of the second book. There is much relevant analysis in the three volumes of *Critique of Everyday Life,* translated by John Moore (volumes 1 and 2) and Gregory Elliott (volume 3) (London: Verso, 1991, 2002, and 2006). Related themes are explored in *Rhythmanalysis: Space, Time, and Everyday Life,* translated by Stuart Elden and Gerald Moore (London: Continuum, 2004).

For an account of Lefebvre's relation to Marxism, the only major texts available in English are *Dialectical Materialism,* translated by John Sturrock (reprinted with a preface by Stefan Kipfer; Minneapolis: University of Minnesota Press, 2009), and *The Sociology of Marx,* translated by Norbert Guterman

(Harmondsworth: Penguin, 1968). The latter contains the chapter "Political Sociology: Theory of the State," which provides an initial outline of many of the ideas Lefebvre would develop in *De l'État*. Shorter relevant pieces are included in *Key Writings*, edited by Stuart Elden, Elizabeth Lebas, and Eleonore Kofman (London: Continuum, 2003), which includes other texts that relate to the concerns of this volume. For a late account of Lefebvre's political and theoretical concerns, "Toward a Leftist Cultural Politics: Remarks Occasioned by the Centenary of Marx's Death," in *Marxism and the Interpretation of Culture*, ed. Cary Nelson and Lawrence Grossberg, 75–88 (London: Macmillan, 1988), is helpful.

Of the large amount of Lefebvre's writings as yet untranslated into English we would highlight four major books: *La somme et le reste*, 3rd ed. (Paris: Méridiens Klincksieck, 1989 [1959]); *Espace et politique: Le droit à la ville II*, 2nd ed. (Paris: Anthropos, 2000 [1972]); *Une pensée devenue monde: Faut-il abandonner Marx?* (Paris: Fayard, 1980); and *Le Retour de la dialectique: Douze mots-clefs pour le monde moderne* (Paris: Messidor, 1986). The first offers an autobiographical account of Lefebvre's early career and split from official Marxism and the PCF; the second extends many of his arguments about urban sociology in a more explicitly political register; the third is an impassioned argument for the continuing relevance of Marxist analysis; and in the fourth he reflects on the transformations of modernity by means of a retrospective commentary on some of the "key words" of modern social and political thought. Excerpts from the first and fourth books appear in *Key Writings*; a couple of pieces from the second appear in *Writings on Cities*; and the present volume contains brief selections from the third and fourth.

Publication History

Chapter 1 was originally published as "L'État et la société," *Les cahiers du centre d'études socialistes* 42/43 (1964): 17–29.

Chapter 2 was originally published as "Les sources de la théorie Marxiste–Leniniste de l'État," *Les cahiers du centre d'études socialistes* 42/43 (1964): 31–48.

Chapter 3 was originally published as "L'État dans le monde moderne," *L'homme et la société* 37/38 (1975): 3–23. We are grateful to L'Harmattan for permission to translate and reprint material.

Chapter 4 was originally published as "A propos d'un nouveau modèle étatique," *Dialectiques* 27 (1979): 47–55; translated as "Comments on a New State Form," *Antipode* 33, no. 5 (2001): 769–82. We are grateful to Blackwell for permission to reprint material.

Chapter 5 was originally published as "Henri Lefebvre ouvre le débat sur la théorie de l'autogestion," *Autogestion et socialisme* 1 (1966): 59–70. We are grateful to Éditions Anthropos for permission to translate and reprint material.

Chapter 6 was originally published as "Une Interview d'Henri Lefebvre," *Autogestion et socialisme* 33/34 (1976): 115–26. We are grateful to Éditions Anthropos for permission to translate and reprint material.

Chapter 7 was originally published in *Espaces et sociétés* 1 (1970): 3–12; reprinted in *Espace et politique* (Paris: Anthropos), 49–70. We consulted an earlier translation by Michael J. Enders that was published in *Antipode* 8 (1976):

30–37. We are grateful to Éditions Anthropos for permission to translate and reprint material.

Chapter 8 was originally published in J. W. Freiberg, ed., *Critical Sociology: European Perspectives* (New York: Irvington Publishers, 1979), 285–95. We are grateful to J. W. Freiberg for permission to reprint.

Chapter 9 was originally published as "Le mondial et le planétaire," *Espaces et sociétés* 8 (1973): 15–22. We are grateful to Éditions Anthropos for permission to translate and reprint material.

Chapter 10 was originally published in *Une pensée devenue monde: Faut-il abandonner Marx?* (Paris: Fayard, 1980), 148–61 and 172–74. We are grateful to Fayard for permission to translate and reprint material.

Chapter 11 was originally published as "L'espace et l'état," in *De l'État*, vol. 4, *Les contradictions de l'état moderne: La dialectique et/de l'état* (Paris: Union Générale d'Éditions, 1978), 259–324. A partial translation was previously published in Neil Brenner, Bob Jessop, Martin Jones, and Gordon MacLeod, eds., *State/Space: A Reader* (Cambridge, Mass.: Blackwell, 2003), 84–100. We are grateful to Blackwell for permission to reprint material.

Chapter 12 was originally published as "Kostas Axelos: *Vers la pensée planétaire: Le devenir-pensée du monde et le devenir-homme de la pensée* (Ed. de Minuit)," *Esprit* 338 (1965): 1114–17. *Esprit* lists the subtitle of Axelos's book inaccurately: the final phrase is not "le devenir-homme du pensée" ("the becoming-man of thought") but "le devenir-monde de la pensée" ("the becoming-world of thought"). We are grateful to *Esprit* for permission to translate and reprint material.

Chapter 13 appeared as "Le Monde" in Giuseppe Lissa, Henri Lefebvre, Lambros Couloubaritsis, and Jean Lauxerois, *Pour Kostas Axelos: Quatre études* (Brussels: Éditions Ousia, 2004), 35–49; originally published as "Le monde selon Kostas Axelos," *Lignes* 15 (1992): 129–40. We are grateful to Éditions Ousia for permission to translate and reprint material.

Chapter 14 was originally published in *De l'État*, vol. 4, *Les contradictions de l'état moderne: La dialectique et/de l'état* (Paris: Union Générale d'Éditions,

1978), 413–41. A partial translation appeared in Henri Lefebvre, *Key Writings,* edited by Stuart Elden, Eleonore Kofman, and Elizabeth Lebas (London: Continuum, 2003), 199–205. We are grateful to Continuum for permission to reprint material.

Chapter 15 was originally published in *Le Retour de la dialectique* (Paris: Messidor, 1986), 123–39.

Index

abstract space, 187–88
accumulation: capital, 3, 4, 16, 18, 19, 34, 56–58, 103, 108, 187, 223, 247; political, 110
Accumulation of Capital (Luxemburg), 252n12
Achcar, Gilbert, 47n89
Adorno, Theodor, 105
administrative rationality, 250
advertising, 64, 115
AEAR (Association of Revolutionary Writers and Artists), 299
aero-politics, 275
Africa, 8, 31, 92n11, 230, 295, 298
Agnew, John, 48n90
agrarian phase, 279–80
the agrarian question, 161
agriculture, 156, 178, 179, 186, 212, 279, 305
agro-food industry, 305
Alberti, Leon Battista, 232, 252n6
Algeria, 14, 145, 300
alienation, 10–11, 31, 64, 76–78, 99, 103, 140, 150, 154, 200, 246, 265, 269, 304
Alienation, Praxis and Technē in the Thought of Karl Marx (Axelos), 24, 46n69, 254, 257n1, 272n3
Allende, Salvador, 289n14
Alsace, 179
alterity, 99
Althusser, Louis, 12, 17, 44n33, 45n52, 163n3, 221n1, 253n16

Amin, Samir, 201, 208n4
Amoore, Louise, 48n103
analogic space, 230
anarchism, 14, 85, 89, 105, 139, 141, 278
anarcho-syndicalism, 85, 142
anthropology, 198
Anti-Dühring (Engels), 84
Anti-Oedipus (Deleuze and Guattari), 209n7
antiproductivism, 3, 14, 15, 17–26, 47n85. *See also* productivism
anti-Stalinism, 7, 75
anti-statism. *See* statism
apparatus *(dispositif)*, 213. *See also* ideological state apparatus; state apparatus
appropriation, 150, 186, 192, 288
Arab world, 281
architecture, 3, 21, 179, 197, 202, 224, 232–33, 235, 241, 248, 253, 293, 297; modernist, 233
Aron, Raymond, 154
Aronowitz, Stanley, 43n25
Arrabal, Fernando, 209n7
Arrighi, Giovanni, 48n91
Arthur, C. J., 289n7
Asia, 8, 31, 295, 298
Atlantic Ocean, 251
Attali, Jacques, 38, 127, 136n4, 137n5
Aufhebung. See supersession
authoritarianism, 15, 111

competition states, 34
computers, 127, 131–32, 136n3, 137n4,
171, 244, 283
computer science, 131
Comunidad de Propietarios, 251n3
Comunidad de Vecinos, 251n3
the conceived, 229
concrete universal, 285, 287
Confucius, 294
constitutions, 54, 79
consumer movements, 191
consumer society, 63–65, 118
consumption, 20, 23, 114–15, 131, 177, 188,
213, 224, 235. See also bureaucratic
society of controlled consumption;
consumer society
contradiction, 8, 16, 69, 73, 74
cooptation (recuperation), 155
Le Corbusier, 182, 184n17, 233, 234–35
Corpet, Olivier, 153
cosmological space, 230–31
cosmology, 226, 293
counter-culture, 204, 301
counterrevolution, 120
counter-spaces, 117, 189, 235
creative destruction, 35
crisis, 3, 8, 29, 114, 121, 137n9, 154, 176,
203, 223, 263, 277, 279, 293, 298, 301,
304; economic, 194; Fordist and
Keynesian, 5, 37; theoretical, 106,
198, 203, 231; theory of, 252n8
critical theory, 155
The Critique of Everyday Life (Lefebvre), 10, 43n22, 44n36, 45n50, 136n3
Critique of the Gotha Program (Marx), 9,
18, 19, 68n8, 104, 129, 137n13, 141, 250
Cromwell, Oliver, 57
cubism, 231, 233, 297
Cultural Institute, 299
Cultural Revolution, 106, 293–94
culture, 13, 99, 101, 105, 111, 131, 139, 186,
204, 215, 234, 237, 286, 292–305; state
and, 109, 113, 119, 120, 220

culture industry, 212, 218
cybernetics, 172, 200, 256

Dada, 297, 306n7
DATAR (Délégation pour l'Aménagement du Territoire et l'Action
Régionale), 167, 183n13
de-alienation, 150
death of God, 277
decision-makers (décideurs), 180
Declaration of the Rights of Man and
of the Citizen, 75, 92n15. See also
rights of man; rights of the citizen
decolonization, 23, 92n11, 145
Decouflé, A., 151n2
DeGaulle, Charles, 128, 136n1
De l'État (Lefebvre), 2–4, 8, 10, 11, 12,
13–14, 16, 17, 20, 27, 31, 37, 38–39,
41n5, 43n25, 45n52, 51, 95, 124, 129,
153, 223, 254, 274
Deleuze, Gilles, 209n7
delocalization, 116
democracy, 61, 66–67, 69, 76–79, 85–91,
250–51; bourgeois, 18, 57, 85, 87, 295;
direct, 305; grassroots, 16, 17, 37, 160,
202; liberal, 17–18; movement for,
61; political, 150; proletarian, 87;
radical, 37–38; social, 4, 11, 12, 13, 17–
19, 34, 85, 125, 127, 130, 299; spatial,
193; state, 118; struggle as, 135. See
also autogestion; democratization;
grassroots control; socialism
democratization, 15, 38, 61
dépassement. See supersession
depoliticization, 150, 301
Desan, Wilfrid, 272n5
Desroche, Henri, 150–51, 152n16
de-Stalinization, 52
d'Estaing, Giscard, 136n1
determinism, 143, 199, 266, 295, 305
deterritorialization, 35, 116
the dialectic, 6, 39, 104, 120, 250, 257,
262, 263, 265, 303; autogestion and,

Henri Lefebvre (1901–91) was a French Marxist philosopher and sociologist. The author of more than sixty books, he worked in a wide range of fields, including philosophy, sociology, urban studies, political economy, geography, and literary studies. His best-known works are *The Critique of Everyday Life*, *The Production of Space*, and *The Urban Revolution* (Minneapolis: University of Minnesota Press, 2003).

Neil Brenner is professor of sociology and metropolitan studies at New York University. He is author of *New State Spaces: Urban Governance and the Rescaling of Statehood* (Oxford: Oxford University Press, 2004).

Stuart Elden is professor of political geography at Durham University in England. He is author of *Understanding Henri Lefebvre: Theory and the Possible* (London: Continuum, 2004) and *Terror and Territory: The Spatial Extent of Sovereignty* (Minneapolis: University of Minnesota Press, 2009).

Gerald Moore is a lecturer in languages in the Faculty of Science and Technology, Université Paris–XII (Val de Marne). Among his translations are works by Michel Foucault and Georges Didi-Huberman, and he has published on Jacques Derrida, Jean-Luc Nancy, and recent French philosophy of economics.